The Praeger Handbook
of Media Literacy

Credits

Advisory Board

Frank Baker
Renee Hobbs
Elizabeth Thoman
Kathleen Tyner

Contributing Editors

Project Manager: Lisa Marcus
Threads:
Media Literacy Organizations: Shirley Brinker
Notable National Media Literacy Figures: Alex Detrick
International Media Literacy Programs: Kit Jenkins and Kathleen Marie
    Straubinger
Media Literacy Resources: Debra Finkel and Caitlin Leahy
Editing: Angela Sherman
Entries: Kim William Gordon and Lisa Marcus
Research: Donald Miller, Devin Hurst, Andrew Smith, Jessica Bellomo,
    LeeAnn Tapscott, Robert Armbrister, and Patrick Hughes

The Praeger Handbook of Media Literacy

VOLUME 1

Art Silverblatt, Editor

 **PRAEGER**

AN IMPRINT OF ABC-CLIO, LLC
Santa Barbara, California • Denver, Colorado • Oxford, England

Library of Congress Cataloging-in-Publication Data

The Praeger handbook of media literacy / Art Silverblatt, editor.
   volumes cm
  Includes bibliographical references and index.
  ISBN 978-0-313-39281-8 (hardcopy : alk. paper) — ISBN 978-0-313-39282-5 (ebook)
1. Media literacy—United States.   2. Mass media in education—United States.   3. Media literacy.   I. Silverblatt, Art, editor of compilation.
  P96.M42U5846   2014
  302.23—dc23   2013022536

ISBN: 978-0-313-39281-8
EISBN: 978-0-313-39282-5

18 17 16 15 14   1 2 3 4 5

This book is also available on the World Wide Web as an eBook.
Visit www.abc-clio.com for details.

Praeger
An Imprint of ABC-CLIO, LLC

ABC-CLIO, LLC
130 Cremona Drive, P.O. Box 1911
Santa Barbara, California 93116-1911

This book is printed on acid-free paper ∞
Manufactured in the United States of America

To my latest rung of friends—Jessica B., Bill M., LeeAnn T., Frank B., Janet L., and Deborah A.

And to my silent partners—Jack and Chubbie

Contents

Preface

The Praeger Handbook of Media Literacy is a reference work focusing on the discipline of media literacy in the United States, with secondary attention to media literacy around the world. This reference book consists of six sections. Because these sections cover key topics that run throughout media literacy and bind it together as a discipline, they are called *threads*. These threads include the following:

- Thread 1: Media Literacy Concepts, Approaches, and Education
- Thread 2: Monographs by Media Literacy Scholars
- Thread 3: Media Literacy Organizations
- Thread 4: Notable National Media Literacy Figures
- Thread 5: International Media Literacy Programs
- Thread 6: Media Literacy Resources (Web Sites, Books, Videos, Articles)

These categories can be found throughout the discipline of media literacy. For instance, Notable National Media Literacy Figures (Thread 4) may be connected to Media Literacy Organizations (Thread 3). Consequently, research using the *Handbook* may require the use of various threads. To illustrate, a monograph in Thread 2 may expand on aspects of a media literacy concept found in Thread 1.

Thread 1: Media Literacy Concepts, Approaches, and Education focuses on media literacy principles, qualitative and quantitative strategies for media literacy analysis, and topics related to media literacy education. The section comprises short entries on a wide range of topics. These entries are arranged alphabetically for ease of use. These approaches are examples of *disparate analysis*, in which the principles and strategies found in established disciplines are applied to the discipline of media. It is hoped that these entries will serve as a springboard for additional attention.

Thread 2: Monographs by Media Literacy Scholars consists of a series of scholarly articles that expand on an aspect of a media literacy issue, concept, or approach presented in Thread 1. These monographs are written by some of the finest media literacy scholars in the field: Erica Weintraub Austin, Marieli

Rowe, Renee Hobbs, Marjorie Hogan, Victor Strasburger, Sam Nkana, Frank Baker, David M. Considine, Bob McCannon, Faith Rogow, Don Corrigan, Rob Williams, Kathleen Tyner, and Elizabeth Thoman. Some monographs have been previously published (and are included for their importance), whereas others were written expressly for the *Handbook*.

Thread 3: Media Literacy Organizations focuses on current national organizations that actively promote media literacy. This thread is representative, if not comprehensive. Moreover, it is fluid, as new organizations emerge and old ones become inactive.

Thread 4: Notable National Media Literacy Figures identifies individuals who have made a significant contribution to the discipline of media literacy in the United States. The information is based on an online project organized by the Center for Media Literacy titled *Pioneer Voices in Media Literacy*. The individuals included in the project consist of people who began to make a significant contribution to the field of media literacy in the United States before 1990. The print versions of those interviews are included here, with the permission of the Center for Media Literacy.

Thread 5: International Media Literacy Programs features media literacy programs from around the world. Efforts were made to contact as many countries as possible with media literacy programs. Surveys were sent to individuals in these countries identified as active and prominent in the field of media literacy. Although not all countries that are involved in media literacy are included in this section, the countries included provide insight into the historical, cultural, and political contexts that promote national media literacy programs.

Thread 6: Media Literacy Resources directs readers to numerous print and non-print resources on media literacy. Given the quick-paced evolution of the field of media communications, works on media literacy, including Web sites, organizations, books, and digital materials, are outdated almost as soon as they are published. However, it is hoped that this information can serve as the basis of future research on these topics. Indeed, the author hopes that there might be ways in the future to maintain the currency of this thread. Some of the titles were suggested by members of the advisory board, but this is just a sampling of works available on media literacy and related topics.

Many thanks to the contributing editors whose names appear in the front of the *Handbook*, particularly Lisa Marcus who, in addition to other editing responsibilities, acted as Project Manager. Other contributors to the book include: Alex Detrick, Kim William Gordon, Kit Jenkins, Kathleen Marie Straubinger, Debra Finkel, Caitlin Leahy, Shirley Brinker, and Angela Sherman (contributing editors); and Don Miller, Devin Hurst, Andrew Smith,

Jessica Bellomo, LeeAnn Tapscott, Robert Armbrister, and Patrick Hughes (research assistants).

Moreover, I would like to acknowledge the support and direction of our illustrious advisory board: Frank Baker, Renee Hobbs, Elizabeth Thoman, and Kathleen Tyner.

And, as usual, thanks to my wife Margie and daughter Leah for their support and, of course, Jack, Ozzie, and Chubbie.

An Introduction to Media Literacy

The traditional definition of *literacy* applies only to print: "having a knowledge of letters; instructed; learned." However, in light of the emergence of the channels of mass communications (i.e., print, photography, film, radio, television, and digital media), this definition of literacy must be expanded. *Media literacy* may be defined as follows:

1. Media literacy is a critical thinking skill that enables people to make independent choices with regard to (1) which media programming to select and (2) how to interpret the information they receive through the channels of mass communication.

Media literacy is, first and foremost, a critical thinking skill that is applied to the source of most of the information we receive: the channels of mass communication. However, for a variety of reasons, we often blindly accept the information that we receive through the media—with disastrous results. We develop brand loyalties that have little to do with the quality of the product. We take the word (or pictures) of journalists to provide us with a clear understanding of our world. And we vote for candidates on the basis of "gut reactions" to political spots devised by clever political media consultants.

One of the criteria of becoming an educated person is developing the critical faculties to understand one's environment—an environment that, increasingly, is being shaped by the media.

2. Understanding the process of mass communication.

By itself, a medium is simply a channel of communication and, consequently, is neither good nor evil. A number of factors determine the impact of a media presentation, including an understanding of the elements involved in the process of media communications: (1) *media communicator*, who is producing the presentation; (2) the *function* (or purpose) behind the production of the presentation; (3) *comparative media*—the distinguishing characteristics of each medium; and (4) the intended *audience*.

3. An awareness of the impact of the media on the individual and society.

The media have transformed the way we think about the world, each other, and ourselves. Media presentations convey cumulative messages that *shape*, *reflect*, and *reinforce* attitudes, values, behaviors, preoccupations, and myths that define a culture. Media literacy education has had a demonstrable impact on young students' behaviors and attitudes with regard to alcohol consumption, tobacco usage, and eating disorders.

In addition, media literacy "interventions" have helped curb aggressive and antisocial behaviors among third- and fourth-grade children.

4. The development of strategies with which to analyze and discuss media messages.

Media literacy provides strategies that enable individuals to decipher the information they receive through the channels of mass communication. These keys also provide a framework that can facilitate the discussion of media content with others—including children, peers, and the people responsible for producing media programming.

5. An awareness of media content as a "text" that provides insight into our contemporary culture and ourselves.

Media presentations often provide insight into the attitudes, values, behaviors, preoccupations, patterns of thought, and myths that define a culture. Conversely, an understanding of a culture can furnish perspective into media presentations produced in that culture.

6. The cultivation of an enhanced enjoyment, understanding, and appreciation of media content.

Media literacy should not be considered merely as an opportunity to bash the media; critical analysis can heighten an awareness of media at its best: insightful articles, informative news programs, and uplifting films.

7. In the case of media communicators: the ability to produce effective and responsible media messages.

To be successful, media professionals must have a mastery of production techniques and strategies. But to truly improve the media industry, media communicators must also be aware of the challenges and responsibilities involved in producing thoughtful programming that serves the best interests of the public.

Key Media Literacy Terms, Concepts, and Principles

The following media literacy terms, concepts, and principles are critical to an understanding of media literacy:

- *Levels of meaning: manifest and latent messages.* Manifest messages are direct and clear to the audience. We generally have little trouble recognizing these messages when we are paying full attention to a media presentation. But in addition, latent messages are indirect and beneath the surface, and, consequently, escape our immediate attention. Latent messages may reinforce manifest messages, or they may suggest entirely different meanings. For example, "G.I. Joe" commercials promote their line of war toys. However, the G.I. Joe ad campaign conveys latent messages glorifying war and equating violence with masculinity.
- *Cumulative messages* occur with such frequency over time that they form new meanings, independent of any individual production. Consistent messages recur throughout many media presentations with regard to gender roles, definitions of success, and racial and cultural stereotypes. As an example, taken by itself, *The Chronicles of Riddick* (2004) is simply an action-entertainment film. However, this macho image, repeated in countless other media presentations, sends an aggregate message about the ideal of masculinity.
- *Point of view* refers to the perspective on events. In any media presentation, there can be a range of points of view:
  - The media communicator
  - The characters in the presentation
  - The prevailing point of view of the period in which it was produced
  - The point of view of audience members

Point of view has an impact on (1) how a story is told, (2) what information is conveyed, and (3) how the audience responds to the information being presented.

- *Media presentations are constructions of reality.* According to the Association for Media Literacy at the Request of the Ontario Ministry of Education, one of the major principles of media literacy is that all media are *constructions* (or versions) of reality.

In its ability to instantaneously preserve a moment of time in space, a media image creates the illusion of *verisimilitude*, or lifelike quality. We must remember, however, that the media can capture only a brief instant, without the context that gives it meaning. Indeed, the very *presence* of the media often affects what is being recorded. Subjects often act differently when they know that they are being photographed.

- *Affective strategies.* Visual and aural media (photography, film, television, radio, and digital media) are particularly well suited to emotional appeals. Production elements such as color, shape, lighting, and size convey meaning by evoking emotional responses in the audience. Media communicators can influence the attitudes and behavior of audiences by appealing to their emotions.

- *Embedded values.* Media content may reflect the value system of the media communicator, as well as widely held cultural values and attitudes that, in turn, reinforce and shape attitudes and values among members of the audience. Media communicators convey meaning by manipulating production elements such as editing decisions, point of view, and connotative words and images. Thus, a consideration of these elements can reveal the values of the media communicators.

THREAD 1

Media Literacy Concepts, Approaches, and Education

Thread 1 focuses on media literacy principles, qualitative and quantitative strategies for media literacy analysis, and topics related to media literacy education.

Advertising—Media Literacy Analysis

Advertising is a pervasive influence in American culture. By age 20, the average American has seen 1 million commercial messages (Simon, 1997). On average, each of us will spend one full year of our lives watching TV commercials (Simon, 1997). Consequently, advertising has emerged as a primary focus of media literacy analysis.

Innovations in media technology have added to the challenges facing advertisers. For example, although advertisers spend about $70 billion a year on television commercials, digital video recorders enable viewers to skip ads altogether. At the same time, the Internet has increased ways for advertisers to reach their target audiences. Digital advertising allows advertisers to focus on niche markets and target individual users. Data mining provides information about an individual's online search habits and information from a user's profile to select which ads appear in the user's browser.

The new media environment has necessitated innovative approaches to advertising. Consider the following:

Ubiquitous advertising is a technique in which every conceivable space is dedicated to advertising. For instance, "placed-based video screens" are set up on free spaces, wherever a person takes a moment to focus attention. Ads on gas pumps, ATM machines, health clubs, movie theaters, and elevators can reach many more people than ads on prime-time television. As an example, as of 2007, video screens were located in 20 percent of all grocery stores and 11 percent of all office buildings (Story, 2007).

Cell phone advertising has become an efficient mode of advertising. Although the vast majority of people surveyed say they are averse to having advertisements text-messaged or otherwise sent to their cell phones, nearly a quarter of the people who have received such ads say they have responded to such an advertising appeal at least once (Mindlin, 2008).

By tracking the individual's activities on the Internet, marketing specialists are able to create *personalized ads* that individualize personal advertising messages for their target audience. As an example, advertisers design digital billboards that instantaneously customize their message to the drivers of passing vehicles, by identifying the demographic and psychographic information about the drivers, as well as information about the cars that they are driving. Similarly, digital signs at malls customize information regarding in-store sales to the people strolling by their store, based on the tags in the merchandise that they bought (as well as on the old clothes they are wearing).

Search advertising is a method of locating online advertisements on Web pages, using search engines such as Google or Yahoo. Search advertisements are matched with keywords that are placed in the search engines. Reporter Saul Hansell (2003) discusses the benefits of search advertising as follows:

> The main reason that search advertising has been successful is that it presents advertising that consumers might actually want to see. Someone searching for information on arthritis may well be as interested in ads by drug companies and chiropractors as the reports by medical foundations and information sites found by the search engines.
>
> A less obvious driver of search ads, but perhaps as important in the long run, is that they sell themselves. Rather than negotiating with an ad salesman, the advertiser buys search ads on a Web Site by entering a search term and price it is willing to pay. The highest-bidding ads are displayed, and the advertisers only pay when a user clicks on the ad to visit their Web page.

Product placement refers to an advertising strategy in which the products are incorporated into media presentations. In 1982, Reese's Pieces were visually displayed in the film *E.T.*, as young earthling Elliott used the candy to mark a trail for his alien friend to follow. Within a month of the premiere of the film, sales for the candy jumped by 65 percent (Demarest, 1982).

Since then, product placement in advertising and media presentations from television and film to video games and other media sources has become commonplace. Even during the difficult economic period, product placement in 2008 saw $3.61 billion in spending. In 2008, NBC's *The Biggest Loser* featured 6,804 occurrences of brands such as Brita and 24 Hour Fitness. Paid product placement has a presence in everything from music videos such as Lady Gaga's "Telephone" to brand mentions in song lyrics such as the Black Eyed Peas's jingles for Pepsi or Chris Brown's single for Wrigley, "Forever" (Grover & Lowry, 2009).

Using merchandise as a prop or part of the set legitimizes the product and is therefore an effective form of persuasion. Product placement is now becoming commonplace in many media, such as books, video games, and the lyrics of popular music.

Product placement has become increasingly sophisticated and specialized. *Product integration* is a subtle form of product placement in which products are cleverly embedded into the narrative, conveying the message that these items are essential to the characters (and the audience as well). In addition, product placement is also becoming central to character development

Product placement is an advertising strategy in which the products are incorporated into media presentations. Product placement can be found in a range of media programming, including television programs, films, books, video games, and the lyrics of popular music. (Photo by Lisa Marcus)

in scripts. Indeed, in some cases, the entire storyline has simply become a vehicle for product placement. In 2011, Condé Nast Publications developed an original reality television series produced exclusively for the iPad that enables viewers to pause the program and purchase items of clothing worn by the characters, directly from Gap.com.

Advertisers direct product placement at specific target audiences, including children. Some genres are particularly well suited for product placements. For instance, the reality genre lends itself to product placements, in part because the sets must include branded products as part of their "real" look. Product placements now appear even in newscasts.

However, some writers and producers complain that the imperative to slip product promotion into a script can undermine the integrity of the story. In 2005, a collective of show business unions, including the Writers Guild of America, West; the Writers Guild of America, East; and the Screen Actors Guild, denounced the practice of "stealth advertising" and called for a code of conduct to govern this practice. The group issued a position paper saying, "We are being told to write the lines that sell this merchandise, and to deftly disguise the sale as story. Our writers are being told to perform the function of ad copywriter, but to disguise this as storytelling" (Waxman, 2005).

Neuromarketing is a field of marketing that applies physiological principles to the study of consumer behaviors. Companies such as Google, CBS, Disney, Frito-Lay, and A&E Television, as well as some political campaigns, have used neuromarketing to test consumer reactions to ad content. Reporter Natasha Singer (2010) provides this explanation of neuromarketing:

WHAT happens in our brains when we watch a compelling TV commercial?

For one thing, certain brain waves that correlate with heightened attention become more active, according to researchers who have used EEGs, or electroencephalographs, to study the brain's electrical frequencies. Brain waves that signal less-focused attention, meanwhile, tend to subside.

Neuromarketing's raison d'être derives from the fact that the brain expends only 2 percent of its energy on conscious activity, with the rest devoted largely to unconscious processing. Thus, neuromarketers believe, traditional market research methods—like consumer surveys and focus groups—are inherently inaccurate because the participants can never articulate the unconscious impressions that whet their appetites for certain products.

Neuromarketing researchers study consumers' sensorimotor, cognitive, and affective responses to marketing stimuli, using a range of technologies that track eye movement, heart rate, skin resistance, and brainwaves (EEG). Singer (2010) provides the following example of eye-tracking research:

Volunteers . . . wear a fabric cap that houses EEG sensors and an eye-tracking device while they look at a commercial, use a Web site or view a movie trailer. The dual devices enable researchers to connect the volunteers' brain patterns with the exact video images or banner ads or logos they're viewing.

Studies show that emotionally connected customers were four times as likely to shop first at their preferred retailer than customers who were merely familiar with a retailer ("Connect Emotionally to Boost Sales," 2011). Consequently, marketing firms are then in a position to design ads that generate the desired consumer responses.

Convergence television sets have been transformed into large computer screens. The left-hand side of this "entertainment appliance" is reserved for continuous advertising. The world on-screen has thus become a virtual display window; if viewers fancy a pair of shoes that an actor or actress is wearing on a situation comedy, they will be able to click on the image and order the item.

Viral marketing is a marketing phenomenon in which an advertisement is passed along from person to person, often using the tools of social media, to develop a distinctive message. Reporter Mary Jo Feldstein (2006) explains: "To make an impact on these consumers, you have to look for new ways of reaching them and speaking to them on their terms. . . . If they're not talking about you, you're not getting the message out."

The formula for viral marketing involves putting humorous, entertaining, or shocking video material on the Internet and hoping that this advertising vehicle will be picked up and passed along—like a virus. To illustrate, in 2009, Orabrush posted a funny video about bad breath on YouTube that advertised their product—a tongue cleaner called Orabrush. Reporter Claire Cain Miller (2010) notes,

> A year later, people have viewed Orabrush's YouTube clips 24 million times, watching weekly appearances by a giant tongue named Morgan. Orabrush has sold $1 million worth of the $5 tongue brushes through YouTube, and major drugstores are beginning to stock it on their shelves.
>
> . . . Each week brings a new installment of "Diaries of a Dirty Tongue," in which an actor dressed in a grotesque pink tongue costume rolls on a floor with a librarian or fumbles in social situations. In other videos, an actor dressed in a lab coat and glasses talks about "halitophobia, the irrational fear of bad breath," and lures unsuspecting passers-by to take bad breath tests.

According to Orabrush CEO Jeff Davis, a former executive at Procter & Gamble, viral marketing reverses the classic marketing blueprint:

> "What P.& G. taught me is a different model—you have an idea, build a prototype, have a test market, scale the product, find a retailer and distribution, then turn on marketing," he said. "This was the reverse. We basically launched the entire brand on YouTube and Facebook." (Miller, 2010)

Media Literacy Strategies

A media literacy approach to advertising can be considered from the following lines of inquiry.

- The *process* of constructing and deciphering advertising
  - The role of the media communicator
  - Identifying the function, or purpose, of the advertising message
  - The impact of *audience* on advertising strategy, style, and content
- Advertising as *historical* and *cultural text*
- The impact of a *medium* (e.g., Internet) on advertising
- Analysis of *affective response* and *explicit content* advertising strategies
- Advertising *production elements* as a way to convey or reinforce ad messages

Function

Advertising performs a variety of manifest (or surface) functions:

- Informing the public about a product
- Attracting the attention of the consumer to the product
- Motivating the consumer to action
- Stimulating markets
- Supporting the business community
- Establishing and maintaining a lasting relationship between the consumer and a company

But in addition, advertising serves a number of *latent* functions (i.e., subtle purposes that escape the conscious attention of the audience):

- *Persuasion.* Advertising cannot convince consumers to purchase something that they truly don't want, but in cases in which the customer is already shopping for a product, ads are designed to steer the consumer to their particular brand. Moreover, advertisers try to convince us that we don't merely want a product but, in fact, *need* it. Indeed, advertising copy is often phrased in the form of an imperative, or command (e.g., "Buy it today!").
- *Establishing standards of behavior and lifestyle.* Advertising is in the business of establishing standards of behavior—how to look, where to go, and what to do with our time.

- *Fostering consumer culture.* Beyond any specific product endorsement, the cumulative message of the advertising industry exhorts the public to adopt a consumer mentality. In the world of advertising, personal problems are transformed into consumer needs. Advertising positions products as keys to emotional well-being and happiness. This conditioning begins early. Advertising equates the purchase of goods with parental love and approval. Advertisers encourage the audience to think of themselves in terms of their consumer behavior. Advertising promotes membership in a group (e.g., "The Pepsi Generation"), united by common consumer habits. By wearing designer labels or sweatshirts with commercial logos, consumers have been transformed into walking billboards, advertising these products.

As an example, *search engine optimization* is a technique in which advertisers insert links and key words designed to bring a particular company to the top of a search engine's list, thus "optimizing" the chances that a person conducting a computer search will find them. The fluid nature of interactive media makes it easy to camouflage the advertising function, so that advertising is often difficult to detect. As a result, advertising links may be inserted into editorial copy without being labeled accordingly, so that individuals seeking additional information on a topic instead find themselves in an advertiser's Web site. Consequently, it is important to consider function—*why* particular ads come up first during a Web search.

Advertising as Historical and Cultural Text

Historical text. To reach people in the most immediate manner possible, advertising is extraordinarily sensitive to historical events. These events provide a context of meaning for the commercial message. For instance, after the terrorist attack of 9/11, Calvin Klein altered its campaign from a sexy appeal to film clips, in-home video style, of family moments, shot in retro black and white, set to the 1960s Burt Bacharach song, "What the World Needs Now Is Love."

Cultural text advertising is part of a cultural conversation that (a) discloses areas of cultural interest and concern; (b) furnishes perspective into *cultural preoccupations*, such as aging, sex, and cleanliness; and (c) serves as a barometer of cultural change. In many ads, what is really being sold is the *worldview* of the commercial. Purchasing a product somehow admits the consumer as a member of the world of the ad.

Moreover, ads frequently position their product as the center of the world of the commercial, suggesting that it is an essential part of the situation presented in the advertisement. For instance, in beer ads, the product is placed in the middle of the activity. Consequently, these ads convey the message that beer not only accompanies a good time but that it is impossible to have fun without a provision of beer. Thus, an interesting mode of analysis is to mentally airbrush the product out of an advertisement to identify the worldview surrounding the product. Imagine the beer commercial, in which young people are cavorting on the beach. Now, mentally delete the product from the scene. What remains is a delightful social occasion, replete with plenty of music, flirting, and celebrating. But when the product is placed in the center of the activity, the ad conveys the message that beer is central to this good time—indeed, you can't really have a party without someone bringing a keg.

Beyond the promotion of specific products, ads convey cumulative messages about the world of advertising:

- *A material world.* The worldview of ads is reduced to what we can see, feel, touch—and buy.
- *An uncomplicated world.* This world offers simple solutions to complex problems: all issues can be resolved by purchasing the right product.
- *World of immediate gratification.* A sense of urgency permeates the world of advertising. In commercials, people cannot postpone their gratification for more than thirty seconds.
- *A self-absorbed world.* In this narcissistic world, satisfaction does not stem from helping others but from helping yourself to as many products as you can afford.
- *A competitive world.* Consumers are asked to compare themselves with others, based on goods and services.
- *An optimistic world.* In the worldview of advertising, even the most troublesome problems can be resolved through the acquisition of consumer goods.
- *A class-segmented world.* The world of advertising is divided into two groups: the haves and the have-nots.
- Questions to ask with regard to *worldview* in advertising include the following:
  - What kind of world is being depicted in the ad?
  - What kind of lifestyle is promoted in the ad? Consumers may actually be attracted to the lifestyle depicted in the ad, of which the product is only a small part.

- What is the role of the product within the worldview of the ad? Imagine the ad without the product to see whether that consumer item is indeed an essential part of that world.
- If you did not know what product was being promoted, what would you think was being advertised? Consumers who are interested in the primary product may also be compelled to purchase the other consumer items depicted in the ad.

Affective appeals. Ads are designed to tap into a reservoir of emotional needs, concerns, and fears to sell a product. Despite working within a very limited format (e.g., a thirty-second TV spot), these ads trigger emotions and then manipulate these feelings to sell the product. Ads may be directed at one of the following intrinsic *psychological motivations*:

- *Search for identity.* From the moment we are born, we are engaged in a quest for self-discovery. Thus, one effective ad strategy promotes the product as the culmination of this search for identity; products assume a significance because they tell you (and others) exactly who you are.
- *Love.* Consumer products are positioned as tangible symbols of affection, affirming the depth, sincerity, and permanence of a person's love.
- *Need for approval.* From infancy, human beings share a longing for approval. Thus, a persistent latent message in advertising is that a person's need for acceptance can be satisfied through their consumer behavior.
- *Guilt.* American culture can be characterized as exceedingly guilt-ridden. We feel remorse for any number of real and imagined transgressions. Advertisers capitalize on these irrational feelings to promote products. When confronted by *guilt-provoking ads*, ask the following questions:
  ○ Why am I feeling guilty?
  ○ How will purchasing the product assuage my guilt?
  ○ Is the choice of brand important?
  ○ Could an advertiser exploit these feelings of guilt to sell me other products?

Examining *explicit content* can reveal the following inconsistencies, fallacies, and incongruities in advertisements: (a) *Illogical premise* (an ad may be based on a premise that, on close examination, is illogical); (b) *False and misleading ads*; (c) *Incomplete or distorted message*; (d) *The Big Promise* (claims that are far beyond the capacity of the product); (e) *Hyperbole* (using exaggeration or absurd overstatement to make a point); (f) *Parity statement* (a technique in which ads are worded in a way that suggests that a product is unique, when what the ad is *actually* stating is that the product is indistinguishable from its competition); (g) *Unfinished statements* (making implied claims that advertisers are unable to stand behind. Instead, they leave it to the consumer to complete the statement); and (h) *Qualifier words* (information added inconspicuously to an ad, which discloses important—but often contradictory—information about a product not contained in the main message of the ad).

See also: Cultural Context; Digital Media Literacy; Function; Medium Theory; Production Analysis Approach

References

"Connect emotionally to boost sales." (2011, September 1). *Neuromarketing—Where Brain Science and Marketing Meet.* Retrieved from http://www.neuroscience marketing.com/blog/articles/connect-emotionally.htm

Demarest, M. (1982, July 12). "Living: Ah, How Sweet It Is." *Time* Magazine. www .com/time/magazine/article/0,9171,925564,00.html

Feldstein, M. (2006, September 29). "Mark Schupp got bug for viral advertising on the cutting edge." *St. Louis Post-Dispatch*, B5.

Grover, R., & Lowry T. (2009, April). "TV Shows with the Most Product Placement." *Businessweek.* Retrieved from http://images.businessweek.com/ss/09/04/0423 _tv_product_placements/index.htm

Hansell, S. (2003, December 29). "More Businesses Are Turning to Paid Listings on Search Engines." *New York Times.* Retrieved from http://www.nytimes .com/2003/12/29/business/media/29search.html?scp=1&sq=Hansell%20and%20 %22More%20Businesses%20Are%20Turning%20to%20Paid%20Listings%20 on%20Search%20Engines%22&st=cse

Miller, C. C. (2010, September 26). "To Fix Bad Breath, a Gadget Seen on YouTube." *New York Times.* Retrieved from http://www.nytimes.com/2010/09/27/business/ media/27adco.html

Mindlin, A. (2008, August 11). "It's Not the Ad; It's Getting the Bill." *New York Times.* Retrieved from http://www.nytimes.com/2008/08/11/business/media/11drill.html

Silverblatt, A. (2008). *Media Literacy: Keys to Interpreting Media Messages* (3rd ed.). Westport, CT: Praeger.

Simon, S. (1997, September 19). "Affluenza." KETZ/PBS Special.

Singer, N. (2010, November 13). "Making Ads That Whisper to the Brain." *New York Times.* Retrieved from http://www.nytimes.com/2010/11/14/business/14stream.html

Story, L. (2007, March 2). "Away from Home, TV Ads are Inescapable." Retrieved from http://www.nytimes.com/2007/03/02/business/media/02adco.html?_r=0

Story, L. (2008, March 10). "To Aim Ads, Web Is Keeping Closer Eye on You." *New York Times*. Retrieved from http://www.nytimes.com/2008/03/10/technology/10privacy.html

Waxman, S. (2005, November 14). "Hollywood Unions Object to Product Placement on TV." *New York Times*. Retrieved from http://www.nytimes.com/2005/11/14/business/14guild.html

Affective Response Analysis

Affective response analysis is an approach to the study of media literacy that asks audience members to focus on their emotional reactions at various stages of a media presentation as a springboard to critical analysis.

Although it is often overlooked as a means of acquiring knowledge, affective response represents a primal way in which individuals process information. Indeed, it is often forgotten that when Alan Bloom's *Taxonomy of Educational Objectives* was first published in 1956, *Affective Analysis* (referred to as "feeling, heart") was included as one of the three principle ways for teachers to systematically assess the effectiveness of their teaching strategies.

Affective response is a surprisingly effective communications tool in the mass media as well. Visual and aural media (i.e., photography, film, television, radio, and the Internet) are particularly well suited to emotional appeals. Production values such as color, shape, lighting, and size trigger emotional responses that reinforce or convey messages. Consequently, one-year-old children have demonstrated the ability to decode specific emotional cues delivered on television (Goode, 2003).

In addition, identifying the *function*, or purpose, behind an affective appeal can furnish perspective into a media presentation. Sometimes generating an affective response is the chief function, or purpose, behind the production of a media presentation. To illustrate, *feel-good* movies have emerged as a distinct genre. In like fashion, *chick flicks* are movies designed to trigger particular emotions that are commonly associated with women's emotional landscapes in Western culture. Consequently, a useful line of inquiry focuses attention on how the media communicator wants the audience to be feeling at particular points in the presentation. The next step involves considering *why* a media communicator is attempting to elicit a particular emotional response from the audience. Finally, focusing on an individual's emotional reactions to a media presentation can serve as the basis for critical self-analysis, providing insight into his or her own personal belief system.

Another line of inquiry examines the impact of particular emotions on individuals' attitudes and behaviors. To illustrate, the emotion of surprise can affect people's receptivity to new ideas and information. Chip and Dan Heath explain,

> Surprise makes us want to find an answer—to resolve the question of why we were surprised—and big surprises call for big answers. If we want to motivate people to pay attention, we should seize the power of big surprises. (Heath & Heath, 2007: 69)

In contrast, fear can undermine rational thought. Gregory Berns (2008), a neuroeconomist who has used brain-scanning technologies to decode the decision-making systems of the human mind, has found that fear "does strange things to decision making":

> The most concrete thing that neuroscience tells us is that when the fear system of the brain is active, exploratory activity and risk-taking are turned off. . . . While fear is a deep-seated and adaptive evolutionary drive for self-preservation, it makes it impossible to concentrate on anything but saving our skin
> . . . Ultimately, no good can come from this type of decision making. Fear prompts retreat. It is the antipode to progress. Just when we need new ideas most, everyone is seized up in fear, trying to prevent losing what we have left.

A third line of inquiry involves considering the role and impact of affective response in particular genres or applications of content. To illustrate, media communicators often strive to elicit an emotional reaction from their audience for dramatic purposes or to promote certain behaviors from the target audience. Examples include *political communications* and *advertising.*

Political media strategists have learned to construct media presentations that generate feelings of fear in the audience as a way of inducing voters to support their candidates and issues. Political ads tap into a range of fears: attack by enemies, fear of change, mistrust of politicians, and fear of differences.

Emotion-evoking media presentations have been employed with great success by totalitarian governments—most notably with the propaganda strategies of militaristic regimes such as Nazi Germany. But more recently, nationalistic political groups have employed this approach to influence policies in their countries. As an example, in 2009, Switzerland held a referendum to reconsider the construction of minarets in their country. A minaret is a tall tower attached to Islamic mosques and is the place from which the faithful are called to prayer. Significantly, the referendum banning minarets passed, even though it is hardly a major problem; only four minarets were located in Switzerland at the time of the vote. Much of the success of the anti-immigrant campaign can be attributed to the powerful affective response generated by posters circulated by the anti-immigration Swiss People's Party. The posters featured minarets depicted as missiles rising from the Swiss flag. Written in big, black letters, **"Stop"** appears beside the missiles. Alexander Segert, who designed the poster, commented, "Minarets and the Swiss flag sent the message we wanted because they don't fit together. A person looks and thinks, 'This must be changed' " (Kimmelman, 2010).

Anthony Pratkanis makes the following recommendations for critical analysis of *affective campaign strategies*:

- Keep track of your emotions while viewing the ad.
- Ask yourself, "Why am I feeling (this way) now?"
- If you feel yourself getting manipulated this way, turn off the ad. (Golman, 1992)

Advertising is often approached with the purpose of triggering emotions and then manipulating these feelings to sell the product. Despite working within a very limited format (e.g., a 30-second TV spot), ads are able to evoke intense emotional reactions among members of the audience. Consequently, ads often strive to accentuate the *emotional benefits* of a product. For instance, the phone company is not merely selling a communications system but furnishes the means through which you can "reach out and touch someone" you love. The advertiser hopes that the consumer will then transfer these positive feelings to the product.

Emotional ads also may be directed at one of a number of intrinsic *psychological motivations*, including the following:

- *Need for approval.* From infancy, all human beings share a longing for approval. A persistent cumulative message in advertising is that people can satisfy their need for acceptance through their consumer behavior. One particularly effective version of this appeal centers around the complex relationship between children and their parents. For example, a Michelin Tire advertising campaign featured the slogan, "Because so much is riding on your tires," accompanied by a picture of a cute infant sitting on one of their products. In this case, the ad was directed at young parents, capitalizing on their protective instincts.

- *Guilt.* American culture can be characterized as exceedingly guilt-ridden. We feel remorse for any number of real and imagined transgressions. Advertisers capitalize on these irrational feelings to promote their product.

Fear is an emotional appeal that is often used in advertising. Zeitlin and Westwood (1986) found that to be most effective, fear-based messages should present a mild to moderate threat and provide a manageable solution. These ads begin by emphasizing a threat to the target audience. The ad then positions the product as a means of alleviating the source of the fear. It should be noted that if the audience is too frightened or if the ad does not follow up with a reasonable solution, audience members will not be able to surmount their sense of dread and process the advertising message. Consequently, the source of the fear may not be life-endangering, such as fear of rejection. Although the fear-based appeal may not be rational, audience members respond emotionally to the message.

One effective advertising strategy involves tapping into the prevailing emotional climate of the culture, which is inspired by historical events. For instance, in 2010, a number of television ads reflected the angry mood of the country. Segments of the population were frustrated by the economic recession, which caused massive layoffs and the loss of personal savings while corporate CEOs were collecting enormous bonuses. Stuart Elliott (2008) declared, "The tone and attitude of the ads are part rant, part battle cry, part manifesto and part populist appeal."

For instance, a 2010 Southwest Airlines ad campaign attacked rival companies who charged their customers extra fees. The campaign carried the slogan "Fees don't fly with us." In one print ad, a chart shows how much money other airlines charged for extraneous services, such as extra bags. "What have they been smoking?" the headline asks, referring to the rivals. "Apparently, your rolled-up $20s." Derek Pletch, creative director at Idea City, part of the Omnicom Group, explained that the goal of the ad campaign was "to do something disruptive" that reflected the frustrations of fliers. Another ad featured a mock coupon that read, "Don't #$*!% me over," which appeared above a declaration that "Southwest is the only airline that accepts this coupon" (Elliott, 2008).

Sentiment analysis is an emerging field, in which computer software systematically identifies and tracks reactions to information being conveyed through channels of mass communication to measure consumers' emotional responses to information that appears in the media. Media communicators can then respond to audiences with marketing and public relations strategies that address these emotional responses. Reporter Alan Wright (2009) provided the following example:

A search for Wal-Mart reveals that recent sentiment about the company is running positive by a ratio of slightly better than two to one. When that search is refined with the suggested term "Labor Force and Unions," however, the ratio of positive to negative sentiments drops closer to one to one.

Moreover, software companies are developing sophisticated algorithms that not only evaluate sentiments about particular topics but also identify the most influential opinion holders. Such tools could serve the following functions:

- Pinpoint the impact of specific issues on audience perceptions, attitudes, and behaviors
- Identify how individuals feel about particular topics, organizations, places, people, and themes
- Anticipate trends in opinions about products, services, or topics

See also: Advertising—Media Literacy Analysis; Political Communications, American

References

Berns, G. (2008, December 7). "Preoccupations: In Hard Times, Fear Can Impair Decision-Making." *New York Times*. Retrieved from http://www.nytimes.com/2008/12/07/jobs/07pre.html

Elliott, S. (2008, June 26). "A Spate of Ads Gives Vent to That Howard Beale Feeling." *New York Times*. Retrieved from http://www.nytimes.com/2008/06/26/business/media/26adco.html?pagewanted=all

Goleman, D. (1992, October 27)."Voters Assailed by Unfair Persuasion." *New York Times*. Retrieved from http://www.nytimes.com/1992/10/27/science/voters-assailed-by-unfair-persuasion.html?pagewanted=all&src=pm

Goode, E. (2003, January 21). "Behavior; Babies Pick Up Emotional Clues from TV, Experts Find." *New York Times*. Retrieved from http://www.nytimes.com/2003/01/21/health/behavior-babies-pick-up-emotional-clues-from-tv-experts-find.html

Heath, C., & Heath, D. (2007). *Made to Stick*. New York: Random House.

Kimmelman, M. (2010, January 17). "When Fear Turns Graphic." *New York Times*. Retrieved from http://www.nytimes.com/2010/01/17/arts/design/17abroad.html?pagewanted=all&_r=0

Wright, A. (2009, August 24). "Mining the Web for Feelings, Not Facts." *New York Times*. Retrieved from http://www.nytimes.com/2009/08/24/technology/internet/24emotion.html?pagewanted=all

Zeitlin, D., & Westwood, R. (1986, October/November). "Measuring Emotional Response." *Journal of Advertising Research 26*, 34–44.

Audience Analysis

Understanding the role of audience in the communication process is of paramount importance in the analysis of media and media programming. The analysis of audience consists of three areas of study: (1) Audience Identification, (2) Comprehension of Media Content, and (3) Audience Behavior Patterns.

Audience Identification

The ability to accurately identify the audience is critical to the construction of media messages. The better a media communicator "knows" the audience, the better he or she can tailor the information to the individuals receiving the media message. It is not much of an overstatement that advertisers can sell you *anything* if they know you well enough. Advertisers are expert in defining the needs and concerns of the target audience and then positioning their product to meet those needs. Thus, a dandruff shampoo is a cure for loneliness, and a grocery store provides "peace of mind."

Two techniques are commonly employed in audience identification. *Demographic research* refers to the study of human populations. Media communicators use demographic data to adjust their media strategy or content to most effectively reach their audience. Demographic considerations such as geographic location, age, gender, income, education, occupation, race, religion, and family size play a large role in how individuals respond to media programming. Advertisers know that demographic considerations are significant factors in consumer buying patterns. Political consultants also use demographic data as a way of determining their candidates' strength among specific populations. Communications professor Joseph Turow (2006) commented on ways in which media communicators take advantage of audience demographics:

The ads you see on the Web are increasingly tailored to what market-ers perceive as your demographic—based on your age, where you live, your education, and your movements online and off. The latest technol-ogy . . . enables websites to customize the selection of articles and vid-eos that reach you depending on what they know about you from your registration data, your movements on their site, and even information about you that they've purchased from a third party. . . And Stop & Shop supermarkets in New England has tested a "shopping buddy" that can change the discounts it offers you as you walk through the store based on your buying history.

Psychographic research is an audience-identification mechanism that iden-tifies the attitudes, values, and experiences shared by groups falling within various demographic categories. Media communicators tailor their message to meet the psychological profile of their target audience. Advertisers rely on audience-identification strategies to *anticipate* consumer buying patterns and tailor their messages to promote their products.

In 2009, a team of anthropologists conducted *ethnographic* research on the target audience for Disney entertainment. Disney used this information to connect more effectively with 6- to 14-year-old boys. Reporter Brook Barnes (2009) covered ethnographic research conducted by Kelly Peña and a team of anthropologists and psychologists by looking at living environment of "Dean," a 12-year-old boy:

This kind of intensive research helps the media communicators to pro-duce content that has meaning for individuals like Dean. Actors have been instructed to tote their skateboards around with the bottoms facing outward. (Boys in real life carry them that way to display the personal-ization, Ms. Peña found.) The games portion of the Disney XD Web site now features prominent trophy cases. (It's less about the level reached in the game and more about sharing small achievements, research showed.) . . . This research is profitable. . . . Viewership among boys 6 to 14 is up about 10 percent. (Barnes, 2009)

Media programming may be targeted simultaneously at both a *manifest* and a *latent* audience. Saturday morning commercials, for instance, are obvi-ously directed at children. However, the latent audience consists of *parents*, who are pressured to purchase the products featured in the commercial for their children.

Audience identification assumes a major impact on the communication *strategy*, *style*, and *content* of media presentations.

An astute media communicator is able to adapt the communication strategy to the target audience. For instance, a computer ad appearing in a magazine specializing in digital technology will emphasize technical information, whereas an ad in a general entertainment magazine will emphasize trendiness, convenience, or the snappy color of the unit. In like fashion, the style is tailored to the audience. For example, in a television ad for an automobile, the choice of models, costumes, and music will vary, depending on the target audience. Finally, content responds to the interests of the intended audience. For instance, the preponderance of films dealing with the trials and triumphs of adolescence can be attributed to the audience, which consists primarily of people between the ages of 18 and 24. As a result, film projects are selected and developed only *after* the audience has been identified.

Indeed, one way to identify audience involves working backward: What does the *communication strategy, style*, and *content* of a media presentation tell us about the intended audience?

Comprehension of Media Content

Comprehension of media content refers to the processes through which an audience member filters information and derives meaning from media content. Two schools of thought provide differing explanations with respect to the role of the audience in the interpretation of content: (a) the hegemonic model and (b) reception theory.

According to the hegemonic model, the media communicator establishes a *preferred reading* in which the text dictates the responses of the audience. Production elements such as music, lighting, and angle clearly establish the perspective and orientation of the heroes and heroines.

On the other hand, reception theory posits that the audience assumes an active role in *negotiating*, or interpreting. the information they receive through the channels of mass media, based on the following factors:

- Demographic Profile
  - National origin
  - Gender
  - Race
  - Ethnic origin

- ○ Age
- ○ Education
- ○ Income
- Psychological Profile
  - ○ Self-concept
  - ○ Primary relationships
  - ○ Significant life experiences
  - ○ Ways of relating to others
  - ○ Ways of dealing with emotions
  - ○ Personal aspirations
- Individual's Stage of Development
  - ○ Chronological
  - ○ Cognitive
  - ○ Emotional
- *Familiarity with subject.* How much does the audience already know about the subject?
- *Interest level.* How interested is the audience in the subject? How attentive is the audience?
- *Predisposition.* What is the attitude of the audience toward the subject (positive or negative) going into the conversation?
- *Priorities.* What issues are of particular concern to the audience? Why?
- *Communications environment*
  - ○ What is the size of the audience?
  - ○ What are they *doing* while they are receiving the information?

Members of subcultures may respond differently to a media, based on their shared backgrounds. For instance, women may be more sensitive to media messages about violence against females than men. This same principle applies to groups that are defined by common experiences. People who consume alcohol are more likely to remember seeing anti–drunk driving PSAs and moderation ads than teetotalers (Ognianova & Thorson, 1998).

Consequently, skilled media communicators are able to construct memorable messages by anticipating the interests and concerns of the target audience. Thus, according to the reception theory, when considering the ways in which the audience responds to media content, it is important to consider the following questions:

- What values, experiences, and perspectives are shared by the audience?
- Do these shared values, experiences, or perspectives influence their understanding or interpretation of the media presentation?

Conversely, how people respond to a media presentation can provide insight into an individual's values, background, and experiences.

Which perspective on audience interpretation is correct, the hegemonic model or the reception theory? Probably both. Although audience members are encouraged to assume the point of view of the preferred reading, they also negotiate their own meaning, based on their individual backgrounds, orientations, and experiences.

An individual's stage of life is another important consideration with regard to the audience's comprehension of media content. A 1979 study by W. Andrew Collins provides considerable insight into children's comprehension of media content. Collins found that being able to identify *explicit* and *implicit* content is an essential step in the systematic analysis of media messages.

Explicit content consists of the significant events in a narrative, answering the question: What is this story about? Thus, an individual constructs meaning by first selecting the essential pieces of information in the story. Collins found that children often have difficulty remembering explicit details and identifying important scenes.

Collins found that children's comprehension of explicit story material was surprisingly limited:

- Second graders recalled an average of only 66% of the scenes that adults had judged as essential to the plot.
- Fifth graders recalled 84% of the scenes that adults had judged as essential to the plot.
- Eighth graders recalled 92% of the scenes that adults had judged as essential to the plot. (Collins, 1979: 27)

Implicit content refers to those elements of plot which remain under the surface:

- The motives behind characters' decisions and actions
- The connection between events that occur in the narrative
- The connection between characters in the narrative
- The consequences for characters' action

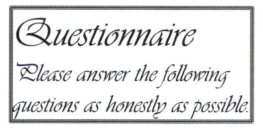

Studies indicate that the ease with which individuals process media content can affect their response to the information. For example, people tend to answer survey questions less honestly if the survey is displayed in a font that they find difficult to read. (Graphic by Lisa Marcus)

In Collins's (1979) study, children had even greater difficulty identifying *implicit* than *explicit* content:

- Second graders had an overall score of fewer than half (47%) of the items that adults had agreed upon. Interestingly, the girls outperformed the boys, "who appear to be performing at about chance level (between 30% and 40%) on this level of inference" (p. 29).
- Fifth graders recalled 67% of the items that adults had agreed on.
- Eighth graders recalled 77% of the items that adults had agreed upon.

Collins explained,

Young children fail to comprehend observed actions and events in an adult-like way because they arrive at different interpretations of the various actors' plans or intentions. . . . Thus, it is possible that second and third graders take away not only a less complete understanding of the program than fifth and eighth graders do, they may also be perceiving the content of the program somewhat *differently* because they retain (and work off of) a different set of cues. (Collins, 1979: 28)

These results suggest that young children are developmentally incapable of recognizing *why* events occur in a story, as well as the connections between events and people. And despite the best intentions of the media communicator to attach a moral to programs, children may be seeing a world without consequence.

Psychological Principles

Several psychological principles help explain (and predict) how individuals comprehend media content.

Cognitive dissonance refers to the principle that individuals tend to selectively remember messages (or parts of messages) in media presentations that reinforce their preexisting beliefs. The principle of cognitive dissonance has several implications for the analysis of media content. As reporters Sam Wang and Sandra Aamodt observe, "Consumers of news, for their part, are prone to selectively accept and remember statements that reinforce beliefs they already hold" (Wang & Aamodt, 2008).

Selective retention refers to individuals' inclination to selectively remember messages (or parts of messages) that are perceived to be relevant to the audience member. An individual's personal experiences, goals, preferences, and beliefs operate together to form a strategy for coping with incoming information. According to Donohew and Tipton's flow model of information seeking, avoiding, and processing (Donohew & Tipton, 1973; Donohew, Tipton, & Haney, 1978), every step of this process involves active decision making:

- Whether to accept or reject that information
- Where to place it in the levels of priority
- Whether to revise it, perhaps seeking out more information

Selective exposure refers to the tendency for individuals to gravitate toward information that supports their own points of view. As a result, selective exposure has an impact on how individuals gather information; we seek out information that reinforces our prejudices, experiences, and predispositions.

This principle also helps to account for the popularity of ideologically driven media, such as Fox News (conservative) and MSNBC (liberal). Reporter Nicholas Kristof (2009) explains,

When we go online, each of us is our own editor, our own gatekeeper. We select the kind of news and opinions that we care most about.

Nicholas Negroponte of M.I.T. has called this emerging news product The Daily Me. And if that's the trend, God save us from ourselves.

That's because there's pretty good evidence that we generally don't truly want good information—but rather information that confirms our prejudices. We may believe intellectually in the clash of opinions, but in practice we like to embed ourselves in the reassuring womb of an echo chamber.

Group polarization refers to a principle in which an individual who holds moderate views will shift in whatever direction the majority favors (in those cases in which the group holds strong beliefs). To illustrate, Tierney cites the following 2005 experiment:

> Groups of Coloradans convened separately in Boulder and Colorado Springs to discuss global warming, affirmative action and civil unions for same-sex couples. Before the discussions, the people in Boulder were on average more liberal than the ones in Colorado Springs, but there were also moderates in both places whose opinions overlapped.
>
> After the group discussions, the people in Boulder moved to the left, and those in Colorado Springs moved to the right. The researchers—David Schkade, Cass Sunstein and Reid Hastie—concluded that "the major effect of deliberation was to make group members more extreme than they were before they started to talk." (Tierney, 2006: A6, p. 21)

According to Tierney, media communicators are *also* products of group polarization: "In fact, most journalists do try to be objective, but as a group they, too, can become polarized by spending most of their time talking to fellow journalists and experts with similar views" (Tierney, 2006).

Cognitive fluency is a psychological principle in which individuals prefer to think about things that are easy, as opposed to those that are difficult—particularly in situations in which they are called on to evaluate the information. Psychologist Adam Alter explains,

> Every purchase you make, every interaction you have, every judgment you make can be put along a continuum from fluent to disfluent. If you can understand how fluency influences judgment, you can understand many, many, many different kinds of judgments better than we do at the moment. (Bennett, 2010)

Mass communicators have begun to apply the principle of *cognitive fluency* in the construction of media messages.

The easier they make it to examine the message, the more inclined people are to accept it. Studies demonstrate that the ease with which an individual processes media content can affect how he or she responds to the information:

- When subjects were exposed to a series of nonsense words or abstract geometric patterns, they expressed a preference for material that had been presented multiple times, and therefore felt familiar (Bennett, 2010).
- Individuals thought that familiar faces, animals, or objects were more attractive than things that were unfamiliar (Bennett, 2010).
- People tend to answer a questionnaire less honestly if it appears in a font that is difficult to read than if it is more legible.
- When presenting people with written descriptions of moral transgressions, increasing the contrast between text and background to make it easier to read the description made people more forgiving (Bennett, 2010).

Thus, the *style* of a media presentation—putting information into rhymes, avoiding jargon that is difficult to pronounce, and employing visually friendly fonts—can affect the audience's receptivity and agreement with the content, as well as their impressions of the communicator. Applying the principle of cognitive fluency can provide insight into the construction of media messages. For instance, a study conducted by Piotr Winkielman and others found a correlation between a person's mood and the desire for fluency. Winkielman found that style affects the receptivity to content; unhappy people responded to familiar, "fluent" presentations.

To illustrate, the 2010 Superbowl ads, which appeared in the midst of a tough economic climate, were populated by familiar faces: Don Rickles for Teleflora, Abe Vigoda and Betty White for Snickers, Chevy Chase and Beverly D'Angelo for HomeAway, Lance Armstrong for Michelob Ultra, Charles Barkley for Taco Bell, Brett Favre for Hyundai, Kool and the Gang for Honda, and Bill Withers for the Dante's Inferno video game. Even old, familiar childhood toys Sock Monkey and a teddy bear sold products. Reporter Stuart Elliott commented on the emphasis on nostalgia and the need for familiar messages:

> The salutes on Sunday to bygone eras reached a peak perhaps not seen since the last time Fonzie said "Ayyyy" on "Happy Days." The reason is, of course, the economy and the belief along Madison Avenue that tough times call for familiarity rather than risks. . . . Sigh. It may take

an economic recovery, even a boom, for Super Bowl advertisers to start taking chances again. (Elliott, 2010)

Audience Behavior Patterns

What are audience members doing while they are receiving media messages? Audience behavior patterns refer to an individual's aggregate experience while exposed to a media presentation.

Competing Activities

Audience members are frequently engaged in competing activities while receiving media messages (driving while listening to the radio, for instance). A study conducted in 2005 found that the subjects (representing a broad range of age) were *multitasking* about a third of the time they were using media. Colleen Fahey Rush, executive vice president for research at MTV Networks, notes, "Our research showed that people somehow managed to shoehorn 31 hours of activity into a 24-hour day. That's from being able to do two things at once" (Waxman, 2006).

Unfortunately, the brain appears to have a finite amount of space for all of the tasks that require concentrated attention. A study using magnetic resonance images of brain activity reveals that engaging in competing activities impairs an individual's ability to perform *either* task effectively.

Although your brain can become more proficient at carrying out multiple tasks, your performance levels are never as high as when the tasks are carried out independently (Blakeslee, 2001). Because of this divided attention, you may be not be giving critical attention to either activity. Studies show that drivers who talk on cell phones are four times more likely to be in a crash and drive just as erratically as people with an 0.08 percent blood alcohol level. In one study cited by the highway safety agency, "drivers found it easier to drive drunk than to drive while using a phone, even when it was hands-free" (Dowd, 2009).

Consequently, you may be susceptible to subtle messages that can affect your attitudes and behaviors. Despite their years of training, young people are overwhelmed by this barrage of images, sounds, and messages. Andrew Blau (2004) declares,

There is more media produced than can ever be seen. . . . Even young people who can multitask in ways that make older heads spin will not be able to keep up with the growing amount of media available on the growing number of surfaces, devices, and screens of all kinds.

This multitasking often involves *multiple media* activities:

- About 80% of teens regularly use more than one media type at a given time.
- More than 60% of teens say they regularly go online while watching TV.
- Nearly 60% use instant messaging, and about 35% listen to the radio while watching TV. (Downey, 2003)

This can lead to a lot of confusion with regard to distinct media messages.

Furthermore, studies indicate that half of the audience leaves the room at least once during the course of a TV show—while the media communicator is "talking" to the audience. And approximately one-third of the audience deserts the typical hour-long program before it is over, switching to another channel or turning off the television (Downey, 2003). Consequently, if you answer the phone or leave the room for a portion of a telecast, the text has been altered; if you miss the ending of a police drama, before the criminals are caught, you may be left with the message that crime *does* pay.

Much of an individual's consumption of media is *involuntary*. Voluntary media consists of times when *you* choose a particular medium or program., Involuntary media refers to the times when someone *else* has made a media selection, and you are exposed to messages beyond your control (e.g., someone blasting the radio in the next room while you are trying to sleep). As a result of this merging of images, printed text, dialogue, and music, an individual may be receiving an altogether *different* message than was originally intended by the media communicator.

Involuntary media activity also may be *embedded within* a voluntary media activity. As an example, *product placement* is an advertising strategy in which the products are incorporated into media presentations. Using products as props or part of the set legitimizes the product and is therefore a subtle form of persuasion. On a per-episode basis, the number of product placements is staggering. In 2006, the telecasts of the reality show *Contender* averaged 500.9 individual occurrences of products placed in its shows—almost 30 times that of traditional commercial messaging (Mindlin, 2006).

Questions to ask regarding media consumption include the following:

- How much of your media activity was voluntary?
- How much media activity was involuntary?
- How much involuntary media activity was *embedded* in voluntary media?

Another focus of audience behavior analysis involves examining media usage by different subcultures. For instance, a breakdown of social media usage by *age* finds that in 2010, people aged between 18 and 33 outpaced other groups, increasing from 67 percent to 83 percent between December 2008 through May 2010. However, during the same period, adults 74 and older who were online *quadrupled* their social networking presence (although their total number is significantly lower than the younger group—16 percent (Wayne, 2010).

Audience behavior also differs significantly between ethnic groups. For instance, in 2010, African Americans watched television for an average of 7 hours, 12 minutes per day. In contrast, Asian Americans watched television for an average of 3 hours, 14 minutes per day. The types of programming also differed according to ethnicity. Football was the most-watched programming among African Americans, Asian Americans, and Caucasians; in contrast, soccer and the Latin Grammys were most popular among Hispanics (Mindlin, 2011).

See also: Advertising—Media Literacy Analysis

References

Blakeslee, S. (2001, July 31). "Car Calls May Leave Brain Short-Handed." *New York Times*, F1.

Barnes, B. (2009, April 14). "Disney Expert Uses Science to Draw Boy Viewers." *New York Times*. Retrieved from http://www.nytimes.com/2009/04/14/arts/television/14boys.html?pagewanted=all

Bennett, D. (2010, January 31). "Easy=True." *Boston Globe*. Retrieved from http://www.boston.com/bostonglobe/ideas/articles/2010/01/31/easy__true

Collins, A. A. (1979). "Children's Comprehension of Television Content." In E. Wartella (Ed.), *Children Communicating*. Beverly Hills, CA: Sage.

Donohew, L., & Tipton, L. (1973). "Conceptual Model of Information Seeking, Avoiding and Processing." In P. Clarke (Ed.), *New Models for Mass Communication*. Beverly Hills, CA: Sage.

Donohew, L., Tipton, L., & Haney, R. (1978). "Analysis of Information-Seeking Strategies." *Journalism Quarterly, 55,* Spring, 25-31.

Dowd, M. (2009, July 21). "Whirling Dervish Drivers." *New York Times*. Retrieved from http://www.nytimes.com/2009/07/22/opinion/22dowd.html

Downey, K. (2003, September 25). "Huge Challenge for Advertisers to Get Noticed," Media Life.

Elliott, S. (2010, February 8). "In Super Bowl Commercials, the Nostalgia Bowl." *New York Times*. Retrieved from http://www.nytimes.com/2010/02/08/business/media/08adco.html.

Kristoff, N. (2009, March 18). "The Daily Me." *New York Times*. Retrieved from http://www.nytimes.com/2009/03/19/opinion/19kristof.html

Mindlin, A. (2006, March 20). "Increasingly, the Message Is in the Medium." *New York Times*. Retrieved from http://www.nytimes.com/2006/03/20/business/media/20drill.html

Mindlin, A. (2011, April 17). "Tracking TV Habits by Ethnic Groups." *New York Times*. Retrieved from http://www.nytimes.com/2011/04/18/business/media/18drill.html

Ognianova, E., & Thorson, E. E. (1998). "Evidence for selective perception in the processing of health campaign messages." Paper submitted to the Communication Theory & Methodology Division of the Association for Education in Journalism and Mass Communication for its 1998 conference.

Tierney, J. (2006, November 7). "Must We Talk?" *New York Times,* A6, p. 21.

Turow, J. (2006, August 27). "Hidden Messages: Is New Technology Empowering Consumers—or Marketers?" *Boston Globe*. Retrieved from http://www.boston.com/news/globe/ideas/articles/2006/08/27/hidden_messages/

Wang, S., & Sandra Aamodt, S. (2008, June 27). "Your Brain Lies to You." *New York Times,* p. A19.

Waxman, S. (2006, May 15). "At an Industry Media Lab, Close Views of Multitasking." *New York Times*. Retrieved from http://www.nytimes.com/2006/05/15/technology/15research.html?pagewanted=all.

Wayne, T. (2010, September 26). "Age Gap Narrows on Social Networks." *New York Times*. Retrieved from http://www.nytimes.com/2010/12/27/business/media/27drill.html

Autobiographical Analysis

Autobiographical analysis is an approach to the study of media literacy that promotes personal discovery and growth. The autobiographical approach is *audience driven*; that is, individuals use their own experiences with the media as a springboard for self-analysis. This approach emphasizes *process* and *exploration*—ways of looking at media content—rather than set answers.

At the same time, juxtaposing one's personal experiences with media depictions can furnish insight into the analysis of characterization, plot conventions, worldview, and media messages about success, violence, and gender roles. In addition, this approach promotes the discussion of media as a representation of reality, as individuals contrast moments in their own lives with media presentations.

This approach is an extension of the *reception theory*, a construct that maintains that the audience assumes an active role in interpreting information. Audience members filter the information they receive through the media, taking into account factors such as gender; racial, ethnic, or class identity; stage of development; and social context. As a result, an individual's interpretation can be entirely different than the "preferred" reading dictated by the media communicator.

Because discussion and analysis begin with personal responses to media content, this approach can be particularly effective in nonacademic settings involving community groups, older adults, church organizations, and "at-risk" teenagers. Although residents of retirement centers may not have the capability or inclination to apply themselves to the academic rigor of a formal media literacy course, the autobiographical approach is educational in a broader sense, by promoting personal reflection.

The autobiographical approach also offers a way to initiate insightful family discussions. Responding to a program that parents and children watch together can lead to valuable "teachable moments." For instance, talking about a television commercial can lead to the following discussions:

- *Function*: What is the purpose of the TV spot?
  From there, it can be useful to focus on latent functions in advertising—although the manifest (i.e., surface) function may be to entertain, the latent (under the surface) function is to generate a profit.
- *Affective Response*: How does the ad make you feel?
  This discussion can lead to a conversation about how ads frequently present scenarios that trigger emotions and then manipulate these feelings to sell their products.

The autobiographical approach can also serve as an effective diagnostic counseling tool. Although at-risk adolescents are often uncomfortable talking about themselves, these teenagers (primarily boys) can be encouraged to talk about media programs.

Identification analysis is a line of inquiry in which individuals examine their own attitudes, values, lifestyles, and personal decisions within the context of media presentations. Two types of identification analysis are character identification and narrative identification.

Character identification involves examining the characters in a media presentation as a springboard to an examination of an individual's own personal experience and social environment. Children often discover personality traits in themselves by recognizing them in others. Psychologist Gloria Johnson Powell (1982) explains,

> After the early differentiation of self from the animate and inanimate worlds, the process of self-concept development becomes more social in nature. It begins to involve identification with others, introjection from others, and expansion into interpersonal relationships. (1982: 107)

Within this context, audience members' identification with particular characters can furnish insight into their interests, aspirations, and values. This approach includes the following steps:

- Ask the subjects to identify favorite characters and explain what they liked and disliked about the characters.
- *Clarify the nature of the character identification*: *likeness* (the subject sees a resemblance with the character) or *aspiration* (the subject would like to emulate the character). This strategy can provide insight into the individual's perceived gender, ethnic, racial, and class identification, as well as information about what the subjects consider attractive or engaging behaviors, values, and attributes.
- *Name additional attributes of the character that the subject did not include in his/her original list of attributes*. This may lead to discussion about qualities that may not be readily apparent but are, nevertheless, essential to the overall character portrait. This also can serve as a springboard for discussion about cultural values, as subjects identify with "negative" attributes (such as violent tendencies) that are seen in a positive light by the respondent.
- *Discuss the role that the attributes of the character play in the outcome of the story.* For instance, a violent temperament often is presented in media programs as essential to resolving problems. Subjects can then examine the role that this attribute plays in their own life "narratives": Does being tough or violent guarantee success?
- Furthermore, it can be useful to consider whether there are *missing* attributes that prevent some characters from succeeding in the narrative. At the same time, other attributes may help the individual succeed within the context of the narrative—some of which, perhaps, the audience member does not identify with or immediately think about.
- Discuss whether there are missing attributes in some characters that prevent them from succeeding within the context of the narrative.

- *Name characters to whom subjects* cannot *relate.* This can stimulate discussion about expectations: what can be regarded as unrealistic or "too perfect" characters or characters with attributes that the student may regard as unobtainable in their own lives.
- *Discuss how the subjects relate to villains.* In some cases, audience members are more attracted to the character traits of the villains than those of the heroes. One way to account for this phenomenon is that audience members identify with some of the flaws of the antagonists. Another possibility is that characterization (and human personality) is more complex than the absolute distinctions presented in the media: there can be evil in good and good in evil. Indeed, villainous characters may display an energy, creativity, and sexuality that audience members find attractive. Finally, these traits may account for their success in the narrative.

Narrative identification is a line of inquiry in which individuals examine their own personal experience in response to choices made by characters in media programs.

Narrative reconstruction and *narrative forecasting* are strategies that can furnish perspective into an individual's interests, values, and concerns.

Narrative reconstruction refers to a process in which individuals recount a story they have seen, heard, or read in the media. This strategy is rooted in the experience of the individual, providing insight into how individuals make sense of the programming they have watched, heard, or read. Asking individuals to focus on the *explicit content* of a media presentation can be an excellent way to learn about their interests and preoccupations. Explicit content refers to the essential events and activities in a story that are displayed through visible action. Thus, one way to learn about a person's interests and preoccupations involves asking individuals to recount a story they have seen, heard, or read in the media: What is the story about?

In retelling stories, young children often have difficulty deciding on the essential points in the narrative. They may omit parts of the story that adults judge to be essential content and also may include pieces of the story deemed nonessential. In reconstructing the essential elements of a narrative, young children often embellish a story with their own experiences, inserting themselves into the narrative. For instance, in describing a James Bond movie, a young child may devote an extraordinary amount of attention describing the Austin Healy driven by the British agent, reflecting his or her interest in cars. In recounting a media narrative, individuals may also add their editorial commentary (e.g., "This was neat"). Thus, a child's narrative reconstruction of the Bond movie may reveal more about the interests of the child than about the film itself.

Narrative forecasting is an approach that enables individuals to examine their own values system in response to choices made by characters in a media presentation. One effective technique involves presenting a scene from a media program to subjects. Subjects then put themselves in the situation depicted in the media program by responding to the following questions:

- What do you think will happen next? Why?
- How will the characters be affected? Why?
- How would you feel about being in that situation?
- How would you react if it happened to you?

Then invite students to compare the narrative to their *own* experience:

- Does the situation remind you of your own life?
- How would the characters handle *your* situation?
- Would it work? Why or why not?
- What would happen to you if you behaved in the way that the characters did in the presentation?

A related mode of analysis focuses attention on the *limits* of identification. Although film, television, and the other media may appear to reflect the audience's experience, the media construct a reality that is impossible to emulate in real life. Production elements such as editing present selected moments that make actors always look perfect. Special effects and stunt specialists enable characters to perform astonishing acts of strength and daring. And because the action is scripted, our heroes and heroines never miss a line, accidentally spill their food, or die while the narrative is in progress.

Moreover, through the use of makeup, editing, lighting, and digital manipulation, actors always look perfect. The members of the audience cannot possibly measure up to these idealized figures.

Questions to ask to examine the limits of narrative reconstruction (de-identification) include the following:

1. In what ways does the media presentation construct a reality that is different from your everyday experience?
2. What production elements are used to construct this reality?
3. Are the actions of the characters unrealistic? Explain.

Media Chronicles

In the 1970s, scholars began to conduct *oral histories* in which they recorded the personal reminiscences of older citizens as a means of studying personal and cultural history. Within this context, media chronicles can be an effective method of triggering personal recollections.

Media programming often assumes a personal significance that transcends its aesthetic or entertainment value. Individuals frequently associate media presentations with significant moments in their lives. Indeed, recalling popular media programming can bring past experiences into the present.

In conducting a media chronicle interview, the facilitator presents clips of popular media programs from a particular era and asks the following questions:

- What does this program remind you of? (Be specific.)
- How old were you when the program was popular?
- What were you doing when it was popular?
- Can you describe the environment in which you watched the program?
  - With whom did you watch the program?
  - Where did you watch the program?
  - What were you doing while you heard (or were watching) the program?
- Can you recall the first time you saw (or heard) the program?
- Can you recall how you felt (scared, amused) while you watched (or listened to) the program?
- Does the program remind you of any people or experiences in your life?
- Are there any cultural artifacts (e.g., cars, dress) or behaviors in the program that had personal significance in your own life? Explain.
- Do you remember any of the characters?
  - Which characters did you like? Dislike? Why?
  - Did you identify with any of the characters? Why?

As the media chronicles demonstrate, watching old films or TV shows or listening to radio programs can spark personal recollections of otherwise forgotten pieces of the past. Hearing an old song on the radio may awaken memories of a summer long ago, perhaps, or of old friends or a first romance.

Media programs also may kindle personal recollections about particular stages of life. For instance, a person may embrace films, songs, and television programs that they associate with their adolescence. Media programs may also be associated with seasonal activities. As an example, Christmas music and movies often evoke memories of family and past holiday seasons.

In addition to stimulating personal recollections, media chronicles can furnish insight into cultural history. Presenting snippets of programs may trigger personal memories about the culture. Media can also be associated with social movements. For instance, the cult film *Easy Rider* (1969) assumes a significance for members of the 1960s counterculture. Seeing this film many years later may evoke memories about the social and political experiences of this social group.

See also: Affective Response Analysis; Audience Analysis; Character Analysis; Production Analysis Approach; Values Clarification Approach

Reference

Powell, G. J. (1982). "The Impact of Television on the Self-Concept Development of Minority Group Children." In Gordon L. Berry and Claudia Mitchell-Kernan (Eds.), *Television and the Socialization of the Minority Child*. New York: Academic Press.

Business Models, Journalism

As a product of the American economic system (as well as a significant player), the journalism industry experienced a state of economic crisis between 2008 and 2010. During this period, newspaper circulation decreased by more than 10 percent. The industry sold about 44 million copies a day—fewer than at any time since the 1940s. As an example, circulation at *The San Francisco Chronicle* declined by 25.8 percent on weekdays, to about 252,000—less than half what it was six years earlier. Moreover, during the first quarter of 2009, advertising revenue was down 30 percent at some newspapers (Perez-Pena, 2009c). Many papers folded, leaving vast regions without a newspaper with roots in their communities. In addition, large media conglomerates like the Tribune Company, which operates *The Chicago Tribune*, *The Los Angeles Times*, and six other daily papers, filed for bankruptcy protection (Swensen & Schmidt, 2009).

Amid all of this chaos, a number of business models have emerged. Although some models will surely fall by the wayside, others will ultimately work to the benefit of the newspaper industry—and its readers.

1. Free Model

One of the byproducts of the development of the Internet is that a great deal of information is available to the public without charge. Consequently, although more people are exposed to news programming than ever before, the companies that produce the news are not realizing a profit. Rupert Murdoch, who once vowed to make *The Wall Street Journal*'s Web site free, reversed course in 2009 and proposed charging readers for access to online newspapers:

> Quality journalism is not cheap, and an industry that gives away its content is simply cannibalizing its ability to produce good reporting. The digital revolution has opened many new and inexpensive distribution channels but it has not made content free. We intend to charge for all our news Web sites. (Carr, 2009)

Significantly, in a 2009 survey of regular Internet users in the United States, 48 percent said that they were willing to pay to read news online, including on mobile devices (Perez-Pena, 2009d).

2. "Less-Is-More" Model

At some newspapers, management decisions have been designed to maximize the profitability of the newspapers—often at the expense of the quality of the news coverage. In some cases, distribution schedules have been reduced. For instance, the *Flint Journal*, the *Saginaw News*, and the *Bay City Times* slashed their daily publication to Thursdays, Fridays, and Sundays only.

Furthermore, some national papers have eliminated their national and international bureaus. In November 2009, *The Washington Post* announced that it planned to close its three remaining national bureaus; instead, the newspaper will cover national stories by traveling from its base in Washington. In a memo to the staff, Executive Editor Marcus W. Brauchli cited "limited resources and increased competitive pressure" for the move (Carter, 2009). Moreover, only a handful of American newspapers now operate foreign bureaus.

The most drastic cuts have come at the expense of personnel. *The Seattle Times* cut its staff from 375 to 210 reporters over a five-year period. Executive Editor David Boardman declared, "We're about at the floor of what we feel we can have and still put out a *Seattle Times* we can be proud of. We've had to be more thoughtful in choosing what we do, but I'm not one to claim that less is more. Less is less" (Perez-Pena, 2009b). The reporters with the highest salaries have also been "downsized," so that papers are staffed by the least experienced journalists. Moreover, these newspapers increasingly rely on wire services such as the Associated Press, contributing to the homogenization of news content.

Unfortunately, this strategy often leads to a cycle in which the decline in quality is accompanied by a shrinking audience, necessitating further cutbacks.

3. Advertising Revenue Model

Some newspapers have continued to rely on advertising as their primary source of revenue. Beginning in 2010, advertising revenue has rebounded, in print, broadcast, and Internet journalism. For instance, Publicis, which owns agencies such as Saatchi & Saatchi and Leo Burnett, reported an 8 percent increase in its revenue for 2010 (Pfanner, 2011).

Some newspapers have begun to implement an Internet advertising strategy that involves selling data on consumers for targeted ads. Another Internet advertising strategy consists of selling *hyperlinks* for purposes of cross-promotion. Walter Isaacson (2009) explains,

> Hypertext—an embedded Web link that refers you to another page or site—had been invented by Ted Nelson in the early 1960s with the goal of enabling micropayments for content. He wanted to make sure that the people who created good stuff got rewarded for it. In his vision, all links on a page would facilitate the accrual of small, automatic payments for whatever content was accessed. (Isaacson, 2009: 54)

4. Subscription Model

Newsday and the *Wall Street Journal* are examples of publications that successfully charge a monthly subscription fee for their online editions. In 2008, paid subscriptions for the *Journal*'s Web site increased by 7 percent despite the recession.

The key question, however, remains: How do you get consumers to pay for a subscription to a publication that they have grown used to getting for free? The answer may involve offering the consumer something *extra*.

- *Additional features* such as e-mail alerts, blogs, discussion forums and video. Indeed, in 2006, *The Washington Post* became the first newspaper to win an Emmy for its video.
- *Additional content* online that is not available elsewhere (including the media organization's print edition).
- *Improved content.* News organizations try to persuade readers that they provide something more valuable than the aggregators and blogs that attract newsreaders online.

5. Micropayment Model

The micropayment model consists of a system in which an individual pays a small sum for each article or program that they receive. A newspaper might charge a fraction of a penny for an article, a nickel for that day's full edition, or $2 for a month's worth of Internet access. For instance, the *Financial Times* has added a plan to accept micropayments for individual articles as an alternative to a full subscription.

The most notable example of the micropayment model is iTunes. The consumer of online music purchases, who was used to free services such as Napster, has generally become comfortable with the concept of paying 99 cents to download a single tune.

The keys to successful micropayment model are *convenience* and *transparency*. Walter Isaacson, president and CEO of the Aspen Institute, a nonpartisan educational and policy studies institute based in Washington, DC, declares,

> The key to attracting online revenue . . . is to come up with an iTunes-easy method of micropayment. We need something like digital coins or an E-ZPass digital wallet—a one-click system with a really simple interface that will permit impulse purchases of a newspaper, magazine, article, blog or video for a penny, nickel, dime or whatever the creator chooses to charge. (Isaacson, 2009)

6. Nonprofit Model

In a nonprofit organization, the goal is something other than making a profit, such as promoting social welfare. Nonprofit newspapers benefit from Section 501(c)(3) of the Internal Revenue Service code, which provides exemption from taxes on income and allows tax deductions for people who make contributions to eligible organizations.

Another advantage of the nonprofit model is that the editorial staff is insulated from advertisers and stockholders. David Swensen and Michael Schmid (2009) explain, "The greater stability and enhanced independence [of this model] . . . allow them to serve the public good more effectively."

A related strategy involves building an endowment that would insulate the media organization from market pressures.

How large an endowment would a major newspaper need? Swensen and Schmidt estimate that the *New York Times* would require a $5 billion endowment:

> The news-gathering operations at the *New York Times* cost a little more than $200 million a year. Assuming some additional outlay for overhead, it would require an endowment of approximately $5 billion (assuming a 5 percent annual payout rate). Newspapers with smaller newsrooms would require smaller endowments . . . (This would be) supplemented by Hard Copy Sales and Online Subscriptions. (Swensen & Schmidt, 2009)

The great disadvantage of the nonprofit business model is that endowed institutions are prohibited from trying to "influence legislation" or "participate in any campaign activity for or against political candidates." This would appear to undermine one of the chief functions of newspapers—to present *editorials* on the eve of elections that endorse candidates and issues.

One derivative nonprofit model involves journalism sites dedicated to investigative projects, in collaboration with established news outlets. For instance, ProPublica and the Center for Public Integrity are examples of online nonprofit journalism sites devoted to investigative journalism. The partnership between ProPublica and the *New York Times* produced two big stories in 2009: a front-page examination of failures in American reconstruction efforts in Iraq and a story about how Siemens, the German engineering firm, paid millions of dollars in bribes around the world. Indeed, ProPublica won a share of the 2010 Pulitzer Prize for investigative reporting, in partnership with the *New York Times Magazine*, for a story about the critical decisions made by doctors at a New Orleans hospital during Hurricane Katrina.

Another variation of the nonprofit model is the Low-profit Limited Liability Company (L3C), which combines foundation funding and for-profit investment to pursue a social or charitable purpose. These nonprofit hybrids are founded on the premise that more investment capital will flow to charitable organizations that are able to offer a "double bottom line"—a social benefit and a financial return.

A successful L3C includes the following key elements:

- A charitable mission that takes precedence over maximization of profit
- Revenue from operations
- A financial model that contemplates funding from foundations and others

- An entity that has owners with an economic stake in the enterprise (in contrast to a non-profit whose members do not have an economic stake) (Moody, 2008)

Tom Moody, who works with businesses, investors, and equity firms to set up L3Cs, explains,

> The companies that are able to create this kind of leverage will be giving private foundations the kind of long-term return they want to see—the possibility of some financial return, but, more importantly, long-term social benefits that will result from the organization's expanded operations and greater financial self-sufficiency. (Moody, 2008)

In 2008, Vermont became the first state in the United States to enact a law permitting the formation of L3Cs. An L3C organized under the laws of the State of Vermont must meet the following criteria:

- The company significantly furthers the accomplishment of one or more charitable or educational purposes and would not have been formed but for the company's relationship to the accomplishment of charitable or educational purposes.
- No significant purpose of the company is the production of income or the appreciation of property; provided, however, that the fact that the company produces significant income or capital appreciation is not, in the absence of other factors, conclusive evidence of a significant purpose involving the production of income or the appreciation of property.
- The company is not organized to accomplish one or more political or legislative purposes. (Moody, 2008)

7. Niche Market Model

Over time, the media market has grown to the point that it has become profitable to direct messages at specialized interests, tastes, and groups. In 2009, *Newsweek* responded to the economic downturn by targeting a small but affluent readership base, actually lowering its rate base (the circulation promised to advertisers) from 3.1 million to 2.6 million, with a plan to lower the base to 1.5 million by January 2010. The editors of *Newsweek* hoped to make up for this overall loss of audience by raising its subscription rate from less than $25 to $50 a year (Perez-Pena, 2009a).

Newsweek's change in its identity was accompanied by a new design. The magazine replaced its thin paper with heavier stock that is more appealing to advertisers and readers and will also put more emphasis on photography.

In addition, by focusing on a niche market, *Newsweek* altered its content. Rather than emphasizing the week's biggest event, articles were reorganized under four sections: *Short Takes*, *Columnists and Commentary*, *In-depth* pieces (such as the cover articles), and *Culture*. A new graphic feature on the last page, "The Bluffer's Guide," tells readers how to sound as if they are knowledgeable on a current topic.

A related niche strategy is *localization*, targeting local subcultures such as ethnic and racial groups, as well as religious affiliations. According to Ellen Sherberg, publisher of the *St. Louis Business Journal*, the key to its success is addressing the interests and concerns of the local community:

> It's all about the "niche" we hold, providing information you can't find anywhere else, including our Top 25 lists for business growth, people on the move, network tips and our own event series. And in this "Great Recession," we can tell you how to get your piece of the stimulus or which companies are hiring.
>
> Business news is important. And because over 80 percent of business is local, local business news is even more important. (Sherberg, 2009)

Indeed, *Newsday* has taken this strategy a step further, tailoring its news stories to the readers' zip codes (Perez-Pena, 2009a).

8. Collaborative Model

Over the years, the journalism industry has looked to the collaborative model as a way to share expenses. The passage of the Newspaper Preservation Act of 1970 enabled competing newspapers in a geographic area to combine business operations while maintaining separate—and competitive—enterprises. During the recent economic downturn, several media operations pooled their resources as a cost-saving measure. For example, in North Carolina, the *Charleston Gazette*, a family-owned newspaper, has entered into a joint operating agreement with the *Charleston Daily Mail*, which is owned by the Media News Group.

More recently, collaborative efforts between newspapers of business operations have taken several forms:

- *Printing schedules*—two newspapers are printed on the same presses at different times of day
- *The consolidation of classified advertising*
- *Distribution*—two newspapers share the same distribution agent (i.e., delivering the papers)
- *Sharing content*—as an example, in February 2009, five newspapers in New York and New Jersey announced plans to share articles and photographs

9. Investment Capital Model

This business model is predicated on the assumption that the media company is a sound investment. As an example, in 2009, the political news Web site *Talking Points Memo* announced a plan to attract investors that involved increasing site staff. Unfortunately, the investment model lends itself to a climate that can encourage influence peddling. In 2009, *The Washington Post* issued invitations to lobbyists to sponsor off-the-record "Salons" where they could mix with what a promotional flier called "the right people" to "alter the debate." The "right people" consisted of White House officials, members of Congress, and the *Post*'s own journalists. The Salons were to be held in the home of the paper's publisher, Katharine Weymouth. Accepting this invitation cost between $25,000 and $250,000.

But after the Salons were reported on the Web site *Politico*, they were canceled. The *Post*'s ombudsman called the Salons an "ethical lapse of monumental proportions" (Rich, 2009).

10. Employee-Driven Model

This model has hardly progressed past the conceptualization stage but does offer some intriguing potential. The underlying principle is that employees are familiar with an operation in a way that investors—or the company's own executives—are not. Thus, employees could run a cost-efficient organization. Moreover, longtime employees have a passion for the field and a commitment to maintaining a quality newspaper. One way to proceed is for a union to purchase the newspaper, thus making the employees co-owners.

11. University Model

Historically, university journalism programs have served as learning laboratories that educate aspiring reporters. By working on their school newspapers, students learn to research, write, and edit journalism stories. But in addition, a new model has emerged in which university media programs work with journalism organizations on projects as part of their curriculum, the object being to produce publication-worthy articles. For instance, in 2009, the University of California-Berkeley's Graduate School of Journalism entered into a partnership with a $5 million initial grant from F. Warren Hellman and the news staff of KQED-FM to create a nonprofit local news Web site for the San Francisco area.

See also: Journalism; Ownership Patterns, Media

References

Carr, D. (2009, August 10). "For Murdoch, It's Try, Try Again." *New York Times*. Retrieved from http://www.nytimes.com/2009/08/10/business/media/10carr.html

Carter, B. (2009, November 25). "Washington Post to Shut U.S. Bureaus." *New York Times*. Retrieved from http://www.nytimes.com/2009/11/25/business/media/25post.html

Isaacson, W. (2009, February 5). "How to Save Your Newspaper." *Time Magazine*, 53–56.

Moody, T. (2008). "The L3C—Facilitating Socially Beneficial Investing." Burlington, VT: Downs Rachlin Martin PLLC. Retrieved from http://www.linkingmissiontomoney.com/documents/L3CArticle-Moody.pdf

Perez-Pena, R. (2009a, February 9). "*Newsweek* Plans Makeover to Fit a Smaller Audience." *New York Times*. Retrieved from http://www.nytimes.com/2009/02/09/business/media/09newsweek.html

Perez-Pena, R. (2009b, August 10). "Seattle Paper Is Resurgent as a Solo Act." *New York Times*. Retrieved from http://www.nytimes.com/2009/08/10/business/media/10seattle.html?pagewanted=all

Perez-Pena, R. (2009c, October 27). "U.S. Newspaper Circulation Falls 10%." *New York Times*. Retrieved from http://www.nytimes.com/2009/10/27/business/media/27audit.html

Perez-Pena, R. (2009d, November 16). "About Half in U.S. Would Pay for Online News, Study Finds." *New York Times*. Retrieved from http://www.nytimes.com/2009/11/16/business/media/16paywall.html

Pfanner, E. (2011, March 27). "Digital Strategy Paying Off for Publicis." *New York Times*. Retrieved from http://www.nytimes.com/2011/03/28/business/media/28levy.html?pagewanted=all

Rich, F. (2009, July 26). "And That's Not the Way It Is." *New York Times*. Retrieved from http://www.nytimes.com/2009/07/26/opinion/26rich.html?pagewanted=all

Sherberg, E. (2009, December 4–10). "Paper Thrives, Circ Rises, Readers Profit." *St. Louis Business Journal, 30* (14), 1.

Swensen, D., & Schmidt, M. (2009, January 27). "News You Can Endow." *New York Times.* Retrieved from http://www.nytimes.com/2009/01/28/opinion/28swensen .html?pagewanted=all&_r=0

Careers, Media Literacy

Increasingly, students across the United States are developing a passionate interest in the field of media literacy. But although these students clearly understand the value of this area of study, they are faced with a practical consideration—namely, what careers are available for those who study media literacy. This entry identifies trends that can help media literacy students look for professional applications for their interests and skills. By no means do the organizations cited in the entry represent a comprehensive list. The information is designed to serve as a springboard for further investigation into careers in media literacy.

Generally speaking, the discipline of media literacy prepares individuals for any profession requiring critical thinking, research, and writing skills. But more specifically, media literacy students may pursue careers in the following fields.

Education

In the United States, language pertaining to media literacy is included in the educational standards—what students are expected to know by graduation—in all 50 states. However, relatively few elementary or secondary schools actually teach media literacy, for a variety of reasons:

- With requirements such as No Child Left Behind, teachers feel overwhelmed.
- Media literacy content does not appear on the state standardized tests—and, consequently, isn't taught.
- Teachers are not prepared to teach the material.

However, in this era of educational accountability, it is reasonable to expect that media literacy will become part of the curriculum of elementary and secondary schools in the foreseeable future. Furthermore, although the upper-level grades are filled with requirements, there is, generally, more opportunity for media literacy education between grades 5 and 9. As a result, there will be a growing demand for teachers who have a background in media literacy.

Moreover, media literacy is frequently integrated into established disciplines such as English and social studies. As a result, media literacy pedagogy is incorporated into the course content of these disciplines.

Faculty positions at the college level should be opening up as well. A 2007 survey found that more than 180 schools of higher education (community colleges, colleges, and universities) throughout the United States offer coursework or programs in media literacy.

Most media literacy courses can be found in departments of communication. However, schools such as Appalachian State University and Webster University offer media literacy degrees through their departments of education. As more elementary and secondary school districts begin to implement media literacy requirements, there will be an increasing demand for education departments to teach the teachers about this discipline.

In addition, Morehead State University and Wesley College have added media literacy courses to their general education requirements for all of their students. If this trend catches on, the additional number of course offerings will further increase the demand for instructors in this field.

Numerous organizations promote media literacy education in the United States, including the National Alliance for Media Literacy Education (NAMLE), the Center for Media Education, the Media Education Foundation, and the National Council for Teachers of English (NCTE).

In addition, enterprising media literacy graduates may work in one of a number of *nontraditional educational venues*, which introduce media literacy to audiences normally not reached through the conventional educational system. For example, media literacy classes have been offered through Oasis, a national organization for people aged older than 50 years that subscribes to the mission of "promoting successful aging through lifelong learning, health plans, and volunteer engagement" (www.oasis.org/AboutUs.aspx).

Another nontraditional educational avenue involves speaking to parents' groups such as parent/teacher organizations (PTOs) about the value of media literacy education, which has the added benefit of enlisting support for media literacy education in the schools. Administrators may not be attentive to the recommendations of teachers, but they are extremely responsive to parental concerns.

Other nontraditional educational opportunities include the following:

- *Conducting professional development workshops for teachers*. School districts routinely offer professional development programs to enhance their teachers' instructional skills. Because most current teachers haven't been exposed to media literacy curricula, professional development sessions introduce teachers to the principles of media literacy and assist instructors in developing classroom lessons.

- *Developing classroom materials for teachers.* Teachers frequently lack the time to develop relevant and timely lesson plans and curricula. These teaching materials could be distributed over the Internet on a subscription basis.

- *Teaching parents about strategies for media analysis.* Media coverage of news events, new films, advertising campaigns, and Internet developments provides innumerable "teachable moments" that illustrate and extend the principles of media literacy. Organizations such as Parents as Teachers reach two nontraditional audiences at once: small children and parents. In the process, both young children and their parents become more sensitive to media-related issues, such as messages in video games and violence in the media. Even young children can become aware of the influence of production values such as music in a media presentation.

Business

In 2009, the average American consumed approximately 34 gigabytes of data and information each day—an increase of about 350 percent over about three decades. At the same time, however, the amount of time that individuals spend reading has actually declined (Bilton, 2009). Consequently, many companies now place a value on employees who have the ability to interpret and construct messages, using the various "languages" of media, such as film, television, audio, and the Internet.

At University of Southern California, 60 academic courses require students to create term papers and projects that use video, sound, and Internet components. According to Elizabeth Daley, dean of the School of Cinema-Television at the university, "The greatest digital divide is between those who can read and write with media, and those who can't. Our core knowledge needs to belong to everybody" (Van Ness, 2005).

The curricula in business schools are now designed to educate students to construct and interpret messages using the various "languages" of media (i.e., print, photography, audio, film, television, and digital media).

Moreover, for the first time, at the Massachusetts Institute of Technology's annual entrepreneurial competition, contestants were able to submit their start-up ideas not just on paper and in person but also in 60-second videos on YouTube. Universities such as Harvard, Rice, and the University of Chicago competed for the $100,000 prize, presenting 60-second *elevator pitches* via YouTube. In addition, video pitches came from universities in Taiwan, Cameroon, India, and Pakistan.

MBA student Kourosh Kaghazian, who organized the contest, notes, "It's really important for start-ups that have limited resources to be able to use social media platforms to . . . promote their products or services, to recruit talent or raise funding" (Hartman, 2011). The 60-second elevator pitch has three key ingredients: (1) the problem, (2) explanation of how your solution works in the marketplace, and (3) a closer—something catchy to seal the deal.

In addition, premier business schools such as Harvard, Stanford, and the Rotman School of Management at the University of Toronto have redesigned their curriculum to emphasize *critical thinking*—the foundation of media literacy. Garth Saloner, dean of Stanford's Graduate School of Business, declares, "If I'm going to really launch you on a career or path where you can make a big impact in the world, you have to be able to think critically and analytically about the big problems in the world" (Wallace, 2010).

Steve McConnell, a managing partner of NBBJ, an architecture firm based in Seattle, has noticed a distinctly different approach in the Rotman students he has hired. "They seemed to be naturally free of the bias or predisposition that so many of us seem to carry into any situation. And they brought a set of skills in how you query and look into an issue without moving toward biased or predetermined conclusions that has led to unexpected discoveries of opportunity and potential innovation" (Wallace, 2010). Recognizing this connection, business and management majors at Webster University can supplement their program of study with an 18-hour certificate in media literacy.

Media Activism

Media activism is a prominent sector of media literacy, committed to taking steps to democratize the communications environment, both nationally and globally.

Media literacy educators have extended the notion of "democracy" beyond its political connotation. The New Mexico Media Literacy Project regards media literacy as democratic in terms of challenging established ways of thought:

> The New Mexico Media Literacy Project wants to remain the most successful grassroots media literacy project in the United States . . .

(W)e want to promote democracy through citizen and parent activism by eroding corporate censorship and passive consumption of the media. (Nkana, 2010)

The Aspen Institute National Leadership Conference on Media Literacy presented media activism as a logical next step to the media literacy process:

Is media literacy important only to the extent that it enables one to be a better citizen in society? What is the role of ideology in the process? To what extent is an individual "media literate" if she just appreciates the aesthetics of a message without going further with it? (Nkana, 2010)

Media activism is rooted in the educational sector but then goes a step further, asking the question: Given the information about the media and media messages, what can be done to improve the media industry?

Media reform organizations have been formed that analyze the political and economic impact of the media industry and identify strategies to implement change. In some cases, public policy organizations work in partnership with educational institutions, community organizations, and media literacy associations to promote changes in media policy.

Thanks to the efforts of organizations such as Free Press (www.free-press.com) and Action Coalition for Media Education (ACME), media activists from across the country employ different strategies that share a common goal, broadening and diversifying ownership of the media industry. In 2006, thanks largely to a grassroots movement organized by Free Press, a two-year moratorium was established that preserved the principle of *Net Neutrality* as part of an agreement for a merger between AT&T and the Bell companies.

In 2007, a landmark Media Reform Conference was held in Memphis, Tennessee. Three thousand activists from around the country gathered to share ideas with respect to the democratization of the U.S. media industry. Workshops included the following topics:

- Effective Grassroots Lobbying
- How to Challenge a Broadcast License
- Connecting Community-based Media Organizations across America
- Get Radio: What You Need to Know to Start Your Own Station

Media justice is a movement designed to enable the voice of the masses to be heard by the media. According to the media justice organization Reclaim the Media, the work of the media justice movement is "pursuing a more just society by transforming our media system and expanding the communication rights of ordinary people through grassroots organizing, education, networking and advocacy" (Reclaim the Media, 2010).

Media activism also includes lobbying state and federal educational agencies, although identifying funding agencies willing to lend their support is an ongoing challenge.

A related form of media activism involves working in the public policy sector, instituting legislation that protects the goals of media literacy or, in some cases, revamps existing legislation that is undermining the objectives of media literacy.

Community Media Activities

The explosion of digital media has given individuals immediate access to global sources of information. But lost amid the national and international media are local media. As a result, many local outlets have suffered from shrinking audiences and income, either shrinking or folding altogether. However, community newspapers, radio stations, and television stations play a pivotal role in the life of the community.

For example, in St. Louis, Missouri, the vacuum created by the contraction of the *St. Louis Post-Dispatch* has been offset by community papers. The *Suburban Journal*, *Webster-Kirkwood Times*, and *West-end World* have continued to thrive, providing information about the community, such as weddings and road construction. These newspapers are free and available to all residents, deriving their income solely through advertising.

In addition, newspapers also cater to other communities defined by ethnicity, race, and religion. In St. Louis, newspapers cater to Bosnian and Chinese readers, African Americans, and Catholics.

Graduate Study

Undergraduate coursework in media literacy provides a solid foundation for graduate study in media literacy and media studies (e.g., journalism, media studies, film studies, and production programs in video, film, and digital media). But in addition, the discipline of media literacy is excellent preparation for graduate programs requiring research and critical thinking skills, such as public policy or law school.

Research

Media literacy students have become proficient at conducting research. A number of research centers affiliated with universities conduct analysis of the media industry and media coverage of issues. In addition, privately funded organizations examine ongoing coverage of issues in the media. Media literacy students can also apply these research methodologies in a variety of other fields requiring qualitative and quantitative research skills, such as marketing.

Writing

A surprising amount of media literacy analysis appears in the popular press. For instance, many newspapers and magazines include media critics on their staff. Some of these critics have a narrow conception of their role, providing superficial reviews of films and television programs. However, others have broadened their discussions to examine cultural trends, as reflected through media programming.

Entertainment journalism and feature stories occasionally examine media content as a cultural barometer. To illustrate, in 2005, columnist David Carr filed a story focusing on the image of journalists in Hollywood films, finding that the image of reporters is of "sleazy bystanders who take people down as a matter of general practice. . . . When Hollywood has a role requiring greasy self-interest, it knows it can insert a fast-talking guy with a notebook and soup stains on his tie" (Carr, 2005).

This portrait is based on journalists found in numerous films. Carr explains,

> *King Kong* offers a . . . typical scenario. The poor gorilla is chained to a stage for the entertainment of others and photographers shower him with flashbulbs until he goes ballistic, flattens New York and then tumbles to his death. And, oh yeah, the journalists are there to climb atop the carcass for some more pictures. Not much has changed in public perception of the craft since the original *King Kong* was made back in 1933. In *Capote*, the journalist sells out his subject, while in *Munich* a frantic electronic press in pursuit of the story tips off the terrorists.
>
> . . . Often, journalists are the handmaidens to evil: Danny DeVito as a sleazy reporter blackmailing left and right in *L.A. Confidential*, Sally Field, a malpracticing scribe who trashes the reputation of the character

played by Paul Newman in *Absence of Malice*, or the witless careerists of *Broadcast News* or *To Die For*. Dustin Hoffman, playing a ambitious reporter in *Mad City* put it rather succinctly, "I don't want to cross the line, I just want to move it a little bit." (Carr, 2005)

Media Literacy Organizations

Media literacy organizations such as the National Telemedia Council and Center for Media Literacy assemble and disseminate media literacy information, as well as sponsor programs and conferences throughout the country. Other organizations, such as Action for Children's Television, promote goals associated with media literacy.

In addition, organizations sponsored by the newspaper, film, and television industries have instituted programs that promote critical understanding of the media. Programs such as Creating Critical Viewers, which is sponsored by the National Academy of Television Arts and Sciences, is a powerful and effective voice for media literacy outreach, lending valuable expertise and legitimacy to media literacy.

Media Production

An awareness of the principles of media literacy helps media professionals produce responsible and informative programming. The study of media literacy, in combination with production areas, prepares students for careers in broadcast and print journalism, advertising, radio, television, film, and interactive media. News and documentary programs such as *Frontline* and *On the Media* heighten the awareness of the impact of the media on our culture.

The evolution of cheaper and more accessible digital media has made it easier to produce online content. In addition, independent video companies produce educational materials that support media literacy curricula. For example, the Media Education Foundation has produced the following presentations:

- *Killing Us Softly: Advertising's Image of Women*
- *Understanding HookUp Culture*
- *Codes of Gender*
- *Consuming Kids*
- *Mean World Syndrome: Media Violence & the Cultivation*

Advertising and Marketing

Media literacy can also be an asset to a career in marketing. The quantitative and qualitative methodologies employed in the discipline of media literacy can help define audiences—the primary objective of marketing.

In addition, a background in media literacy can be beneficial to the field of advertising. Media literacy approaches media presentations as *cultural text*— a way to assess cultural attitudes, preoccupations, and behaviors.

As an example, in 2008, Webster University was corecipient of a grant to produce a public service ad meant to discourage youngsters from smoking. The project comprised the following groups: (1) one college class in media literacy; one college class in advertising; a junior high school class from the St. Louis school district, which supplied the actors; and KDHX, the community radio station, which produced the spot.

The media literacy students examined a range of popular media presentations to determine which approaches would be most effective. What they determined wouldn't work was an ad in which 14-year-olds discussed the long-range risks of cancer. Instead, they selected the following scenario: a group of girls are in a mall, gathered in a circle, talking to each other while talking and texting on their cell phones. A young boy approaches one of the girls; he is smoking a cigarette. As the girl turns toward him, she exclaims, "Ooh, you *smell*." This ad strategy is effective, reflecting the cultural preoccupation with appearance found throughout popular media programming.

See also: Integrated Approach to Media Literacy Education; Ownership Patterns, Media; Sectors, Media Literacy

References

Bilton, N. (2009, December 9). "Part of the Daily American Diet, 34 Gigabytes of Data." *New York Times*. Retrieved from http://www.nytimes.com/2009/12/10/technology/10data.html

Carr, D. (2005, December 12). "Hollywood Gives the Press a Bad Name." *New York Times*. Retrieved from http://www.nytimes.com/2005/12/12/business/media/12carr.html?adxnnl=1&adxnnlx=1134401997-C5fXlsLZCu5NWB4hJhvfoA

Hartman, M. (2011, May 10). "The Art of the Elevator Pitch." Retrieved from Marketplace Morning Report. http://www.marketplace.org/topics/business/art-elevator-pitch

Nkana, S. (2010, March). "Media Literacy Education: A Case Study of the New Mexico Media Literacy Project." Unpublished PhD dissertation, Andrews University, Berrien Springs, MI.

Reclaim the Media (2010). "What We Do." Retrieved from www.reclaimthemedia
  .org

St. Louis Oasis. Retrieved from http://www.oasisnet.org/Cities/Central/StLouisMO
  .aspx

Van Ness, E. (2005, March 6). "Is a Cinema Studies Degree the New M.B.A.?" *New
  York Times*, March 6, 2005. Retrieved from http://www.nytimes.com/2005/03/06/
  movies/06vann.html

Wallace, L. (2010, January 10). "Multicultural Critical Theory. At B-School?" *New
  York Times*. Retrieved from http://www.nytimes.com/2010/01/10/business/10mba
  .html?pagewanted=all

Character Analysis

Character Analysis is an approach to media literacy that examines aspects of characterization as a means of deriving insight into media content. The strategy follows five lines of inquiry: (1) Character Identification; (2) Ideological Orientation; (3) Historical Context; (4) Character Development; and (5) Values Hierarchy. These lines of inquiry are employed in other qualitative approaches but, together, provide a distinctive approach to media literacy analysis.

Character Identification

Audience members' identification with particular characters can be a valuable source of information about what they consider attractive or engaging behaviors, values, or attributes. As a result, this line of inquiry frequently is applied in the Autobiographical Approach to media analysis, furnishing perspective into individuals' interests, aspirations, and values.

This approach is based on Social Learning Theory of Personality Development. Identification is a widespread and normal part of the process of identity formation. According to philosopher John Locke, children are like a blank slate as they undergo the process of preparation for adult roles; that is, human beings tend to imitate the actions, attitudes, and emotional responses they witness in others. This preparation occurs all the time that the child is awake and active—even when he and the person with whom he interacts are not consciously concerned with the formation of character.

Social learning consists of the following stages:

- An individual is exposed to a portrayal of a behavior, leading to identification with people or situations.

Media images can serve as a public declaration of personal identity. For instance, a person who wears a T-shirt with the peace sign is making a statement about his lifestyle, values, and positions on political and social issues. (Photo by Lisa Marcus)

- The person attempts to reproduce the behavior in a relevant situation.
- This behavior is reinforced by the individual's ability to handle situation successfully.
- This behavior is then adopted on a lasting basis as a means of coping with repetitions of the situation.

Media presentations serve as a primary source of *observational learning* and modeling behaviors. Audience members frequently measure their own lives in relation to what is happening to their favorite characters in a film, television show, or tabloid news story. People look to actors, actresses, and sports figures as role models. This process enables individuals to "try on" aspects of personality that they admire in a media figure.

The character identification process operates in one of the following ways:

- Identifying with media figures or characters they perceive as possessing common traits
- Identifying with those they aspire to be like

- Adopting the point of view of the person with whom they identify
- Identifying with situations in which the characters find themselves
- Reacting to what is happening to the character as if it was happening to them
- Emulating behaviors exhibited by the characters with whom they identify
- Identifying with the worlds these characters inhabit
- Measuring their own lives in relation to what is happening to their favorite characters
- Identifying with a situation facing a character and reacting to the course of action taken by that character
- Responding to the characters' actions according to their own moral codes and value systems
- Understanding the motivation of a character's action based on perceived common values systems

This process is facilitated by the sense that the audience knows and trusts the media figures they select as role models. Within this context, exposure to characters in media presentations can more or less simulate primary interaction. This impression of intimacy is reinforced by efforts of media communicators to cultivate a *parasocial relationship* with their audience, which refers to the *appearance* of a close interpersonal relationship. The producers encourage this sense of familiarity by putting the media communicator on a first-name basis with the audience. For instance, viewers are invited to watch *Conan* (O'Brien) every night. In addition, the close-up shot employed in film and television simulates an intimate one-on-one conversation, so that the audience feels that they have a personal relationship with Conan.

Children sometimes engage in *fantasy participation*, in which they insert themselves into the program. Fantasy participation can help children prepare for the world off-screen, as they picture what they would do in those circumstances to alter the situation.

In addition, identifying with a media figure can serve as a public declaration of Self. For instance, a young man who wears a T-shirt with the likeness of Bono on it is displaying his taste in music. But in addition, wearing the shirt is making a statement about his lifestyle, attitudes, and positions on political and social issues.

Some critics have expressed concerns that identification with media personalities can lead directly to imitative behavior. But although identification is a *precondition* of imitation, it is not a *guarantee* that people will adopt the modeling behavior. Indeed, modeling behavior can be a positive, healthy stage of personality formation.

Media Literacy Strategies: Character Identification

Character identification is an approach that can provide insight into media presentations and furnish perspective into an individual's belief system. Critical analysis of character analysis asks individuals to respond to the following questions:

- *Who are your favorite characters in a media presentation? Who are your least favorite characters in the program? What do you like and dislike about them?* These questions may lead to discussions about qualities that may not be readily apparent but are, nevertheless, essential to the overall portrait of the character. This also can serve as a springboard for a discussion about cultural values, as individuals identify with "negative" attributes (such as violent tendencies) that are perceived in a positive light by the respondent.
- *What is the nature of your identification with a character?* Focus on:
  - *Likeness*: Ways in which an individual sees a resemblance with a character
  - *Aspiration*: Ways in which an individual would like to emulate a character

This strategy can provide insight into the individual's perceived gender, ethnic, racial, and class identification, as well as information about what they consider attractive or engaging behaviors, values, and attributes.

- *What role do the attributes of the character play in the successful outcome of the story?* For example, in many media presentations, a violent temperament is central to resolving problems. From this point, individuals may consider the role that these attributes play in the outcome of their own life "narratives." Does being tough or violent guarantee success?
- *Are there attributes in a character that **prevent** him or her from succeeding in the narrative?*
- *Are there characters with whom you **cannot** identify?* This question can stimulate discussion about expectations: what can be regarded as unrealistic or "too perfect" characters, or characters with attributes that the individual may regard as unobtainable in their own lives.

- *Are there characters whose depiction is illogical?* This question leads to discussion of the *irreality* of a character depiction. In some media presentations, characters prevail despite their attitudes, values, and behaviors. They succeed because they are the heroes and are *supposed* to succeed.
- *How do you relate to villains in the media presentation?* Individuals are often attracted to some of the character traits of the antagonists. Villainous characters often display an energy, creativity, and sexuality that members of the audience may find appealing. One way to account for this response is that audience members identify with some of the flaws of the antagonists. But another possibility is that human nature is more complex than the absolute dichotomy of good and evil depicted in media presentations. There can be good in evil, just as there can be evil in good characters.

Ideological Orientation

This line of inquiry, which is utilized in the Ideological Approach to media analysis, operates on the premise that people tend to identify with characters that epitomize *success* as defined by the culture. Heroes and heroines often epitomize the qualities that a society considers admirable.

Examining the popularity of characters can serve as a barometer of enduring cultural issues. As an example, there have been 80 film and television versions of Robin Hood, which shows the appeal of organized resistance against the upper class (i.e., stealing from the rich and giving to the poor; Applebome, 2009).

Indeed, the contests between heroes and villains sometimes are the embodiment of idelogical conflicts. To illustrate, at the seventh biennial meeting of the International Association for Robin Hood Studies held at the University of Rochester in 2009, topics included "African-American Traditions and the Robin Hood Ballads," "Robin Hood for the PlayStation Generation, or Every Age Gets the Robin Hood It Deserves," and "Robin Hood and the 2008 Presidential Election" (Applebome, 2009).

In addition, it can be useful to trace the reemergence of heroic figures, as a reflection of changes in a culture. For instance, reflecting on the Robin Hood legend, reporter Applebome observes, "Maid Marian, it turns out, was barely there at the beginning, but is pretty much a co-star now and a template for much feminist theorizing" (Applebome, 2009).

An extension of Ideological Analysis is *Oppositional Identification* in which individuals identify with a character other than the protagonist: a member of a subculture, a member of the opposite sex, or a supporting character. The analysis could, then, follow the following line of questioning:

- What could you accomplish as one of *these* characters?
- What opportunities would be available to you?
- What advantages would you have?
- What could you "get away with" because of your position?
- What conclusions can you draw from this analysis?

Historical Context

Characterization can serve as a reflection of historical events. For instance, the 2009 version of *Robin Hood* is set within the historical context of an era characterized by bankruptcies and CEO bonuses. Reporter Peter Applebome declares, "Still, here in the golden era of stealing from the poor and giving to the rich, it's perhaps no accident that Robin is around like never before. If you Google 'Obama' and 'Robin Hood' you get about 945,000 hits" (Applebome, 2009).

At the same time, historical events may influence the character development in popular media presentations. In the wake of the 9/11 tragedy, for example, DC comics produced a new series, *In the Line of Duty*. Instead of a superhero or suave character à la James Bond, the comics featured everyday heroes such as firefighters and police officers.

In addition, several dramatic series featured characters who were "average guys"—the types who served so heroically in the aftermath of the attack. These heroes had all been wounded—either physically or emotionally—by the 9/11 attack. In the TV drama *CSI: New York*, Mac Taylor (Gary Sinise) is a character whose wife had been killed during the terrorist attack. Consequently, his character is emotionally withdrawn, which TV critic David Kronke describes as "Sinise's bottled quietude; he barely speaks above a whispered monotone" (Kronke, 2004).

Character Development

This approach considers ways in which characters have changed as a result of the events in a narrative. Examining what the characters have learned as a result of their experience is a useful method for detecting themes and media messages.

During the course of a narrative, characters often discover a new outlook on life, engage in self-discovery, or develop new skills that enable them to prevail at the conclusion of the story. This character development gives an artist an opportunity to make a thematic statement.

Consequently, critical analysis of character development focuses on the following questions:

- Have the major characters changed as a result of the events in the story?
  - How?
  - Why?
- What have the characters learned as a result of their experience?

Values Hierarchy

Values Hierarchy is a line of inquiry employed in the Values Clarification Approach to media analysis. Characters can be considered personifications of values. Heroes and heroines epitomize those qualities that society considers admirable, whereas villains generally represent negative values. The text establishes a *preferred reading*, which dictates how the audience is to respond. For instance, the choice of music signals that certain characters are protagonists and others are villains.

Daniel Chandler (n.d.) cites the following examples of oppositions that are personified by characters in a narrative:

Nature/Culture	Freedom/Constraint	Knower/Known	Inner/Outer
Animal/Human	Individual/Society	Old/New	Private/Public
Mind/Body	Gay/Straight	West/East	Insider/Outsider
Art/Science	Producer/Consumer	Black/White	Weak/Strong
Male/Female	Old/Young	Us/Them	Rich/Poor
Inclusion/Exclusion	Dominant/Subordinate		

Within this context, plot conflicts can be regarded as values oppositions, as embodied by the characters in the program (Chandler, n.d.: 77). The conclusion of the production establishes a hierarchy of values. For instance, at the conclusion of a police drama, as the good guys win and justice prevails, a system of values has been firmly established.

See also: Autobiographical Analysis; Cultivation Analysis; Ideological Analysis; Narratology; Values Clarification Approach

References

Applebome, P. (2009, October 26). "A Hero (or Villain) for the Left (or the Right)." *New York Times*. Retrieved from http://www.nytimes.com/2009/10/26/nyregion/26towns.html

Chandler, D. (n.d.). *Semiotics for Beginners*. Retrieved from http://www.aber.ac.uk/media/Documents/S4B/semiotic.html

Kronke, D. (2004, September 22). "Crit-O-Matic; TV Reviews." *Daily News of Los Angeles*. Retrieved from http:www.dailynews.com

Citizen Journalism

One of the major developments of digital journalism, *Citizen Journalism* refers to audience-driven news production and distribution that circumvents traditional gatekeepers of news and information. The audience has an expanded role in this process. Due to the innovations of media technology, citizen reporters are able to document events that otherwise would go unreported by the mainstream media. These "correspondents" are now a pervasive presence, taking photographs and videos on their cell phones and posting information on their blogs or on sites such as YouTube. As *Washington Post* staff writer Howard Kurtz (2006) explains,

> Citizen journalism encourages individuals to conduct their own research on the Internet to become informed on a topic. Consequently, the audience can learn about a subject in depth, while at the same time seeing the impact of the event. The audience has unprecedented control, deciding what features (e.g., video or photos) they want to see or hitting a "hot link" to learn more about particular aspects of a story. The good news is that the average consumer can in effect create his own news, picking and choosing from sources he trusts and enjoys rather than being spoon-fed by a handful of big corporations.

To illustrate, during the bombing tragedy in Boston in 2013, conditions prevented many news organizations from covering the crisis in a timely manner. In this news vacuum, many of the citizens who were living in those areas posted video and photos on the Internet; much of this coverage was consequently picked up by major newsmakers.

As members of the community, citizen correspondents often have unique access to news stories that are unavailable to outsiders. Mainstream reporters covering the wars in Afghanistan and Iraq frequently employ local residents, out of concern for their own safety, as well as the welfare of interviewees. Furthermore, citizens of those countries are less likely to be candid with Western reporters than they are with their neighbors.

In large measure, the establishment of the citizen journalism movement is a result of the dissatisfaction with the performance of the mainstream press as a societal watchdog. Contributors sometimes include professional journalists who are discouraged by what they see as the corruption of the American journalism system, activists, and amateurs with an interest in the field of journalism or a specific interest in an issue. Consequently, citizen journalism calls attention to important information that is underreported by the mainstream media and puts this information into meaningful perspective. To illustrate, a video clip of the death of an Iranian woman, Neda Agha-Soltan, became a symbol of the Iranian opposition movement after the country's disputed 2010 presidential election. Ms. Agha-Soltan collapsed on the street, apparently the victim of a sniper. A succession of people were responsible for getting the video clip out of Iran, illustrating how the Internet successfully bypasses traditional borders. The man who first witnessed the event and captured it on video (who wished to remain anonymous) sent the clip to a doctor (also anonymous), who then forwarded the video clip to acquaintances outside of Iran, with the message "Please let the world know." The clip was then uploaded to YouTube and other Web sites, where it has been viewed by millions of people.

Media technology also enables citizen journalists to gather and distribute information in a timely fashion. For instance, within hours of the 2006 Mumbai train bombings, citizen journalists began listing phone numbers of hospitals where victims were taken (Sengupta, 2006). These publications are relatively inexpensive to produce, because Web journalists are spared the costs of printing and distribution.

The 2007 perjury trial of I. Lewis "Scooter" Libby Jr., aide to former Vice President Dick Cheney, established online citizen journalism as a legitimate news vehicle. To cover the trial, Firedoglake.com assembled a team of citizen journalists, consisting of six contributors in rotation. They included a former prosecutor, an active defense lawyer, a PhD business consultant, and a movie producer. Throughout the trial, one member of the team provided a real-time transcript of the testimony. *New York Times* reporter Scott Shane noted, "With no audio or video feed permitted, the Firedoglake 'live blog' has offered the fullest, fastest public report available. Many mainstream journalists use it to check on the trial" (Shane, 2007). Shane continued, "For blogs, the Libby trial marks a courthouse coming of age. It is the first federal case for which independent bloggers have been given official credentials along with reporters from the traditional news media."

The audience following the trial on Firedoglake grew to more than 200,000 visitors—approximately the size of a midsized daily print newspaper. The citizen journalists, many of whom took vacation time from their jobs or had flexible schedules, were all unpaid.

But along with the positives of citizen journalism, this phenomenon continues to face some challenges in its efforts to be a serious journalistic conduit:

- Quality standards and practices haven't yet been established. As a result, while some blogs are carefully researched and fair in their coverage of issues, others are merely personal reflections.
- Citizen journalists generally are not trained in the profession, which can lead to inconsistencies in coverage.
- Articles authored by citizen journalists may not provide citations or references. In addition, there may be no information on the reporter—background, qualifications, or motive for contributing.
- The "correspondents" are often unpaid, which leads to issues of exploitation on the part of the "publishers."

See also: Digital Media Literacy; Journalism

References

Kurtz, H. (2006, March 13). "The Big News: Shrinking Reportage." *Washington Post*. Retrieved from http://www.washingtonpost.com/wp-dyn/content/article/2006/03/12/AR2006031201300.html

Sengupta, S. (2006, July 19). "You Won't Read It Here First: India Curtails Access to Blogs." *New York Times*. Retrieved from http://www.nytimes.com/2006/07/19/world/asia/19india.html

Shane, S. (2007, February 15). "For Liberal Bloggers, Libby Trial Is Fun and Fodder." *New York Times*. Retrieved from http://www.nytimes.com/2007/02/15/washington/15bloggers.html

Communication Models

Communication Models identify how information is conveyed from one party to another. These communication models have changed as a result of the introduction of the mass media into the lives of individuals.

Interpersonal Communications Model

The Interpersonal Communication Model consists of the following elements:

- The *communicator:* the person who delivers the message
- The *message:* the information being communicated

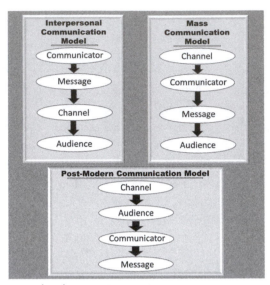

(Graphic by Lisa Marcus)

- The *channel:* the passage through which the information is being conveyed (e.g., voice, eyes, and facial expressions used as channels for interpersonal communication)
- The *audience:* the party that receives the message

In mass communication, the media—newspapers, photographs, film, radio, television, and the Internet—serve as channels for the communication of information to large groups of people who are separated in time and/or space from the media communicator.

Mass Communication Model

When Marshall McLuhan declared, "The medium is the message," he was suggesting that the media have reconfigured the traditional communications model. The channels of mass communications assumed a primary role in determining the choice of communicator, the message, and the audience.

Thus, the reconfiguration of the Mass Communication Model is as follows:

- *The channel* (In mass communication, the media—newspapers, photographs, film, radio, television, and the Internet—serve as channels for the communication of information to large groups of people who are separated in time and/or space from the media communicator.)
- Communicator

- Message
- Audience

To illustrate, in broadcast news programming, the medium of television dictates the choice of communicator. Anchorpersons must be likable, convincing, and attractive. Moreover, television affects the message. Television lends itself to the entertainment sensibility of the medium. Television news programs favor events-oriented news stories, as opposed to the detailed presentation of complex issues characteristic of print journalism. Finally, the choice of medium has a significant impact on the audience: Television is the most credible source of news, including word of mouth.

Postmodern Communication Model

The emergence of digital communication has, once again, reconfigured the communications model, incorporating the distinctive interactive characteristics of the media. Digital media fosters an *interactive participation* that media scholar Kathleen Tyner characterizes as "critical, investigatory, and creative uses of information" (Tyner, 1998: 90).

Consequently, the audience has become a factor at an earlier stage of the communication process. One of the distinguishing features of interactive media is that audience members are able to bypass traditional media gatekeepers and act as their own content providers. As an example, consumers can now access "television" programs on their computers, selecting the programs they want, at the time that they choose to watch. Ironically, the postmodern communications model brings us back to the pre-Copernican conception of the universe, in which the earth (you) are the center of the universe. Author Nick Bilton (2010) explains,

> If you pull out your smartphone and click the button that says "locate me" on your mapping application, you will see a small dot appear in the middle of your screen.
>
> That's you.
>
> If you start walking down the street in any direction, the whole screen will move right along with you, no matter where you go.
>
> This is a dramatic change from the print-on-paper world, where maps and locations are based around places and landmarks, not on you or your location. In the print world people don't go to the store and say, "Oh, excuse me, can I buy a map of me?" Instead, they ask for a map of New York, or Amsterdam, or the subway system. You and

I aren't anywhere to be seen on these maps. The maps are locations that we fit into.

But today's digital world has changed that. Now, we are always in the center of the map, and it's a very powerful place to be.

The Postmodern Communication Model has transformed the American political landscape, with social networking emerging as an effective (and uniquely democratic) means of reaching citizens. One of their most important achievements of the Obama campaign during the 2008 presidential election was transforming social media into a grassroots organization, bypassing the mainstream news media and taking messages straight to the public. As president, Barrack Obama has extended this postmodern communications approach to his approach to governance. Reporters Jim Rutenberg and Adam Nagourney explain:

> The most prominent example of the new strategy is his weekly address to the nation—what under previous presidents was a speech recorded for and released to radio stations on Saturday mornings. Mr. Obama instead records a video, which on Saturday he posted on the White House Web site and on YouTube; in it, he explained what he wanted to accomplish with the $825 billion economic stimulus plan working its way through Congress. By late Sunday afternoon, it had been viewed more than 600,000 times on YouTube. (Rutenberg & Nagourney, 2009)

Sending unedited information from the president directly to his constituents is an effective way of building public opinion. But in addition, this approach represents an opportunity to form a relationship between the president and the public. David Plouffe, Obama's 2008 campaign manager, declares,

> So it's: "Here's the president's speech today on the economy. Here are some talking points. . . . If someone who has never been involved in politics before—or is an independent or a Republican—makes this case with their circle of people, that has more impact. (Rutenberg & Nagourney, 2009)

However, at the same time, members of the mainstream media express concern that this model could serve as a public relations vehicle because citizens only receive the point of view of the communicator/politician. Bill Kovach, chair of the Committee of Concerned Journalists notes,

They're beginning to create their own journalism, their own description of events of the day, but it's not an independent voice making that description. It's troublesome until we know how it's going to be used and the degree to which it can be used on behalf of the people, and not on behalf of only one point of view. (Rutenberg & Nagourney, 2009)

This concern reflects the media literacy principle that the media are simply a channel of communications and can be used in a positive or negative fashion. Consequently, it is essential that individuals consider who is presenting the message (identification of media communicator) and why that person is presenting the message (the function, or purpose, behind the media presentation).

See also: Digital Media Literacy

References

Bilton, N. (2010, September 12). "A Tech World That Centers on the User." *New York Times*. Retrieved from http://www.nytimes.com/2010/09/13/technology/13future.html?pagewanted=all

Rutenberg, J., & Nagourney, A. (2009, January 26). "Melding Obama's Web to a YouTube Presidency." *New York Times*. Retrieved from http://www.nytimes.com/2009/01/26/us/politics/26grassroots.html?pagewanted=all

Tyner, K. (1998). *Literacy in a Digital World*. New York: Erlbaum/Routledge.

Content Analysis

Content Analysis is a quantitative methodology that looks for patterns with regard to messages, symbols, language, art forms, and potential biases in print and electronic media. This methodology measures how often (i.e., how many times per page or episode) a given kind of behavior (e.g., violence or stereotypical behavior) is observed. Paul F. Lazarsfeld and Harold D. Lasswell, in the 1920s, were the first to begin writing about quantitative content analysis as a methodology.

Conducting a content analysis consists of the following stages:

1. defining the categories to be studied;
2. tabulating and summarizing the data; and
3. making *inferences*—that is, drawing conclusions from the patterns you have identified.

Content analysis may be used to gather the following types of information:

- To infer something about the communicators (e.g., Are journalists biased?)
- To discover something about the volume (amount) of information carried by a particular medium
- To investigate content differences by medium (e.g., Which medium contains a representation of minorities most similar to that in the general population?)
- To examine the depiction of particular subjects and characters
- To find out what kinds of behaviors audiences are being exposed to (e.g., How much violence on TV cartoons are children exposed to on Saturday mornings?)

This type of approach can detect behaviors that are useful indications of stereotypes, as well as making individuals more sensitive to the portrayal of groups in the media.

One of the most challenging aspects of conducting this kind of research is to ensure consistent data entries on the part of the researchers. Some of the demographic categories (e.g., specific age) or behavior characteristics require estimation. Moreover, drawing inferences from data can be subjective, in that categories are classified through behaviors. Thus, patting a person on the head can be regarded as an instance of nurturing behavior but could also be an example of a condescending attitude. Consequently, extensive pretesting must be conducted to ensure clarity of criteria and consistency in categorization.

An example of a content analysis is a study by Indiana University media researcher Mike Conway, who examined 115 episodes (six months' worth) of Bill O'Reilly's "Talking Points Memo" editorials, which Reilly refers to as a "No Spin Zone" (Ingram, 2007). Conway found that O'Reilly used a derogatory name to describe a person or a group on average of once every 6.8 seconds. That is nearly nine times every minute during the opening editorials of his program each night. After tabulating the research data, Conway and coworkers concluded, "Our results show a consistent pattern of O'Reilly casting non-Americans in a negative light. Both illegal aliens and foreigners were constructed as physical threats to the public and never featured in the role of victim or hero" (IU News Room, 2007).

A related quantitative approach is *culturomics*. The most basic version of culturomics content analysis recognizes basic patterns, from which the researcher can draw inferences. Erez Lieberman Aiden and Jean-Baptiste Michel formed a research team at Harvard that, working with Google, has assembled a database comprising 500 billion words contained in 5.2 million digitized books published between 1500 and 2008, in English, French, Spanish, German, Chinese, and Russian—nearly 4 percent of all books ever printed (Cohen, 2010). The analysis focuses on a tabulation of the number of appearances of short words and phrases, which involves tabulation and analysis of a vast digital database. Reporter Patricia Cohen describes how "the warehouse of words makes it possible to analyze cultural influences statistically in a way previously not possible":

> A simple online tool allows anyone with a computer to plug in a string of up to five words and see a graph that charts the phrase's use over time With a click you can see that "women," in comparison with "men," is rarely mentioned until the early 1970s, when feminism gained a foothold. The lines eventually cross paths about 1986.
>
> You can also learn that Mickey Mouse and Marilyn Monroe don't get nearly as much attention in print as Jimmy Carter; compare the many more references in English than in Chinese to "Tiananmen Square" after 1989; or follow the ascent of "grilling" from the late 1990s until it outpaced "roasting" and "frying" in 2004. (Cohen, 2010)

Lieberman Aiden, one of the scholars who, along with Michel and Steven Pinker, spearheaded the culturomics research project to demonstrate the scholarly applications of vast digital databases, commented, "The goal is to give an 8-year-old the ability to browse cultural trends throughout history, as recorded in books" (Cohen, 2010).

To illustrate, Dr. Nathan DeWall conducted a computer analysis of hit songs between 1980 and 2007 and found a statistically significant trend toward narcissism in the lyrics of popular music. According to a personality inventory administered over the past several decades, the level of narcissism has been rising since the early 1980s (Tierney, 2011). This attitude is reflected in the lyrics of popular music. DeWall found that the words "I" and "me" appear more frequently, along with a corresponding decline in "we" and "us." Reporter John Tierney explains,

> Today's songs, according to the researchers' linguistic analysis, are more likely be about one very special person: the singer. "I'm bringing sexy back," Justin Timberlake proclaimed in 2006. The year before, Beyoncé

exulted in how hot she looked while dancing—"It's blazin', you watch me in amazement." And Fergie, who boasted about her "humps" while singing with the Black Eyed Peas, subsequently released a solo album in which she told her lover that she needed quality time alone: "It's personal, myself and I." (Tierney, 2011)

Other applications of this quantitative approach include the following:

- A way to identify the duration of a cultural phenomenon. As an illustration, researchers measured the duration of fame, finding that written references to celebrities faded twice as quickly in the mid-20th century as they did in the early 19th. The study relied on a data set that started in 1800, enabling the researchers to project trends (Cohen, 2010).
- A way to determine the interval between the time when an innovation is introduced to a culture and when it becomes popular. For instance, researchers found that inventions took, on average, 66 years to be adopted by the larger culture in the early 1800s and only 27 years between 1880 and 1920 (Cohen, 2010).

In addition, a second generation of research, known as "Culturomics 2.0," makes use of a 30-year translated archive of international news reports, combining three massive news archives:

- The complete *New York Times* from 1945 to 2005
- The unclassified edition of Summary of World Broadcasts from 1979 to 2010
- An archive of English-language Google News articles spanning 2006 to 2011

This archive, totaling more than 100 million articles worldwide, creates a "network" of more than 10 billion people, places, things, and activities connected by more than 100 trillion relationships.

Although the initial culturomics approach simply tabulates the frequency of its usage over time, Culturomics 2.0 enables researchers to forecast cultural and historical events, on the basis of the tabulation and analysis of global news media. The culturomic software identifies the *latent tone* of a large digital news archive—the emotional response that reveals the subtle attitude of the media communicator *toward* the topic. Research focuses on "mapping" strategies to determine the average tone of all articles mentioning specific *entities* (i.e., location, event, or person). These entities are color-coded on a map, from bright green (high positivity) to bright red (high negativity), based on the average tone of all articles mentioning that entity. These mapping strategies identify:

- Positive and negative references to locations
- Relationships with other geographic locations

This approach assesses the global mood about each country in the world. As an example, the *New York Times*, which published 2.9 billion words between 1945 and 2005, mentions one location every 200 to 300 words in a typical article. Thus, 369,000 locations are mentioned more than 10.4 million times, which equates to around one location every 279 words (Leetaru, 2011). Similarly, one geographic reference is made for every 215 spoken words in broadcast news programming. Consequently, with 1.2 billion words spoken in news broadcasts between 1979 and 2010, 201,000 unique locations were mentioned roughly 5.81 million times (Leetaru, 2011).

In addition, research can identify relationships, as reflected by articles that mention *two* entities (i.e., locations, events, or persons). For example, each article mentioning two or more cities together creates a link between those cities, and the average tone of all articles mentioning both cities is color-coded.

Reporter Robert Johnson provides the following illustration of how culturomics culturomics predicted the revolution in Egypt:

On 25 January 2011, popular dissent with the Egyptian state culminated in mass protests that continued through President Mubarak's resignation on 11 February. Figure 2 shows the average tone by month from January 1979 to March 2011 of all 52,438 articles captured by *SWB* mentioning an Egyptian city anywhere in the article. Only articles explicitly mentioning an Egyptian city were included to filter out casual references to Egypt to return only articles reporting on the country in more detail. To normalize the data, the Y axis reports the number of standard deviations from the mean, with higher numbers indicating greater positivity and lower numbers indicating greater negativity. January 2011 reports only the tone for 1 January through 24 January, capturing the period immediately preceding the protests. Only twice in the last 30 years has the global tone about Egypt dropped more than three standard deviations below average: January 1991 (the U.S. aerial bombardment of Iraqi troops in Kuwait) and 1–24 January 2011, ahead of the mass uprising. The only other period of sharp negative moment was March 2003, the launch of the U.S. invasion of neighboring Iraq. (Johnson, 2011)

This methodology was also successfully employed to forecast further unrest during the Arab Spring of 2011 and to estimate Osama bin Laden's final location within a 200-kilometer radius (Johnson, 2011).

A third generation of culturomics research offers unique research capabilities by using social media as a database. The "sample" consists of all primary materials, such as Tweets, eliminating the possibility of error that stems from drawing conclusions from a small sample. Instead, the "sample" size of Facebook (500 million people) and Twitter (175 million people) is larger than many nations. Furthermore, this computer software facilitates the ease of ongoing research.

The data from Facebook and Twitter reveal patterns that can forecast various events. One study found that by analyzing the positive or negative sentiments expressed in 2.8 million Twitter messages about 24 movies, they could predict how the films would perform at the box office. Another study found that they could forecast changes in the Dow Jones Industrial Average by classifying 9.7 million Twitter posts as falling into one of six mood categories (happiness, kindness, alertness, sureness, vitality, and calmness) (Gertner, 2010).

But as is the case with Content Analysis, drawing inferences from the data can be a subjective process and, therefore, requires systematic analysis. As Cohen (2010) observed, "Aware of concerns raised by humanists that the essence of their art is a search for meaning, Mr. Michel and Mr. Lieberman Aiden emphasized that culturomics simply provided information. Interpretation remains essential."

See also: Affective Response Analysis; Content Analysis; Cultural Context; Effects Theories, Media Literacy; Fame

References

Cohen, P. (2010, December 16). "In 500 Billion Words, New Window on Culture." *New York Times*. Retrieved from http://www.nytimes.com/2010/12/17/books/17words.html?pagewanted=all

Gertner, J. (2010, December 17). "Social Media as Social Index." *New York Times Magazine*. http://www.nytimes.com/interactive/2010/12/19/magazine/ideas2010.html#Social_Media_as_Social_Index

Ingram, P. (2007, May 16). "O'Reilly Study Generates National Attention." Indiana University School of Journalism. Retrieved from http://journalism.indiana.edu/news/oreilly-study-generates-national-attention

IU News Room. (2007, May 7). "Content Analysis of O'Reilly's Rhetoric Finds Spin to Be a 'Factor.'" Retrieved from http://newsinfo.iu.edu/news/page/normal/5535 .html

Johnson, R. (2011, September 12). " 'Culturomics' Predicted the Arab Revolutions—And Now It Predicts Global Unrest." *Business Insider.* www.businessinsider.com/ culturomics-predict-revolution-2011-9

Leetaru, K. H. (2011, September 6). "Culturomics 2.0: Forecasting Large-Scale Human Behavior Using Global News Media Tone in Time and Space." *First Monday, 16* (9-5). Retrieved from http://firstmonday.org/ojs/index.php/fm/article/ view/3663/3040

Tierney, J. (2011, April 25). "A New Generation's Vanity, Heard through Lyrics." *New York Times*. Retrieved from http://www.nytimes.com/2011/04/26/science/26tier .html

Cultivation Analysis

Cultivation analysis is an approach to the study of media content that explores the extent to which media consumers' beliefs about the world around them are shaped by exposure to repetitive and pervasive media messages. Cultivation analysis, which was first conceived by George Gerbner in the late 1960s, is founded on the premise that the media "cultivates" perceptions of reality for audiences that are consistent with the world depicted in media presentations. Indeed, the presence of the media can alter the event itself, affecting the reality of the moment.

To illustrate, Gerbner found that frequent TV viewers exhibited behaviors that displayed more fear of their environment than occasional viewers. For instance, when measured against the behaviors of occasional television viewers, heavy TV viewers were more likely to have bought dogs for protection and installed locks in their homes.

Rather than focusing on the causes and effects of individual messages or programs, Gerbner examined the *cultivation of collective consciousness* in relation to the rapid growth of media outlets. Mass communication is the distribution and consumption method of cultural stories that establish a society's agenda of priorities, values, and relationships. Individuals select programming that supports and shapes their personal vision, tastes, views, and preferences. Thus, assessment of the media system is a first step toward investigating the role of message systems in establishing and maintaining stable conceptions of reality. This approach focuses on what is most broadly shared across genres and what large groups of otherwise heterogeneous viewers have in common (Gerbner, 1985).

Early cultivation research was mainly concerned with the issue of television violence, but over the years, investigations have been expanded to include other media (e.g., photographs, film, the Internet) and issues (e.g., gender roles, images of aging, political orientations, and attitudes toward the environment).

The three primary approaches to cultivation analysis are as follows:

- *Projective techniques* ("Projective Techniques," 2001) create an environment that discloses the views, expectations, and values (conscious or unconscious) of the subject. The best-known projective test is the Rorschach test (or "inkblot test") created in the 1920s by Swiss psychologist Hermann Rorschach. These tests provide information on the basis of subjects' reactions to visual stimuli, ability to complete sentences, or word associations. Because of the leeway provided by the tests, the subjects project their own personalities onto the stimulus, which provides insight into personal conflicts, motivations, coping styles, and other characteristics.
- *In-depth interviews* focus on an individual's views, expectations, and values and relate these to media reception patterns, as well as demographic and psychographic information about the respondent. This approach is often used to help advertising researchers understand a consumer's attitudes toward certain products and why consumers purchase certain brands. Clotaire Rapaille (2006), a well-known marketing expert, uses in-depth interview technique to understand the system of culture codes that people acquire while growing up in a particular culture. These codes then help advertisers know the best way to get media consumers to buy their product.
- *Periodic questions* on sample surveys are administered as a way of establishing a national probability sample of respondents. For years, Nielson Media Research used periodic diaries to collect information about what television programs are being watched before converting to a computer-based system.

See also: Character Analysis; Culture Code

References

Gerbner, G. (1985). "Mass Media Discourse: Message System Analysis as a Component of Cultural Indicators." In G. Smitherman-Donaldson, and T. A. Van

Dijk (Eds.), *Discourse and Communication; New Approaches to the Analysis of Mass Media Discourse and Communication* (pp. 13–25). Berlin: Walter de Guyter.

"Projective Techniques." (2001). *Gale Encyclopedia of Psychology* (2nd ed.). Retrieved from http://findarticles.com/p/articles/mi_g2699/is_0002/ai_2699000273

Rapaille, C. (2006). *The Culture Code: An Ingenious Way to Understand Why People around the World Live and Buy as They Do*. New York: Random House.

Cultural Context

Cultural context is a qualitative approach to media literacy analysis that focuses on media presentations as cultural text. Because U.S. media is a market-driven industry rooted in popular culture, their media communicators must be responsive to the needs and interests of their audience. The term *popular* connotes acceptance, approval, and shared values among large numbers of people. We admire the popular set because of who they *are* (attitudes and values) and for what they *do* (behaviors). This notion of popularity also applies to media presentations. People only watch programs that meet their approval. An individual who is truly offended by violent programs won't watch them. And in the market-driven media industry, programming with low ratings are soon cancelled.

As a result, media programming can be regarded as a text that *reflects* the attitudes, values, and behaviors that define a culture. For example, in an article focusing on the image of journalists in Hollywood films, columnist David Carr found a pattern of "sleazy bystanders who take people down as a matter of general practice" (Carr, 2005). This image of journalists is, to a large extent, a reflection of behaviors exhibited by the American press. Carr recalls the following examples:

> Myriad plagiarism scandals, most notably one involving the *New York Times* and Jayson Blair and CBS's failure to verify a memo related to President Bush's National Guard service, conjure their own images of journalistic malfeasance.
>
> There were the travails of Judith Miller, the former reporter for *The Times,* and now even Bob Woodward of *The Washington Post*—whose work with Carl Bernstein provided grist for *All the President's Men*, a journalistic paean—is starring in a far less praiseworthy role. (Carr, 2005)

At the same time, cultural attitudes, values, and behaviors are *reinforced* through the countless hours of media programming that repeats, directly or indirectly, the cultural script. The portrait of journalists discussed above is based on *cumulative messages*; that is, similar depictions of journalists in numerous films. Author Edward Jay Epstein explains, "The constant images of a news media whose entire existence is based on harassing innocent people and popular celebrities has an effect much like a drop of water constantly hitting the public's head. It creates the impression that journalists are at best unnecessary" (Carr, 2005).

Finally, the media does not merely *reflect* or *reinforce* culture but in fact *shapes* thinking by introducing people to ideas and attitudes. To illustrate, during the 1950s, teenage fans of Elvis Presley were, at the same time, becoming fans of black culture. Part of Elvis's appeal was that he was a white singer who incorporated elements of black culture into his style. Similarly, rap and hip-hop, which originated in the streets as an expression of the concerns of young inner-city African American males, have become popular among white teenagers; the trappings of rap and hip-hop, such as speech, dress, and dance moves have been incorporated into mainstream culture.

In addition, media presentations can reflect (as well as reinforce and shape) *cultural preoccupations*—that is, the relative importance that a culture places on particular issues. For instance, concerns about body image are widespread in Western culture. Much of this dissatisfaction is due to the influence of media celebrities. Moreover, this media pressure to attain the perfect body begins early. In 2009, *The Daily Telegraph*, a British newspaper, reported that an issue of *Practical Parenting and Pregnancy*, a periodical for young parents in the United Kingdom, had included a cover photograph in which the image of a baby had been altered, removing her "baby fat" (Graff, 2009).

Media presentations may also reflect (as well as reinforce and shape) cultural *changes*. For example, a 2010 television ad for Pampers disposable diapers features football star Drew Brees, acknowledging the changing role of fathers in American culture. On his blog, *Rebel Dad*, Brian Reid notes, "The fact that Pampers . . . thinks it's worth the time and effort to get Drew Brees to talk to dads, makes it seem that they realize that this is a market segment that can't be ignored" (Newman, 2010).

Worldview

Worldview is a line of inquiry that focuses on the question: What kind of world is depicted in the media presentation?

Popular artists construct a complete world out of their imaginations. The critical analysis of worldview focuses on the following questions:

- What culture or cultures populate this world?
  - What kinds of people populate this world?
  - What is the ideology of this culture?
- What do we know about the people who populate this world?
  - Are characters presented in a stereotypical manner?
  - What does this tell us about the cultural stereotype of this group?
- Does this world present an optimistic or pessimistic view of life?
  - Are the characters in the presentation happy?
  - Do the characters have a *chance* to be happy?
- Are people in control of their own destinies?
  - Is there a supernatural presence in this world?
  - Are the characters under the influence of other people?
- What hierarchy of values is in operation in this worldview?
  - What embedded values can be found in the production?
  - What values are embodied in the characters?
  - What values prevail through the resolution?
- What does it mean to be a success in this world?
  - How does a person succeed in this world?
  - What kinds of behavior are rewarded in this world?

The worldview of a media presentation frequently assumes a disarming naturalness in the narrative; the correctness of this order is never questioned by the heroes and heroines with whom we identify.

Every genre presents its own distinct worldview that attracts its intended audience. Indeed, it can be argued that the fundamental appeal of some genres is not the plot, but rather, their worldview. Fans of Westerns are attracted to the worldview of the genre—wide-open spaces, rugged individualism, and the code of western justice. Moreover, in many ads, what is really being sold is the *worldview* of the commercial. When consumers buy a designer shirt or sunglasses, they are purchasing membership in the upscale and trendy world depicted in the ad campaigns. The inference is that purchasing the product somehow admits the audience into the world of the ad.

Representation of Subcultures

Media presentations disclose cultural attitudes toward particular groups. Critical analysis of the issue of representation focuses on the following questions:

- How frequently are subcultures presented in media presentations (compared with their actual presence in the population)?
- How are these groups depicted?

Media Stereotyping focuses on how particular groups are depicted in the media. A stereotype is an oversimplified depiction of a person, group, or event. Stereotyping is an *associative* process; that is, ideas about groups are based on a shared understanding about a group. People often base their opinions about a person on one distinctive characteristic, which becomes the basis of the stereotype.

Stereotyping is a common coping mechanism. Even people who are victims of stereotyping in turn stereotype others. Thus, stereotyping serves as a kind of shorthand that enables us to make everyday decisions in our lives.

To be sure, some stereotypes are positive (e.g., the Japanese are good in math, the Russians are proficient in chess, the Germans are efficient and punctual). However, this grouping principle is frequently inaccurate, negative, and dangerous. William B. Helmreich (1983) observes, "Approximately one third of stereotypes can be said to have a good deal of truth to them. . . . The accurate stereotypes are predominately positive, whereas those that seem highly inaccurate tend by and large to be negative."

The media industry is particularly well suited for stereotyping. Media communicators do not have the luxury of time to develop a unique set of characters. Indeed, over the past ten years, the amount of time in which a network television program could run before facing cancellation has been reduced from 13 to 4 weeks—hardly a time frame during which the audience can become familiar with a full cast of complex, unique characters. Consequently, media communicators tap into the cumulative experience of the audience through stereotypes; audience members recognize a character who appears on screen because they have seen him (or a character like him) dozens of times before.

Media communicators may also rely on stereotypes to compensate for their limited ability to collect information firsthand. To illustrate, as it became dangerous for correspondents covering the Iraq War to venture out of the protected "Green Zone," reporters increasing relied on official military briefings for their information or hired untrained Iraqis to go out into the field and bring back stories. As a result, coverage of the conflict reflected only a general, stereotyped understanding of the Iraqi communities.

One of the troubling issues of media stereotyping involves editing decisions—what to omit or include in a media presentation. The concern is not that particular behavior by members of a group is depicted by the media, but rather that this is the *only* character trait presented. For instance, it may appear harmless to depict an African American man as silly and bumbling; after all, these qualities are central to comedy—and certainly, it is easy to find corresponding examples of buffoonery among white male performances. For instance, "slacker" films feature white males who are annoying, crude, and clueless. However, if these character traits were the *only* way that white males are presented in media presentations, then this characterization would perpetuate a cultural stereotype.

As an example, the stereotypical Arab is a depicted in film and television programs as a villain—often a terrorist—who belongs to an extremist Muslim sect. However, Moustapha Akkad, an Arab American film producer declares, "We cannot say there are no Arab and no Muslim terrorists. Of course there are. But at the same time, balance it with the image of the normal human being, the Arab-American, the family man. The lack of anyone showing the other side makes it stand out that in Hollywood, Muslims are only terrorists" (Goodstein, 1998).

See also: Fame; Hierarchy of Appearance; Media and Social Change; Singularity

References

Carr, D. (2005, December 1). "Hollywood Gives the Press a Bad Name." *New York Times*. Retrieved from http://www.nytimes.com/2005/12/12/business/media/12carr.html?adxnnl=1&adxnnlx=1134401997-C5fXlsLZCu5NWB4hJhvfoA

Goodstein, L. (1998, November 1). "Hollywood Now Plays Cowboys and Arabs." *New York Times*. Retrieved from http://www.nytimes.com/1998/11/01/movies/film-hollywood-now-plays-cowboys-and-arabs.html

Graff, A. "Some Magazines Airbrush Baby Images." (2009, November 18). *San Francisco Chronicle*. Retrieved from http://www.sfgate.com/cgi-bin/blogs/sfmoms/detail?entry_id=51878&tsp=1#ixzz0Z17hKRQ3

Helmreich, W. (1983). *The Things They Say Behind Your Back: Stereotypes and the Myths Behind Them*. New Brunswick, NJ: Transaction.

Newman, A. A. (2010, June 22). "Getting Dad to Do Diaper (Buying) Duty." *New York Times*. Retrieved from http://www.nytimes.com/2010/06/23/business/media/23adco.html

Cultural Insulation

Cultural insulation is a phenomenon in which individuals are becoming immersed in a few, selected areas of personal interest, remaining completely uninformed and disinterested in other cultural spheres. As a result, individuals know more and more about less and less.

One of the unintended consequences of the media industry's shift from broadcasting to narrowcasting is the slow but inevitable cultural segregation of the population. In the early days of American media, when the overall audience was limited, the mass communicator had to appeal to the broadest possible audience to generate a profit. To illustrate, television variety shows in the 1950s such as the *Ed Sullivan Show* routinely featured puppet shows, comedians, opera singers, and rock stars in the course of one telecast to appeal to everyone in the mass audience.

The next stage of the evolution of a medium is the move from broadcasting to narrowcasting. At this stage, the media market has become so large that it is now profitable to direct messages at specialized interests, tastes, and groups. As an example, ESPN realized that it didn't have to attract all cable television viewers—only sports fans.

Today, digital communications is so specialized that the media is characterized by a *microcasting* system, in which information is individualized to the specific tastes and interests of the individual audience member. This trend further insulates individuals within their particular spheres of interest. Instead of the narrowcasting model of directing messages at sports fans, the microcasting model directs messages to individuals on particular sports, such as soccer or lacrosse. Even ads that are aimed at a general audience are presented in a style that fits the particular interests of the audience member. For instance, McDonald's commercials may have a country, soul, or rock flavor, depending on the musical interests of the consumer.

The Internet has opened up virtual libraries of information on a specific topic. Furthermore, hyperlinks are embedded in articles, giving the audience the opportunity to delve further into a particular topic. As an example, a digital article on presidents may include a sentence about Harry Truman that captures the interest of the reader. By hitting the hyperlink, the audience member is catapulted into an article furnishing more detailed information about Truman. But unfortunately, the reader may never make it back to the original article about all of the presidents.

Social media and "apps" represent extensions of this trend. Each individual media device is being defined by a set of distinctive characteristics (apps) that, in turn, influences the presentation of information. Reporter Steve Lohr (2011) explains,

> These applications often tap into Web sites for information on all manner of things. But they do not reside on the open Web, and cannot be

searched and linked to one another in the same way Web applications can. Think of the apps tailored for Apple's iPhones and iPads, or those made for Google's Android operating system. Social networking sites like Facebook and Twitter have similar characteristics, as walled gardens that are connected to the open Web but are separate from it.

In 2010, Tim Berners-Lee, the Web's creator, warned that even the existence of the Web is threatened. "The Web as we know it is being threatened." The danger, he added, is that "the Web could be broken into fragmented islands" (Lohr, 2011):

Several threats to the Web's universality have arisen recently. Cable television companies that sell Internet connectivity are considering whether to limit their Internet users to downloading only the company's mix of entertainment. Social-networking sites present a different kind of problem. Facebook, LinkedIn, Friendster and others typically provide value by capturing information as you enter it: your birthday, your e-mail address, your likes, and links indicating who is friends with whom and who is in which photograph. The sites assemble these bits of data into brilliant databases and reuse the information to provide value-added service—but only within their sites. Once you enter your data into one of these services, you cannot easily use them on another site. Each site is a silo, walled off from the others. Yes, your site's pages are on the Web, but your data are not. You can access a Web page about a list of people you have created in one site, but you cannot send that list, or items from it, to another site.

The isolation occurs because each piece of information does not have a URL. Connections among data exist only within a site. So the more you enter, the more you become locked in. Your social-networking site becomes a central platform—a closed silo of content, and one that does not give you full control over your information in it. The more this kind of architecture gains widespread use, the more the Web becomes fragmented, and the less we enjoy a single, universal information space.

Thus, *Cultural Insulation* undermines the very foundation of culture, which is built on common understandings, experiences, and values. Instead, individuals are insulated within their particular spheres of interest, so that they remain completely uninformed and disinterested in other cultural spheres. For instance, fans of hard rock are unlikely to tune in to other types of music, such as opera, gospel, or 1940s big band. Unfortunately, audiences can become locked into this demographic straitjacket and never be exposed to other types of music. More importantly, society will be populated by individuals who are incapable of making meaningful connections with other members of the culture.

Finding ways to break out of this industry-imposed cultural isolation is essential to preserving our sense of cultural cohesiveness, which is built on common understandings, experiences, and values. Consequently, one of the principal goals of media literacy education is to expose students to other subcultures and interests by encouraging them to look beyond the confines of their particular media "diet." For instance, one type of assignment asks students to analyze a range of radio formats to learn about different types of musical offerings. Using the translation feature on newspapers' Web sites, students can also examine ethnic newspapers directed at recent immigrants to the United States (e.g., Russian, Chinese, or Bosnian papers) to be exposed to the points of view of different subcultures. Similarly, students also become exposed to media presentations with different ideological perspectives, such as liberal magazines such as *The Nation* and conservative publications such as the *National Review*.

See also: Cultural Context; Historical Analysis, Media: Systems Approach

References

Berners-Lee, T. (2010, November 22). "Long Live the Web: A Call for Continued Open Standards and Neutrality." *Scientific American.* Retrieved from http://www.scientificamerican.com/article.cfm?id=long-live-the-web

Lohr, S. (2011, March 27). "In a New Web World, No Application Is an Island." *New York Times.* Retrieved from http://www.nytimes.com/2011/03/27/business/27unboxed.html

Cultural Studies

Cultural studies is a critical approach to communication analysis that focuses on the connections between communication and culture. According to cultural studies scholar James Carey (1988),

> Culture . . . is the meaning and significance particular people discover in their experience through art, religion, and so forth. . . . But what is called the study of culture also can be called the study of communications, for what we are studying in this context are the ways in which experience is worked into understanding and then disseminated and celebrated. . . .

At the same time, communication is a process through which a shared culture is created, modified, and transformed.

The focus of cultural studies is not on aesthetic aspects of text but rather at communications as a cultural "text": what these texts reveal in terms of the social system. Carey observed:

Our task is to construct a "reading" of the text. The text itself is a sequence of symbols—speech, writing, gesture—that contain interpretations. Our task, like that of a literary critic, is to interpret the interpretations. (1988: 60)

According to Carey, culture is made up of multiple realities: "Culture . . . is never singular and univocal. It is like nature itself, multiple, various, and varietal. It is this for each of us. Therefore we must begin . . . from the assumption of multiple realities" (1988: 65). Within this context, the media is a reflection of the multiple realities that compete for attention in our society. Carey notes:

Culture . . . is never singular and univocal. It is like nature itself, multiple, various, and varietal. It is this for each of us. . . . The analysis of mass communication will have to examine the several cultural worlds in which people simultaneously exist—the tension, often radical tension, between them, the patterns of mood and motivation distinctive to each, and the interpretation among them. (1988: 65–67)

It would not be stretching Carey's thinking by very much to expand his notion of multiple realities to include the many subcultures which make up American society. The media is a valuable "text" through which we can understand the distinctive values, concerns, and priorities of subcultures such as women, adolescents, and African Americans in American culture.

Cultural studies scholars argue that the media do not merely reflect or reinforce culture but in fact shape thinking by promoting the dominant ideology of a culture through *cultural hegemony*; that is, the ability of the dominant classes to exercise social and cultural leadership to maintain economic and political control over the subordinate classes. Rather than imposing its will on the subordinate class through force, the members of the dominant class cultivate a worldview that supports their interests. In adopting this worldview, the subordinate class willingly consents to the continued preeminence of the dominant class.

As Alan O'Connor explains, these "approved ways of understanding and experiencing the everyday world (i.e., *cultural hegemony*) have important political consequences" (O'Connor, 1995: 36), by controlling cultural responses to the text.

Media presentations contain their own *preferred readings*, based on the social position/orientation of the media communicator. In this way, the sympathies of the audience are aligned with the values and beliefs of this dominant culture. O'Connor declares that the media serve as "processes of persuasion in which we are invited to understand the world in certain ways but not in others" (Silverblatt, 2007: 10). Thus, the media create (or re-create) representations of reality that support the dominant ideology as a means of maintaining cultural control.

Cultural Studies and Media Literacy

Although cultural studies scholars have provided a conceptual framework, they have not been specific about a methodological approach for the study of mass communications. Carey suggests that "the task of the cultural scientist is closer to that of a literary critic or a scriptural scholar, though it is not the same, than it is to a behavioral scientist" (Carey, 1988: 60).

The following assumptions apply the principles of cultural studies to the field of media literacy:

- There is an inequitable distribution of power in our cultures; as a result, it is possible to detect race, gender and class power profiles.
- Forces of domination and subordination are central in our social system.
- All meanings are *intertextural*, in that any one text is necessarily read in relation to others and the reader brings a range of textural knowledge to bear upon it.
- The same ideology is repeated in a variety of texts.
- Cultural studies looks at cultural commodities of our culture (particularly our media "text") to find meanings and values.
- A society's economic system reproduces its ideology in its (media) commodities, but it is not very visible; it appears to be the natural way that things are.
- Subordinate groups make their own culture out of the commodities that are supplied by the dominant system.
- The dominant culture turns this process to its advantage (as evidenced in some advertising).

- The conflict of interests that emerge from the sense of social difference result in an ongoing struggle for power, which results in social change.
- Audiences bring this cumulative information to new material, which reinforces this dominant ideology.

Cultural studies focuses attention on the role of the media as a principal means by which ideology is introduced and reinforced within contemporary culture. One of the central tenants of Cultural studies is that the media promote the dominant ideology of a culture. The media industry is owned by those people, groups, and interests that maintain economic and social control of the culture.

Examples of the hegemonic process can be found in cumulative messages conveyed through the media. For instance, one of the messages conveyed through U.S. media regarding success is that success is tied to virtue: Those who attain material success are morally superior, and people who do not succeed according to these standards somehow deserve their fate. This lesson is taught repeatedly in children's programs, such as Disney's *Aladdin*, in which the goodness of the young hero is parlayed into position, wealth, and the princess of his dreams.

See also: Cultural Context; Ideological Analysis

References

Carey, J. W. (1988). *Communication as Culture: Essays on Media and Society*. New York: Routledge Press.

O'Connor, A., and J. Downey. (1995). *Questioning the Media* (p. 35). Beverly Hills, CA: Sage Publications.

Silverblatt, A. (2007). *Media Literacy: Keys to Interpreting Media Messages* (3rd ed.). Westport: Praeger Publishing.

Culture Code

Culture code is a qualitative approach to media literacy analysis that furnishes perspective into the relationship between media and culture. This is an example of a *disparate* approach to media analysis, in which the principles of another discipline are applied to the interpretation of media content. Developed by anthropologist Clotaire Rapaille, a code is "the unconscious meaning we apply to any given thing—a car, type of food, relationship, even a country—via the culture in which we are raised" (Rapaille, 2006: 5).

Culture codes can be considered as a kind of *cultural semiotics* in which individuals develop associations with their environment, creating an *emotional imprint* that, according to Rapaille, "give[s] us a distinctive glimpse of why we do the things we do and provide[s] us with a new set of glasses that allows us to view our behavior afresh" (Rapaille, 2006: 191).

To illustrate, the culture code for coffee in the United States is *domesticity*, based on the early recollections of home associated with the smell of coffee brewing. As reporter Jack Hitt (2000) explains,

> There is a little window of time when you are young in which to imprint the idea of "coffee." . . . It occurs usually around age two in America, when your mother is cooking breakfast. Your mother loves you. You are happy. . . . This is the American code for coffee's aroma: "home."

Indeed, many real estate agents make use of this cultural imprint, brewing coffee when they hold open houses to create a positive domestic atmosphere.

The media often reinforces culture codes. For instance, the day after Thanksgiving has been designated as "the busiest shopping day of the year." The lead story in both print and broadcast news programs routinely features images of shoppers, arms filled with packages, finding bargains in this, the first "unofficial" shopping day of the Christmas season. However, this culture code has been manufactured as a result of a collaborative effort between the business community and the media, sanctioning the event as part of America's national consciousness. As columnist David Carr (2008) explains,

> In partnership with retail advertising clients, the news media have worked steadily and systematically to turn Black Friday into a broad cultural event. A decade ago, it was barely in the top 10 shopping days of the year. But once retailers hit on the formula of offering one or two very-low-priced items as loss leaders, media groups began to cover the post-Thanksgiving outing as a kind of consumer sporting event.

The methodology employed in the culture code consists of a "discovery session," in which participants respond to a series of words, going back to their first conscious memory of a concept.

- *Step One* consists of an interview with the focus group, listening to what people *say* about a product, place, or idea.

- In *Step Two*, participants sit on the floor and use scissors and a pile of magazines to make a collage of words about the subject. Rapaille observes, "The goal here [is] to get them to tell me stories with these words that would offer further clues [about the 'deep meaning' of the concept]." (Rapaille, 2006: 15)
- In *Step Three*, Rapaille creates a relaxed environment; participants lie on the floor with pillows, while soothing music plays in the background. She then allows subjects to identify and discuss their earliest and/or significant memories. The goal is to bring participants back to "their first imprint" and the emotion attached to it. Rapaille explains,

> The relaxation process employed during the discovery sessions allows participants to access this (dreamlike) state. . . . People regularly report that memories come back to them during these sessions that they had forgotten for years. (2006: 15)

At that point, participants' responses are analyzed to identify *patterns* in word choice, tone, and messages. "We discover the Codes when we find these common messages" (2006: 25).

Cultural Relativism

Every culture has its own interpretation (or code) that reflects its distinct character. Rapaille (2006) explains, "All cultures have a language, a habitat, a history . . . all these elements . . . create the unique identity of each culture. . . . There is an American mind, just as there is a French mind" (pp. 20–22, 27). Thus, examining, a country's culture code can furnish perspective into the characteristics of that culture.

To illustrate, the culture code for food in France is *pleasure*. In that country, a meal is regarded as a social occasion; people linger over their meals in restaurants, tour the kitchens, and engage the chefs in conversations about their meal. In addition, the French appreciate the aesthetics of food preparation. Patrons appreciate the "presentation" of the food. Quality, rather than quantity, is of major importance in French culture. Thus, the portions at French restaurants are considerably smaller than their American counterparts.

In contrast, the culture code for food in the United States is *fuel*. The chief American contribution to international cuisine is "fast food," which is designed for quick and expedient consumption.

According to Rapaille (2006), the American culture code for food can be traced to its "humble beginnings":

Though we are the richest country in the world, . . . at the reptilian level, we consider ourselves poor. We start out with nothing and we labor to achieve wealth, and even though we may succeed, the hand-to-mouth attitude remains. The response of poor people to food is consistent throughout the world: they eat as much as they can when they can, because they don't know whether they will have the opportunity to eat the next day. . . . When someone eats huge quantities, we sometimes say he "can really put it away." Unconsciously, this is exactly what he is doing. He is storing as much food as he can to forestall starvation (though the chances of starvation are extremely slim). (2006: 141-142)

Rapaille (2006) observes, "At the conclusion of dinner, Americans end a meal by saying, 'I'm full.' The French end a meal by saying 'That was delicious'" (p. 142). Indeed, as Rapaille points out, the mini-grocery stores in gas stations are the perfect metaphor for American food.

Thus, an understanding of culture code can provide insight into American ads for fast food. These ads rarely show the product, instead emphasizing other reasons to eat. For instance, Taco Bell touches on the melding of food and mobile lifestyle with its slogan, "Run for the Border."

Alternative Culture Codes

One limitation in Rapaille's methodology is that it can be difficult for one "code" to encompass all of the complexities of a culture. In a multifarious culture, there may be several alternative culture codes. As an example, Rapaille (2006) identifies one code for *beauty* in American culture—*man's salvation*:

When asked to go back to their first and most powerful memories of their own beauty, [women participants] recalled moments of romance, of attraction, of getting a man's attention. . . . Many of the stories revealed something even deeper. Statements such as "He was proud to be with me," "He made a fuss," and "I was the most special person to the other person" suggested that beauty not only attracted a man but also changed him in a substantial way at the same time . . .

If a woman can impress her beauty upon a man permanently, if she can stay beautiful in his eyes, she can make him a better human being. She is doing more than keeping herself visually appealing to him: she is elevating him from a rutting animal to something more exalted. (Rapaille, 2006: 60)

Rapaille (2006) cites an example of this culture code from the film *Pretty Woman* (1990):

In that movie, Julia Roberts played a prostitute hired by a hardhearted tycoon played by Richard Gere. While she looks like a hooker, she's nothing more than a plaything to Gere. However, when he needs her to accompany him to a formal function and when she dresses elegantly and makes herself as beautiful (rather than provocative) as possible, she wins Gere's heart. She saves him from a life of emotional emptiness.

Another even more blatant sign of the Code at work in popular culture is with the TV show *Baywatch*. In this series, gorgeous women (most famously Pamela Anderson) perform the function of lifeguards, literally saving men (and women, too, of course) from drowning and other dangers of the water. These women perform heroic acts while appearing as though they have run into the bay straight out of the *Sports Illustrated* swimsuit issue. (Rapaille, 2006: 60–61)

However, other definitions of beauty can be found in American culture as well, as evidenced in the media examples cited by Rapaille:

- *Identity*: In the United States, people's identity is tied to their appearance. Indeed, studies reveal that attractive people are treated differently:
  - Parents give more attention and supervision to their pretty offspring.
  - Good-looking people get a "beauty premium" in the workplace—an extra 5 percent an hour—while there is a "plainness penalty" of 9 percent in wages. Meanwhile, obese women tend to get substantially lower wages than women of average weight (Dowd, 2010). This preferential treatment affects an individual's sense of identity—how others see them and how they see themselves. For instance, Rapaille makes the point that in the TV series *Baywatch*, the female lifeguards were members of an exclusive group, defined by their appearance.
- *Power*: Beautiful people are able to exert control over their environment and other people. In *Pretty Woman*, the transformation of Vivian Ward (Julia Roberts) changes the balance of power between herself and her "employer" Edward Lewis (Richard Gere). In one scene, Vivian dons an elegant evening gown, which has a visible effect on Edward. No longer cold and demanding, Edward is rendered powerless by her beauty. However, the beautiful heroine uses her power judiciously, treating her admirer with kindness and generosity.

- *Reflection of internal virtue:* In novels of the Victorian age, the physical beauty of the heroines was presented as the embodiment of their virtue. Similarly, in *Pretty Woman*, the audience recognizes that despite her circumstances, Vivian Ward is a good and moral person.

In addition, it should be noted that, over time, the addition of the *beautiful temptress* character in soap operas and reality shows reflects changes in American culture. Thus, it can be useful to broaden the scope of the analysis by considering alternative culture codes as they appear in media presentations.

Media Literacy Strategies

Culture code is an approach that can follow several lines of inquiry, as detailed in this section.

1. Providing insight into the study of international communications
The culture code approach focuses on the following aspect of international communications:

- *A media presentation that is popular in another country can provide insight into possible connections between the two cultures.* For instance, an American hero who is popular abroad is "on code" with regard to that culture. Moreover, media figures from one country who are not accepted in another culture may signal disconnects between the two cultures.
- *Examining a country's culture codes for another country in its media presentations can indicate how one country thinks of that country.* To illustrate, according to Rapaille (2006), the following countries have different code for America:
  ○ In *England,* Americans are depicted as "big, loud, powerful, vulgar, extreme, and determined to win at any cost. . . . In speaking about America, the notion of quantity came up with great regularity. . . . The English code for America is *Unashamedly Abundant*" (Rapaille, 2006: 175).
  ○ "[*French* respondents] characterized [Americans] as childlike and naïve, but powerful at the same time. When the French spoke of Americans, it was almost as though they were speaking about an alien race. . . . The Code for America in France is *Space Travellers*" (Raipelle, 2006: 172).

○ "*Germans* see themselves as superior in education, engineering, and creating order. They see Americans as primitive, yet they understand that Americans have been able to do things on a world level that they have not—and that confounds them. . . . They've imprinted us as liberators and benevolent cowboys. . . . The Code for America in Germany is *John Wayne*" (Rapaille, 2006: 174).

2. *Furnishing perspective into cultural attitudes, values, behaviors, preoccupations, and myths.* To illustrate, as discussed above, Rapaille defines the American code for beauty as *man's salvation*. However, other cultures have their own codes for beauty:

- In Arab cultures, which are dominated by men, women's appearance is regarded as a reflection of her man's success.
- In Norway, beauty is a reflection of the natural world.
- In Latin America, beauty is age-appropriate. Thus, an elderly male or female may be regarded as beautiful.

3. *Furnishing perspective into cultural self-concept: how a culture sees itself.* As an example, Rapaille (2006) has identified the culture codes that the following countries have assigned to themselves:

- *England*: *Class*—there is a strong sense among the English that they are of a higher social stratum than other people. This arises from England's long history of world leadership ("the sun never sets on the British Empire") and from the messages passed down from generation to generation that being English is a special privilege that one receives at birth (p. 176).
- *France*: *Idea*—raised on stories of great French philosophers and thinkers, French children imprint the value of ideas as paramount and refinement of the mind as the highest goal (p. 176).
- *Germany*: *Order*—over many generations, Germans perfected bureaucracy in an effort to stave off the chaos that came to them in wave after wave, and Germans imprinted early on with this most powerful of codes (p. 177).

4. *Providing insight into a country's culture codes.* Journalist Jack Hitt explains,

Once you understand the Rapaille method, you start noticing just how often in our mediated day some emotional depth charge is set to go off—whether it's a television commercial, a [political] speech or a Hollywood film. For years, there was a certain telephone commercial that had me by the throat. I am talking about that damp little melodrama involving a middle-aged black woman sitting in a chair as she receives her first phone call from her son, newly arrived to his dorm in college. I simply had to watch it. If it came on in a room, I would turn away from what I was doing or whomever I was talking to in order to experience this tiny emotional whippet. Now I see that it wasn't merely the surface sentimentality of the mother-son bond that was plucking my heartstrings. A Rapaille reading would interpret this vignette as an immigrant morality story tailored for the American psyche—where blackness stood for our country's ongoing sense of striving to better yourself; college was the signifier for having made it. This wasn't sentiment; it was patriotism. (Hitt, 2000)

5. Providing insight into media presentations. Analysis of a culture code can provide considerable insight into the construction of media messages. According to Rapaille, a key to the popularity of media presentation is that it is "on code," as well as furnishing an explanation for why we watch particular programs. In addition, Rapaille contends that heroes prevail in media programs because they are "on code."

In addition, culture code can be a useful way to discover the "meaning" behind popular shows. As an example, in 2009 Wheaties cereal devised a marketing strategy and advertising campaign for a new brand that reflects the culture code (as defined by Rapaille) for food in America as *fuel*. The marketing strategy for this new brand, Wheaties Fuel, involved assembling a panel of accomplished male athletes, who discuss how their bodies are machines that must be "fueled" to maximize performance. Quarterback Peyton Manning declares, "I learned what I need to perform at my best . . . carbohydrates [for energy]." Thus, the campaign was based on the idea that the ads were "on code" with Wheaties' target audience for the concept of food.

Critical analysis of media presentations focuses on the following questions:

- Where does a culture code appear in a narrative?
- In what ways are concepts "on code"?
- In what ways is culture code tied to thematic concerns?
- In what ways is culture code tied to characterization?

6. Tracing shifts in a culture. Examining changes in the culture code can provide insight into corresponding changes in a culture. For example, in post–World War II, the culture code for doctor was *deity*. In the 1960s' television series such as *Dr. Kildare* and *Ben Casey*, the physicians are infallible and often dispensed advice beyond their field of expertise.

Over time, as HMOs have become the primary health care entity in the United States, doctors have lost status. Doctors are limited in terms of the kinds of treatments that they can administer. Furthermore, the number of malpractice lawsuits brought against doctors has undermined the cultural myth of infallibility. Consequently, it can be argued that the culture code for doctors has changed to *mechanic*.

7. Identifying the treatment of a particular topic. Examining the culture code can provide insight into a particular topic. Consider that, in the United States, the ritual of courtship is framed as a conflict, often being referred to as the "battle between the sexes." In particular, wooing makes males feel very uncomfortable. Thus, Rapaille's choice of culture code for courtship/seduction is *manipulation*. An alternative culture code is *confrontation*.

In Italy, courtship is considered an elaborate and joyous *game*. According to Rapaille (2006), "Playing is much more important than winning" (p. 45). Italian males enjoy the experience—even if it is not successful. "If a woman doesn't reciprocate his interest, he'll merely smile, shrug, and move along" (p. 45).

8. Identifying the use of culture code in the construction of media messages. Examining the culture codes can be a useful way to approach the analysis of narrative elements, such as theme, character, and plot conventions. According to Rapaille, the heroes of media presentations succeed because they are "on code." In addition, the plot convention of the comeback is "Code for Perfection. . . . Trying, failing, learning from our mistakes, and coming back stronger than ever is an essential part of the American archetype" (p. 135).

9. Using culture codes to construct effective media programming. The strategic use of culture codes can be used in the construction of media messages. A media presentation that is "on code" can affect how the audience responds.

10. Evaluating marketing strategies. Advertisers frequently position their product to fit a country's culture code. As Rapaille (2006) observes, "Awareness of the Code offers clear-cut ways to market . . . products" (p. 102). For instance, American advertisers frequently promote health products by playing off of its code: *movement*. Thus, ads that are "on code" promote mobility or action, whereas ads that are "off code" suggest *constraints* on movement (pp. 84–85).

This approach is particularly useful in the arena of international marketing. According to Rapaille, advertising an imported product requires a *two-step* marketing approach. First, advertisers tap into the cultural code of the country of origin to market the product to an international audience. Rapaille observes, "A global strategy requires customizing for each culture, though it is always important that the strategy embrace the culture in which it is marketing the product" (2006: 179). At that point, international advertisers position the product in terms of the culture code for the foreign culture. Rapaille explains,

> [It is] essential that [advertisers] not run away from their "American-ness" in building a marketing strategy in each culture. . . . If the English expect abundance from Americans, it is important to highlight that. Products should come "fully loaded" and "super-sized." If the Germans expected John Wayne, products should help "save the day" without asking anyone to change who they are. . . . [Thus], if the French expect us to be space travelers, then the products we bring them should have an otherworldly quality; they should feel new and unusual. (p. 176)

Thus, Chrysler's marketing campaign in France followed this successful two-step process:

> Chrysler fulfilled the American role as space travelers by introducing a car that looked like nothing else on French roads. They then marketed the car in a way that was completely On Code for the French. Their ads spoke of the 150 new ideas that went into the creation of the PT Cruiser, with different ads detailing several of these ideas. (Rapaille, 2006: 178)

11. Examining the use of culture codes in political campaigns. Political media consultants could make use of culture codes as they map out strategies for their candidates. To illustrate, much of the success of the 2008 Obama campaign can be attributed to its ability to identify the on-code messages of *change* and *hope.*

See also: Cultural Context; Hierarchy of Appearance; International Communications, Media Literacy Approach

References

Carr, D. (2008). "Media and Retailers Both Built Black Friday." *New York Times.* Retrieved from http://www.nytimes.com/2008/12/01/business/media/01carr.html?pagewanted=all

Dowd, M. (2010, June 5). "Dressed to Distract." *New York Times.* Retrieved from http://www.nytimes.com/2010/06/06/opinion/06dowd.html

Hitt, J. (2000, May 7). "Does the Smell of Coffee Brewing Remind You of Your Mother?" *New York Times Magazine*. Retrieved from http://www.nytimes.com/2000/05/07/magazine/does-the-smell-of-coffee-brewing-remind-you-of-your-mother.html?pagewanted=all&src=pm

Rapaille, C. (2006). *The Culture Code*. New York: Broadway Books.

Curriculum Developments in Higher Education, Media Literacy

The discipline of media literacy has begun to make significant inroads in U.S. colleges and universities. According to a 2003 study, approximately 180 colleges and universities offer coursework or programs in media literacy at both the undergraduate and graduate levels—nearly three times the number recorded five years earlier (Webster University Media Literacy Web site, 2008). As this discipline matures, patterns are emerging in regard to curriculum development that may be key to continued growth and success in U.S. colleges and universities. The following sections consider these factors.

1. An Integrated Approach to Media Literacy

The traditional approach to media literacy education involves offering *stand-alone* classes in media literacy, such as Introduction to Media Literacy or Approaches to Media Literacy. In these classes, media literacy is the primary focus of attention.

Renee Hobbs was among the first media literacy scholars to discuss the relative merits of an *integrated pedagogical model* verses *stand-alone* media literacy courses in primary and secondary school curricula. In the Integrated Approach, media literacy principles are incorporated into established disciplines, such as language arts, social studies, art, and health. Hobbs explains, "Because mass media artifacts are relevant to science, social studies, the visual and performing arts as well as reading/language arts, teachers can easily make connections which stretch across subject areas by teaching with media and teaching about media" (1996).

Advocates of the integrated approach use the analogy of foreign language instruction, pointing out that offering classes in Latin, French, or Chinese once or twice a week is not nearly as effective as becoming immersed in the language by traveling to a foreign country. Furthermore, they note that required courses and standardized tests have limited the opportunity to offer new courses such as media literacy.

In colleges and universities, the discipline of media literacy generally is offered in separate, stand-alone courses. However, the integrated approach is also an effective way to incorporate media literacy education into higher education. In this application, traditional media communications classes are presented from a media literacy perspective.

To illustrate, the introductory class in international communications typically identifies the structure and types of media systems around the world, from authoritarian to libertarian models of mass communications. A media literacy approach also considers these international communications models. But in addition, a media literacy perspective provides students with strategies to interpret and discuss the messages being conveyed by the channels of international communications. A media literacy approach to international communications also focuses on the following areas of study:

- Ways in which international media presentations provide insight into a country's cultural attitudes, values, behaviors, preoccupations, and myths
- The impact of global media on traditional cultures
- An analysis of a national media system by identifying the following defining characteristics of a country
  - Political system
  - Geographical factors
  - Ethnic composition
  - Religious composition
  - Educational system
  - System of media ethics

A third approach is a *hybrid model* of media literacy curriculum, which combines specialized media literacy courses with the Integrated model of media literacy curriculum. To illustrate, Webster University's Bachelor's in Media Communications with emphasis in Media Literacy consists of the following stand-alone media literacy courses:

MEDC 1630, *Media Literacy*—Prerequisite Class
MEDC 2630, *Media Literacy II*
MEDC 3900, *Studies in Media Literacy*
MEDC 4100, *Media and Digital Culture*
MEDC 4850, *Seminar in Media Literacy*—Capstone Class

In addition, the curriculum includes the following traditional media communications courses that are taught from a media literacy perspective:

SPCM 2600, *Nonverbal Approaches to the Media*
MEDC 3260, *International Communications*
MEDC 3850, *Television: A Critical Study*
MEDC 4220, *Approaches to Genre Study*
JOUR 4400, *Media Criticism for Publication*
MEDC 4500, *Political Communications*

These courses reinforce media literacy concepts and principles as they are applied to these discrete fields of study.

2. A Media Literacy Course as Theoretical Prerequisite Class

Introduction to Mass Communication is generally the prerequisite theory class required for students majoring in media communications or related fields, such as video production, advertising, journalism, digital media, film theory and production, or audio recording. This theoretical introduction to media focuses on the following areas of study:

- The process of mass communication
- Distinguishing elements of various media
- The influence of ownership on media content
- The impact of the media on individuals and society
- The history of individual media systems (i.e., print, photography, radio, film, television, and the Internet)

The initial media literacy class also considers these areas of study, with the exception of the unit on media history. However, some media literacy texts now include the analysis of media history, identifying patterns in the evolution of various channels of mass communication.

But in addition to the above areas of analysis, the introductory media literacy class provides students with the theoretical tools to conduct primary research of the media and media content. As a result, media literacy students learn to decipher media messages, based on systematic analysis of media presentations.

Indeed, there is considerable overlap between the content of these two courses. To illustrate, *Introduction to Mass Communication—Media Literacy and Culture,* by Stanley J. Baran (2010) is a textbook that takes a media literacy approach to the Introduction to Mass Communication course.

3. Teaching Media Production Classes from a Media Literacy Perspective

Teaching media literacy through production courses can be an effective mode of instruction. Taking a hands-on approach to the construction of media messages reinforces the concepts and principles of media literacy. Students discover that the production choices they make (e.g., what to include or omit, camera angles, and the selection of images) reinforce the manifest message of the media communicator or, in some cases, convey independent messages.

This approach is an extension of the integrated model discussed earlier, adding a media literacy dimension to traditional coursework in photography, film, audio, video, and digital media. As an example, at Webster University, VIDE 1810, Video Production I, is approached from a media literacy perspective. The initial stage of this class is identical to the traditional approach in that students learn the production techniques, such as lighting, camera proximity, and editing. But in the media literacy version, students are then asked to consider what *messages* are conveyed by these production choices. For instance, students are given an exercise in which they are asked to select production techniques (e.g., lighting and camera angle) that make the subject look authoritative and his or her point of view legitimate. In this way, students learn that using bright lighting and shooting up at the subject convey positive messages, whereas darkness and shadows, as well as a downward camera angle, convey negative messages about the subject and his or her point of view.

Significantly, there is some indication that teaching production classes from a media literacy perspective can help to achieve the original learning objectives of these courses. For instance, Video I instructors at Webster University report that the final projects produced in these classes are of higher quality than their counterparts in sections of the course that rely on the traditional instructional approach. In addition to mastering the various production techniques, students are asked to apply critical analysis to the production process, deciding when particular production techniques are most appropriate.

4. Media Literacy Class as General Education Requirement

Part of becoming an educated person is having the ability to make sense of one's environment. In the modern era, in which our environment is shaped by and brought to us through the media, it is vitally important that students develop the skills to become intelligent consumers of media.

Thus, in recognition of the value of the discipline, institutions of higher education have begun to add media literacy to their general education requirements. Some schools furnish a list of courses that meet their general education requirements. St. Louis Community College-Meremac includes a media literacy course in its general education list. Other institutions, such as Webster University, offer a set of courses that are *process driven*. Thus, at Webster University, media literacy is included in the set of courses that fulfill the general education requirement of "critical thinking."

5. As a Complementary Area of Study

Media literacy is an academic discipline that complements other fields of study. For example:

- Business and management majors at Webster University can supplement their program of study with a 15-hour certificate in media literacy, in recognition of the linkage between these two disciplines. Studies show that although people are consuming more information than ever before, their reading has *declined*. Consequently, it behooves business students to learn how to construct and interpret messages, using the different "languages" of media, such as video and interactive media (Bilton, 2009).
- Advertising majors are advantaged by learning how to examine media presentations as a text that reflects cultural attitudes, values, behaviors, preoccupations, and myths. Identifying these messages can be invaluable in the process of developing advertising campaigns. It is also essential that advertising students consider ethical considerations before actually encountering situations as media professionals.
- Political science majors benefit from media literacy coursework because they learn to apply media literacy strategies to the analysis of political campaigns. Media literacy can also help political science majors learn to construct political advertising. Media literacy also focuses attention on the impact of the media on the American political process, including the following:
  - Campaign finance
  - Party politics
  - Political advertising
  - Debates
  - Selection of candidates
  - Media consultants
  - The scrutiny of the media

As an example, Webster University offers programs in media literacy that complement a major course of study. A minor in media literacy consists of 18 hours of coursework in the discipline. Another ancillary program is a certificate of media literacy, which is 15 hours of specified media literacy courses.

See also: Careers, Media Literacy; Definition, Media Literacy; Historical Analysis, Media: Systems Approach; Integrated Approach to Media Literacy Education; Production Analysis Approach; Sectors, Media Literacy

References

Baran, S. J. (2010). *Introduction to Mass Communication—Media Literacy and Culture* (6th ed.). New York: McGraw-Hill Humanities/Social Science/Languages.

Bilton, N. (2009, December 9). "Part of the Daily American Diet, 34 Gigabytes of Data." *New York Times*. Retrieved from http://www.nytimes.com/2009/12/10/technology/10data.html

Hobbs, R. (1996). "Expanding the Concept of Literacy." Retrieved from http://jcp.proscenia.net/publications/articles_mlr/hobbs/expanding.html

Webster University Media Literacy Web site. (2008, July 8). Retrieved from http://www.webster.edu/medialiteracy

Definition, Media Literacy

As the media have evolved, so has the definition of media literacy. In 1946, Edgar Dale was among the first to define a new kind of literacy:

What do I mean by the term "literacy" and the "new" literacy? I mean by literacy the ability to communicate through the three modes: reading and writing, speaking and listening, visualizing and observing—print, audio, and visual literacy. This literacy, broadly speaking, can be at two levels. First, is at the level of training, initiative reaction. Here we communicate the simple, literal meaning of what is written, said or visualized. . . . Or second, we can have creative interaction, can read between the lines, draw inferences, understand the implications of what was written, said, or spoken. We then learn what the speaker, writer or visualizer "meant to say," which requires a greater degree of literacy. And finally, we learn to read beyond the lines, to evaluate, and apply the material to new situations. We use the message in our own varied ways.

I would also classify responses as uncritical or accepting, or as critical and evaluating. The new literacy involves critical reading, critical listening, and critical observing. It is disciplined thinking about what is read, heard, and visualized. (Dale, 1946)

Since that time, numerous definitions of media literacy have emerged. A close examination of the various descriptions of media literacy by scholars and educators reveals a pattern of common elements that, together, form a definitive definition of the discipline.

1. Media Literacy Is A Critical Thinking Skill That Is Applied to the Source of Much of Our Information: The Channels of Mass Communication

At the 1992 Aspen Institute of Media Literacy, a conference that helped launch the Medial Literacy movement in the United States, Patricia Aufderheide authored a report containing the following definition of media literacy: "The ability to access, analyze, evaluate, and create messages in a variety of forms" (1993: 3).

The National Association for Media Literacy Education (NAMLE, n.d.) calls for critical thinking in its "Implications for Practice":

Media literacy education . . . actively encourage(s) critical thinking in all classrooms . . . Media literacy education teachers do not train students to ask IF there is a bias in a particular message (since all media messages are biased), but rather, WHAT the substance, source, and significance of a bias might be.

Media literacy promotes the critical thinking skills that empower people to make independent judgments and informed decisions in response to information conveyed through the channels of mass communications. Educator and scientist Steven Schafersman defines critical thinking as follows:

Critical thinking means correct thinking in the pursuit of relevant and reliable knowledge about the world. . . . It is reasonable, reflective, responsible, and skillful thinking that is focused on deciding what to believe or do. . . . A person who thinks critically can ask appropriate questions, gather relevant information, efficiently and creatively sort through this information, reason logically from this information, and come to reliable and trustworthy conclusions about the world that

enable one to live and act successfully in it. . . . True critical thinking
is higher-order thinking, enabling a person to, for example, responsibly judge between political candidates, serve on a murder trial jury,
evaluate society's need for nuclear power plants, and assess the consequences of global warming. Critical thinking enables an individual to
be a responsible citizen who contributes to society, and not be merely a
consumer of society's distractions. (Schafersman, 1991)

An essential element of critical thinking found in media literacy is *inquiry*;
that is, the ability to use critical thinking skills to view, question, analyze, and
understand issues presented overtly and covertly in movies, videos, television, and other visual media.

Critical thinking strategies also encourage students to think *dialogically*—
that is, the ability to move back and forth between opposing points of view
or frames of reference. Thus, as applied to media literacy, critical thinking
includes the following skills:

- Distinguishing between verifiable facts and value claims
- Determining the reliability of a claim or source
- Determining the accuracy of a statement
- Distinguishing between warranted and unwarranted claims
- Detecting bias
- Identifying stated and unstated assumptions
- Recognizing logical inconsistencies
- Determining the strength of an argument
- Assessing and/or instituting systematic application of concepts

Renee Hobbs and Richard Frost found that the study of media literacy
improves students' comprehension of print, audio, and video texts, message
analysis, and interpretation:

At the center of media literacy education must be the pedagogy of
inquiry, which is the act of asking questions about media texts. . . . The
cultivation of an open, questioning, reflective, and critical stance towards
symbolic texts should be the pole of the media literacy umbrella, as it
is the concept most likely to ensure its survival. (Hobbs & Frost, 2003)

As a critical thinking skill that is applied to the study of media, media
literacy education also promotes critical thinking skills in traditional disciplines such as mathematics, history and geography. Furthermore, media

literacy education also enhances students' general *critical* and *creative* thinking skills. Frank Baker provides the following example:

> A three-year research project (2003–2006) involving two middle schools in the San Francisco area revealed that students' critical and creative thinking skills measurably increased following their participation in a media literacy curriculum. Educational researcher Michael Cohen reported that "the results of the evaluation clearly indicate that those students exposed to the Media Education, Arts and Literacy (MEAL) curriculum showed significant increases in their acquisition of knowledge in core curriculum areas—and even shifts in attitudes toward learning." (Baker, 2010)

2. Media Literacy Furnishes Individuals with the Tools to Make Independent Choices with Regard to (1) Which Media Programming to Select and (2) Interpreting the Information That They Receive through the Channels of Mass Communication

According to W. James Potter, media communicators frequently lull audience members into a state of *automaticity*,

> where our minds operate without any conscious effort from us. . . . A great deal of the time, media exposure is done mindlessly . . . [Media communicators] use programming strategies to condition you into habitual exposure states and then reinforce those habits. (Potter, 2005)

In contrast to this passive mindset, the National Telemedia Council states that media literacy fosters "mindful viewing, reflective judgment. . . . Media literacy is the ability to choose, to understand—within the context of content, form/style, impact, industry and production—to question, to evaluate, to create and/or produce and to respond thoughtfully to the media we consume" (National Telemedia Council).

In this sense, media literacy is a process-oriented discipline. Rather than imparting a set interpretation of a media presentation, media literacy-educated students are equipped to apply strategies in order to decipher media messages.

FCC commissioner Michael Copps observes that encouraging a critical independence is particularly valuable in the development of children and adolescents:

> [The study of media literacy] teaches kids not only how to use the media but how the media uses them. Kids need to know how particular

messages get crafted and why, what devices are used to hold their attention and what ideas are left out. In a culture where media is pervasive
and invasive, kids need to think critically about what they see, hear
and read. No child's education can be complete without this. (Media
Clearinghouse)

An adolescent's ability to question the motives and methods of advertisers
will make them less susceptible to the preferred reading of media communicators in magazines and movies ("Children Are Still Making the Decision to
Smoke," 2006).

3. Media Literacy Furnishes Insight into the Impact of Various Contexts on the Construction of Media Messages

As British media scholar Cary Bazalgette observes, "Evaluating content . . .
rests on a substantial body of knowledge regarding the broader social, cultural, economic, political, and historical contexts in which media content is
produced" (1989). Influences on the media include historical, geopolitical,
economic, and cultural context, as well as the impact of the media industry
and the traditions and formulae of media genres.

4. Understanding the Process of Mass Communication

Beyond teaching about particular texts, media literacy fosters an understanding of the process of media communications: (a) the function (or purpose) of
a media presentation, (b) the media communicator, (c) comparative media—
the distinguishing characteristics of each medium, and (d) the audience.

5. An Awareness of the Impact of the Media on the Individual and Society

The media have transformed the way we think about the world, each other,
and ourselves. Media presentations convey cumulative messages that *shape,
reflect,* and *reinforce* attitudes, values, behaviors, preoccupations, and myths
that define a culture.

The media have assumed a major role in the lives of individuals. Photographs, DVDs, and videos document and preserve personal identity. In addition, the media transmit family histories to succeeding generations, recording
significant events such as birthdays, anniversaries, graduation, and weddings.
Language, fashion, and social activities revolve around the media.

Our common cultural experience is defined largely through media consumption. People must remain current on popular programs to maintain membership in particular subcultures. The media also help to define popular taste. For instance, the mechanized sitcom laughs during a prime-time season set the norm for what is funny.

In addition, the media play an increasingly prominent role in the socialization process. At times, an individual's contact with the outside world has become dependent on the media. In her study of media usage in retirement centers, Mary Cassata (1967) described aging as a process of "social disengagement" from family, friends, job, and health. Cassata found that members of retirement centers rely on the media in response to the vacuum created by these disengagements.

Furthermore, the media play an increasingly prominent role in the establishment and enforcement of social norms. Which is the proper salad fork? How should you approach a woman or gentleman you would like to meet? What athletic shoes should you wear? All of these questions can be answered through careful attention to media programming.

6. An Awareness of Media Content as a "Text" That Provides Insight into Our Contemporary Culture and Ourselves

The study of media presentations can have a *hermeneutic*, or interpretive, function, furnishing a means of understanding culture. Because the Western media is a market-driven industry, mass communicators must offer popular programming that attracts a large audience share. The term *popular* connotes acceptance, approval, and shared values among large numbers of people. Successful media communicators have learned to anticipate the interests and concerns of the audience. However, if we are truly offended by violent television programs, we won't watch them; programming with low ratings is soon cancelled. Consequently, the study of media presentations can provide insight into the cultural issues, concerns, patterns of thought, and myths that define a culture. Conversely, an understanding of a culture can furnish perspective into media presentations produced in that culture.

7. The Development of Strategies with Which to Analyze and Discuss Media Messages

Media literacy provides strategies that enable individuals to decipher the information they receive through the channels of mass communications. The National Association for Media Literacy Education states, "Media literacy is the ability to encode and decode the symbols transmitted via media and the ability to synthesize, analyze and produce mediated messages."

These keys also provide a framework that can facilitate the discussion of media content with others—including children, peers, and the people responsible for producing media programming.

W. James Potter (2005) has identified the following seven skills of media literacy:

1. Analysis: breaking down a message into meaningful elements.
2. Evaluation—judging the value of an element; the judgment is made by comparing the element to some standard.
3. Grouping—determining which elements are alike in some way; determining which elements are different in some way.
4. Induction—inferring a pattern across a small set of elements, then generalizing the pattern to all in the set.
5. Deduction—using general principles to explain particulars.
6. Synthesis—assembling elements into a new structure.
7. Abstracting—creating a brief, clear and accurate description capturing the essence of a message in a smaller number of words than the message itself. (Potter, 2005)

Media literacy education is not about replacing students' perspectives with someone else's (your own, a teacher's, a media critic's, an expert's, etc.). Sharing a critique of media without also sharing the skills that students need to critically analyze media for themselves is not sound media literacy education practice. This includes presenting media literacy videos, films, books, or other curriculum materials as a substitute for teaching critical inquiry skills (NAMLE, n.d.).

Thus, in becoming familiar with various critical approaches as tools, individuals are able to systematically analyze media content (with support from the media "text"). In all cases, media literacy education trains students to use document-based evidence and well-reasoned arguments to support their conclusions.

8. In the Case of Media Communicators: The Ability to Produce Effective and Responsible Media Messages

To be successful, professionals in the field of media must have a mastery of production techniques and strategies. The production choices that are made can reinforce messages and, in some cases, convey independent messages.

Moreover, to truly improve the media industry, media communicators must also be aware of the challenges and responsibilities involved in producing thoughtful programming that serves the best interests of the public.

9. The Cultivation of an Enhanced Enjoyment, Understanding, and Appreciation of Media Content

Media literacy should not be seen merely as an opportunity to bash the media. Instead, media literacy should increase the individual's understanding and enjoyment of the media—particularly in light of the limited resources and time or space constraints facing the media communicator.

The media are simply channels of communication. As such, the media are neither good nor evil. At its best, the media offer insightful articles, informative news programs, and uplifting films. What determines the value and effectiveness of a media message includes who is producing the message, what the function is, and the target audience.

10. The Ability to Comprehend, Interpret, and Construct Messages, Using the Different "Languages" of Media

Each medium is defined by a set of distinctive characteristics that influence how it presents information. For instance, radio obviously cannot employ visuals in transmitting information. However, the radio producer can appeal to listeners' imaginations through creative use of words and sound effects. NAMLE calls attention to the importance of recognizing the distinctive characteristics of individual media systems:

> Each medium has different characteristics, strengths, and a unique "language" of construction. . . . Media Literacy Education enables students to express their own ideas through multiple forms of media (e.g., traditional print, electronic, digital, user-generated, and wireless) and helps students make connections between comprehension and inference-making in print, visual, and audio media. (NAMLE, n.d.)

Neil Postman and Charles Weingartner declared, "Being illiterate in the processes of any medium (language) leaves one at the mercy of those who control it" (Postman & Weingartner, 1969).

In 2009, the average American consumed approximately 34 gigabytes of data and information each day—an increase of about 350 percent over about three decades. Significantly, at the same time, the amount of time individuals spent reading actually *declined* (Bilton, 2009). Consequently, many corporations now place a value on employees who have the ability to interpret and construct messages, using the different "languages" of media (i.e., photographs, video, audio, and the Internet).

11. Anticipating Changes in the Media Landscape

Media literacy education prepares individuals to examine the current state of the media. But in addition, studying patterns in the development of media systems and examining the vision of media artists are stratagies that can help to make sense of this rapidly changing media landscape.

See also: Affective Response Analysis; Cultural Context; Key Principles and Concepts, Media Literacy; Medium Theory; Production Analysis Approach

References

Aufderheide, P. (1993). *National Leadership Conference on Media Literacy: Conference Report.* Washington, DC: Aspen Institute, 1993.

Baker, F. W. (2010). "Curriculum 21: Essential Education for a Changing World." ASCD (formerly the Association for Supervision and Curriculum Development), 2010. Retrieved from http://curriculum21.ning.com

Bazalgette, C. (Ed.). (1989). *Primary Media Education: A Curriculum Statement.* The British Film Institute: BFI Education Department.

Bilton, N. (2009, December 9). "Part of the Daily American Diet, 34 Gigabytes of Data." *New York Times.* Retrieved from http://www.nytimes.com/2009/12/10/technology/10data.html

Cassata, M. (1967). "A Study of the Mass Communications Behavior and the Social Disengagement Behavior of the 177 Members of the Age Center of New England." PhD dissertation, Indiana University, Bloomington.

"Children Are Still Making the Decision to Smoke." (2006, October 26). *Miami Herald*, p. 6.

Dale, E. (1946). *Audiovisual Methods in Teaching.* New York: Holt, Rinehart, and Winston.

Hobbs, R., & Frost, R. (2003, Spring). "Measuring the Acquisition of Media Literacy Skills." *Reading Research Quarterly.* http://www.mpls.k12.mn.us

Media Literacy Clearinghouse (2012 September). http://www.frankwbaker.com Retrieved September 2012.

National Association for Media Literacy Education (formerly AMLA). (n.d.). Retrieved from http://www.NAMLE.net

National Telemedia Council. Retrieved from http://www.nationaltelemediacouncil
.com

Postman, N., & Weingartner, C. (1969). *Teaching as a Subversive Activity.* New
York: Delacorte Press. Retrieved from the Clearinghouse of Media Literacy:
www.frankwbaker.com/ml_quotes.html

Potter, W. J. (2005). *Media Literacy* (3rd ed.). Thousand Oaks, CA: Sage, 2005.

Schafersman, S. D. (1991). *An Introduction to Critical Thinking.* Retrieved from
http://www.freeinquiry.com/critical-thinking.html

Dialectical Analysis

Dialectical analysis is an approach that identifies and analyzes contradictions that exist in the construction of media messages. Growth, change, and development take place through a naturally occurring struggle of opposites. For example, one could argue that winter gives meaning to spring; people who live in tropical climates cannot appreciate warm weather with the same fervor as individuals who endure a cold winter every year.

Thus, dialectical analysis has a number of useful *functions*, or purposes, including the following:

- Exposing the underlying assumptions in the construction of a message
- Identifying critical points of contention in a media presentation
- Providing a stimulus for bridging seemingly irreconcilable opposites
- Promoting creativity (i.e., finding a synthesis that is better than the trade-off between the opposites)

Inquiry—or dialectics—can be traced back as far as 3,000 years ago and has appeared in numerous cultures. The Value Based Management Web site (www .valuebasedmanagement.net) provides the following historical overview:

In Asia, the idea that everything is made of opposites—yin and yang— dates back to the I Ching around 3,000 years ago and the Taoist master Lao Tzu around 2,500 years ago.

Taoism holds that change is the only constant. Taoist philosophy also understood that "gradual change leads to a sudden change of form (*hua*)." Also around 2,500 years ago in ancient Greece, Heraclites advanced the idea that all change comes through the struggle of opposites. The Aztecs also held the idea of nature being made of opposites, as did the Lakotas in North America. In Plato's dialogues, Socrates typically "argues" by means of cross-examining someone else's assertions in order to draw out the inherent contradictions within the other's position. (Management.net)

The idea that the synthesis of opposites demarcates meanings appeared in Western thought with philosophers Immanuel Kant and Georg Wilhelm Friedrich Hegel at the turn of the eighteenth century. The Hegelian dialectic formed the basis of *dialectical materialism*, the foundation of Marxist philosophy developed by Karl Marx and Friedrich Engels, in which social change is regarded as a dialectical process involving the following steps:

- Stating a *thesis*
- Developing a contradictory *antithesis*
- Combining or resolving these contradictions into a coherent *synthesis*

Applications

Dialectical inquiry has emerged as a useful research instrument. In an article titled "The Effects of Dialectical Inquiry: Devil's Advocacy, and Consensus Inquiry Methods in a GSS Environment," authors Lai Tung and Alan R. Heminger (1993) drew a distinction between *structured conflict* (the basis of dialectical inquiry) and a *consensus approach*:

> Most (research) has been created around a common approach to group work, which can be characterized as consensus. However, research in the manual group literature suggests that a consensus approach does not always produce the best outcomes. *Structured conflict* may provide superior performance when the issues under consideration contain multiple or unclear underlying assumptions. (Tung & Heminger, 1993)

Eli Berniker and David E. McNabb (2006) employed dialectical inquiry as a qualitative research method for studying participant models of organizational processes. The research challenge was to "make sense" of this secondary data. Berniker and McNabb set up a dialectic consisting of a thesis and its antithesis to explain the facts and data. These oppositions stem from different assumptions. According to Berniker and McNabb, "The point of the dialectic is to posit antithetical theories and models as a method of elucidating the assumptions underpinning those theories and models."

Media Literacy Strategies

The dialectical approach to media literacy can provide insight into the analysis of media and media content. One exercise that focuses attention on the dialectical inquiry method involves the following steps:

1. A decision-making group is divided into two subgroups, each of which will be involved in the analysis and solution of the problem at hand.
2. One subgroup develops recommendations and supports them with all key assumptions, facts, and data, all of which are provided to the other subgroup.
3. The second subgroup develops plausible/alternate assumptions that negate those of the first, and then uses new assumptions to construct counter-recommendations.
4. The debate continues until they agree on a set of assumptions—and then unite to develop recommendations.

The dialetical approach offers the following lines of inquiry for the analysis of media and media content:

Points of View

Dialectical inquiry can focus on *points of view* in a media presentation, furnishing the following perspectives into media and media content:
- The prevailing point of view of the media presentation
- The *assumptions* that constitute this point of view
- Counter-perspectives; what are the opposing points of view
- The *assumptions* that constitute this opposing point of view
- The impact of oppositional points of view on content and message

Conclusion as Resolution of Values

In a narrative, characters can be considered embodiments of ideological positions, based on whose interests they represent. Professor Henry A. Murray (1960) explains, "The forces that are aligned with the group's welfare, with its hopes for the future, being beneficent in direction, are exalted as the good powers. The opposing and hence maleficent forces are portrayed as evil" (p. 78).

Within this context, Daniel Chandler (n.d.) provides the following examples of ideological oppositions found in characters:

Nature/Culture	Freedom/Constraint	Knower/Known	Inner/Outer
Animal/Human	Individual/Society	Old/New	Private/Public
Mind/Body	Gay/Straight	West/East	Insider/Outsider
Art/Science	Producer/Consumer	Black/White	Weak/Strong
Male/Female	Old/Young	Us/Them	Rich/Poor
Inclusion/Exclusion	Dominant/Subordinate		

The triumph of good over evil in the conclusion generally is dependent on the characters' adherence to the values and goals of dominant culture. Consider the *Iron Man* series of films (2008–2013) in which Tony Stark/Iron Man (played by Robert Downey Jr.) is a character who embodies dominant culture: he is white, male, rich, and a corporate insider. Thus, the triumphant conclusion of each episode of *Iron Man* reinforces the ideology of the dominant culture.

Oppositional Analysis

Even though media presentations offer a *preferred reading*, all texts are open to alternative interpretations. This line of inquiry, which is also utilized in the ideological approach to media analysis, sets up dialectical opposition, in which audience members assume the point of view of one of the subordinate characters in the narrative: a member of a subculture, a member of the opposite sex, or a supporting character.

These subordinate characters are often members of the underclass (e.g., African American, females, or Latinos). These characters literally play "supporting roles" to the main characters, who generally are members of the dominant culture.

An oppositional analysis follows the following line of questioning:

- Adopt the perspective of the members of the dominant culture presented in the media presentation:
  - What opportunities are available to you?
  - What advantages do you have?
  - What do you "get away with" in the story because of your position?
  - What conclusions can you draw from this analysis?
- Adopt the perspective of a member of the subordinate culture:
  - What could you accomplish as one of *these* characters?
  - What opportunities would be available to you?
  - What advantages would you have?
  - What could you "get away with" because of your position?
  - What conclusions can you draw from this analysis?

In this way, media presentations can be examined as microcosms of the social systems that operate in the world outside of these fictional narratives.

See Also: Ideological Analysis; Values Clarification Approach

References

Berniker, E., & McNabb, D. E. (2006, December 4). "Dialectical Inquiry: A Structured Qualitative Research Method." *The Qualitative Report, 11*, 643–664. Retrieved from http://www.nova.edu/ssss/QR/QR11-4/berniker.pdf Pacific Lutheran University Tacoma, Washington.

Chandler, D. (n.d.). *Semiotics for Beginners*. Retrieved from http://www.aber.ac.uk/media/Documents/S4B/semiotic.html

Murray, H. (1960). "The Possible Nature of a 'Mythology' to Come." In *Myth and Mythmaking*. New York: George Braziller.

Tung, Lai Lai, & Heminger, A. R. (1993). "The Effects of Dialectical Inquiry, Devil's Advocacy, and Consensus Inquiry Methods in a GSS Environment." *Information & Management, 25,* 33–41.

Zain Online Books. Dialectical Inquiry. (2012). Retrieved from http://www.zane booksonline.com

Digital Media Literacy

Digital media literacy is a primary focus of media literacy analysis. Digital media refers to a wide range of interactive media devices, including the Internet, cell phones, social media (including Facebook and Twitter), instant messaging, and digital still- and video-imaging devices. A useful definition of digital media communications is as follows:

Digital media communications refers to communication between an Initiator and Receiver, in which long-established media are combined with computer technology through a transparent machine to emulate humans' communication patterns.

It might be helpful to break down this complex definition and expand on its major features:

Communication between an Initiator and Receiver

Digital media is interactive; we both *retrieve* and *impart* information. As is the case with interpersonal communications, our role changes as we move from media communicator (the person initiating the dialogue) to audience (the recipient of information—both solicited and unsolicited) and back again.

. . . using a combination of long-established media

Although digital media is considered a discrete mass medium, it is actually the ultimate *hybrid*, combining all of the established media: print, photography, graphics, audio, and video.

. . . to emulate humans' patterns of thought and expression

Like no other medium, digital communication approaches the dynamics of interpersonal communications. The communication style of human beings can best be described as *dynamic* and *nonlinear*. We often jump from one subject to another or elect to focus our attention on a particular facet of a topic. Unlike the old analogue model, which presents information in a set linear order from beginning to end, digital technology enables individuals to jump from subject to subject or go into one topic in-depth—simulating the process of human communication.

. . . through a transparent machine

It wasn't long ago that the technology of the computer was terribly intrusive. We had to attach the connection to an outside source (often through the phone line), boot up the computer, log on, and contend with technical delays and interruptions. Today, computers are handheld, wireless, and portable. Moreover, we have moved into the stage of *ubiquitous computers*, in which computers are fully integrated into our personal environment. The next generation of interactive devices will include *virtual presence systems*, in which microprocessors installed in your home will monitor your heart rate and blood pressure the moment you enter the house and automatically contact emergency services if they detect any irregularities. And while dining at a restaurant, an electronic menu may help you order, taking into account any of your medical or dietary restrictions.

The *digital communications model* comes into play most visibly in the world of digital communications. Digital media empowers the audience like never before by enabling individual audience members to bypass the traditional media gatekeepers. Individuals can now produce their own media presentations, edit, and distribute them over the Internet. Commerce sites like eBay are virtual flea markets in which individuals barter and sell goods, free of corporate intervention.

Media literacy involves the ability to make independent choices about the selection and interpretation of content. As writer David Allen observes, "Technology is a great servant but it is a terrible master" (quoted in Fallows & Shelley Hayduk, 2011). Although journalists Hayduk and Fallows regard digital media technology as the cause of stress, at the same time, they also regard media technology as a solution to this problem. "Achieving serenity is about taking control and leveraging all the information that surrounds you, rather than it controlling you." This observation touches on another fundamental tenant of media literacy. The digital medium is simply a channel of information, which is neutral in nature. What determines whether a medium is "bad" or "good" depends on who is using it and for what purpose or function.

Cultural Context

A significant focus of media literacy analysis examines the impact of digital media on individuals and society. For example, digital communications are linked to a growing *generational schism*. Communications patterns vary widely between generations. Reporter Jill Colvin explains,

> Many see the shift away from voice mail as part of a generational divide, in which younger people are substituting text for talk, while older folks yammer on. Text messaging has increased more than tenfold over the last three years. . . . Young people have overwhelmingly been the most enthusiastic adopters. According to Nielsen Mobile, users 13 to 17 now send or receive an average of 1,742 text messages a month, versus 231 cellphone calls, and they spend nearly the same amount of time on their phones texting as talking.
>
> . . . By contrast, 91 percent of people under 30 respond to text messages within an hour, and they are four times more likely to respond to texts than to voice messages within minutes, according to a 2008 study for Sprint conducted by the Opinion Research Corporation. (Colvin, 2009)

Not only do generations use different media, they use the media *differently*. According to Amanda Lenhart, senior research specialist at the Pew Research Center, "Adults aren't texting in the same way adolescents are. Teens don't expect people to call—texting has become the default way to connect" (Colvin, 2009). As a result, the generations aren't likely to communicate with each other, reinforcing this generational schism.

Indeed, the generation gap has accelerated so markedly that American culture is now characterized by a series of "mini-generation gaps." Lee Rainie, director of the Pew Research Center's Internet and American Life Project explains,

People two, three or four years apart are having completely different experiences with technology. College students scratch their heads at what their high school siblings are doing, and they scratch their heads at their younger siblings. It has sped up generational differences. (Brad Stone, 2010)

For instance, psychology professor Larry Rosen has drawn a distinction between the *Net Generation*, born in the 1980s, and the *iGeneration*, born in the 1990s and the first decade of the millennium:

Now in their 20s, those in the Net Generation . . . spend two hours a day talking on the phone and still use e-mail frequently. The iGeneration— conceivably their younger siblings—spends considerably more time texting than talking on the phone, pays less attention to television than the older group and tends to communicate more over instant-messenger networks.

Dr. Rosen said that the newest generations, unlike their older peers, will expect an instant response from everyone they communicate with, and won't have the patience for anything less. "They'll want their teachers and professors to respond to them immediately, and they will expect instantaneous access to everyone, because after all, that is the experience they have growing up. They should be just like their older brothers and sisters, but they are not. (Stone, 2010)

As a result, college students may be out of touch with the media habits of brothers and sisters still in high school. Reporter Brad Stone declares,

These mini-generation gaps are most visible in the communication and entertainment choices made by different age groups. According to a survey last year by Pew, teenagers are more likely to send instant messages than slightly older 20-somethings (68 percent versus 59 percent) and to play online games (78 percent versus 50 percent). (Stone, 2010)

Digital Media as Cultural Text

Digital media also provide insight into cultural attitudes, values, behaviors, and preoccupations that define a culture. As an example, in 2010, a popular Japanese video game, *Rapelay*, exploited the young audience's preoccupation with sex and violence. In the course of the game, players' *avatars* rape women on a train and try to impregnate underage girls. Players are awarded extra points if they can convince their victims to get abortions. *Rapelay* was eventually taken off the shelves, due to its offensive content; however, young fans of the game simply downloaded it from the Internet.

Cyber Warfare

Because computers have now been incorporated into security and weapons systems, war tactics have shifted to disabling these computer programs:

- In 2010, a Stuxnet computer worm apparently wiped out a part of Iran's nuclear centrifuges and delayed its ability to produce nuclear fuel. Although no entity has acknowledged being the source of the poisonous code, some evidence suggests that the virus was an American-Israeli project.
- In March 2011, South Korea was the target of a cyber-attack by an unidentified assailant, in which forty Web sites were attacked by a computer virus. This *denial of service* attack overwhelmed targeted sites with a surge of traffic that crashed their servers.

Richard A. Falkenrath, former deputy Homeland Security adviser to President George W. Bush observes, "This new form of warfare has several implications that are only now becoming apparent, and that will define the shape of what will likely become the next global arms race—albeit one measured in computer code rather than firepower" (2011). Indeed, military aid to allies now includes antivirus software designed to defend against cyber-attacks.

eCommerce

The Internet has extended the business-to-consumer (B2C) model, making it easier for consumers to seek out a product, as well as allowing businesses to offer a large number of products in a single online location. In addition, the consumer-to-consumer (C2C) model allows individuals to sell or auction their products or services to anyone with access to the Internet. Some of the most significant eCommerce platforms include Google, eBay, Amazon.com, YouTube, iTunes, and BlackBerry. Amazon.com is a virtual shopping mall, offering a vast array of products for convenient shopping at home.

Regulation Issues

The relationship between a media system and government regulatory policy has a major impact on the quality and diversity of media messages. Every country maintains its own policies on the content and dissemination of information through the channels of mass communication. Because the Internet is an international channel for communication and commerce, one country's customs and laws don't apply across national borders.

Digital media censorship occurs when access to information conveyed over the Internet is restricted. The extent of government control varies across the globe. For example, the Chinese government prohibits searching the Internet for information pertaining to the subjects of human rights, Taiwanese independence, and democracy. Significantly, U.S. companies Microsoft and Google have been complicit in helping China develop censorship tools.

In the United States, censorship can be imposed by either private or public entities. Internet content has been censored by employers, parents, and schools. Censored content can include anything from pornography to the voicing of opinions that challenge an authoritarian government. Most Internet content is protected as free speech in the United States. However, obscenity, libel, and misuse of intellectual property are categories of content that are subject to regulation. The Justice Department has filed pornography charges against several people it accused of using computers to transmit child pornography. But while the U.S. Telecommunications Bill expressly prohibits the distribution of pornographic material to minors over computer networks and imposes penalties for violators, it clearly has no international jurisdiction.

In attempting to protect intellectual copyright, in 2008, Wikileaks.org, a whistleblower site that anonymously posts classified documents, was temporarily censored by a court injunction in the State of California. However, the injunction was later lifted, the court citing first amendment and jurisdiction concerns.

Most Internet censorship is maintained via a firewall that blocks specific words or Web sites. Critics of Internet censorship argue: that (a) access to the Internet is a basic right, (b) the software used to censor content slows down the Internet, (c) censorship can mistakenly restrict access to legitimate sites, and (d) censorship is easily circumvented by those who are technically savvy—frequently young people.

Spyware describes programs and scripts that have been created to infiltrate interactive media devices and exploit user data without informed consent. Some forms of spyware collect and distribute personal information, and other types of invasive software take over the functions of the media device. Spyware can be triggered by a number of innocuous procedures, such as *peer-to-peer file trading*, e-mail attachments, browser cookies, and infected software installation. According to the Pew Internet and American Life Project,

Overall, 43% of Internet users, or about 59 million American adults, say they have had spyware, adware, or both types of programs on their home computer. . . . [T]here is a very strong likelihood that a big portion of those who have had computer problems have been victimized by spyware or more aggressive computer viruses without their knowing the cause of their problems. (Fox, 2005)

Strategies for avoiding spyware include (a) only installing software from trusted sources, (b) scanning e-mail attachments before opening, and (c) using antivirus software.

As public access to digital media increases, so does concern for the privacy of personal information. This information includes but is not limited to an individual's name and address, financial records, memberships, buying and browsing habits, religious and political beliefs, and medical history. The exploitation of this kind of information is not new but the digital media environment greatly increases the ease with which personal information can be collected, analyzed and abused. Therefore, it is important to understand how a person's information will be used by those entities to whom the information is given, such as online communities, wireless and cellular service providers, retailers, and social networks.

Privacy awareness and education. Organizations such as the Electronic Privacy Information Center, Electronic Frontier Foundation, the American Civil Liberties Union, and the Privacy Rights Clearinghouse inform citizens about abuses of personal information on the Internet. Common among Internet privacy advocates is a call for users to be conscientious about what they open, share, and install while using digital media communication. With a proactive approach, users can make educated decisions about what information they share and how that information is to be used.

Media Literacy Strategies

Media literacy is a discipline that provides individuals with strategies for the systematic analysis of media content. These research tools enable individuals to conduct *primary research*, so that they are not merely citing what others have written but are able to conduct independent analysis. Key to successful media literacy research is (a) applying the methodology in a systematic manner and (b) providing examples that support and extend insights.

Lines of inquiry that are particularly useful in digital media analysis include the following:

Document Analysis. Among the resources that can be found on the Internet are Web sites that are repositories for primary documents. For example, Pastebin.com houses unedited information on a variety of topics. Reporter Noam Cohen (2011) explains,

> In a fashion, [Pastebin] is offering direct, anonymous "publishing". . . . The service could not be simpler—there is a "bin" (an empty input box) into which text is pasted. No registration is required. . . . The site (has) slowly gained notoriety as a way to place information—often anonymously—into the public information stream.

Individuals interested in conducting research have direct access to these documents. One of the subject areas found at Pastebin, for example, is a collection of documents that pertain to the Occupy Wall Street movement. According to Cohen (2011), Pastebin has emerged as "the de facto open-source bible of the protests":

> At Pastebin.com, you can search for the personal information of the police officials who have used force against the Wall Street protesters; or what purports to be e-mail addresses of bank executives; or guides on how to spot an agent provocateur or undercover officer in your midst; or lists of other Occupy movements around the country and the world.

Keyword searches on the Internet enable researchers to trace the growth and development of issues and social movements. This analysis also enables researchers to detect patterns in the stories, furnishing perspective into the media coverage of these events and issues.

For instance, the Pew Research Center found that until the beginning of October, cable news and radio almost entirely ignored the Occupy Wall Street movement. Approximately four weeks after the beginning of the demonstrations, coverage of the movement was, for the first time, roughly equivalent to early coverage of the Tea Party movement in early 2009. Reporter Brian Stelter (2011) explains,

> As the Occupy Wall Street message of representing 99 percent of Americans has spread across the country, news media coverage of the Occupy movement has spread, too, to the front pages of newspapers and the tops of television newscasts. . . .

In the first full week of October, according to Pew's Project for Excellence in Journalism, the protests occupied 7 percent of the nation's collective news coverage, up from 2 percent in the last week of September. Before then, the coverage was so modest as to be undetectable by the Project for Excellence in Journalism, which surveys 52 news outlets each week to produce a weekly study of news coverage.

In addition, polls can provide insight into public attitudes toward these events and issues. For instance, a poll conducted by the Pew Center found that between October 6 and 9, 2011, 42 percent of the public began paying serious attention to the protests (Stelter, 2011). Moreover, the poll discovered a generational gap with regard to interest in the protests. Eleven percent of respondents between the ages of 18 and 29 cited the protests as the story they followed the most closely between October 6 and 9, whereas only 3 percent of respondents age 65 and older mentioned Occupy Wall Street as their top story. Furthermore, this research can identify patterns with regard to media content. The majority of the stories appearing during the first week of October focused on the mass arrests of protesters in New York, for example (Stelter, 2011).

Thus, it appears that media organizations—particularly visual media such as television, film, and video/film appearing on the Internet (e.g., YouTube)—are more inclined to cover *events* than *issues*. Consequently, organizers of social movements should note that arranging events like protests (and arrests) that bring the issue to public consciousness will attract media attention they seek.

Finally, the analysis of the networks' millions of posts and status updates can serve as a cultural barometer that *anticipates* cultural changes. Reporter Jon Gertner (2010) notes,

In October [2009], a team led by Johan Bollen at Indiana University reported that by classifying 9.7 million Twitter posts as falling into one of six mood categories (happiness, kindness, alertness, sureness, vitality and calmness) they could predict changes in the Dow Jones Industrial Average. As Bollen explains, when he began his study, he expected that the mood on Twitter would be a reflection of up and down movements in the stock market. He never imagined it would be a precursor. (Gertner, 2010)

In addition, many of the approaches that heretofore have been used in the analysis of established media and media presentations can also be applied to the study of digital media.

To illustrate, understanding the *function,* or purpose, behind an interactive communications exchange is a vital consideration—both on the sending and receiving end of the process. A digital media communication activity may be motivated by many *functions*, or purposes, such as information exchange, expression, persuasion, and entertainment. The *manifest*, or surface, function behind the communication offers the obvious or primary reason behind the media presentation. However, there may also be *latent* functions; that is, instances in which the media communicator's intention may not be immediately evident to the audience.

For instance, many articles on the Internet that appear to have an informational or entertainment function are actually designed to generate advertising profits through a strategy called *Search Engine Optimization* (SEO). Internet ad companies place articles on the Internet with the purpose of generating "hits" on keywords and links, thereby "optimizing" the chances that a person conducting a computer search will find them. The more "hits" that a site receives, the higher it appears on the Google search list—thereby boosting its advertising rates. Reporter David Segal (2011) describes the process of SEO:

> If you own a Web site, for instance, about Chinese cooking, your site's Google ranking will improve as other sites link to it. The more links to your site, especially those from other Chinese cooking-related sites, the higher your ranking. In a way, what Google is measuring is your site's popularity by polling the best-informed online fans of Chinese cooking and counting their links to your site as votes of approval.

Thus, although the manifest function of SEO may be information or entertainment, the latent function is *profit.* Most importantly, one must consider the *function* behind the appearance of the article on the Internet.

For example, in 2010 a media literacy class at Webster University was given an assignment to apply a selected "Key to Interpreting Media Message" (Silverblatt, 2008) to the analysis of social media. The students' analyses of Facebook and Twitter generated by these keys included the following insights (student names are given in parentheses):

- *Overview*
    - "Social media is basically a present day journal where everyone writes their activities and thoughts—only now the whole world can view them." (Derek Dressel)

- *Media communicator: Who is responsible for creating the media production?*
  - "The last media communicator is the hardest to identify. This would be the anonymous communicator. On Facebook, a user can message anyone else who has an account. This means that they might not be able to view all of the other person's information without being their friend, but they can still write them. Also, the recipient can see the anonymous person's name and picture, but can never be certain that any of that information is reliable. Another example of this is an application on Facebook called the *honesty box*. The honesty box is where one user sends a totally anonymous message to another user. Moreover, the person who receives the message cannot see the writer's name, picture, age, etc. This application brought on a huge dilemma to those receiving these kinds of messages." (Alexandra Hage)
- *Function:*
  - *What is the purpose behind the production?*
    - Does the media communicator want you to think or behave in a particular way as a result of receiving the information?
    - *Does the production contain any **latent functions**?* (Latent function refers to instances in which the media communicator's intention may not be immediately obvious to the audience.)
  - Overview—Function
    - "A step to understanding Facebook is to look at its *function*: why does the site command such a large Internet presence? The site has grown beyond its original purpose, which was to help users keep in touch with friends and family. Now users can play games, use applications, and even shop on Facebook. It has also become a source of news and events. . . . Because it is a text-based website, it also functions as a way to store information. Things the user may have otherwise forgotten through oral conversation are forever immortalized in text or image somewhere on the site." (Alexandra Hage)
  - Functions
    - "Facebook provides an opportunity for individuals to become new members of a community centered around friends, family, and common interests." (Jaime Gaal)
    - "Another function is creative expression. While on Facebook, a user can upload, share, comment on, and edit pictures." (Jaime Gaal)
    - "Facebook is a great way to get information to large groups of people. For example, musical groups can make pages and send

out information about their group and upcoming events without making flyers or other advertisements. . . . Working as a social network, Facebook rekindles old friendships and helps to develop new ones . . . through pictures, comments, and a user's personal information." (Kathryn Sharp)

○ Latent Functions
  - "The function of social media is to keep everyone in touch with each other. This is the most basic underlying purpose of social media; however, social media is continually evolving. Now social media is becoming more and more of a marketing and advertising channel. Now there are advertisements and company logos all over Facebook." (Derek Dressel)
  - "More than ever, people need to feel as if they are connected to the outside world and to other people." (Alexandra Hage)
  - "The large user base also allows news to spread quickly. Users can discover new interests through posting to each other's news feed." (Alexandra Hage)
  - "To show everyone just who they are. . . . On social networks, you have the opportunity to create an online image of yourself." (Kathryn Sharp)

○ Negative Impact of Function
  - "Although Facebook can at times be a good thing, this site can also be used in a negative way. Allowing people to have so much access into the personal lives of other people, some of whom they have never actually met in person can cause privacy issues. It can also lead to people being bullied, spied on, and harassed. . . . Some victims of harassment have felt so upset that they have taken drastic measures to avoid the humiliation." (Sarah Maas)
  - "Social media encourages users to spend time interacting with each other in its cyber universe, instead of doing so in reality." (Alexandra Hage)
  - "Because it is less intimidating and semi-anonymous, many users are emboldened to act on and say things they would not say in real life. For instance, it has become a common trend to break up with a Significant Other on Facebook, instead of real life." (Alexandra Hage)

- *Audience*
  - *For whom is the media presentation produced?*
  - *Is there more than one intended audience?*

– *What values, experiences, and perspectives are shared by the audience? Do these shared values, experiences, or perspectives influence their understanding or interpretation of the presentation?*

– *How do the experiences and perspectives of the individual audience member affect his/her interpretation of the presentation?*

– *How does the choice of audience influence the strategy, style, and content of the media presentation?*

– *Do the strategy, style, and content of the media presentation provide insight into the intended audience(s)?*

◦ "The audience of Facebook is another way we can garner information about the site. Originally intended only for college students, the site is now open to all private users, as well as companies. This means Facebook has now become ripe for use as a business tool to make connections or advertise to a large audience. . . . Because of the explosive growth of the Internet and the availability of information and products, businesses are being forced to switch to a business model which caters directly to the individual, and Facebook provides the perfect venue for that. Users can 'like' a page and then receive information on that product, person, etc. in regular updates. They choose who and what to follow, and are increasingly becoming choosy about the media they consume." (Alexandra Hage)

◦ "Businesses now have the ability to connect with their clients in ways they never could. . . . Customer feedback is almost instant with the press of a 'like' button. . . . Facebook members are more likely to view a business' site after seeing it on Facebook than seeing it displayed in other search engines such as Google or Yahoo. Facebook has implemented several strategies to enhance the promotion of businesses. Their first strategy was 'Groups,' allowing businesses to share company information, such as products, areas of progress, and services, to a specific audience." (Kathryn Sharp)

• *Cultural Context: Examining the relationship between digital media and culture*

  ◦ As Reflection of Cultural Attitudes, Behaviors

   • "Cultural attitudes are moving toward a society in which the desired information is largely personal." (Alexandra Hage)

   • "There is also an interest in popularity and recognition. Users can view how many friends each user has, and their relationship with each individual." (Alexandra Hage)

- "Through the use of groups and pages, users can reinforce their personal values through discussion with other similar users." (Alexandra Hage)
- "Facebook reveals an increasing cultural preoccupation with the personal lives of others." (Alexandra Hage)
- "It also shows a need for recognition as an individual and a desire to be noticed." (Alexandra Hage)

  ○ Shifts in Cultural Attitudes, Behaviors . . .

  - "Cultural changes and attitudes are shown in people's pictures and statuses. People dress according to what other people are wearing in their pictures and choose to go to places seen in their friends' pictures. If people feel a certain way they can persuade others and provide people with information through their page." (Amy Raimondo)

  ○ Worldview: What kind of world is depicted in the media presentation?

  - "A world in which popularity is valued." (Amy Raimondo)

- *Production Elements*:
  - *Do the production values employed in interactive media serve a clear purpose appropriate for the intended audience?*
  - Production elements to consider include:
    - Web page composition
    - Inclusion and omission of information
    - The selection of links
    - The combination of media such as print, graphics, audio, and video to convey messages.

    ○ "The top left corner of Facebook's homepage says that it 'helps you connect and share with the people in your life.' The placement of this sentence conveys a message with regard to its importance. The words are larger than the other text on the page, and it is in a position where it is the first thing people see.

    "[In addition], when looking deeper into this sentence, word choice is very important. Two connotative words in particular stand out. First, Facebook used *connect* when they could have easily used *talk*. Both words share the same primary connotative definition: 'To establish communication between. . . .' However, some additional definitions for *talk* are 'to chatter, discuss, and express in words.' At the same time, other definitions of *connect* are 'to join, link, or fasten together; to unite or bind' and 'to associate with mentally or emotionally.' Thus, when comparing these two words, talking is a measure of having a simple conversation, whereas connecting gives the word a deeper, more meaningful definition that people love to feel.

"The second connotative word is *share*. Again, why did Facebook use this word when they could easily have used a synonym, such as *exchange*. Under these two words, the same definition appears: 'to divide and distribute.' Other definitions for share are 'to use, participate in, enjoy, apportion, and receive equally.' Other definitions for exchange are 'to give up, replace, and barter.' When in comparison, *exchange* sends a message of giving up something only because there is something wanted in return. *Sharing*, on the other hand, means that giving and taking of different things is wanted and appreciated. Overall, sharing is a more personal and positive word, and one can bet Facebook knows this as well." (Jaime Gaal)

- Conclusion
  - "Social media is ever-changing and constantly adding new features to cater to the changing interests of its users. However, with the use of media literacy keys, no matter the changes to these sites, we can use these tools to effectively analyze the intentions and manifest and latent functions of websites such as Facebook." (Alexandra Hage)

Other approaches for the systematic analysis of digital media and digital media content include:

- *Structure*
  - What patterns of ownership are emerging on the Internet?
  - What is the impact of these patterns on the content that appears on the Internet?
- *Veracity of Content*
  - How can an individual evaluate the information that is available on the Internet?
  - Criteria for evaluating content include:
    - Verifiable documentation
    - Currency of information
    - Use of reliable sources
    - Objectivity
    - Consistency
- *Historical Context*
  - Which historical events discussed on the Internet are of interest and concern to the public?
  - Do patterns emerge in Internet discussion venues that reveal prevailing attitudes toward these historical events?

- *Introduction*: *What is the function of the homepage?*
  - ° Does the homepage succeed in establishing the identity, or "personality" of the host?
  - ° How would you describe the "personality" of the site as reflected in the homepage?
  - ° What information does the homepage provide?
  - ° What information does it omit? What does the homepage reveal about the values of the host?
  - ° What does the homepage reveal about the intended audience?

See also: Advertising—Media Literacy Analysis; Communication Models; Cultural Context; Function; Media and Social Change; Political Communications, American; Social Networking

References

Allen, D. (2011) in James Fallows and Shelley Hayduk, "The Secret to Digital Sanity." *The Atlantic Monthly*. Retrieved in: http://www.theatlantic.com/technology/archive/2011/03/the-secret-to-digital-sanity/72550/

Cohen, N. (2011, October 9). "A Fluid Protest Movement Finds a Forum to Match." *New York Times*. Retrieved from http://www.nytimes.com/2011/10/10/business/media/pastebin-helps-occupy-wall-street-spread-the-word.html?_r=0

Colvin, J. (2009, April 2). "You've Got Voice Mail, but Do You Care?" *New York Times*. Retrieved from http://www.nytimes.com/2009/04/02/fashion/02voicemail.html?pagewanted=all

Falkenrath, R. A. (2011, January 26). "From Bullets to Megabytes." *New York Times*. Retrieved from http://www.nytimes.com/2011/01/27/opinion/27falkenrath.html

Fallows, J., & Hayduk, S. (2011). "The Secret to Digital Sanity." *The Atlantic Monthly*. Retrieved from http://www.theatlantic.com/technology/archive/2011/03/the-secret-to-digital-sanity/72550

Fox, S. (2005, July 6). *Spyware: Part 2. Threats Affect Online Behavior*. Pew Internet and American Life Project. http://www.pewinternet.org/Reports/2005/Spyware/04-Threats-Affect-Online-Behavior.aspx?view=all

Gertner, J. (2010, December 17). "Social Media as Social Index." *New York Times*. Retrieved from http://www.nytimes.com/interactive/2010/12/19/magazine/ideas2010.html#Social_Media_as_Social_Index

Segal, D. (2011, February 12). "The Dirty Little Secrets of Search." *New York Times*. Retrieved from http://www.nytimes.com/2011/02/13/business/13search.html?pagewanted=all

Silverblatt, A. (2008). *Media Literacy: Keys to Interpreting Media Messages* (3rd ed.). Westport, CT: Praeger.

Stelter, B. (2011, October 12). "A News Story Is Growing With 'Occupy' Protests." *New York Times*. Retrieved from http://www.nytimes.com/2011/10/13/us/occupy-wall-street-protests-a-growing-news-story.html

Stone, S. (2010, January 9). "The Children of Cyberspace: Old Fogies by Their 20s." *New York Times*. Retrieved from http://www.nytimes.com/2010/01/10/weekin review/10stone.html?pagewanted=all

Discourse Analysis

Discourse analysis refers to the formal and orderly expression of thought, using spoken or written language such as a conversation or a newspaper article. J. P. Gee (1996) explains,

> A discourse . . . is composed of ways of talking, listening (often, too, reading and writing), acting, interacting, believing, valuing, and using tools and objects in particular settings at specific times, so as to display and recognize a particular social identity. (p. 128)

Discourse analysis considers ways in which people craft messages to influence the audience's ability to recall information, color their interpretations, or facilitate the processing of information. This qualitative approach is based on the assumption that people draw on cultural and linguistic resources as they construct versions of their experiences. Thus, discourse analysis focuses on the tools and strategies people use when engaged in communication, such as slowing one's speech for emphasis, use of metaphors, choice of particular words to display affect, and so on.

Because language use is an important form of social interaction, discourse analysis is concerned with the *social context* in which discourse is embedded. Gee (1996) observes,

> Discourses create "social positions" (perspectives) from which people are "invited" (summoned) to speak, listen, act, read and write, think, feel, believe and value in certain characteristic, historically recognizable ways, combined with their own individual styles and creativity. (p. 128)

Consequently, the dynamics and environment of a communications exchange can have a bearing on how it is interpreted by the audience. As a result, a primary focus of discourse analysis is the underlying social structure that may be assumed or played out within the conversation or text.

Indeed, discursive formations can be considered *systems of thought*, of which language is the central mode of expression. Media literacy scholar Kathleen Tyner (1998) observes that the work of educator Paulo Freire "reflected the belief that the constrained discourse of schooling was created to perpetuate social inequity":

> [According to Freire] the dominant culture defines literacy, and therefore the reading and writing skills that are acknowledged by mainstream society and sanctioned in the schooling process are only those that reinforce the status quo. (p. 30)

Media Literacy Strategies

Discourse analysis is a qualitative methodology that can be applied to the study of the media and media content. According to Eamon Fulcher (2012), researchers look for linguistic patterns: "The investigator attempts to identify categories, themes, ideas, views, roles, and so on, within the text itself. The aim is to identify commonly shared discursive resources (shared patterns of talking)." The method of analysis involves examining transcripts of conversations and systematically coding the discursive patterns. Areas of analysis include the following:

- How the discourse helps us understand the issue under study
- How people construct their own version of an event
- How people use discourse to maintain or construct their own identity (Fulcher, 2012)

Ideological Line of Inquiry

One useful line of inquiry involves examining the ideological meaning, or belief system, contained in discourse; that is, sets of verbal and/or visual statements that express the meanings and values of an institution and the power relations that operate within and define that institution.

Gee provides insight into the relationship between discourse and ideology:

- Discourses are inherently ideological.
- Discourses are intimately related to the distribution of social power and hierarchal structure in society. . . . Control over certain Discourses can lead to the acquisition of social goods (money, power, status) in a

society. . . . Discourses that lead to social goods in a society (can be called) *dominant Discourses* . . . those groups that have the fewest conflicts when using them, *dominant groups*.

- Discourse-defined positions from which to speak and behave . . . are standpoints . . . in relation to other, ultimately opposing discourses . . .
- A Discourse puts . . . forward certain concepts, viewpoints, and values at the expense of others. . . . (Gee, 1995: 29)

The following discursive elements provide ways to examine the ideological messages in a media presentation:

- *Rate* (success, failure) of character types
- *Source*—nonverbal and verbal cues, gender, age, income, etc.
- *Context*—the situated nature of interaction consists of those surrounding elements that shape meaning
- *Message*—features in the text that contribute to one's interpretation of the information
- *Receiver Features*—the role of the audience in the construction of meaning

Discourse can be used to impose dominant ideology on a culture in the following ways:

Masking—discourse can conceal class exploitation in a specific manner, to the extent that all trace of class domination is systematically absent from its language.

Displacement occurs when emphasis is shifted from the sphere of production to the sphere of exchange of consumption.

Fragmentation—discourse identifies the audience not as members of a collective group but rather as individuals with no meaningful connection to others. The only group cohesion offered through discourse is a consumer identity.

Discursive Patterns

Another line of inquiry involves identifying patterns in the appearance of discursive elements in a body of data. These discursive elements include the following:

- *Themes.* The researcher looks for recurring themes in the media presentation.

- *Active Voicing.* Using the same wording in different versions of a presentation affirms the veracity of a statement, proving that it was really said (Hutchby & Wooffitt, 1998).
- *Expressions of Uncertainty.* According to scholar Jonathan Potter (1996), when a narrator initially expresses doubt about the truth of his or her claim ("I don't have much experience with this"), this comment conveys the message that the speaker is attempting to distance herself from the statement.
- *Externalizing Device.* Expressions such as "What I've read is . . . " conveys the message that his or her grasp of the information is impersonal and dispassionate; the individual has no personal involvement in the content.
- *Three-Part Lists.* This refers to the significance of things coming in threes. Examples include the following:
  - *Here, There, and Everywhere* (song by the Beatles)
  - Every Tom, Dick, and Harry (Potter, 1996)
  Three-part lists are mystical in derivation, suggesting a level of existence beyond everyday experience, instead standing for something more timeless and everlasting.
- *Outsider Status.* Referring to people as "others" and "them" separates the speaker from the people in the media presentation.
- *Normalizing Devices.* Devices used to establish themselves as "ordinary people" affected by extraordinary events or people.

See also: Ideological Analysis; Labeling Theory

References

Fulcher, E. (2012). "What Is Discourse Analysis?" Retrieved from http://eamonfulcher.com/discourse_analysis.html

Gee, J. P. (1996). *Social Linguistics and Literacies: Ideology in Discourses.* London & Bristol, PA: Taylor & Francis.

Hutchby, I., & Wooffitt, R. (1998). *Conversation Analysis.* Oxford, UK: Polity Press.

Potter, J. (1996). *Representing Reality: Discourse, Rhetoric and Social Construction.* London: Sage.

Tyner, K. (1998). *Literacy in a Digital World: Teaching and Learning in the Age of Information.* London: Lawrence Erlbaum Associates.

Dramatological Analysis

Dramatological analysis is an approach to media literacy designed to provide insight into how performance elements of media presentations shape the construction of messages. This mode of analysis is based on the work of Erving Goffman, who looked at social interaction as drama in which people play a variety of roles in different social settings. Notions of performance, scene setting, and role-play become central to interpretations of people in a public setting (Goffman, 1976).

This approach also examines the merging of public and private performance for those covered by the media. Obviously, many media presentations are performance-based presentations that adhere to the formulae and conventions. However, performance elements are also major considerations—in professions such as broadcast journalism, in which on-air reporters are presumably not judged as performers but, rather, their skills as journalists.

The evolution in media has restructured the relationship between physical place and social place, altering the ways in which we transmit and receive social information. By providing greater access to, and awareness of, backstage behavior, electronic media have served as an instrument of demystification, leading, for example, to a decline in the image and prestige of political leaders.

At the same time, media communicators have become aware of the importance of performance in their total communications effort. For instance, political candidates are schooled in verbal and nonverbal performance elements and are cautioned to be always on guard, because backstage behavior has been all but eliminated by the all-pervasive camera.

Media Literacy Strategies: Function

A performance can serve a number of functions (or purposes). A performance can also fulfill more than one function (or purpose). Finally, a performance can serve *latent* functions; that is, a purpose that is not immediately obvious to the audience.

Critical analysis of performance focuses on the following question: *What is the function (or purpose) of performance in the media presentation?*

- As a clarification device: to emphasize points
- To describe (or act out) verbal content
- To indicate degree of involvement on the part of the performer (e.g., attentiveness, interest, emotional engagement)
- As a persuasive device
- To establish roles
  - Status
  - Authority
  - Dominance and submission

- To establish or reinforce personal association
  - ◦ To foster intimacy (e.g., romantic gaze)
  - ◦ To establish or maintain distance
  - ◦ To establish a *parasocial* relationship (the appearance of an intimate relationship)
- To express emotional response
- To help regulate conversation (e.g., turn-maintaining, turn-requesting, and turn-taking cues)
- To create an impression
- To establish credibility
- To establish "likeability"
- To convey competence
- To establish trustworthiness

Performance analysis focuses on four general areas:

- What are the *nonverbal* messages within the verbal communication?
  - ◦ Physical appearance
    - How are the characters dressed and what does this tell you about the character (social class, education, ethnic orientation)?
    - What artifacts does the character wear?
  - ◦ Gesture and movement
    - What are the characters' postural styles (rigid, relaxed, nervous, calm, friendly, contentious, attentive)?
    - What messages do these postures convey?
    - Do the postures match the verbal communication?
  - ◦ Face and eye behavior
    - What are the facial expressions and what do they convey (frown, head tilt, scowl, smile)?
    - How do you interpret the eye movements (staring, threatening, loving, or avoidance)?
    - Is the face expressing something different that the spoken words?
  - ◦ Body shape
    - What is the shape of the body (obese, thin, muscular)?
    - What does the body type tell you about the character?
    - What are the comparative heights of the characters?
    - Does this signify anything as to a dominant/subordinate relationship?
- What *vocalic* messages are in the media presentation?
  - ◦ What tone of voice is used?

- ○ Is there an accent or dialect?
- ○ How fast does the character speak?
- ○ Are there long silences or pauses and what does this mean?
- How do the characters interact with the *environment*?
  - ○ Space
  - ○ What is the physical distance between the characters? What does this signify?
  - ○ Where is the action set?
  - ○ What does the architecture tell you about the characters lifestyle?
  - ○ What perception to you get from the environment (warm, formal, private, familiar, distant, confining)?
  - ○ What is the dominant color in the overall production and what does it convey?
  - ○ Does any scene offer a contrasting color theme? What is the color change telling you?
- What are the *interaction patterns* of the characters?
  - ○ Do the characters touch each other?
  - ○ How would you characterize the touching behavior?
    - Reassuring
    - Loving
    - Hostile
    - Sexual
    - Other
  - ○ Who initiates the touching behavior? What does this signify?
  - ○ What does performance reveal about the relationship between characters?
    - Is it friendly, hostile, loving? How is this manifested nonverbally?
    - What are the distinctive characteristics of the relationship?
    - What are the nonverbal interactive patterns?
    - What are the nonverbal clues for status?
    - What are the distinctive characteristics of the subordinate?
    - Can you define the differences in nonverbal behavior patterns between cultures?

See also: Function; Political Communications, American

References

Gee, J.P. *Social Linguistics and Literacies: Ideology in Discourses*. London and Bristol, PA: Taylor & Francis, 1996.

Goffman, E. (1976). "Gender Advertisements." *Studies in the Anthropology of Visual Communication*, *3*, 65–68.

Dream Theory Approach to Media Analysis

Dream theory is a qualitative approach to media analysis that offers strategies for discussing and interpreting media content. This is an example of a *disparate approach to media analysis,* in which the principles of another discipline are applied to the interpretation of media content.

From its earliest days, the media have drawn comparisons to dreams. Paul Lippmann describes media presentations as "the modern embodiment of ancient dreamlife":

> It is quite possible to conclude that dreams, rather than being merely buried in modern life, also have been absorbed and transformed in the modern world. . . . Dreams resurface as TV and film in the modern world. (Lippmann, 2006: 123–125)

According to Lippman (2006), "film was born in direct imitation of dreams and modeled itself closely on the ways of dreams":

> In the late 1890s, at the same time that Freud was beginning the writing of his dream book in Vienna, nearby in Paris, the Lumière brothers— August and Louis—were significantly advancing the technology of the infant art and science of film. Also, with the money they earned from their technological successes, they began to create dozens of short films that directly imitated, portrayed, and depicted dreams.
>
> The Lumières deliberately and consciously explored the possibilities of moving the private dream into a shared and social experience, explored the possibilities of exchanging the inner screen for an external screen—one they could play on for the delight, amusement, and edification of paying customers. (p. 124)

Indeed, the film experience—sitting in a darkened theater, immersed in sound and images—inspires a dreamlike state of consciousness. Within this context, a dream theory approach to media analysis can furnish perspective into media content, in the following ways:

- As a bridge between conscious and unconscious worlds
- As a reflection of an individual's concerns and preoccupations
- As a way to account for the popularity of a media presentation
- As a way to account for the recurrence of characters, plots, and themes in media presentations
- As insight into collective fantasy

Water is a universal symbol that is frequently incorporated into both dreams and media presentations. Water is a primal element that reflects the dreamer's unconscious, internal state of mind. (Photo by Lisa Marcus)

Externalization

Both dreams and media presentations act as expressions of internal processes, through the process of externalization. Tony Crisp (1990) explains how this process works in dreams:

> In the world of dreams, our most intimate fears and longings are given an exterior life of their own in the form of the people, objects, and places of our dream. . . . The external person or object in a dream is actually the dreamer's own internal feelings. . . . While asleep, the world in which their dream appears as exterior is actually their own internal thoughts, feelings, and psychological functions. . . . Each aspect of the dream, each emotion, each landscape and environment are materalizations of our own feeling states. . . . Dreams frequently portray intimate parts of ourselves which have never been made fully conscious or verbalized—even to ourselves. (pp. 12–14)

These feelings often are such a source of anxiety to the dreamer that his/her subconscious disguises the content in the dream. Martin Grotjahn explains, "The dream tendency, heavily censored, undergoes disguise and symbolization in order to pass the censorship of the preconscious. Only then is the dream hallucinated to become a pictorial adventure" (Grotjahn, 1957). Thus, dreaming is an "externalization" process that creates the necessary psychological distance to enable the dreamer to process disturbing issues.

As an example, Crisp (1990) asserts that dreams in which the protagonist suffers from some sort of physical abnormality are an expression of an internal conflict:

> Even if parts of one's body or face are shown in a dream to be distorted or abnormal, such a dream is not usually referring to the physical body. Our own idea or image of what sort of person we are is translated in dreams into our body form. We might dream our face looks abnormal mentally, or our body has strange areas. This refers to an internal sense of ourself [*sic*] not having developed to our full potential or of psychological hurts having distorted some aspect of ourself [*sic*]. (p. 17)

Visual media such as video, film, and interactive media operate on this same principle of externalization by serving as the external expression of the media communicator's personal experience. To illustrate, Molly Ringwald, who starred in several of filmmaker John Hughes's "youth culture" films in the 1980s, made the following observation about the director shortly after his death in 2009:

> The Hughes films . . . [specifically *Sixteen Candles* and *The Breakfast Club*] were the most deeply personal expressions of John's. In retrospect, I feel that we were sort of avatars for him, acting out the different parts of his life—improving upon it, perhaps. In those movies, he always got the last word. He always got the girl. (Ringwald, 2009)

For example, one formulaic plot device commonly employed in film and video narratives consists of situations in which characters are trapped or behave in a confused manner. These external events symbolize the fear of loss of control. The violence in popular films, television programs, and video games can also be regarded as metaphorical expressions of internal conflicts experienced by the media communicator. Tony Crisp explains, "Each of us are implicated in killing—by denying, repressing, controlling some part of our own nature" (1990: 261).

In addition, the *audience members* become involved in the externalization process by identifying with the characters, thereby making the presentation *their* dream/vision as well. Colin McGinn (2005) explains, "The Self is not so absent from the movies as may initially appear. . . . Whatever you do, there is always someone on the screen whose place you are imaginatively occupying; and without this your involvement would be greatly diminished" (p. 163). Indeed, the identification process often transcends physical or typical demographic categories. McGinn (2005) observes,

> When I watch *Brief Encounter* (probably my favorite film), I feel a strong sense of identification with the female lead, Laura . . . and less with the male lead, Alec . . . probably because I feel a stronger resemblance of personality between Laura and myself. (p. 165)

Media presentations also serve as a form of *dream-telling*. As its name implies, dream-telling refers to the process of communicating a dream to oneself or to others. According to Anthony Stevens, dream-telling involves the process of *amplification*—creating an environment that enables dreamers "to walk about (in the dream), allowing them to reveal their different facets of consciousness" (1994: 109). At the same time, dream-telling is a *dissociative* process, creating the *psychological space* that enables people to deal with potentially disturbing issues.

Media presentations function in much the same way as dream-telling. Media narratives are stories that, on the surface, are about somebody else. Consequently, the media functions as a safe haven in which individuals are able to explore boundaries in safety.

Function

Examining the function (or purpose) of dreams can provide considerable insight into media presentations as well. Lippmann (2006) states that

> [d]reams once were the private experience that informed, educated, explored, entertained, delighted, frightened, solved problems, looked into the future, reworked the past, provided access to forbidden experience, excited, played, provided release, expressed emotion, rehearsed for death. . . . Film and TV perform these identical functions (of dreams) but from the outside in. (p. 124)

Some of the shared functions of dreams (and, by extension, media presentations) include the following.

Guide to Self-Knowledge

Psychologists agree that dreams can serve as a key to understanding the self. Dreams furnish an opportunity for individuals to work out issues that are buried within their subconscious. Anthony Stevens (1994) notes,

> Freud believed that during sleep forbidden wishes are liberated from their daytime inhibition and seek to gain admission to consciousness. However, the "forbidden" nature of these wishes means that they are experienced by the ego as disturbing, and are therefore capable of waking one up. It is the *function* of dreams, in Freud's view, to prevent this from happening. (p. 102)

Both dreams and media can provide emotional catharsis. According to McGinn (2005),

> Emotions are inherently energetic, even explosive, and they seek an outlet; dreams seem to offer one type of outlet. . . . You don't need to be a Freudian to believe that emotions are often repressed and seek an outlet. By producing visual images in narrative form, with an emotional theme, movies and dreams convert those repressed and free-floating emotions into visible form, giving them shape and definition. (pp. 107–108)

Thus, both the process of dreaming and receiving media presentations can be considered healing processes. Gary Solomon (2001) writes,

> Movies can unlock the doors to some of those memories that you might have been trying to process in your dreams. If I can get you to watch a movie that helps you deal with your healing, you may find that a dream is a continuation of that healing process or that previous dreams are similar to what you see and feel by watching the movies. The movies may help you put to rest those conflicting feelings that you have been carrying around for so many years. . . . You will be quite amazed at the outcome when you let yourself feel free to heal. And part of that healing will be in the dreaming process and movie watching. (p. 14)

Preparation

Psychologist Alfred Adler held that, in dreams, "anticipatory sensations" not found in our conscious thinking, enable individuals to see the world in a new light. Indeed, ancient civilizations such as Egyptians, Jews, Greeks, and

Romans regarded the dream state as having prophetic implications, acting to foreshadow future events (Adler, 1927/2006: 215).

In like fashion, media presentations enable individuals to "anticipate" events by preparing audience members to contend with events, issues, and people they may encounter. Thus, to extrapolate from Adler, media presentations serve as a problem-solving blueprint, as the audience members witness how the characters respond to familiar situations on screen.

Narrative Analysis

According to Freud, the elements of a dream are arranged in such a way that "they form an approximately connected whole, a dream composition" (1911/1952: 42). Indeed, dreams and media presentations share the same narrative structure. Carl Jung divided the basic structure of a dream into four stages:

- The exposition, which sets the place and often the time of the action, as well as the dramatic personae involved
- The development of the plot, in which the situation becomes complicated and "a definite tension develops because one does not know what will happen"
- The culmination or peripeteia, when "something decisive happens or something changes completely"
- The lysis, the conclusion, the solution, or result of the dream work (Jung, 1953–1978)

Freud maintained that, in dream analysis, the first step involves breaking the dream into narrative elements such as characterization, plot, and theme. The next step involves identifying the commonalities in these elements. Freud observed,

> A dream superimposes the different components upon one another. The common element in them then stands out clearly in the composite picture, while contradictory details more or less wipe one another out. (Freud, 1911/1952)

The psychical material of the dream habitually includes recollections of distinctive experiences, sometimes dating back to early childhood. According to Freud, these elements may consist of "disconnected fragments of visual images, speeches and even bits of unmodified thoughts" (1911/1952: 40). This accounts, to some degree, for the inconsistencies in dream narratives, such as sudden switches in locations and characters. To illustrate, Freud cited a dream of his, in which an acquaintance touched him in a familiar fashion. In his analysis, Freud observed, "The intimate laying of a hand on my knee belonged to a quite different context and was concerned with quite other people. This element in the dream was in turn the starting point of two separate sets of memories—and so on" (1911/1952: 28).

In like fashion, while media presentations may appear disjointed, the emotional context provides the foundation of the narrative structure. McGinn (2005) comments, "When the image on the screen transforms and flows, it mirrors the ebb and flow of emotion, the lulls and rushes that characterize emotional consciousness" (pp. 105–106).

Thus, applying the analysis of dreamic plots to media presentations focuses on the following questions:

- Can you identify the plot fragments?
- What do these plot fragments refer to?
- Why are these disparate fragments connected together in the dream?

In addition, dreamic plots (and by extension, media presentations) often represent a personal response to a universal situation. For instance, *initiation stories* are tied to the discovery of Self. As an example, in the classic film *Wizard of Oz* (1939), Dorothy embarks on a wondrous quest to make a discovery about Self. Crisp (1990) explains,

> Although we might meet the heights of religious experience as well as the depths of human despair on the journey in simple terms it is primarily a journey into a confrontation with our own potential, our own fear, our own prison bars of thought and habit, our own ability to lift perception beyond what we have known before and look at the world, and our life in it, from new perspectives. (p. 25)

Furthermore, many dreamic plots (and media presentations) correspond with stages in the maturation process of human beings. For example, one dream narrative common to the adolescent stage of development consists of parents appearing drunk, incapable, or foolish. According to psychologist Rollo May, these dreams represent "another means of gaining independence from internalized values" (Crisp, 1990: 162).

Finally, media programs are often success stories, in which the protagonists do everything that we "dream" about. In that sense, many dream plots can be regarded as a form of wish fulfillment, as defined by the *optative clause* "if only":

- "If only I had been on time to catch the train."
- "Oh, if only I had called Aunt Carol."
- "If only I had purchased that particular stock on Thursday."

According to Freud (1911/1952), these dreamic plots go further than mere hypothetical positing:

> They show us the wish as already fulfilled; they represent its fulfillment as real and present and the material employed in dream representation consists principally, though not exclusively, of situations and of sensory images, mostly of a visual character. Thus, even in this "infantile" group, a species of transformation, which deserves to be described as dram work, is not completely absent; a thought expressed in the optative has been replaced by a representation in the present tense. (pp. 24–25)

For instance, the film *It Could Happen to You* (1993) is built on the following premise: What if you won the lottery. Michael Feller (n.d.) has contributed the following plot synopsis on the Internet Movie Database:

> Charlie and Muriel Lang have led simple lives—for most of their existence. That's until they win $4 million on the lottery! There is a problem, however. Prior to winning the lottery, Charlie had eaten at a cafe and hadn't been able to tip the waitress. He had promised her, jokingly, that if he won the lottery he'd give her half of it. This is why his wife, Muriel decides to leave him. She doesn't want the waitress to get a cent of their money. In fact, she wants all $4 million for herself!

In this case, the film contains a second optative clause: What if you borrowed the money to purchase the lottery ticket. Would you make good on your pledge to split the winnings with the lender?

Characterization

Dreams often include composite figures, combining the features of two (or more) people. Characters can be combined in the following ways:

- Giving a character the features of two people
- Giving a character the form of one person but think of it in the dream as having the name of another person

- Having a visual picture of one person, but put it in a situation that is appropriate to another character
- Imbuing a person with the characteristics (e.g., name, physical characteristics) of one character but the behavior/context of another character.

Thus, one line of inquiry involves identifying the composite characters, as well as considering the common elements between the collective figures:

- Who are the separate characters that were the models for the composite figures?
- What common elements are shared between the models for the composite figures?
- What have the common elements to do with the narrative?

Characters appearing in dreams may also represent the externalization of the Dreamer. Tony Crisp (1990) notes, "The hero/ine frequently depicts our initiative and unexpressed potential. We might see our highest ideals as coming from an exterior figure. . . . What happens to the hero/ine shows how one's own creativity and expressed love fare" (p. 199). Thus, character identification can determine points of perceived similarity (e.g., responses to situations, mannerisms) between the individual and characters in a media presentation.

Thematic Analysis

According to Jungian analysis, the characters in dreams are striving to achieve a psychic balance. Thus, a thematic line of inquiry involves identifying the central problem of the (dream/media presentation) and determine how it was resolved.

Common themes in dreams also found in media presentations include the following:

- The *retribution theme* is a wish-fulfillment tied to empowerment dreams.
- The *self-actualization theme* is an expression of the process involved in maturation. Crisp observes, this "is not only that of becoming a person but also expanding the boundaries of what we can allow ourselves to experience as an ego. . . . A drive toward the growth of our personal awareness, toward greater power, greater inclusion of the areas of our being which remain unconscious" (1990: 221).

To illustrate, *American Heart* is a 1993 film that tells the story of Jack (Jeff Bridges), a man who has just been released from prison and his efforts to become a responsible father to Nick (Edward Furlong). Solomon has identi-fied the following "healing themes" associated with this film:

- Growing up without a parent
- Coping when one of your parents drinks
- Being abandoned by someone you love
- Feeling like you have no place to go
- Being told you're not wanted
- Taking on the responsibilities of being a parent

John Hesley and Jan Hesley have assembled a list of films that touch on primal themes:

- Parent–Child Relationships
  - *The Great Santini*
  - *To Kill a Mockingbird*
  - *Ordinary People*
  - *I Never Sang for My Father*
- Family Conflicts
  - *The Brothers McMullen*
  - *Hannah and Her Sisters*
  - *Home for the Holidays*
  - *Long Day's Journey into Night*
  - *Marvin's Room*
- Sibling Rivalry
  - *Eating*
  - *The Myth of Fingerprints*
  - *Ordinary People*
  - *Soul Food*
  - *A Thousand Acres*
- Death and Dying
  - *My Life*
  - *Nothing in Common*
  - *Terms of Endearment*
  - *Shadowlands*
- Romantic Entanglements
  - *The Accidental Tourist*
  - *Bye, Bye Love*
  - *First Wives Club*
  - *Starting Over*

Setting

Setting refers to the environment in which a dream takes place (e.g., in a church vs. outer space). Settings often have symbolic properties. For instance, different rooms of a house can correspond to sides of Self. Tony Crisp (1990) explains,

> A house nearly always refers to oneself, depicting one's body and attributes of personality. Thus if we take a large house with its many functional rooms, the library would represent the mind, the bathroom cleansing or renewal of good feelings, the bedrooms one's sexuality or intimacy, the roof one's protectiveness or "coping" mechanisms. Large public buildings such as hospitals, factories, blocks of flats, depict particular functions suggested by their nature. (p. 204)

Consequently, dramatic shifts in the landscape of a dream can serve as an expression of internal unrest or conflict.

Context can play a significant role in the particular meaning attached to a setting. For instance, a door can be a barrier, entrance, or an opportunity.

Setting plays a similar role in media presentations. In films, certain types of activities occur in particular locations. As an example, the roof is close to heaven, so that it is a fitting locale for scenes featuring a revelation or a triumph. In contrast, scenes that dramatize the evil side of human nature may take place in a basement—close to Hell.

Symbols are part of human prehistory, existing before language. Indeed, symbols are intuitive, irrational, multilayered, and poetic and, consequently, are difficult to explain through language. Significantly, Freud draws connections between dream symbols and popular culture (which would include media as well):

> Dream symbolism extends far beyond dreams: it is not peculiar to dreams but exercises a similar dominating influence on representation in fairy tales, myths and legends, in jokes and in folklore. It enables us to trace the intimate connections between dreams and these latter productions. (1911/1952: 74)

An understanding of dream symbolism is essential to the interpretation of universal dreams; that is, dreams that are shared by many people, reflecting our common experience. To illustrate, water contains universal symbolic properties that can be found in dreams as well as media presentations. Crisp (1990) provides the following description:

Emotions, moods, and flow of feeling energy. . . . The nature of water
. . . lends itself to depicting aspects of how we relate to emotions; for
instance, one can "drown" in or feel swept away by some emotions, at
other times we can feel cleansed and refreshed. (p. 402)

Indeed, in many ads, the symbolic meaning, although latent, is the primary
message. For instance, in a radio spot for a Bank of America St. Louis Cardinals credit card, the product is positioned as a symbol of *identity*: purchasing the product is a way "to show the world" you are a St. Louis Cardinals
baseball fan.

Genre generally corresponds to the types of fantasies commonly found
in dreams. For example, the horror genre is associated with nightmares.
McGinn (2005) observes that horror programs typically are "not the rational
terror of ordinary waking life—wars, demons, accidents—but the irrational
fantasy terror of dream life" (p. 130). In contrast, the romance genre is tied to
wish fulfillment, celebrating the possibilities of life. And the adventure genre
features stories of empowerment on the behalf of the hero.

Production Elements

In dreams, meanings are formulated through production elements. Stevens
(1994) explains, "Why then do dreams need to be interpreted? Not because
they are disguises but because their meanings are formulated in a pictorial
'language' that is rendered comprehensible to the ego only when put into
words" (p. 106).

At the same time, the very insubstantiality of media presentations (i.e.,
the intangibility of image and sound) is dreamlike. McGinn (2005) explains,

What we see on the screen is a kind of idealized and transformed replica
of a real person: weightless, odorless, unified, and marvelous. And just
as the spiritual body is conceived as mind incarnate—what mind would
be if it were to achieve perceptible form—so the screen image gives us
the human form as a repository of human feeling and thought. This is
the human form infused with spirit. It is the soul in the guise of matter,
taking the form it must if it is to appear to human eyes at all. (p. 72)

Furthermore, digital special effects have created a dreamworld that defies
the laws of nature. Lippman (2006) explains, "Dreams serve as a model for
the expanding virtual world and for our electronic revolution (i.e., disembod-
ied, separated from the natural world, wish-fulfilling, magically connecting
with any and all)" (p. 125).

Significantly, production elements that appear in media presentations mirror many aspects of consciousness. Hugo Munsterberg (2005) observes that "production elements mimic the mind's processes by containing analogues of key psychological functions: the close-up mirrors attention, the flashback is memory, the flash forward is imagination or expectation" (p. 68).

Editing

The "editing" that takes place in dreams requires a subconscious recognition of relationships and points of commonality that escape the attention of an individual during their waking hours. Freud observed,

> Dreams take into account the connection which undeniably exists between all the portions of the dream thoughts by combining the whole material into a single situation. They reproduce logical connection by approximation in time and space. . . . Often when they show us two elements in the dream content close together, this indicates that there is some specially intimate connection between what correspond to them among the dream thoughts. (1911/1952: 41)

In dreams, these interrelationships transcend the conventions and laws of nature that "normally" remain beyond the recognition of the conscious mind.

In media presentations, editing is employed to draw connections between characters, significant moments, and locations in ways that are impossible to achieve in "real life." Film editor Walter Murch states,

> The instantaneous displacement achieved by the cut is not anything that we experience in ordinary life. . . . So *why do cuts work?*. . . Although "day to day" reality appears to be continuous, there is that other world in which we spend perhaps a third of our lives: the "night-tonight" reality of dreams. And the images in dreams are much more fragmented, intersecting in much stranger ways that approximately at least, the interaction produced by cutting. Perhaps . . . we accept the cut because it resembles the way images are juxtaposed in our dreams. (cited in McGinn, 2005: 110)

Discussing the film technique of montage (i.e., assembling a series of images), McGinn (2005) noted, "This capacity for imaginative sequencing is surely a mark of dream images strung together which have never been encountered together in perceived reality but which form a nexus of meaning for the dreamer" (p. 112).

Indeed, editing techniques such as flashbacks can be considered *dissociative devices* that make audience members feel safer and more secure as they are engaged in the media presentation—much like a dream.

In addition, the analysis of editing examines the messages that are conveyed by connecting seemingly unrelated points of information. In the interpretation of dreams, therapists look for *causality*—why certain events appear, as well as determining the relationship between two events. However, causality is often left unrepresented in dreams. Consequently, according to Freud, analysis invariably reveals the "associative links connecting these trivialities with things that are of the highest psychical importance in the dreamer's estimation" (1911/1952: 36).

Some of the subtle clues in dreams that indicate causality include the following:

- According to Freud (1911/1952), causality may be replaced by a *sequence* of two pieces of dream of different lengths. Freud explained, "Here the representation is often reversed, the beginning of the dream standing for the consequence and its conclusion for the premise" (Freud, 1911/1952: 42).
- An immediate *transformation* of one thing into another in a dream seems to represent the relation of *cause and effect* (Freud, 1911/1952: 42).
- In cases of dream displacement, the dream may have a *different center* from its dream thoughts; that is, the significant center has been replaced by a trivial one (Freud, 1911/1952: 35).

Significantly, identifying causality remains one of the most challenging aspects of media analysis. In many media presentations, heroes do not appear to be responsible for the destruction that they inflict in the course of the narrative. In advertising, however, connections are made between two unrelated events, suggesting a causality that, in fact, doesn't exist: for instance, if you buy a certain shampoo, you will not instantly become popular and successful.

Thus, applying observations about causality in dreams to media presentations (e.g., noting the messages conveyed by transformation) can furnish insight into the "scripted" notion of causality, as well as direct attention to issues of cause and effect in the media presentation.

Movement

Movement in media presentations is also dreamic in nature. Freud brought up the meaning behind movement in dreams: "The sensation of inhibition of movement (frozen) which is so common in dreams also serves to express a contradiction between two impulses, a conflict of will" (1911/1952: 42).

In films and television programs, the media communicator can alter the rate and rhythm of movement to give scenes a feeling of irreality. McGinn (2005) observes, "The exaggeration of movement found in Asian martial-arts films is part of the same tendency (of) magnifying movement to dreamlike levels of intensity" (p. 128).

Furthermore, in the production elements line of inquiry, it can be worthwhile to consider *why* other production elements, such as lighting, angle, scale, and sound are employed at certain points of a media presentation.

Dreams in Media Presentations

The appearance of dreams in media presentations is another area requiring further exploration. Dreams have played a significant role in many media presentations, as a way to express the internal state of the characters. McGinn (2005), for example, discusses the meaning behind *The Wizard of Oz* as dream:

> *The Wizard of Oz* is about a dream: the main color section simply is Dorothy's dream. Her house hurtles through space, hoisted by a tornado, lands in Munchkinland, on top of an unfortunate witch and there she begins a journey along the yellow brick road. As she dances the road, red ruby slippers sparkling, the movement never ceases, with flying witches, a stumbling straw man, an ambling lion, a haling tin man, and airborne monkeys. The entire film has the hyperkinesis of the dream, even ending with a balloon flight. The theme of an anxiety-ridden journey, full of obstacles and delays, is utterly dreamlike—and of course it is a dream. (p. 128)

See also: Formulaic Analysis; Function; Genre Study, Media Literacy Approach; Mass-Mediated Reality; Nonverbal Approach to Media Analysis

References

Adler, A. (2006). "Dreams and Dream Interpretation." In *The Practice and Theory of Individual Psychology*. Translated by P. Radin. London: Kegan Paul. (Original work published 1927)

Crisp, T. (1990). *Dream Dictionary*. New York and Avenel, NJ: Wings Books.

Feller, M. (n.d.). Plot summary for *It Could Happen to You*. Internet Movie Database (IMDb). Retrieved from http://www.imdb.com/title/tt0110167/plotsummary

Freud, S. (1952). *On Dreams*. New York: W. W. Norton. (Original work published 1911)

Grotjahn, M. (1957). *Beyond Laughter: Humor and the Subconscious*. New York: McGraw-Hill.

Hesley, J. W., & Hesley, J. G. (2001). *Rent Two Films and Let's Talk in the Morning* (2nd ed.). New York: John Wiley.

Jung, C. G. (1953–1978). *The Collected Works of C. G. Jung* (20 vols.). H. Read, M. Fordham, & G. Adler (Eds.). London: Routledge.

Lippmann, P. (2006). "The Canary in the Mind: On the Fate of Dreams in Psycho-analysis and in Contemporary Culture." *The American Journal of Psychoanalysis, 66*, 113–130.

McGinn, C. (2005). *The Power of Movies: How Mind and Screen Interact*. New York: Pantheon Books.

Munsterberg, H. (2005). "Why We Go to the Movies." In McGinn, C. *The Power of Movies: How Mind and Screen Interact*. New York: Pantheon Books.

Ringwald, M. (2009, August 11). "The Neverland Club." *New York Times*. Retrieved from http://www.nytimes.com/2009/08/12/opinion/12ringwald.html?pagewanted=all

Solomon, G. (2001). *Reel Therapy*. New York: Lebhar-Friedman Books.

Stevens, A. (1994). *Jung: A Very Short Introduction*. New York: Oxford University Press.

Effects Theories, Media Literacy

Effects theories refer to theories that examine the impact of the mass media on individuals and society. Effects theories range from direct/immediate effects to indirect/cumulative effects, which include the formation of attitudes toward groups and issues.

Direct and immediate effects theories were prominent from the early 20th century through the 1930s and were based on assumptions about the passivity of the audience. Media scholar Elizabeth M. Perse observes that the public response to the *War of the Worlds* radio broadcast "reinforced beliefs that mass communication could instill extreme emotions and reactions in the audience" (Perse, 2008: 24).

The "Magic Bullet," or "Hypodermic Needle" theory was an extension of the stimulus-response model drawn from psychology and mass society theory. According to media communications scholar John Fiske, this model of the relationship between the media and audience regarded the media as " 'injecting' values, ideas, and information into each individual in a passive and atomized audience, therefore producing a direct and unmediated effect" (O'Sullivan et al., 1994: 137).

Limited effects theories, which emerged in the 1940s and 1950s, were based on the premise that the media have only a limited influence on the audience. The rationale for limited effects theory is the *reception theory*, which holds that the audience selectively chooses and uses media content. The media's main and most common impact was believed to be *reinforcement* of cultural attitudes and values.

The limited effects approach grew out of persuasion and election research of scholars such as Paul Lazarsfeld, who found that social connections among people draw people together and can lead to shared interpretations of media messages. The media's impact is also influenced by the people in the flow of information from mass media. Finally, personal experiences and attributes can lead them to seek out media content.

According to Tim O'Sullivan, the *two-step flow model* is an example of the "complex network of steps and influences involved in the transmission of media messages through group relations" (O'Sullivan et al., 1994: 322). The two-step flow model operates as follows:

- Interested people pay attention to specialized media and pass along that information to others to whom they are socially connected.
- Researchers found that media messages flow from opinion leaders to family members, friends, and, even casual coworkers.

The two-step flow model has several significant implications. First, individuals may be influenced by media messages that they have not directly encountered. In addition, the information passed along by opinion leaders is not necessarily identical with the messages delivered by the media. Opinion leaders themselves are affected by the following *selectivity processes*:

- Selective exposure, or control over what individuals watch, listen to, or read in the media
- Selective attention, or control over which elements of media messages individuals pay attention to

- Selective perception, or control over how messages are interpreted
- Selective recall, or control over how and what was learned from the media (Perse, 2008: 25)

Indeed, the personal influence represented by the two-step flow can be an especially powerful barrier to the enhancement of media effects.

Another significant contribution to this school of thought was Joseph Klapper's identification of two conditions under which the media could influence the audience: (1) if normal barriers to effects are not operating and (2) if mediating factors are congruent with media's influence (Perse, 2008: 25).

The *uses and gratifications model* holds that people use the media to fulfill specific gratifications. Theorists focus on the specific uses that people make of the media and how the media compete against other information sources for viewers' gratification.

The 1970s witnessed a return to the notion of *immediate* and *observable* effects of mass media. A fundamental assumption is that the audience reacts involuntarily, automatically, and uniformly to media content. Furthermore, it is assumed that the audience is incapable of countering the impact of the media (Perse, 2008: 29).

Media scholarship during this period was largely based on *social learning theory*, which holds that learning is often achieved through imitation and identification. This can be accomplished through *modeling*, or direct imitation of media content or *identification*, in which observers do not exactly copy what they have seen but make a more generalized but related response. In some cases, the impact of the media is *inhibitory*, in that seeing a model punished for a particular behavior reduces the likelihood that the observer will perform that behavior.

Social learning theory further holds that people are more likely to learn behaviors that are presented realistically. The impact of the media is contingent on the following variables:

- Structural features
- Content features
- Arousal
- Realism (Perse, 2008: 31)

Conditional affects theory holds that impact is contingent on the *audience*. Perse observes,

The model is called conditional because when effects do occur, they are conditional on some attribute of the audience The audience can avoid exposure and reject influence. (Perse, 2008: 33)

Conditional effects theory is similar to the limited effects model in terms of their perception of the role of the audience. In addition, both approaches are based on notions of *selectivity*. However, the chief difference is that whereas the limited effects model is confined to *reinforcement*, the conditional affects model goes beyond reinforcement to *change*. When change effects occur, they are conditional on some attribute of the audience. Although selectivity is often seen as a barrier to effects, audience characteristics may act as lenses, focusing the influence of the media. Audience characteristics are, therefore, conditions of influence.

Social categories such as age, gender, and income are significant variables that affect the audience's response to media content. Other influential demographic factors include religious, political affiliations, and social relationships.

Perse explains that the conditional effects model "recognizes that all media exposure is not bound to result in media effects" (Perse, 2008: 33):

The audience has the power to avoid exposure and reject influence. And when media effects occur, they are certainly not uniform. People may be affected differently by the same media content. [The conditional effects model] . . . focuses mainly on the individual audience member (and) can be used to explain almost any media effect at an individual level. The individual is the focus of media effects because of the individual's power to be selective. The audience member is central to the Conditional Model (and media content is ignored, for the most part) because of selectivity processes that act as barriers to intended media effects. (p. 34)

Finally, the *cumulative effects model* holds that the impact of the media is not due to a single event but rather to continuous exposure to the same media messages.

Criticisms of Effects Theory

Many respected scholars question the efficacy of effects theory. Perse notes,

Scholars who hold critical and cultural studies perspectives argue that the study of media effects is limited and the results of those studies obscured because of faulty assumptions. [Todd] Gitlin (1978) explained that the dominant paradigm in the study of media effects is a behaviorist approach that directs scholars to be concerned with a very narrow definition of "effects." Because behaviorism focuses on outcomes that can be observed, much research has been limited to short-term manifestations of "effects" that can be easily measured in laboratories or in surveys. Effects have been defined in most studies as attitude change or in specific, discrete behaviors. This means that, for the most part, research has not considered the effects of long-term, cumulative media experience.

. . . Administrative research . . . also places value on short-term media impact that can be identified in pretests designed to help prepare campaigns or in post-campaign evaluations. Moreover, administrative media effects research is typically interested in variables . . . that can be manipulated or controlled, such as media production variables or frequency of exposure. Structural variables that may shape media production and content, are rarely studied in connection with media effects, so their impact are rarely considered. (Perse, 2008: 14–15)

Media Literacy Effects Theories

Effects theory takes yet another turn within the context of media literacy. Media literacy encourages *active learning*, as students apply critical thinking skills to the media and media presentations. According to media literacy educator Robert McCannon, media literacy education provides students with a knowledge base with regard to media techniques and functions: "Tobacco users and nontobacco users gained knowledge of tobacco ads' techniques of persuasion, becoming better able to resist them" (McCannon, 2009: 532).

A 2003 report issued by the Henry J. Kaiser Family Foundation cites studies finding that media literacy "interventions" can influence attitudes and behaviors with regard to tobacco and alcohol usage, as well as issues related to body image (Kaiser Family Foundation, 2003). McCannon (2009) explains,

Currently, media literacy "interventions" are incorporated into an incredibly wide variety of programs and curricula—everything from standard school disciplines to antidrug programs, smoking prohibition, antipoverty efforts, positive body image, antiviolence, sobriety, nutrition education, and help-the-homeless efforts. Many activists and organizations are attempting to use media literacy to control absenteeism, raise grades, promote self-esteem, reduce teacher/student parent friction, and more. (p. 524)

According to the Kaiser Report, "Studies suggest that even a single media literacy intervention can help children and adolescents understand the persuasive appeals of tobacco advertising messages and make a difference in their intention to use tobacco, at least in the short-term" (Beltramini & Bridge, 2001).

One of the most significant "effects" of media literacy education is that media literacy education enhances *critical thinking skills*. According to Renee Hobbs and Richard Frost (2003), media literacy instruction can enhance critical thinking in *other* disciplines:

The first large scale empirical study measuring the acquisition of media literacy skills in the United States concluded that incorporating media message analysis into secondary level English language arts curriculum . . . improved students' reading, viewing and listening comprehension of print, audio and video texts, message analysis and interpretation, and writing skills. (p. 340)

The current media literacy "effects" studies fall into the following categories:

Impact on Attitudes

One area of media literacy research examines the influence of media literacy education on subjects' perception of media and reality. A study by Nathanson and Cantor (2000) found that a media literacy intervention altered how children viewed characters and the violence in media presentations. Young children, especially boys, were more likely to identify with the victim. The children also thought the violence was less justified (Nathanson & Cantor [cited in McCannon, 2009: 535]).

Another study found that media literacy education had a positive impact on subjects' self-esteem. In a media literacy class focusing on media messages and body image, the subjects demonstrated an increased a sense of self-acceptance and empowerment (Piran, Levine, & Irving, 2000).

Media literacy education also helps individuals to develop an *independence* from the information being conveyed through the media. Several studies demonstrate that subjects develop an autonomy that enables them to make choices with regard to the media and media programming:

- Students who had completed a media literacy course felt that they were less susceptible to peer pressure toward smoking (McCannon, 2009: 528).

- Learning to deconstruct media messages has helped juvenile offenders develop strategies to resist antisocial impulses (Moore et al., 2000).
- A media literacy "intervention" program for high school male athletes helped these students develop a healthy skepticism about steroids and supplements, while building knowledge about strength-training (Goldberg et al., 2000).
- In a study focusing on media literacy and tobacco use, subjects were less likely to identify with people in ads who smoked (McCannon, 2009: 528).

Furthermore, McCannon (2002, 2009) has identified attitude changes in regard to health issues:

- Demonstrated changed attitudes toward alcohol and tobacco advertising (persuasion appeals)
- Awareness of public exploitation by tobacco companies (accompanied by resentment of this exploitation)
- A desire to live a healthier lifestyle

Impact on Behaviors

A number of studies have found that media literacy education results in demonstrable changes in behaviors. For instance:

- In one study, third and fourth graders given a course in media literacy decreased their time spent watching TV and playing video games and reduced their use of verbal and physical aggression as judged by their peers (Robinson et al., 2001).
- A study of a year-long critical viewing curriculum found that children in the early grades watched less violent TV after the intervention (Rosenkoetter et al., 2002).
- An evaluation of a classroom-based intervention found that media literacy education influenced students' decision making about drinking alcohol (Austin & Johnson, 1997).

Moreover, one area of research focuses on the influence of media literacy education on the behaviors of individuals at various demographic stages of development, such as age, social class, race, ethnicity, and social class. For instance, a study found that one media literacy session increased third and fourth graders' understanding of the intent of alcohol advertising and decreased the treatment groups' desire to be like the ads' characters (Austin & Johnson, 1997).

Other studies link the efficacy of media literacy education to an individual's personal experiences. As an example, an audit of studies on media literacy and tobacco usage found the following:

Teens who had never tried tobacco became more aware of the persuasive tactics of tobacco advertising and developed skills to resist it and dissuade peers from smoking. Teens who had tried tobacco increased their awareness of how tobacco messages affect themselves and other teens, were less likely to identify with people in ads who smoke, and felt that they were less susceptible to peer pressure to smoke. (Pinkleton et al. [quoted in Kaiser Family Foundation, 2003: 6])

Studies also have found that media literacy education has an impact on behavior at various stages of the decision-making process, including identification and long-term thinking, such as contemplating consequences to certain behaviors.

- *Identification with those engaged in the behavior:* subjects were less likely to identify with people in ads who smoked (McCannon, 2009: 528).
- *Susceptibility to external influences:* subjects felt less susceptible to peer pressure to smoke (McCannon, 2009: 528).
- *Long-term thinking/understanding consequences:* media literacy interventions can help juvenile offenders consider the consequences of risky behaviors, contributing to more responsible decision-making skills (Moore et al., 2000).

McCannon (2009) cites the current limits of media literacy scholarship:

There are fewer than a hundred media literacy studies, compared, for example, to the thousands of studies about media effects or smoking effects. The research is weak and mixed, leaving the question of media literacy's efficacy very much up in the air.

As a relatively new field, funding is scarce. Media literacy studies tend to treat small samples. They are frequently survey based, simple in design, nonrandomized, and short term. Replicated treatments are next to impossible to find.

Careful quasi-experimental studies exist, but there are no longitudinal data about changes in attitude, and positive results on behavioral change are nonexistent or, at best, weak. Many media literacy interventions are done by the intervening group. Most of the studies are quantitative, despite a need for qualitative studies. (McCannon, 2009: 525–526)

However, McCannon (2009) believes that "there is room for enthusiasm" with regard to the findings thus far:

Many practitioners and researchers find that media literacy programs can successfully change attitudes and, sometimes, behaviors. These studies suggest that the content and skills of media literacy can be taught, and they might be able to enhance childhood, culture, and democracy by leading students and citizens to understand, access, and produce media. (pp. 525–526)

Determining the duration of effects through follow-up studies can provide much-needed information about the effects of media literacy education. A few studies suggest that there might be lasting effects of media literacy education. For instance, in 1997, Austin and Johnson conducted a study focusing on third and fourth graders' understanding of the intent of alcohol advertising. McCannon (2009) observes, "Even 3 months later, the study decreased their expectation of positive consequences from drinking alcohol and decreased their likelihood of choosing an alcoholic drink" (p. 527). Another study that used alcohol education and discussion of beer ads among 12- to 17-year-olds produced cognitive resistance after the treatment group voiced a 20-minute sports show with four beer ads. The effect lasted months or years after the (initial study) (McCannon, 2009). However, studies like these are far too rare to be definitive. McCannon adds, "More research is needed on matching media literacy treatments, methods, appropriate content, and duration of intervention with different ages and types of students" (p. 538).

See also: Definition, Media Literacy

References

Austin, E., & Johnson, K. (1997). "Effects of General and Alcohol-Specific Media Literacy Training on Children's Decision Making about Alcohol." *Journal of Health Communication 2*, 17–42.

Beltramini, R. F., & Bridge, P. (2001, Winter). "Relationship between Tobacco Advertising and Youth Smoking: Assessing the Effectiveness of a School-based, Antismoking Intervention Program." *Journal of Consumer Affairs 35*, 263–276.

Goldberg, L., MacKinnon, D., Elliot, D., Moe, E., Clarke, G., & Cheong, J.W. (2000). "The Adolescents Training and Learning to Avoid Steroids Program." *Archives of Pediatric and Adolescent Medicine, 54*, 332–338.

Hobbs, R., & Frost, R. (2003, Spring). "Measuring the Acquisition of Media Literacy Skills." *Reading Research Quarterly 38*, 330–355.

Kaiser Family Foundation. (2003, November 29). *Media Literacy. Key Facts.* Retrieved from http://kff.org/other/fact-sheet/media-literacy

McCannon, R., (2002). "Media Literacy: What? Why? How?" In V. Strasburger & B. Wilson (Eds.), *Children, Adolescents & the Media.* Thousand Oaks, CA: Sage.

McCannon, R. (2009). "Media Literacy/Media Education." In V. Strasburger, B. Wilson, & A. Jordan (Eds.), *Children, Adolescents, and the Media* (2nd ed., pp. 519–570). Thousand Oaks, CA: Sage.

Moore, J., DeChillo, N., Nicholson, B. Genovese, A., & Sladen, S. (2000, Spring). "Flashpoint: An Innovative Media Literacy Intervention for High-Risk Adolescents." *Juvenile and Family Court Journal, 51*, 23–34.

O'Sullivan, T., Hartley, J., Saunders, D., Montgomery, M., and Fiske, J. (1994). *Key Concepts in Communication and Cultural Studies.* Routledge: London and New York Second Edition.

Perse, Elizabeth, M. *Media Effects Theory and Society.* Taylor & Francis (2008).

Pinkleton, B., Austin, E., Cohen, M., & Miller, A. (2003, May). "Media Literacy and Smoking Prevention among Adolescents: A Year-Two Evaluation of the American Legacy Foundation/Washington State Department of Health Anti-Tobacco Campaign." Paper presented at the International Communication Association, Health Communication Division, San Diego, CA.

Piran, N., Levine, M., and Irving, L. (2000, November/December). "GO GIRLS! Media Literacy, Activism, and Advocacy Project." *Healthy Weight Journal,* 89–90.

Robinson, T. N., Wilde, M. L., Navracruz, L. C., Haydel, K. F., & Varady, A. (2001). "Effects of Reducing Children's Television and Video Game Use on Aggressive Behavior." *Archives of Pediatric Adolescent Medicine 155*, 17–23.

Rosenkoetter, L., Rosenkoettr, S., Ozretich, R., & Acock, A. (2002, August). "Mitigating the Harmful Effects of Violent Television." Unpublished report, Oregon State University, Corvallis.

Fame

Fame is a focus of media literacy analysis that provides insight into the role of the media in the development of celebrity culture. According to historian Leo Braudy, seeking fame is a desire "to be known for one's talents or for oneself" (1997: 5). Braudy offers the following description of "the dream of fame":

Like a dim remembrance of unfallen purity, the dream of fame promises a place where private dreams of recognition triumphantly appear in public. Fame allows the aspirant to stand out of the crowd, but with the crowd's approval; in its turn, the audience picks out its own dear individuality in the qualities of its heroes. Famous people glow, it's often said, and it's a glow that comes from the number of times we have seen the images of their faces, now superimposed on the living flesh before us—not a radiation of divinity but the feverish effect of repeated impacts of a face upon our eyes. The ease with which we allow ourselves to be absorbed by such images, the desires to be that way ourselves, confirms that the essential lure of the famous is that they are somehow more real than we and that our insubstantial physical reality needs that immortal substance for support. (p. 6)

The desire to acquire fame is widespread. In the United States, approximately 30 percent of adults report regularly daydreaming about being famous; for teenagers, the rates are higher (Carey, 2006). The degree of infatuation with celebrity in the United States is roughly equivalent to that of residents in metropolitan centers in China and Germany, suggesting that the mass-mediated cultures of large urban communities play a role in shaping their residents' attitudes toward fame.

Characteristics of Fame

Fame can be characterized as follows:

- *A sense of approval* and *personal validation*. Fame is the ultimate form of validation. Reporter Benedict Carey (2006) explains,

    People with an overriding desire to be widely known to strangers are different from those who primarily covet wealth and influence. Their fame-seeking behavior appears rooted in a desire for social acceptance, a longing for the existential reassurance promised by wide renown. . . . "To be noticed, to be wanted, to be loved, to walk into a place and have others care about what you're doing, even what you had for lunch that day: that's what people want, in my opinion," said Kaysar Ridha, 26, of Irvine, Calif., a recent favorite of fans of the popular CBS reality series *Big Brother*.

- *Position of power.* This is what Braudy (1997) refers to as "a liberation from powerless anonymity" (p. 7)—it stems from an unequal relationship in which the celebrity is recognized by people whom he or she has never met.

- *Emblem of success.* Celebrities are celebrated for special talents that make them stand out. A person whose fame is measured in achievement is described in absolute terms: "the most . . ." or "the best." Thus, the conquests of Alexander the Great on the battlefield or John L. Sullivan in the boxing ring cannot be rescinded over time.
- Celebrities are also regarded as the personification of perfection. More-over, celebrities are always shown at their best in mass-mediated culture. Media presentations are carefully edited. In addition, digital manipulation eliminates unwanted pounds and erases wrinkles. And musicians can have their voices enhanced. As a result, celebrities establish an ideal of perfection that is unattainable by the general public.
- In 1990, actress Michelle Pfeiffer appeared on the cover of *Esquire* magazine, in large measure because she is seen as an icon of physical beauty. However, the cover required more than $1,525 of photo touch-ups. Significantly, then, if Michelle Pfeiffer cannot measure up to her own standards of beauty, what chances do the rest of us have? However, to be *too* unique can undermine celebrity. Audiences must be able to identify with a celebrity. As Braudy notes, celebrities must be "imitatible" (1997: 5) or they will lose their audience. Thus, modern celebrities are often models of normality; Tom Cruise looks like everyone else, only better.
- *Association with immortality.* As Braudy (1997) explains, to attain celebrity is "to put one's mark on time" (p. 16):

> The urge to fame originally was the aspiration for a life after death in the words and thoughts of the community. . . . Where one is remembered after they have passed from the earth; to be remembered, celebrated, discussed, *brought to life*. (p. 605)

Thus, celebrities like Marilyn Monroe or Elvis continue to live long after their deaths as a part of the popular culture—through memorabilia and retrospectives of their work. In addition, for some, a dramatic end of life has added to their celebrity. In a column about 19th-century poet Lord Byron, critic Michael Kimmelman observes,

> Lord Byron lacked only one thing to insure his immortality: a really good death. And this came about with perfect filmic melodrama in 1824, while he was leading an ill-planned campaign in Greece's war of

independence against the Turks. He had outfitted a warship (and gone so far as to design the men's uniforms—although even his second in command refused to take his plumed helmet with the Byron crest out of its pink box). Then Byron caught a fever; at the end, abandoned by mutinous troops, he died a gloriously unnecessary death in the marshes at Missolonghi, bled by his doctors. (Kimmelman, 1999)

Celebrities are characterized by an extravagant, controversial lifestyle. Indeed, the talent of celebrities often transcends the boundaries of convention, and their work involves extending boundaries. The wealth that accompanies fame ensures that the celebrity is unburdened by conventional worries, such as paying the phone bill. But even more significantly, because of the approval of the public, the celebrity is not bound by social convention. As a result, the celebrity is free to disregard public opinion. This challenge to conventional manners and behaviors is often regarded as dangerous. In his discussion of Lord Byron, Kimmelman (1999) relates the following anecdote: "Catching sight of [Byron] at St. Peter's, one English lady told her daughter to cast her eyes down: 'Don't look at him, he is dangerous to look at'."

- *Focus on Self.* According to reporter Benedict Carey (2006), the quest for fame is rooted in *narcissism*. A narcissist is characterized as "a devastatingly vulnerable person, compensating for a deeply imprinted inadequacy with a desperate need for admiration, and a grandiose self-image." Columnist David Brooks explains,

  > The narcissistic person is marked by a grandiose self-image, a constant need for admiration, and a general lack of empathy for others. He is the keeper of a sacred flame, which is the flame he holds to celebrate himself. . . . His self-love is his most precious possession. . . . There used to be theories that deep down narcissists feel unworthy, but recent research doesn't support this. Instead, it seems, the narcissist's self-directed passion is deep and sincere. . . . And because he plays by different rules, and because so much is at stake, he can be uninhibited in response. Everyone gets angry when they feel their self-worth is threatened, but for the narcissist, revenge is a holy cause and a moral obligation, demanding overwhelming force. (Brooks, 2010)

These narcissistic impulses not unusual. A study conducted at the National Institutes of Health reveals that 6.2 percent of Americans suffer from narcissistic personality disorder, including 9.4 percent of people in their 20s (Brooks, 2010).

But while the classic form of narcissistic personality disorder is acquired early in an individual's development, in response to feelings of rejection, psychologists have discovered a related syndrome, acquired situational narcissism, which is often developed in the quest for fame. Psychologist Robert Millman explains,

> The view of the world the acquired situational narcissist is getting is, when you think about it, quite reasonable. They are different. They're not normal. And why would they feel normal when every person in the world who deals with them treats them as if they're not? (Sherrill, 2001)

Indeed, some individuals have gone to extreme lengths to attain notoriety. Columnist Alessandra Stanley provides the following examples:

> John Hinckley Jr. said he shot Ronald Reagan to impress the actress Jodie Foster. Mark David Chapman told his first parole board hearing in 2000 that he shot and killed John Lennon to get noticed. ("I was feeling like I was worthless, and maybe the root of it is a self-esteem issue," Mr. Chapman said, according to the transcript. "I felt like nothing, and I felt if I shot him, I would become something, which is not true at all.") (Stanley, 2009)

Historical Context

The analysis of fame can provide considerable insight into a historical period. According to Braudy (1997), a celebrity is a "product of his or her time":

> The history of fame is also the history of the shifting definition of achievement in a social world, achievement often defined by the eyes of others, but just as often by their ostentatious absence. (p. 7)

The nature of fame began to shift in the 18th century, corresponding to dramatic global changes characterized by democratization (with French, Russian, and American revolutions), urbanization, and education, culminating in the development of a popular culture. According to Braudy (1997), these changes were accompanied by "greater and greater disagreement over what constitutes worthy activity—worth doing, worth knowing about, and worth conveying to others" (p. 7).

In the United States, one of the outcomes of this democratic movement was an expanded definition of fame—as an extension of the American Dream.

Instead of being celebrated on the basis of birth and social class, the definition of fame was expanded to individual achievement. Columnist Alessandra Stanley (2009) observes,

> In totalitarian regimes, some people take huge risks for the freedom to be themselves; in this democracy, some people take huge risks for the freedom to be someone else—a celebrity.
>
> Fame has a spellbinding power in American society, the one thing that can trump wealth, talent, breeding and even elected office. Reality shows and social Web sites like Facebook long ago knocked down the barriers that kept ordinary people trapped in obscurity. And instant renown is nothing if not democratic.

In the media age, fame has been transformed from a celebration of human achievement to a sense of *notoriety*. That is, many famous people are *known* for being *known*. Kimmelman (1999) says,

> In Vietnam today there are 1,000 temples dedicated to a cult of Victor Hugo. Which is nothing compared to the number of albums sold by Milli Vanilli, the 80's pop duo who faked their way to stardom by lip-syncing songs recorded for them by other people. The idea of the heroic individual now having devolved into mere celebrityhood, modern magazines and television make people famous simply for having had their pictures taken. Talent isn't necessarily an issue. . . . Fame, stripped of its old spiritual sense of everlasting existence derived from valued accomplishment, accrues these days to Linda Evangelista and Kate Moss, who look good in advertisements.

Within this context, fame has been reduced from recognition of accomplishments to celebration of *style* and *physicality*—sex appeal. Performers like Madonna came to public attention by shocking the audience.

Fame and the Media

Channels of communication have always been essential in spreading the word about the virtues of notable individuals. In that regard, the evolution of the media has influenced both the nature of fame and its role in mass-mediated culture. Artist Andy Warhol's observation that everyone now has 15 minutes of fame turns out to have been prophetic.

The pervasive nature of the modern media adds to the familiarity that the public feels toward a celebrity. Thus, a performer like Lady Gaga appears in all channels of mass communications. Not only is her music featured on the radio but she can be found on the Internet, magazines and newspapers, and entertainment news programs on television. Moreover, she has been a pioneer in developing Backplane, a media platform to manage her fan base by integrating feeds from a variety of online sites, such as Facebook and Twitter.

In the United States, media companies are profit-oriented enterprises, generally owned by large conglomerates. Celebrities are simply products, like shoes or showerheads, to be manufactured and "sold" to the public. Within this context, celebrities are simply products that meet a particular need. Journalist Lynn Hirshberg (2009) explains,

> Historically, Hollywood likes to look for a close (and usually younger) facsimile of its reigning stars. When Julia Roberts became less interested in romantic comedies, those parts went to Sandra Bullock. When Robert Redford was more attracted to directing than to being a leading man, Brad Pitt was waiting in the wings.

Thus, media literacy analysis often reveals that the latent function, or purpose, behind celebrity culture, is *profit*. To illustrate, celebrity "news" presentations have been transformed into a lucrative *product*. Reporter Jim Rutenberg (2011) explains,

> This is how it works in the new world of round-the-clock gossip, where even a B-list celebrity's tangle with the law can be spun into easy money, feeding the public's seemingly bottomless appetite for dirt about the famous. A growing constellation of Web sites, magazines and television programs serve it up minute by minute, creating a river of cash for secrets of the stars, or near-stars. An analysis of advertising estimates from those outlets shows that the revenue stream now tops more than $3 billion annually, driving the gossip industry to ferret out salacious tidbits.

A Media Literacy Approach to the Study of Fame

Media literacy empowers individuals to develop a critical distance from the phenomena of celebrity. Braudy (1997) declares,

> To be aware of fame is to be behind the scenes, and to be behind the scenes is to control rather than be controlled. Whether your particular knowledge is gossip about politicians and movie stars, advance reports

about the newest fashion trends, secret proof of the existence of aliens, or apocalyptic paranoia about the government, the United Nations, or the New World Order, having such knowledge proves that you're special, that you can't be fooled, and that you understand the heart of things. (p. 600)

The following lines of inquiry can furnish perspective into the study of celebrity.

Historical Context

The study of fame enables individuals to be able to recognize and anticipate the stages of fame.

Stage 1: Ascension to Celebrity Status

In this mass-mediated culture, fame is tied to a person's ability to exploit this media industry to his/her advantage. Consider actress Megan Fox admitting that she does not possess an abundance of show business talent; instead, her skill involves an understanding of the process involved in the acquisition of fame. Hirshberg (2009) explains,

Although she just signed a deal with Armani to replace Victoria Beckham as its underwear model, and to serve as its jeans model, Fox does not seem particularly fashion-conscious or interested in style. Instead, she's a student of personalities, of careers, of image. . . . "I'm not one of these people who grew up studying acting or went to theater school . . . I don't know if I'm talented, I don't know what I can do or can't do. I had no skills at all . . . Hollywood is filled with women who have tried to cope. I like to study them. I like to see how they've succeeded. And how they've failed."

Celebrity campaigns involve a process of *branding*, an advertising strategy in which a product is given a distinct identity in the marketplace. Those who aspire to ascend to celebrity status embark on public relations campaigns, in which they apply the principles of branding to themselves. Laura Lake (n.d.) explains,

A strong brand is invaluable as the battle for customers intensifies day by day. It's important to spend time investing in researching, defining, and building your brand. After all your brand is the source of a promise to your consumer. It's a foundational piece in your marketing communication and one you do not want to be without.

Indeed, celebrities often think of themselves as products, referring to themselves in the third person. "I wanted to do what was best for LeBron James and make him happy," announced the basketball star after signing a multimillion contract (Collins, 2011).

A carefully thought-out strategy is designed to attract the attention of the media. Take the 2009 case of Michaele and Tareq Salahi, who snuck into a state dinner at the White House, outwitting the security system of the Secret Service. The couple had a photo taken of them and the Obamas. Mr. and Mrs. Salahi were being considered for a new reality series, *The Real Housewives of D.C.* Thus, their plan was implemented in hopes that they would be selected for the reality series.

Stage 2: Sudden, Immediate Celebrity

Media Scrutiny. Celebrities of the premedia period were defined by their inaccessibility. Alexander the Great and Napoleon were rarely (if ever) seen by the masses. In contrast, fans feel intimately acquainted with their media celebrities, who appear in many media. For instance, thanks to print media such as *Fan Magazine*, fans can follow the everyday exploits of film stars. The Internet has expanded this nearly universal access to celebrities. Braudy (1997) explains, "Part of the fame of Byron and Napoleon was their inaccessibility—the brief glimpse of them that paintings and prints allowed. . . . In contrast, increased accessibility has shrunken the size of fame . . . they lack private mystery" (p. 610). Kaysar Ridha, 26, of Irvine, California, a recent favorite of fans of the popular CBS reality series *Big Brother*, commented, "It's strange and twisted, because when that attention does come, the irony is you want more privacy" (Carey, 2006).

Seventeen-year-old Melanie Oudin provides an example. In 2009, she stunned the tennis world by winning matches at Wimbledon and the U.S. Open, becoming an overnight celebrity. However, this instant fame was quickly followed by media scrutiny that threatened her initial success. Journalist Christopher Clarey (2009) explained,

> The day after her first night match at this United States Open, Melanie Oudin was up by 6 a.m., appearing on two morning television programs and completing plans for a quick trip to California to tape "The Tonight Show" and the Ellen DeGeneres Show. . . . But on the same night that Oudin lost at the Open, SI.com reported that her father, John Oudin, filed for divorce from her mother, Leslie Oudin, on July 24, 2008, and has since claimed in court documents that one of the reasons for his filing was that Leslie Oudin had an affair with Brian de Villiers, Melanie

Oudin's longtime coach. . . . "A lot of the media and stuff, you don't realize how much more it is than just playing tennis," she said, explaining that she was "exhausted."

Isolation and Insulation. At the same time, famous people become insulated by a "celebrity environment. Celebrities frequently employ an 'entourage'— a staff that adds to the celebrity's sense of self-importance." Consequently, celebrities "begin to think they're invulnerable. Some even risk their lives, since the world can't hurt them if it's not real" (Sherill, 2001).

Ironically, then, fame is also characterized by loss of freedom and privacy. Braudy (1997) observes, "the heart of what it meant to 'go public' was to be entrapped by the gaze of others, to be reduced by their definitions, and to be forced into shapes unforeseen in the innocent aspirations to the golden world of fame" (p. 12).

Stage 3: The Mortality of Fame

The fickleness of modern audience means that mass-mediated celebrities operate in a world in which fame is *transitory*. Thus, "One-hit wonders" or celebrities who appear on "has-been celebrity" reality shows are reminders of the mortality of the modern celebrity. The participants in a study who focused on goals tied to others' approval (like fame) reported significantly higher levels of distress than those interested primarily in self-acceptance and friendship (Carey, 2006).

Audience

In addition, media literacy analysis provides insight into the role of audience in celebrity culture. Ultimately, it is the audience that decides who is worthy of attention. Consequently, the study of fame focuses on the relationship between a celebrity and his or her fans. In addition, the study of what the audience finds superlative—worthy of fame—can furnish perspective into a culture. Tim O'Sullivan (O'Sullivan et al., 1994) explains,

> Stars are popular because they are regarded with some form of active esteem and invested with cultural value. They resonate within particular lifestyles and subcultures and are subject to differential forms of identification dependent upon gender or sexuality for example. (p. 297)

Cultural Context

The study of fame furnishes perspective into culture. According to Braudy (1997), fame tells us much about how particular ages defined, promulgated, and understood what a person was or could be. . . . To call someone or something famous essentially means "pay attention to this," and in a world overcrowded with people places, things, and ideas, the problem of what deserves attention is a crucial issue. (pp. 585, 600)

Thus, a celebrity is a cultural icon—the personification the needs, drives, and dreams of American society. O'Sullivan (1994) explains,

Stars, both in the characters and performances they play, in their disclosed "private" lives . . . represent certain ideals of behavior, action, style, sentiment, etc. In this context, they act as powerful signs, images, or types within cultural codes and process. (p. 223)

It can be argued that celebrities are cultural archetypes that hold a fascination with the public. Thus, Lady Gaga is simply the latest incarnation of the "Blonde Bombshell" archetype that includes Jean Harlow, Marilyn Monroe, and Madonna. Braudy (1997) explains,

Long-lived celebrity and fame . . . represent unfinished business in the national psyche, emblems of heroism or villainy, innocence or guilt, that may last for decades, even centuries. (p. 600)

Furthermore, celebrities not only express absolute cultural values but *reinforce* and *shape* cultural values. Braudy (1997) states that "modern fame is always compounded of the audience's aspirations and its despair, its need to admire and to find a scapegoat for that need" (p. 9). Celebrities serve as symbols of the Good Life for all, as well as spokespersons for social movements—whether or not their talents falls within the range of their expertise.
Additional areas of analysis include the following:

- Fame as a media construction
- The impact of individual media systems on the celebrity campaigns
- The interaction of media systems on celebrity campaigns
- The use of new media on celebrity campaigns
- How celebrities use the media to promote themselves and maintain their celebrity status
- The impact of fame on individuals
- Fame and subcultures

See also: Cultural Context

References

Braudy, L. (1997). *The Frenzy of Renown: Fame and Its History*. London: Vintage Books.

Brooks, D. (2010, July 15). "The Gospel of Mel Gibson." *New York Times*. Retrieved from http://www.nytimes.com/2010/07/16/opinion/16brooks.html

Carey, B. (2006, August 22). "The Fame Motive." *New York Times*. Retrieved from http://www.nytimes.com/2006/08/22/health/psychology/22fame.html?pagewanted=print

Clarey, C. (2009, September 11). "Oudin Finds Success at U.S. Open Brings Scrutiny Also." *New York Times*. Retrieved from http://www.nytimes.com/2009/09/11/sports/tennis/11oudin.html

Collins, G. (2011, May 14). "Presidential Primary Book Club." *New York Times*. Retrieved from http://www.nytimes.com/2011/05/14/opinion/14collins.html

Hirshberg, L. (2009, November 15). "The Self-Manufacture of Megan Fox." *New York Times Magazine*. Retrieved from http://www.nytimes.com/2009/11/15/magazine/15Fox-t.html?pagewanted=all

Kimmelman, M. (1999, October 17). "The Lost Art of Immortality." *New York Times*. Retrieved from http://www.nytimes.com/1999/10/17/magazine/the-lost-art-of-immortality.html?pagewanted=all&src=pm

Lake, L. (n.d.). "What Is Branding and How Important Is It to Your Marketing Strategy?" Retrieved from http://marketing.about.com/cs/brandmktg/a/whatisbranding.htm

O'Sullivan, T., Hartley, J., Saunders, D., Montgomery, M., & Fiske, J. (1994). *Key Concepts in Communication and Cultural Studies* (2nd ed.). Routledge: London and New York.

Rutenberg, J. (2011, May 21). "The Gossip Machine, Churning Out Cash." *New York Times*. Retrieved from http://www.nytimes.com/2011/05/22/us/22gossip.html?pagewanted=all

Sherill, S. (2001, December 9). "Acquired Situational Narcissism." *New York Times*. Retrieved from http://www.nytimes.com/2001/12/09/magazine/the-year-in-ideas-a-to-z-acquired-situational-narcissism.html

Stanley, A. (2009, November 28). "For Some, a Search for Celebrity Is Worth Any Risk." *New York Times*. Retrieved from http://www.nytimes.com/2009/11/28/arts/television/28watch.html

Formulaic Analysis

Formula is a fundamental characteristic of popular media presentations. Formula refers to patterns in *premise*, *structure*, *characters*, *plot*, and *trappings*.

Every genre is characterized by its own distinctive formula. Thus, the formula characteristics of soap operas are readily distinguishable from television news broadcasts.

The use of formula in popular genre is tied to *predictability*—that is, working within the experience and expectations of the audience. Formula serves as a guide for the audience, providing clues and cues that help them negotiate meaning as they read a novel or watch the news on television. Early on, children learn the "language" of film: for instance, how to recognize a flashback or identify heroes and villains. Film critic Neal Gabler (2002) explains,

> Formulas are designed to elicit predictable responses through predictable means—predictable because they have worked in the past. You show an audience an attractive young man and woman who playfully bicker at the beginning of a movie and it roots for them to wind up together at the end. Or show a bully pushing around a decent fellow and viewers root for the latter to defeat the former. The audience reacts not because it knows the formula—it reacts because the formula knows the audience.

Thus, despite language and cultural differences, audiences can pick up the cues provided by a program's formulaic elements.

Unfortunately, many *genric* presentations (that is, a program that belongs to a particular genre) are simply repetitions of formula. For instance, many film sequels simply rehash the successful plot elements of the original movie, such as *plot*. Consider John McClane, the lone-wolf policeman from *Die Hard* (1988) who foils yet another terrorist attempt in *Diehard: With a Vengeance* (1995). Another formulaic reprise involves repeating the *relationship dynamics* between the main characters, as in the case of Martin Riggs (Mel Gibson) and Roger Murtaugh (Danny Glover) in *Lethal Weapon 1–4* (1987–1992).

One of the major challenges facing media communicators is their ability to explore complex themes and issues within the constraints of a formula. In the 16th century, Elizabethan poets were judged on their ability to create sonnets within the tight constraints of the formula. A sonnet is a lyric poem of 14 lines, consisting of 4 divisions: 3 quatrains (each with a rhyme pattern of its own) and a rhymed couplet. Thus, the typical rhyme scheme for the English sonnet is *abab, cdcd, efef, gg*. These standard rules establish a frame of reference that determines the artistic merit of the poems (as well as the poets). What distinguished Shakespearian sonnets from those of his contemporaries was his ability to work so magnificently within these artistic limits. In like fashion, what has established *I Love Lucy* and *Seinfeld* as classic TV

Trappings are artifacts that appear so often in media presentations that they have become associated with a genre. For instance, the Stetson hat, horse, and rugged terrain in this photo identify this scene as belonging to the western genre. (Photo by Lisa Marcus)

sitcoms is what these programs were able to achieve within the standard sit-com formula.

Formulaic Twists

Media presentations or entire genres sometimes fall out of favor simply because the audience becomes bored with the formula. For instance, in 2004, Gary Newman, co-president of 20th Century Television, declared, "For a lot of young people, the sitcom format feels retro and tired" (Carter & Elliott, 2004). To revive interest in the genre, media communicators must challenge the parameters of the formula. For instance, *Arrested Development* departed from the usual sitcom formula by featuring running gags extending over several episodes and adding absurd plot twists, surreal flashbacks, and unsympathetic heroes.

But even programs that challenge the parameters of a genre are highly conscious of its formula. For instance, *Arrested Development* played with the audience's expectations for comedic purposes. As an example, the conclusion of an episode often included a "teaser" that previewed the next week's program. However, the teaser often turned out to be a stand-alone joke.

Other formulaic twists occur simply by making changes in narrative elements, including the following:

- *Characters.* In *House, M.D.*, a medical drama, the lead character (Dr. Gregory House) is a blunt nonconformist, a twist on the stock character of the smooth, omnipotent physician.
- *Gender.* The gender of characters can also be switched to give a formula a fresh look. For instance, in *Trial by Jury*, a derivative of *Law and Order*, the dominant roles are played by women.
- *Sexual orientation.* The success of *Queer Eye for the Straight Guy* led to the development of a derivative program: *Queer Eye for the Straight Girl*. The show has the identical premise and format. But instead of five gay men "making over" a straight male, this series involves three gay men and one gay woman transforming a "fashion-challenged" woman.
- *Age.* Changes in the age of the characters can give a show a fresh appearance. For instance, prime-time soap operas, which hearken back to the 1980s heyday of *Dynasty* and *Dallas*, have reemerged in the form of teen-centered dramas like *O.C.*, *One Tree Hill*, and *Skin*.
- *Setting.* A change in setting can create a fresh appearance for a genre. For instance, the dramatic series *The Mountain* is described by critics Bill Carter and Stuart Elliot as "*Dynasty* on skis." The series takes place at a luxury ski resort inherited by a young man. According to *LAX* executive producer, Mark Gordon, the setting makes the difference. "This arena is fresh and different and someplace that we haven't seen before" (Carter & Elliott, 2004: 9).

Formulaic Elements

Formulaic Premise

A *premise* is defined as the initial circumstances, situation, or assumption that serves as the point of origin for a narrative—that is, a characteristic situation in which characters find themselves. This premise furnishes information about what the audience can expect when they come upon a program belonging to a particular genre. One way, then, to identify a premise is to begin with this statement: *"The media presentation presents is a world in which . . ."*

Each genre has its own distinctive formulaic premise. For instance, a situation comedy is characterized by the following formulaic premise: A situation comedy presents a world in which a recurring cast of characters encounters humorous situations based on everyday situations rather than on individual jokes. The characters survive the minor problems—only to face new trials on the next episode.

Identifying the premise of a genre can furnish perspective into cultural issues, preoccupations, and myths. As an example, disaster films such as *The Day After Tomorrow* (2004) and *The Core* (2003) reflect growing concerns about the growing instability of the environment.

Formulaic Structure

Popular genres generally operate within a readily identifiable structure. This formulaic structure reinforces the worldview of the genre. To illustrate, the standard framework found in sitcoms is *order/chaos/order*:

- The beginning of a sitcom finds the world in harmony.
- The initial order of the story is disrupted almost immediately.
- The chaotic stage consumes the majority of the program and is the source of much of its interest.
- The status quo is finally restored in the conclusion.

This formulaic structure conveys the message that problems are all solvable, and justice always prevails. Characters who have violated the moral code of sitcoms (by lying or trying to be something they're not) suffer the consequences. Misunderstandings are cleared up, and characters who have been at odds are reconciled.

As with the sitcom formula, the horror genre typically begins with a sense of order but then quickly descends into the chaos stage. The characters soon discover that this initial order was only an illusion. Behind this fragile façade, evil is lurking—either monsters that had heretofore been dormant or forces that are hidden within human beings. Although the crisis has been momentarily averted, the story raises questions about evil that cannot easily be dismissed. Consequently, the emotional response of the characters combines sorrow and relief, rather than celebration.

Soap operas operate according to a variation of the order/chaos/order formula. Within this "serial" model, a single episode typically consists of several subplots at different stages of development, which are interwoven throughout the episode. Consequently, although each subplot ultimately works according to the order/chaos/order structure, it does not operate within the bounds of a single episode. One subplot may be at the inception stage, two others may be in the process of unfolding, and a final one may be at a point of resolution.

Taken collectively, this model reinforces the worldview of the soap opera, which is characterized by *change*.

Variations on this formulaic structure work off of the expectations of the audience as a dramatic device or to make a thematic statement. As an example, the film noir classic *Double Indemnity* (1944) begins at the end of the film, as Walter Neff (Fred McMurray) speaks into a Dictaphone, confessing to a murder. The film then moves into a flashback to show how the murder occurred. The structure of most murder mysteries move toward the solving of the crime; however, in this film, the audience immediately knows *who* committed the murder. Instead, the focus of *Double Indemnity* is on *why* Neff committed the crime—a far more intriguing mystery of human nature.

Stock characters appear so frequently in a genre that they are instantly recognizable. The appearance of stock characters enables the audience to quickly become involved in the story. Even "unscripted" reality shows employ stock characters:

- The "Good Girl"
- The Bitch
- The Pot-Stirrer (someone who fans the flames of controversy)
- The Groovy Guy

The designation of stock characters can provide insight into attitudes toward particular groups of people. For instance, in 2006, *Valley of the Wolves*, an action/adventure film, was released in Turkey, in which Americans fill the role of the stock villains. The plot of the film involves Turkish gunmen seeking revenge against a tyrannical occupying army. This casting reflected popular sentiment in Turkey about the U.S. role in Iraq. Journalist Sebnam Arsu (2006) notes, "The commander's name is Sam—as in uncle—is a sociopath, killing people without a second's thought and claiming that he is doing God's will. While fictional, some of the movie is based in part on real events, and many of the scenes elicit knowing looks from the audience."

A *convention* is a practice that appears so often that it has become standard. Conventions furnish cues about people, events, and situations. Consequently, identifying conventions provides important tools for deciphering media messages. For example, plot conventions are recurring incidents that appear across a number of genres (e.g., the boy-meets-girl scenario, the love–hate relationship between a couple). Other plot conventions appear so frequently within a particular genre that they have become associated with that genre. Examples include the gun duel in a western, the wedding scene in a romance, or the car chase in the action genre.

Trappings are artifacts that appear so often that they have become associated with a genre. For instance, Stetson hats, horses, and spurs are items that subtly establish the authenticity of the western genre. Trappings furnish cues about people, events, and situations. To illustrate, heroes in westerns are identifiable by their white hats; conversely, villains wear black.

Different trappings may give the illusion of a new genre. For instance, despite its modern trappings, police dramas are actually contemporary westerns. Horses have been replaced by hot cars, and the prairie and rough towns of the Old West have been transformed into the urban landscape. However, the essential conflicts of good versus evil remain the same.

Media Literacy Strategies

The formulaic approach includes the following lines of inquiry:

1. *Defining the formulaic elements that are characteristic of a genre and examining the messages that are conveyed by this formulaic configuration.*
2. *Examining a body of programs belonging to the same genre, focusing on variations that occur within the formula.*
   - Identifying the variations that occur.
   - Analyzing the significance of these variations with respect to themes, worldview, and messages in the program.
3. *Comparing the formulaic patterns in different genres.*
4. *Examining ways in which different cultures make use of the same basic formula.*
5. *Tracing the evolution of a particular formula over a substantial period of time as a reflection of cultural changes.*
6. *Focusing on formulaic analysis as a way to identify similarities in dissimilar programming.*
7. *Considering ways in which the same basic cultural symbolism is used in a variety of formulas (e.g., how the symbolism of crime is used in different formulas, such as the gangster story and the classical detective caper story). The growth and decline of different formulas involving the same symbols suggests shifts in attitude toward the social phenomenon.*
8. *Tracing the evolution of a particular formula to furnish perspective into cultural change.*
9. *Examining ways in which different cultures or periods make use of the same basic formula.*

See also: Character Analysis; Narratology

References

Arsu, S. (2006, February 14). "If You Want a Film to Fly, Make Americans the Heavies." *New York Times*. Retrieved from http://www.nytimes.com/2006/02/14/international/europe/14turk.html?pagewanted=print

Carter, B., & Elliott, S. (2004, May 18). "ABC and WB Announce Lineups They Hope Will Bring a Turnaround from Disappointing Seasons." *New York Times,* Section C, p. 9.

Gabler, N. (2002, August 4). "The Nation: The Illusion of Entertainment; Just Like a Movie, But It's Not." *New York Times*. Retrieved from http://www.nytimes.com/2002/08/04/weekinreview/the-nation-the-illusion-of-entertainment-just-like-a-movie-but-it-s-not.html?pagewanted=all&src=pm

Foundations of Media Literacy Education

Although a diversity of materials and approaches to media literacy education is emerging, some principles are fundamental to all of these approaches:

Fundamental Principles of Media Literacy Education (Len Masterman)

Len Masterman (1985) has identified 18 principles of media education for the systematic and rigorous analysis of media "text":

1. Media education is a serious and significant endeavor.
2. The central unifying concept of media education is that of representation.
3. Media education is a lifelong process.
4. Media education aims to foster critical autonomy.
5. Media education is investigative.
6. Media education is topical and opportunistic.
7. Media education's key concepts are analytical tools rather than an alternative content.
8. Content, in media education, is a means to an end.
9. The effectiveness of media education can be evaluated by just two criteria:
    ○ The ability of students to apply their critical thinking to new situations and
    ○ The amount of commitment and motivation displayed by students.

10. Ideally, evaluation in media education means student self-evaluation, both formative and summative.

11. Media education attempts to change the relationship between teacher and taught by offering both objects for reflection and dialogue.

12. Media education carries out its investigations through dialogue rather than discussion.

13. Media education is essentially active and participatory, fostering the development of more open and democratic pedagogues. It encourages students to take more responsibility for and control over their own learning, to engage in joint planning of the syllabus, and to take longer-term perspectives on their own learning. In short media education is as much about new ways of working as it is about the introduction of a new subject area.

14. Media education involves collaborative learning.

15. Media education consists of both practical criticism and critical practice. It affirms the primacy of cultural criticism over cultural reproduction.

16. Media education is a holistic process.

17. Media education is committed to the principle of continuous change.

18. Underpinning media education is a distinctive epistemology. (Masterman, 1985)

Principles of Media Literacy Education (Center for Media Literacy)

In 1989, under the leadership of Executive Director Elizabeth Thoman, the Center for Media Literacy (CML; formerly called the Center for Media and Values) established a framework for studying and understanding media messages. These five key concepts incorporated ideas previously promoted by media educators in Australia, the United Kingdom, and Canada. CML president Tessa Jolls states:

> It is our dream that by the time they graduate from high school, all students will be able to apply the Five Key Questions almost without thinking. . . . Practicing and mastering the Five Key Questions leads to an adult understanding of how media are created, what their purposes are, and how to accept or reject their messages. (Center for Media Literacy)

Accompanying each concept is a series of questions designed to help students better understand media producers, techniques, and messages:

- Key Concept 1 focuses on *authorship*:
  - What kind of "text" is it?
  - What are the various elements (building blocks) that make up the whole?
  - How similar or different is it to others of the same genre?
  - Which technologies are used in its creation?
  - What choices were made that might have been made differently?
  - How many people did it take to create this message?
  - What are their various jobs?
    (Source: http://www.medialit.org/pdf/mlk/02_5KQ_ClassroomGuide .pdf, p. 14)
- Key Concept 2 focuses on *format*:
  - What do you notice . . . (about the way the message is constructed)?
  - Colors? Shapes? Size?
  - Sounds, Words? Silence?
  - Props, sets, clothing?
  - Movement?
  - Composition? Lighting?
  - Where is the camera?
  - What is the viewpoint?
  - How is the story told visually?
  - What are people doing?
  - Are there any symbols?
  - Visual metaphors?
  - What's the emotional appeal? Persuasive devices used?
  - What makes it seem "real?"
    (Source: http://www.medialit.org, p. 28)
- Key Concept 3 focuses on *audience*:
  - Have you ever experienced anything like this in *your* life?
  - How close is this portrayal to your experience?
  - What did you learn from this media text?
  - What did you learn *about yourself* from experiencing the media text?
  - What did you learn from other people's response?
  - From their experience of life?
  - How many other interpretations could there be?
  - How could we hear about them?
  - Are other viewpoints just as valid as mine?
  - How can you explain the different responses?
    (Source: http://www.medialit.org/pdf/mlk/02_5KQ_ClassroomGuide .pdf, p. 42)

- Key Concept 4 focuses on *content*:
  - What kinds of behaviors/consequences are depicted?
  - What type of person is the reader/watcher/listener invited to identify with?
  - What questions come to mind as you watch/read/listen?
  - What ideas or values are being "sold" to us in this message?
  - What political ideas are communicated in the message? Economic ideas?
  - What judgments or statements are made about how we treat other people?
  - What is the overall worldview of the message?
  - What ideas or perspectives are left out? How would you find what's missing?)
    (Source: http://www.medialit.org/pdf/mlk/02_5KQ_ClassroomGuide .pdf, p. 56)
- Key Concept 5 focuses on *purpose*:
  - Who's in control of the creation and transmission of this message?
  - Why are they sending it?
  - How do you know?
  - Who are they sending it to? How do you know?
  - What's being sold in this message?
    - What's being told?
  - Who profits from this message? Who pays for it?
  - Who is served by or benefits from the message?
    - The public?
    - Private interests?
    - Individuals?
    - Institutions?
  - What economic decisions may have influenced the construction or transmission of messages? (Source: http://www.medialit.org/pdf/ mlk/02_5KQ_ClassroomGuide.pdf, p. 68)

Pedagogical Line of Questioning: Critical Thinking (Frank Baker)

Getting students to be critical thinkers (and viewers) by questioning media messages is one of the chief goals of media literacy education. Media literacy educator Frank Baker has devised the following series of critical thinking questions to encourage critical thinking:

1. Who is the producer/storyteller of the message?

2. What is their purpose/motive/agenda?
3. Who is the intended (primary) target audience?
    ◦ How do you know?
    ◦ Is there another (secondary) audience?
4. What does the message say? How does it say it?
5. How do you know what the message means?
6. What format/medium does the producer use?
7. What are the advantages of the format/medium?
8. What methods/techniques does the producer use to make the message attractive/believable?
9. What lifestyle is portrayed in the message? What clues tell you?
10. Who makes money or benefits from the message?
11. Who/what is left out of the message?
12. Whose interests are served by telling/showing the message in a particular way?
13. Do you agree with the message?
14. How might different people interpret the message differently
15. What do you know; what do you *not* know; what would you like to know?
16. Where can you go to verify the information or get more reliable information?
17. What can you do with the information you have obtained from the message? (Baker, n.d.)

Signpost Questions, Media Literacy Curriculum, Primary Grades (Cary Bazalgette)

Signpost questions provide a theoretical framework for the primary curriculum, Grades 1 through 6. This construct consists of a series of *signpost questions*, which can be applied to media texts:

* *Who is communicating, and why?* (Media Agencies)
  Who produces a text; roles in production process; media institutions; economics and ideology; intentions and results.
* *What type of text is it?* (Media Categories)
  Different media (television, radio, cinema, etc.); forms (documentary, advertising, etc.); other ways of categorizing texts; how categorization-relates to understanding.
* *How is it produced?* (Media Technologies)

What kinds of technologies are available to whom, how to use them; the differences they make to the production processes as well as the final product.

- *How do we know what it means?* (Media Languages)
  How the media produce meanings; codes and conventions; narrative structures.
- *Who receives it, and what sense do they make of it?* (Media Audiences)
  How audiences are identified, constructed, addressed, and reached; how audiences find, choose, consume, and respond to texts.
- *How does it present its subject?* (Media Representations)
  The relation between media texts and actual places, people, events, ideas; stereotyping and its consequences. (Bazalgette, 1991)

Media Literacy Triangle (Eddie Dick)

A framework for teaching media literacy, developed by Eddie Dick of the Scottish Film Council, the Media Literacy Triangle consists of the interaction of three components: *text*, *audience*, and *production*.

1. A text is any media product we wish to examine.
2. Anyone who receives a media text is a member of an audience.
3. Production refers to everything that goes into the making of a media text. (Source: The Perfect Curriculum; http://www.media-awareness.ca/english)

Parental Strategies for Media Literacy

The following techniques and strategies help parents make the most constructive use of the media with their children (Davis, Osborn, & Thoman, 1991). These principles can be employed by parents to help their children attain a critical independence from what they watch on television:

- You're smarter than your TV. Children can—and should—make sense of media messages conveyed through television.
- TV's world is not real.
  - Plots are made up.
  - Characters are actors.
  - Incidents are fabricated.
  - Settings are often constructed.
  - Programs are broadcast to make money.

- ○ Money for programs comes from advertisers purchasing airtime.
- ○ Ads are to sell products to the viewer.
- ○ Audience size determines broadcaster income.
- TV teaches us that some people are more important than others.
- TV keeps doing the same things over and over again. Consequently, it is easy for children to identify patterns with respect to stereotypes, techniques, and messages.
- Somebody is always trying to make money with TV.

Other strategies focus on techniques that teach children to establish their own television viewing patterns:

- Start early to develop good viewing habits.
- Develop planned viewing with specific programs. Talk about why you think some shows are better than others.
- Seek out programs that were made for kids your child's age. Guide your child's choices to appropriate media. You can begin to do this by offering your child a choice among several media you already prefer.
- If possible, have a TV viewing area separate from where the regular family functions occur. If not, consider covering the TV when not in use.
- Differentiate between "make believe" and real-life situations with younger children. When they see disturbing news items, explain to them that tragedies occur in real life, but that they are safe. Not talking about tragedy, or saying that "everything will be all right," can contribute to a child's anxiety.
- Don't let kids use TV as an excuse for not participating in other activities.
- Encourage your child to exercise and do hands-on activities such as folk crafts, cooking, family games, etc.
- Help kids use "alone time" for other purposes than just viewing whatever happens to be on TV.
- Use sensitive TV themes to open up discussion opportunities. These are good times to talk about your own family's beliefs and values.
- Expose deception in TV advertising.
- Discuss ads that emphasize heavy-sugar snack foods. Discourage eating in front of the television.
- Read to your child. Many of the same skills can be used to regulate computer game use, music listening, and other media at home. Wise use of media is a skill that can be fostered early on and is best set through your own example.

Finally, several approaches are designed to help children develop a critical awareness of media content:

- Compare the current episode of a favorite show with previous ones.
- Focus attention on aspects of the plot, special effects, characterization, and acting.
- Turn off the sound to see what can be deduced from the television pictures alone.
- Listen only to the sound to try to guess what the pictures might be.
- Chart the family's viewing behavior.
- Analyze how television reflects society and why it reflects certain facets of society in certain ways.
- Discuss TV industry considerations.
- Discuss the child's understanding of the *explicit content* of the media presentation. Asking a child to give a plot synopsis of the story ("what happened") provides an opportunity for adults to clarify any misconceptions, fill in gaps, and learn about the child's interests and concerns.
- Discuss the child's understanding of the implicit content of the media presentation.
- Asking children to explain *why* things occurred in the story encourages them to examine the relationship between events and the consequences of actions. Children also find it interesting and worthwhile to explore the motives of characters. ("Why do you think he behaved like that?")
- Discuss the child's *affective response* to the media presentation.
  - How did you feel during particular points of the story?
  - How did you feel about certain aspects of the program? For instance, "Did you like (a particular character)? Why?"

See also: Affective Response Analysis; Cultivation Analysis; Curriculum Developments in Higher Education; Institutional Analysis; Key Principles and Concepts, Media Literacy; Production Analysis Approach

References

Baker, B. (n.d.). Retrieved from http://www.frankwbaker.com

Bazalgette, C. (1991). "Signpost Questions." In Andrew Hart, *Understanding the Media: A Practical Guide* (pp. 32–33). London: Routledge.

Center for Media Literacy. http://www.medialit.org

Center for Media Literacy. http://www.medialit.org/reading_room/article661.html

Davis, J. F., Osborn, B., & Thoman, E. (1991). *Parenting in a TV Age*. Philadelphia: Center for Media and Values, 1991.

Dick, E. *Media Literacy Triangle*. Scottish Film Council. The Perfect Curriculum. Retrieved from http://www.media-awareness.ca/english

Masterman, L. (1985). *Teaching the Media*. London and New York: Routledge.

The Perfect Curriculum. http://www.media-awareness.ca/english/resources/educational/teaching_backgrounders/media_literacy/perfect_curriculum_1.cfm

Function

An approach to media analysis involves the identification of the function, or purpose, of a media presentation. The channels of mass communication are, in themselves, neither good nor evil. What determines whether a media message is positive or negative is its *function*, or the purpose behind sending or receiving a message.

Examples occur in the course of everyday conversations. Imagine the following:

> You are engaged in a conversation about a controversial topic—for instance, politics—with a person who subscribes to a different political philosophy (i.e., you are a liberal, he is a conservative). You work on the assumption that the function of the conversation is information exchange. But as the discussion progresses, it becomes evident that the other person is not listening to what you have to say but instead wants to convince you that his position is correct. In this case, while you are engaged in *information exchange*, the function of the other party is *persuasion*. Once you have identified this disparity in function, you are in a position to decide whether to continue participating in the conversation.

In the analysis of media presentations, identifying the communications function is equally crucial in determining the motive of the media communicator and deciding how to interpret media content.

A communication activity may be motivated by many *functions*, or purposes:

- *Information.* The channels of mass communication are invaluable conduits of information. Young people have become remarkably proficient at conducting online research. Cell phones have become portable libraries, giving us more access to information than scholars had in years past.
- *Expression* occurs as people inform their audience of their frame of mind—what they are thinking at that moment, how they are feeling, or

their attitudes toward people and issues. In the world of mass communications, the extemporaneous nature of this function can be the cause of many difficulties. For instance, occasionally politicians and other public figures are be "caught" expressing thoughts and feelings that are not part of their planned remarks, to their embarrassment.

- *Description* refers to occasions in which a communicator elaborates on general statements or provides concrete examples.
- *Instruction* occurs when the purpose of the communication is either to inform someone about a subject with which he or she is unfamiliar or to furnish additional information about a subject with which the audience is already acquainted.
- *Entertainment* diverts individuals from the more serious and pressing matters of the day. Jokes, stories, and gossip are mechanisms that break down traditional social barriers.
- *Creative expression.* Novelists, painters, or experimental videographers express themselves through their art and share their artistic visions with their audience.
- *Persuasion* is a term that can be applied to occasions in which the media communicator's objective is to promote a particular idea or motivate the intended audience to action. Persuasion often occurs in an informal setting in which an individual wants to convert another person to his or her point of view. However, a more organized and systematic category of persuasion is *propaganda*. Propaganda refers to the strategic development and dissemination of information, which is designed to influence public opinion to promote the policies of a particular country, organization, or group.

  However, propaganda is a subjective term. Although propaganda has a negative connotation, it can also promote national interests, pave the way for diplomatic initiatives, and encourage trade, tourism, and investment. In addition, public service announcements that promote drug prevention or tobacco use can also be regarded as a form of propaganda.

  Moreover, organized religions that are involved in missionary activities believe that they are offering a service in the name of salvation, but outsiders might consider their efforts to be a propaganda campaign.

- *Agenda setting.* This function refers to creating awareness of issues through media coverage. Even if the media do not tell the public what to think, they do tell the public what to think *about*. The major factors responsible for the agenda-setting function include (a) perceived credibility of media, (b) reliance on media for information, and (c) exposure to media messages.

The agenda-setting power of the media extends to the following:

- Who is given coverage (and when)
- What issues are covered (or omitted)
- What priorities are given to certain issues in the media
- Which issues are covered on a sustained basis

To illustrate, in 2011, after the Occupy protests began, the use of the words *income inequality* in the news media had *quintupled* (Kristof, 2011). As a columnist who expresses opinion, Nicholas Kristoff (2011) welcomed the upsurge of this concept in the news, acknowledging the agenda-setting function of the media:

> The solution to these inequities and injustices is not so much setting up tents at bits of real estate here or there, but a relentless focus on the costs of inequality. So as we move into an election year, I'm hoping that the movement will continue to morph into: Occupy the Agenda.

Another example is autism, a disorder that has been featured in several Hollywood films, including *Rainman* (1988), *Snow Cake* (2006), *Mozart and the Whale* (2005), and *After Thomas* (2006). In *Rainman*, Raymond Babbett (Dustin Hoffman) is a character whose autism makes the character seem a bit offbeat and engaging. As a result, the audience becomes more sympathetic to the character and the issue.

These films are initiation stories, in which other characters learn to respect and appreciate the autistic character as they learn about the disorder. In the course of the narrative, the audience assumes the role of the protagonist's community, becoming advocates of the autistic character as well.

In addition, the autistic characters serve as metaphors for universal aspects of human nature. Film critic Caryn James observes that in the film *Snow Cake*, Linda (Sigourney Weaver) is a symbol of unfiltered emotional honesty: "Alex (Alan Rickman) tells Linda, 'You are the only person I have ever met I don't have to explain or even justify myself to.' They are two damaged people who find each other" (James, 2007).

Autistic characters also serve as a metaphor for the unconnectedness of human relationships. James (2007) explains,

> Autism as a metaphor for the difficulty of human connections is especially prevalent in films about people who are considered highly functioning, like Ms. Weaver's character, Linda, in *Snow Cake*.

Autism is a disorder that had rarely been mentioned in the media before *Rainman*. However, this increased media attention conveys the cumulative message that autism is not a medical condition to be ashamed of.

In some cases, the agenda-setting function of the media can manufacture a crisis. To illustrate, three incidents of attacks by sharks occurred over the summer of 2001. As horrific as these events were, the saturation of media coverage created the impression that shark attacks were an imminent and dangerous threat. Actually, statistics from the International Shark Attack File of the Florida Museum of Natural History, based at the University of Florida, indicate that the chances of getting bitten by a shark were less than those of being hit by lightning, injured with a power tool, or bitten by an alligator (Page, 2001). Columnist Clarence Page observed, "Nevertheless, we do have something to fear: our tendency to act out of emotion in the absence of facts."

- *Status Conferral.* The mass media have the ability to legitimize ideas, people, or events. Thus, in the contemporary American political system, the first objective of media consultants is to bring their candidates to the attention of the media, so that the public will consider him or her as a serious candidate.
- *Socialization* is the process of preparing individuals to become a member of society. The media are primary sources of modeling, providing role models for their target audience. Author Mark Bennett (Daley, 2000) advises people to look closely at the way that TV characters handle their problems:

  > Anything you want to do, you can use TV as a tool to get there. I think there's nothing better than being able to jump into a favorite character in a real-life situation that might not be so great. It can save you from a bad scene. . . . It works wonders at social functions I can't get out of.

In addition, media programming provides guidelines by which people learn about societal rules and expectations. For instance, the term *tween* refers to a new stage of life that characterizes boys and girls between the ages of 9 and 14. In the 20th century, adolescence emerged as social class that was regarded as a preparation for adulthood. In like fashion, tweens appeared near the beginning of the 21st century and is seen as a preparation for adolescence. Television programs directed at tweens that appear on Nickelodeon and the Disney Channel regulate conduct by dramatizing appropriate and inappropriate behavior.

- *Escape.* The experience of consuming media is a ritual that transcends specific programs. Popular genres permit individuals to explore in fantasy the boundaries between the permitted and the forbidden and to experience in a carefully controlled way the possibility of stepping across this boundary. Watching a gangster program like *The Sopranos* (HBO) enables the viewer to vicariously experience thrills associated with living outside the law without suffering the consequences.

- *Therapeutic Function.* Popular media presentations serve as vehicles through which individuals are able to put their own lives into perspective. In the face of social upheaval, audiences often turn to the media for their predictability. To illustrate, in the aftermath of 9/11, the audience for situation comedies increased over the previous year, in part because the familiarity of the genre provided a degree of comfort to the audience. The media can also provide a safe way for people to cope with uncertainties in their own lives.

- *Fostering Community.* The media provide shared cultural experiences. For example, through social media, individuals have become members of communities centered around common interests and experiences. Indeed, virtual matchmaking sites like eHarmony.com even provide venues for romantic relationships, relying on database profiling systems to identify potential mates.

- *Profit.* In the U.S. market-driven media industry, profit is a major function. This economic imperative has an influence on the content of media programming. To illustrate, during the 1950s, it was expected that the news division of local television stations would *lose* money. The owners thought of news programming as a "lost leader" that fulfilled the networks' mandate as a public service. The TV executives counted on its entertainment programming to make up for the revenue lost by the news division. By the 1970s, the news was considered a "break even" proposition. That is, although they did not require the news division to generate a profit, they didn't expect news programming to lose money either. But today, news divisions are counted on as primary sources of revenue. Indeed, the only original programming produced by local affiliates are the local news and promos for the local news.

Thus, it can be worthwhile to consider *why* a particular topic is being promoted by the media. Possibilities include the following:

- The media communicator may regard the topic to be of cultural significance.

- The topic may reflect a particular agenda or point of view of the media communicator.
- The subject may easily attract a large audience, thus boosting ratings.
- The type of story may lend itself to the medium. For instance, a natural catastrophe such as an earthquake or tsunami is a dramatic event that is covered well by television news.
- The context; is it a "slow news day"?

Manifest and Latent Functions

The *manifest*, or surface function, behind the communication offers the obvious or primary reason behind the media presentation. To complicate matters, a media presentation may also contain a *latent* function (or functions)—instances in which the digital media communicator's intention may not be immediately obvious to the audience.

The manifest (or surface) function is often subordinate to other latent purposes. As an example, the 1955 animated version of George Orwell's *Animal Farm* was markedly different from the original novel. Journalist Laurence Zuckerman explains,

> Many people remember reading George Orwell's *Animal Farm* in high school or college, with its chilling finale in which the farm animals looked back and forth at the tyrannical pigs and the exploitative human farmers but found it impossible to say which was which.
>
> That ending was altered in the 1955 animated version, which removed the humans, leaving only the nasty pigs.
>
> Another example of Hollywood butchering great literature? Yes, but in this case the film's secret producer was the Central Intelligence Agency.
>
> The CIA, it seems, was worried that the public might be too influenced by Orwell's pox-on-both-their-house critique of the capitalist humans and Communist pigs. So after his death in 1950, agents were dispatched (by none other than E. Howard Hunt, later of Watergate fame) to buy the film rights to *Animal Farm* from his widow to make its message more overtly anti-Communist. (Zuckerman, 2000)

Thus, while the manifest function of the film was *entertainment*, the latent function was *persuasion*.

Regardless of the manifest function of a media presentation (e.g., entertainment or information), *profit* has emerged as a significant latent function.

To illustrate, Web sites directed at kids typically include games, with the chance to win free "stuff." However, the contest forms that they fill out are actually marketing surveys that furnish advertising people with invaluable data they can use later, as the kids grow up. Furthermore, marketing companies often sell this information to other companies who want access to this invaluable marketing data. Thus, while the manifest function of a children's game on the Internet may be to entertain or educate, children may be unaware that its underlying purpose is to generate product sales.

In like fashion, video games for adults that appear on iPhones are latent advertisements. Jenna Wortham (2009) explains,

> The iPhone has proved lucrative for some developers. Now, advertising networks are cashing in on the platform. Greystripe, a mobile advertising start-up, takes a different approach to advertising on the iPhone. Rather than simply layer a banner ad across the bottom or top of an application, the company creates advertisements that look like games. For example, one ad for the car company Kia pits players against a ram in a boxing ring. Another ad lets users pop heart-shaped bubbles floating out of a tub in which the Burger King character, the King, is soaking.

Celebrities who dispense advice in the media are often being compensated for their services, unbeknownst to the audience. Reporter Melody Peterson (2002) provides the following example:

> In a rare interview, Lauren Bacall appeared on the NBC "Today" program in March, telling Matt Lauer about a good friend who had gone blind from an eye disease and urging the audience to see their doctors to be tested for it.
>
> "It's just—it's frightening because it—it can happen very suddenly," she said. Ms. Bacall then mentioned a drug called Visudyne, a new treatment for the disease known as macular degeneration. She never revealed that she was being paid to tell the story, and neither did the network, NBC.

The process of identifying communications functions can be complicated by a number of other factors related to function.

Multiple function refers to a communications exchange that serves more than one purpose at a time. For instance, Population Communications International (PCI), a New York-based nonprofit group, focuses on

"Entertainment-Education and social change communications," incorporating social messages into popular genres. PCI explains its approach as follows:

> Media Impact's unique approach to communications combines the principles of Entertainment-Education with the reach of mass media to mobilize individual, community and political action and catalyze positive change. Our programs primarily focus on promoting sexual and reproductive health, prevention of HIV/AIDS, biodiversity conservation, sustainable development, human rights and democracy.
>
> Entertainment-Education (E-E), sometimes called Edutainment, is the process of purposely designing and implementing a media message both to entertain and educate, in order to increase audience members' knowledge about an educational issue, create favorable attitudes, and change overt behavior. By inserting critical information into entertaining media, producers are able to capture the audience's attention and role model desired behavior changes through their favorite characters. Over the course of the series, the audience forms emotional ties to the characters. It's this emotional bond that helps shift individual and collective values and behaviors—the audience learns from the successes and failures of the characters, which are designed to represent them. (http://mediaimpact.org)

Undefined function. On occasion, the media communicator does not have a clear intention in mind. This lack of definition can result in a muddled, directionless presentation. As an example, the release of the western film *Cowboys and Aliens* (2011) was greeted with considerable mirth rather than the exhilarated reaction that director Jon Favreau was going for—a result of confusion on the part of the audience whether the film was supposed to be a comedy or adventure. Journalist Michael Cieply (2010) reports on a preview exhibition of the film:

> Harrison Ford glowered. Daniel Craig glared.
>
> But the crowd at a midnight movie in Santa Monica . . . rocked with laughter as it took in the new theatrical trailer for the potential blockbuster *Cowboys and Aliens* from Universal Pictures and DreamWorks.
>
> Oops. . . .
>
> Mr. Favreau has joined the studio in a campaign to change expectations around the film. By the time the film . . . opens next July, the studio

expects advertising and future promotions to have persuaded almost everyone that Mr. Favreau's movie is a tough-minded adventure on the order of Clint Eastwood's *Unforgiven*—with aliens.

Thus, function focuses on the following questions for critical analysis of media presentations:

- What is the purpose behind the production?
- Does the media communicator want you to think or behave in a particular way as a result of receiving the information?
- Does the production contain any of the following?
  ○ Latent functions
  ○ Multiple functions
  ○ Undefined functions

See also: Advertising—Media Literacy Analysis; Digital Media Literacy; Journalism; Memetic Approach, Media Analysis; Political Communications, American

References

Cieply, M. (2010, November 29). "Question for Big Film: It's Not a Comedy?" *New York Times*. Retrieved from http://www.nytimes.com/2010/11/30/movies/30cowboys.html

Daley, D. (2000, January 5). "Author's Advice: Don't Let Life on TV Become Yours." *The Hartford Courant*, Page C.

James, C. (2007, April 29). "Hollywood Finds Its Disorder Du Jour," *New York Times*. Retrieved from http://www.nytimes.com/2007/04/29/movies/29jame.html?pagewanted=all

Kristof, N. D. (2011, November 19). "Occupy the Agenda." *New York Times*. Retrieved from http://www.nytimes.com/2011/11/20/opinion/sunday/kristof-occupy-the-agenda.html?_r=0

Page, C. (2011, September 9). "Is the Frenzy Over Sharks Justified?" *The Chicago Tribune*. Retrieved from http://articles.chicagotribune.com/2001-09-09/news/0109090229_1_shark-attacks-george-h-burgess-shark-bit

Peterson, M. (2002, August 11). "Heartfelt Advice, Hefty Fees." *New York Times*. Retrieved from http://www.nytimes.com/2002/08/11/business/heartfelt-advice-hefty-fees.html?pagewanted=all&src=pm

Wortham, J. (2009, September 7). "Placing Ads on iPhones." *New York Times*. Retrieved from http://query.nytimes.com/gst/fullpage.html?res=990CE3D81E3AF934A3575AC0A96F9C8B63.

Zuckerman, L. (2000, March 18). "How the C.I.A. Played Dirty Tricks with Culture." *New York Times*. Retrieved from http://www.nytimes.com/2000/03/18/books/how-the-cia-played-dirty-tricks-with-culture.html?pagewanted=all&src=pm

Genre Study, Media Literacy Approach

One of the established content areas in the field of media communications curriculum, which can be approached from a media literacy perspective, is the genre study. The word *genre* simply means "order." As applied to artistic works, a genre is a type, class, or category of presentation that shares distinctive and easily identifiable features. Examples of genres include romances, science fiction, situation comedies, and news programming.

A genre can be identified by its own distinctive patterns in premise, plot, structure, character, worldview, style, formula, and conventions. Because of these characteristic elements, *genric programs* (that is, programs that belong to a particular genre) can be discussed as a discrete body of work. Brian G. Rose (1985) explains, "The term genre implies that these groups of formal or technical characteristics exist among works of the same kind, regardless of time or place of composition, author, or subject matter."

Genres may act as agents of socialization, providing guideposts by which people learn about societal rules and expectations. For example, the media can serve as a primary source of the socialization for tweens, the young demographic between the ages of 9 and 14. Thus, sitcoms directed at tweens can be found on the Disney Channel, instructing the target audience how to be "cool."

Popular genres are also used to convey political and social messages. For instance, in 2005, two miniseries were produced on Arab television stations and broadcast throughout the Arab region, which were timed to coincide with the Ramadan, a period in which families gathered nightly to break their fast—and watch TV. The function of each series was to focus attention on the damage of extremism to the Arab world.

In addition, genres have emerged as a primary vehicle for informing the public about social issues. A joint report by the United Nations program on AIDS and the World Health Organization (2002) concluded that soap operas aimed at AIDS prevention appeared to be making a difference across the globe (Sawyer, 2002).

Lines of Inquiry

A media literacy approach to genre studies provides students with a number of theoretical "lenses" through which they can conduct primary research into the analysis of genre and genric content. Media literacy also enables students to apply these methodologies to areas not generally thought of as genres, such as political cartoons, radio talk shows, and Facebook entries.

Genre analysis offers the following lines of inquiry for the analysis of media content:

Function

Critical analysis of *function*, or purpose for creating and receiving media presentations, focuses on the following questions:

- Why do media communicators produce particular genres?
- What accounts for the ongoing popularity of particular genres?
- What can we learn about a genre by identifying its functions?
- What purposes are served by watching a genre such as a horror film or a reality show?

A genre generally shares a common *manifest function*. Manifest function refers to a clear purpose behind the production or consumption of genric programming. As an example, in news programming (e.g., newspaper articles, news magazine shows, or Sunday-morning interview programs), the clear purpose is to inform the public. But at the same time, a genre may also fulfill a number of *latent functions*. Latent functions are secondary purposes that may not be immediately obvious to the audience. In some cases, the manifest function of a genre is subordinate to its latent purposes. For instance, Web sites directed at kids typically include games, with the chance to win free "stuff." However, the contest forms that they fill out are actually marketing surveys, in which the marketing department is beginning to collect a database of information on these future consumers.

Affective Response

Popular genres correspond to our primal emotions. Comedies make us laugh. Romances make us cry. Action/adventure programs tap into our feelings of anger. And horror genres tap into those dark aspects of life that are fundamentally terrifying to human beings.

Genres provide a controlled environment that enable individuals to confront these elemental emotions in relative safety. By knowing that the danger isn't real, the audience can take the experience of fear to new levels of imagination and enjoyment.

Moreover, genres can provide a safe way for people to confront uncertainties in their own lives. For instance, in the horror genre, the monsters symbolize those dangerous elements within human experience that comprise the underside of life. Moreover, the resolution of the genre, in which the monsters are vanquished, furnishes a ritual by which individuals resolve their own internal conflicts. Of course, taken as a whole, horror films convey the cumulative message that there are always new forms of the same old demons to take their place.

Popular genres permit individuals to explore in fantasy the boundaries between the permitted and the forbidden and to experience in a carefully controlled way the possibility of stepping across this boundary. Thus, watching a gangster program like *The Sopranos* (HBO) enables the viewer to vicariously experience thrills associated with living outside the law without suffering the consequences.

Indeed, the emotional release that accompanies these affective experiences can even provide physical benefits. According to psychologist Jack Vaeth, watching a horror film "releases chemicals including adrenaline and endorphins into your blood, which are similar to opiates. So what we are doing is stimulating ourselves to a point of chemical release which in turn is rewarding to our bodies" (Selby, 2000).

Moreover, a genre can fulfill a cathartic function, giving expression to the destructive feelings that exist in members of the audience—what author D. H. Lawrence called *creative dissolution*. For example, although it is fun for young children to build something with blocks, it can be even more fun to knock down what they've built.

Genres frequently play on the affective responses of the audience to build dramatic tension. For instance, horror films like *The Exorcist* (1973) play on the primal fears of the audience to enhance the terror onscreen.

In addition, genres offer individuals an opportunity to break through their personal isolation. Talk shows like *Dr. Phil* provide a public arena for what formerly were "private" problems, such as spousal abuse and alcoholism.

Formulaic Analysis

Every genre is characterized by its own distinctive formulaic elements— that is, patterns in *premise*, *structure*, *characters*, *plot*, and *conventions*. The success of a genre largely depends on the audience's ability to recognize, identify, and respond to the formula of a genre. Thus, formula is tied to the audience's expectations: what they anticipate when they attend a horror movie or romantic comedy.

As an example, identifying *conventions* provides important tools for deciphering media messages. A convention is a practice or object that appears so often in a genre that it has become standard. Conventions furnish cues about people, events, and situations in a genre. To illustrate, consider the following scenario:

> *A tall, rangy fellow enters a public gathering place. He is wearing a Stetson hat, blue jeans, and cowboy boots. His hat and shirt are white. A six-gun is strapped around his waist. His name is "Tex."*
>
> *The entrance to the building is distinguished by a set of swinging doors. Once he is inside, Tex can hear a lively cowboy song being played on the piano. A long bar extends from one side of the room to the other. People dressed like Tex line the bar, drinking whisky from shot glasses or tall glasses of beer.*
>
> *At several tables, card games are going on. Young women, dressed provocatively, are stationed by the players. At one of the tables, a gentleman sits behind a large stack of chips; he appears to be the big winner. He is wearing a three-piece suit. He has dark hair, slicked back, and is sporting a moustache.*

The conventions clearly designate this program as a western. The saloon (complete with swinging doors, bar, and dance-hall girls) is a conventional setting. The props and costumes are trappings that provide clues about the characters. Heroes in westerns are identifiable by their white hats; conversely, villains wear black. Trappings furnish also cues about people and situations. The gent in the dark suit is a gambler (and is probably dishonest). This moment in the plot represents the first confrontation between good and evil, as represented by Tex and the gambler.

The formulaic line of inquiry focuses on the following areas of analysis:

- Identifying the formulaic elements that are characteristic of a genre.
  - Premise
  - Structure
  - Characters
  - Plot

- ° Conventions
- Examining the messages conveyed by this formulaic configuration.
- Examining a body of programs belonging to the same genre, focusing on variations that occur *within* the formula.
  - ° Identify the variations that occur.
  - ° What is the significance of these variations with respect to themes, worldview, and messages in the program?
- Comparing the formulaic patterns in different genres.
- Identifying similarities in dissimilar genric programming.
- Examining ways in which different cultures make use of the same basic formula.
- Tracing the evolution of a particular formula over a substantial period of time as a reflection of cultural changes.

See also: Formulaic Analysis; Integrated Approach to Media Literacy Education; Narratology

References

O'Brien, S. J. (YEAR, February 27). "The Joy of Destruction," *New York Times*. Retrieved from http://www.nytimes.com

Rose, B. G., ed. (1985). *TV Genres: A Handbook and Reference Guide*. Westport, CT: Greenwood Press.

Sawyer, J. (2002, December 1). "Soap Operas Are Proving Helpful in Informing Public." *St. Louis Post-Dispatch*. Retrieved from http://www.stltoday.com

Selby, H. (2000, September 15). "Eeek! Why People Love to Be Scared (but Not Too Scared) by Films." *Baltimore Sun*. Retrieved from http://www.nytimes.com.

Timberg, B. (1976). "The Rhetoric of the Camera in Television Soap Opera." In Horace Newcomb (Ed.), *Television: The Critical View*. New York: Oxford University Press.

Hierarchy of Appearance

In the United States, popular media programming operates according to a hierarchy of appearance, reflecting Western cultural attitudes toward physical beauty. Attractive people are considered socially desirable, credible, and persuasive. Indeed, attractive people consistently receive preferential treatment from others. A 2005 analysis found that on the job, attractive people and tall people get an extra 5 percent an hour "beauty premium," whereas there is a "plainness penalty" of 9 percent in wages. Another study found that males made $789 more a year for every extra inch of height (Dowd, 2010).

Not only do we admire attractive people, we also identify with them and sympathize with their situations. Thus, even though film stars represent unapproachable ideals of beauty, audience members enjoy projecting themselves into their roles and situations.

In popular media programming, characters often are defined by their appearance. Heroes and heroines are physically attractive, whereas villains often are physically displeasing in some way. Thus, ugliness is equated with evil. This practice can lead to falsely labeling an attractive person as "good" and an unattractive person as "bad." Of course, beautiful but "bitchy" female characters have become a staple of genres such as reality television. This reflects some shifts within the culture because audiences find these characters to be admirable on some level.

Physical beauty also is presented as emblematic of virtue. Thus, heroic characters are attractive because, on some level, they *deserve* it. Handsome heroes assume control of their lives and prevail over the villains—the inference being that these characters are "in the right" precisely *because* they are attractive. The heroes often are called on to protect others—usually an attractive female. The implication is that only beautiful women are worth protecting.

On the other hand, one way we know that supporting characters are not as important as the stars is because they are not as attractive. In romantic comedies, attractive characters are engaged in a quest to find equally gorgeous partners. By extension, unattractive characters are suited only for each other. Comedy (or, worse, tragedy) occurs when people try to seek matches outside of their particular station. The cumulative media message is "know your place" when it comes to appearance.

The hierarchy of appearance is also evident in advertising. Alluring models are typically the center of attention, as ordinary people stare enviously at them (ostensibly because of their appearance, but by implication, because of the product). These ads promote their products as a modern form of alchemy, in which base metals are transformed into gold. In this version, ordinary folks are transformed into the glamorous models—simply by using their products. However, a careful consideration of the ad can uncover this illogical premise.

See also: Nonverbal Approach to Media Analysis

Reference

Dowd, M. (2010, June 5). "Dressed to Distract." *New York Times.* Retrieved from http://www.nytimes.com/2010/06/06/opinion/06dowd.html

Historical Analysis, Media: Systems Approach

A systems approach to the history of media is designed to place events within a broader context, focusing on patterns of development. Details such as names and dates acquire meaning, in terms of how they fit into these developmental patterns. Recognizing patterns that have emerged makes it easier to understand present conditions and anticipate future developments.

Biological Systems

The systems approach to media history uses the analogy of biological principles. Biologists regard living creatures as systems composed of smaller *interrelated* and *interdependent* systems. For example, the cells of the human body have a life of their own, but they also interact to make up larger units, such as the digestive, reproductive, and respiratory systems. Each of these systems depends on the others for selected, specialized functions; the respiratory system, for example, cannot serve the functions of the digestive system. These systems, in turn, are parts of a still larger system—the human body.

In like fashion, the mass media is a complex "system" in which each medium is made up of interrelated and interdependent subsystems. For example, a newspaper is made up of a number of departments, such as the publisher, editorial department, news desk, features, and the advertising division. Each "subsystem" of the newspaper plays a distinct role in the publication of the paper. For instance, the advertising department determines how many news stories can be carried in a particular edition. But at the same time, these departments are interdependent. As an example, it is not uncommon for articles to be "cut" to accommodate the insertion of a last-minute advertisement. Moreover, an ongoing ethical dilemma facing newspaper editors involves how they should treat stories involving prominent clients, on whom the paper depends for advertising revenue.

At the same time, each medium (e.g., film, radio, or the Internet) is part of a larger system, commonly referred to as "the media." As is the case in biological systems, these media are also interrelated and interdependent.

Conglomerates frequently own different media (e.g., newspapers and television stations), so that they share ownership philosophies and resources. For instance, News Corp owns television stations, newspapers, book publishing companies, and Internet sites. Through cross-promotion, programs serve to publicize the programming of other holdings.

In addition, media systems frequently rely on one another as sources of information and programming. For example, nearly three-quarters of all radio stations rely on local newspapers as a primary source of news (Needham, Harper & Steers Advertising).

Media subsystems may also have an overlapping influence on *style*. For instance, print journalism had a profound influence on the literary style of twentieth-century authors such as Ernest Hemmingway. More recently, the medium of film has had an impact on modern literature; current novels are written in a visual, plot-oriented style, which can easily be adapted into film and television scripts.

Finally, "the media" is part of a network of interrelated social institutions that include church, schools, government, and family. Significantly, when Michel Gorbachev initiated social reforms in the Soviet Union in 1987, he began by opening up the media system (under a policy known as *glasnost*). This change led to restructuring the political and economic systems as well.

Principles of Evolution

Evolution refers to patterns by which all species develop from earlier forms of life. According to scientists, life forms began as simple organisms. To adapt to new circumstances and environments, these organisms became more complex. Those life forms that were unable to adapt, like the dinosaur, became extinct.

Natural selection is a related biological principle. During the process of evolution, the best features of an organism are retained and the unnecessary elements are eliminated. To illustrate, the appendix is an organ that has no current physiological function in humans. Scientists believe that at one time, this organ probably aided in cellulose digestion. In other animals, the appendix is much larger and provides a pouch off the main intestinal tract, in which cellulose can be trapped and be subjected to prolonged digestion. Dr. Mabel Rodrigues (2005) speculates that the appendix will gradually disappear in human beings, as our diet no longer includes cellulose.

Just as simple organisms developed, adapted, and became more complex to thrive in new circumstances and environments, media systems (i.e., print, photography, film, radio, television, and the Internet) follow a readily identifiable and distinct pattern of *evolution* that proceeds as follows.

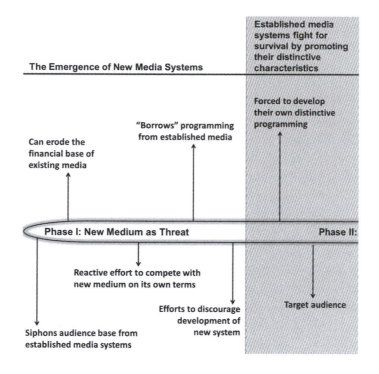

The Emergence of New Media Systems

Established media systems fight for survival by promoting their distinctive characteristics

Forced to develop their own distinctive programming

"Borrows" programming from established media

Can erode the financial base of existing media

Phase I: New Medium as Threat   Phase II:

Reactive effort to compete with new medium on its own terms

Efforts to discourage development of new system

Target audience

Siphons audience base from established media systems

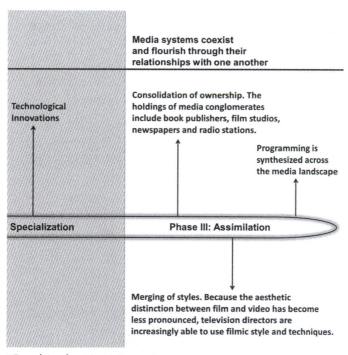

Media systems coexist and flourish through their relationships with one another

Technological Innovations

Consolidation of ownership. The holdings of media conglomerates include book publishers, film studios, newspapers and radio stations.

Programming is synthesized across the media landscape

Specialization   Phase III: Assimilation

Merging of styles. Because the aesthetic distinction between film and video has become less pronounced, television directors are increasingly able to use filmic style and techniques.

(Graphics by Lisa Marcus)

I. The Inception Stage

This initial stage of development consists of the time frame surrounding the invention of the medium. This stage is generally *decentralized*, as individual inventors conduct research independently, in relative isolation. In some cases, several individuals may work on the same invention simultaneously, so that numerous people may be credited for the invention of a particular medium. To illustrate, three men were working on the invention of the television at the same time. In 1923, Russian Vladimir Zworkin invented the inconoscope (camera tube), followed by the kinescope receiving unit in 1926. In 1925, John Logie Baird, a Scottish inventor, achieved the world's first real television picture in his laboratory, which used spinning disks to scan pictures. In 1927, Philo Farnsworth, an American, produced the first all-electronic television picture and on September 7, 1927, transmitted the first electronic television image. During this stage of development, the inventors of these media systems were consumed with the scientific possibilities of their projects, never imagining the commercial implications of their work.

Historical events often play a role in the early stages of media systems. World War I greatly accelerated the growth of the radio industry, as the armed forces began to rely on the communications capability of this medium. By the war's end, more than 100,000 people had been trained as radio engineers.

In contrast, the emergence of television as a popular medium was actually delayed by World War II, while resources were committed to the war effort. Between 1948 and 1952, the American Federal Communications Commission (FCC) imposed a freeze on all new applications for TV stations and the number of station licenses awarded, in order to give themselves time to develop technical standards and procedures for the use of the airwaves.

The invention of the Internet was an outcome of the Cold War. After the Soviet Union's 1957 launch of Sputnik, the first manmade satellite to orbit Earth, the U.S. Defense Department's Advance Research Projects Agency was formed. This agency provided money and computers so that U.S. scientists could compete with their Cold War adversaries. By the mid-1960s, the U.S. Defense Department became concerned about the vulnerability of its defense system. If a targeted area was decimated by a nuclear warhead, all of the defense information at that site would disappear. As a result, the *Arpanet* project (from which the Internet eventually evolved) was created to allow rapid, electronic distribution of defense information.

During the inception stage, the programming is generally designed to demonstrate the capabilities of the medium. For instance, the early films of pioneer filmmakers Auguste and Louis Lumière in the early 20th century were simply celebrations of movement. The title of one film was *Train Coming into Station*; another showed workers leaving the Lumière Factory.

II. The Embryonic Stage

As the commercial potential of a young medium becomes apparent, corporations agree to sponsor the research of these individual inventors and hobbyists. For instance, in 1920, Frank Conrad, an amateur radio operator and engineer for Westinghouse Electric, began broadcasting programs from his garage on amateur station 8XK in Wilkinsburg, Pennsylvania. The broadcasts generated such interest that Westinghouse built KDKA, the first broadcasting station.

Attempts to develop a media system into a profitable industry often evolve into a race between corporations, often becoming an object of dramatic patent wars and monopoly litigation. For instance, in 1919, Radio Corporation of America (RCA) was formed to head off the dominance of the British-dominated Marconi Company.

As television moved into its embryonic stage, RCA wanted to extend its radio monopoly to the new technology. Consequently, the corporation connived to wrest control from inventor Philo Farnsworth. Even though the U.S. Patent Office eventually determined that Farnsworth was the true inventor of electronic television, the massive RCA publicity machine ensured that Sarnoff would receive credit for bringing television to the world. That PR campaign peaked with a much-ballyhooed demonstration of a TV at the 1939 World's Fair. By 1932, NBC installed a television station in the newly built Empire State Building, and Zworykin was employed as director of RCA's electronic research laboratory.

During the embryonic stage, the media hardware (i.e., radio receivers, television sets, computers) was extremely expensive to manufacture and, as a result, nearly prohibitive in cost for the average consumer. For instance, in the early 1950s, television sets sold for more than $1,000; factoring in inflation, this was the equivalent of approximately $8,400 in 2008. In like fashion, in 1985, the first color LCD home computers cost approximately $3,000, which amounted to $5,657 in 2008 (U.S. Department of Labor, 2012).

As a result, media programming at the embryonic stage usually targets the interests and tastes of members of elite culture. To illustrate from a historical example, after Johann Gutenberg invented moveable type (the foundation of the printing press) in 1454, the first printed documents were religious texts and government papers. These materials were directed toward members of the clergy and ruling privileged class. Both audiences were literate, so they could read the materials and were affluent enough to afford to buy these documents, which were expensive to produce. In like fashion, the first commercial radio stations played opera for its rich patrons.

At the same time, the embryonic stage is characterized by experimentation in the style, structure, and content of programming, as the media communicators learn about the possibilities of the medium. Before the formulaic conventions of genres have been established, early work is characterized by innovations that are only seen again after the medium has been well established and the conventions have been thoroughly explored by media communicators. For instance, early filmmaker George Melies experimented with special effects in his work, including stop-action animation. In television, Ernie Kovaks was a comic genius who began experimenting with the medium in the 1940s, before the conventions of television had been established. Kovaks concocted elaborate gags involving camera angles, lenses, music, live audiences, and immediate transmission.

In many instances, media communicators were forced to find creative ways to work within the economic and technological limitations of the medium. Jeff Kisseloff (1998) explains,

> Because no spare parts were available, Arch Brolly used a pickle jar to complete his transmitter and keep WBKB, Chicago's most important station, on the air during World War II. When Brolly's boss, the redoubtable Captain Bill Eddy, needed a camera base that could be raised and lowered, he created one from a barber chair. . . .
>
> When the producers of "Captain Video" needed a ray gun, Charles Polachek, the director, grabbed a spark plug, muffler, rearview mirror and ashtray from the automotive department, glued them together himself and called it the "opticom scillometer."

III. The Popular Stage

During the popular stage, the medium is incorporated into mainstream culture. For example, with the development of the "dry plate" (purchased and ready to use), photography emerged as a popular medium at the beginning of the 20th century, with people taking personal "snapshots." Radio's "golden age" was the decade of the 1930s. In 1930, almost 50 percent of American households had radios. But by 1940, 90 percent of American homes had radios (Gamble & Gamble, 1986).

Moreover, during the popular stage, the media equipment becomes more affordable, in part because mass production reduces the "per unit" cost. In addition, industry executives discover that the greatest source of revenue isn't the "hardware" (the media equipment) but the media "software." To illustrate, during the 1930s, radio companies found that the greatest source of profit was not the radio receiver but the revenue generated by the advertising. Consequently, it behooved the radio companies to lower the cost of the radio set to put a set in every consumer's hands. Indeed, during the Depression, advertising companies sponsored contests as promotions, in which the prizes were radio receivers—a shrewd strategy designed to put more radios in the hands of consumers.

Similarly, the cost of a home computer has steadily dropped, from approximately $2,000 in the 1990s. In 2006, the nonprofit project, One Laptop Per Child announced plans to produce laptops for worldwide distribution at a cost of $150. This type of drastic cost reduction creates a large and profitable market for computer software, as well as goods advertised over the Internet.

During the popularization stage, the various industries pursue a *broadcasting* strategy, in which they strive to appeal to a mass audience. Thus, to ensure a profit, programming is developed that will appeal to the interests and tastes of the majority of the public.

For instance, in the early 1950s, not everyone had a TV set yet, and those who did generally had one set for the entire family, which was stationed in the "TV room." Thus, variety programs such as the *Ed Sullivan Show* flourished during the 1950s. In the course of one hour, the *Ed Sullivan Show* routinely featured puppet shows, comedians, opera singers, and rock stars.

At this stage, the formula of a genre is established. Formula refers to patterns in *premise*, *structure*, *characters*, *plot*, and *trappings*. To illustrate, the evening talk show genre hit its stride with *The Tonight Show, Starring Johnny Carson*, which dominated the genre for 30 years (1962–1992). During Carson's tenure, the basic structure of each program was established:

- First, Carson presented a monologue.
- Carson then moved over to the primary set, consisting of a desk, which the host sat behind, and a sofa for the announcer and guests.
- The pecking order of the guests was also established in order of celebrity. The most renowned guest would appear first, whereas the end of the show was relegated to relative unknowns, such as young comics or authors.

IV. Mature Stage

In this final stage of development, media companies are acquired by large conglomerates. These mega-companies regard media presentations as "products" that generate cash flow for the parent company.

At this stage, media markets have become so large that it becomes profitable to pursue *narrowcasting* strategy, appealing to specialized or minority interests and tastes. To illustrate, cable television features a wide range of channels that appeal to specialized interests, including news, old films, religious programming, cooking shows, and country music.

At the same time, there is considerable competition within each subcategory of programming. For instance, now there is considerable evening and daytime competition for the *Tonight Show*.

At this stage of development, programs often experiment with the established formula of genres to keep it fresh. Ironically, some of these innovations mirror experiments that occur at the embryonic stage of development. For instance, some of the "street activities" on *Late Night with David Letterman* are reminiscent of *The Ernie Kovaks Show* (discussed earlier).

The same stages of development also appear in the media systems of other countries, at the time in which their media systems begin to evolve. Often, in the case of countries in which the development of the media appears later than in the United States, this schedule of development is accelerated. As an example, the pace of change in India is supercharged because the country is catching up to, and in some cases leapfrogging, developments that took decades to play out elsewhere. As Vikram Kaushik, the chief executive of Tata Sky, a satellite-TV, declares, "Everything that happened in the rest of the world in 10 years, is happening here in two years" (Bajai, 2007).

Principles of Ecology

The biological principle of *ecology* offers a useful construct for understanding the complex relationship between media systems. Ecology refers to the biological principle of coexistence. In some cases, organisms are antagonistic to one another. As an example, African lions are predators who feast on a variety of animals, including buffalo, zebra, antelope, giraffe, and warthogs. In other instances, organisms operate in a state of *symbiosis*, in that both organisms prosper through their relationship with one another.

Ecological relations between systems (including media systems) often go through the following stages:

Phase I: New Medium as Threat
Threatened by a loss of cultural control, members of elite culture often dismiss emerging media as detrimental to the culture. For instance, in 1859 poet Charles Baudelaire warned, "By invading the territories of art, this industry

[photography] has become art's most mortal enemy" (quoted in Gernsheim & Gernsheim, 1969).

The development of a new medium poses a threat to existing media on several levels: *An emerging medium "borrows" its programming from the established media, creating an enormous vacuum in the established media systems.* In the early 1950s, for example, situation comedies, soap operas, westerns, and quiz shows moved over to television, causing considerable panic within the radio industry.

The emergence of a new medium siphons the audience base from the established media systems. Recently, video games have taken a toll on television viewership. A 2005 article in *USA Today* explains:

> If video killed the radio star in the 1980s, then it seems video games are trying to do the same thing to TV in this decade. . . . 24% of gamers reduced their TV watching over the past year and 18% expect to cut small-screen viewership next year. Video gamers watched 11.1% less TV than last year, dropping their weekly TV viewership to 16 hours, compared with 18 hours in 2004. ("Gamers' TV Time Going Down the Tube," 2005)

The arrival of a new media system can eat away at the financial base of established media. As an example, the radio industry was faced with a financial crisis in the 1950s, as the sponsors of soap operas moved with the programs to finance their television counterparts. Likewise, in 2006, the film industry found itself in crisis as a result of the competition from "new media."

Initially, the established media react to these threats by trying to compete with the new medium on its own terms; unfortunately, this tactic only makes it clear that the older media do not have the same capabilities as the emerging media. For instance, the traditional news cycle for print newspapers is approximately 12 hours. In contrast, the Internet has virtually eliminated production and distribution time, meaning that there is an open-ended news cycle; stories are immediately posted and continually updated. To compete with this "24/7" deadline of Internet newspapers, the print newspaper industry has altered its standards and practices. Instead of the traditional guidelines of requiring two sources to confirm the facts of a story, editors have reduced this procedure to one source—sometimes with disastrous results. For instance, in their haste to announce the winner of the 2000 U.S. presidential race, CBS announced that the winner of the U.S. presidential election was Al Gore.

Another tactic of the established media industries is to discourage the development of the new system. For instance, in the 1950s, American film studios exerted pressure to prevent their film stars from appearing on television. In addition, the studios refused to release their features for presentation on television. Finally, the film industry launched an intensive publicity campaign, with the slogan "Movies Are Better Than Ever!" to counter the growing popularity of television.

Phase II: Specialization

Eventually, the established media systems fight for their survival by promoting their own distinctive characteristics. This specialization occurs in the following three ways.

1. Technological Innovations

In the 1950s, the film industry introduced a series of technical advances to compete with television, which was then in its "Popular Stage" of evolution. Because television screens were only 13 inches wide, film studios produced movies in widescreen formats such as Cinemascope and Cinerama. Furthermore, during this era, television programming was primarily delivered in black and white; color was introduced in 1954 but was expensive and exclusive until the 1960s. In response, film studios produced movies in Technicolor—a rich, super-saturated color that, again, provided a contrast with black-and-white TV sets. And finally, because the tiny speakers in TV sets could not deliver quality sound, the film industry enhanced their audio delivery systems, including "Surround Sound." The film industry even resorted to technological gimmicks to attract audiences, producing movies in 3-D, "Smellorama," and "Psychorama."

During this period, radio responded to the threat of television with two technical innovations: the transistor and the car radio. The early television sets were bulky and required proximity to an electrical outlet. However, the small, battery-powered transistor radio was transportable and could accompany listeners anywhere—to the beach, or on a picnic. The car radio was another innovation that fit into the American lifestyle. Because Americans were spending an increasing amount of time driving, the car radio was a welcome companion that (unlike television) would not be a distraction for the motorist.

2. Specialized Content

The evolution of a new medium forces the established media to develop their own programming, taking advantage of their own distinctive characteristics. Consider how the development of photography in the 19th century ultimately freed painters to explore other realms of visual expression. Impressionists such as Monet and Manet were free to capture how the world *appeared* to the subjective, human eye.

During the 1950s, the film industry took advantage of the medium's capacity for size by producing grand landscapes in movies like *Around the World in Eighty Days*. In addition, film studios released epics such as *The Ten Commandments* (1956) and *Ben-Hur* (1959) that presented grand themes as well.

3. Target Audience

While the new media system is still establishing its mass audience base, established media direct their programming at target audiences. For instance, as television pursued a broadcasting strategy in the 1950s, radio targeted an adolescent audience in the 1950s through its new "Top Forty" format. Radio played a pivotal role in the popularity of rock 'n' roll and its teen heartthrobs such as Elvis. As a result, despite the gloomy forecasts about the future of the radio industry, the number of radios in use in the United States increased, from 105,300,000 in 1952 to 183,800,000 in 1962 (Biagi, 1988).

Phase III: Assimilation

Eventually, media systems not only coexist but *flourish* through their relationship with one another.

- *Consolidation of Ownership.* The holdings of the major media conglomerates include book publishing companies, film studios, newspapers, and radio stations. For instance, NewsCorp is a media empire that includes 20th Century Fox Film, Fox Television, and a raft of newspapers, such as the London *Times* and *The Wall Street Journal*.
- *Technical Convergence.* Digital technology has resulted in the convergence of all media systems. For instance, digital photography has replaced the traditional chemical process with an electronic process that captures images. In like fashion, digital video and high-resolution television (HDTV) greatly reduce the aesthetic differences between video and film. Recent breakthroughs in digital technology have made it possible to capture movies using high-definition digital video cameras with fidelity comparable to 35-millimeter film and to project them digitally in theaters with no loss of image quality
- *Programming.* Because programming is distributed across the media landscape, individuals can watch television programs and films on their cell phones.

- *Audience.* Audience behavior patterns sometimes consolidate the use of multiple media. For instance, it is not unusual for a person to listen to the radio while reading. In addition, the Internet has added to the overall audience for television by adding an interactive component, known as *event television.* Producers supplement television programs by adding an interactive component. For example, in the reality/performance program *America's Got Talent*, the audience sends texts to vote for their favorite performers.
- *Merging of Styles.* Because the aesthetic distinction between film and video has become much less pronounced, television directors increasingly are able to use filmic style and techniques in their productions.

Cycles

New technological developments can cause a medium to *repeat* the cycle. For instance, digital technology has moved photography from the *mature stage* back into the *popular stage*, as consumers have discovered the application of digital cameras and cell phones.

In addition, a medium may reexperience the same ecological pattern as it adapts to the inception of a new medium. Just as the radio industry had to scramble in the face of the arrival of television in the 1950s, the radio industry again faced competition in 2000—this time from the Internet, which appropriated the environment, format, and structure of radio. Richard Siklos (2006) explains:

> While more than 9 out of 10 Americans still listen to traditional radio each week, they are listening less. And the industry is having to confront many challenges . . . including streaming audio, podcasting, iPods and Howard Stern on satellite radio.
>
> As a result, the prospects of radio companies have dimmed significantly since the late 1990's, when broadcast barons were tripping over themselves to buy more stations. Radio revenue growth has stagnated and the number of listeners is dropping. The amount of time people tune into radio over the course of a week has fallen by 14 percent over the last decade, according to Arbitron ratings.

But once again, the radio industry moved into Phase II: Specialization, as it battled for survival:

- *Programming.* Digital media devices such as IPods appropriated the music format, with the addition of *content accessibility*—listeners can program their own selections. Left with an enormous programming hole, the radio industry responded through the format of talk radio, which offers a type of programming that is unique to this medium. In addition, the radio industry relied more on syndicated programs—not just to save money but as a way to attract a large audience. For instance, superstar Rush Limbaugh reaches 20 million listeners weekly through 500 radio stations.

* *Technology.* The Internet has extended the audience for the traditional radio stations. In addition, satellite radio provided uninterrupted music, in a format of the listener's choice. Moreover, satellite radio offered an exhaustive playlist that introduced the audiences to new songs.

The radio industry is reentering Phase III: Assimilation. Radio is providing content for many of the venues created by digital media. For instance, individuals can download radio programming for play on their iPods. In addition, Internet radio stations have been developed expressly for distribution online. These stations are not subject to FCC license fees and regulations.

See also: Audience Analysis; Digital Media Literacy; Formulaic Analysis; Genre Study, Media Literacy Approach; Ownership Patterns, Media

References

Bajai, V. (2007, February 11). "In India, the Golden Age of Television Is Now." *New York Times*. Retrieved from http://www.nytimes.com/2007/02/11/business/yourmoney/11india.html?pagewanted=all

Biagi, S. (1988). *Media Impact.* Belmont, CA: Wadsworth.

Gamble, M. W., & Gamble, T. K. (1986). *Introducing Mass Communication.* New York: McGraw-Hill.

"Gamers' TV Time Going Down the Tube." (2005, August 8). *USA Today.*

Gernsheim, H., & Gernsheim, A. (1969). *The History of Photography.* New York: McGraw-Hill.

Kisseloff, J. (1998, November 20). "In the Beginning, There Was Risk-Taking." *New York Times*. Retrieved from http://www.nytimes.com/1998/11/29/arts/television-radio-in-the-beginning-there-was-risk-taking.html?pagewanted=all&src=pm

Needham, Harper & Steers Advertising, Washington D.C. Conducted on the Associated Press Broadcasting Services. Yahoo!Internet Life.

Rodrigues, M. (2005, June 29). "Ask a Scientist." *Zoology Archive*. Retrieved from www.newton.dep.anl.gov

Siklos, R. (2006, September 15). "Changing Its Tune." *New York Times* Retrieved from http://www.nytimes.com/2006/09/15/business/media/15radio.html?ei=5088

&en=d2535d0ee447c2f5&ex=1315972800&adxnnl=1&partner=rssnyt&emc=rss &adxnnlx=1158436816-WdbuLZcY+oVLvEevZKmfnw.

U.S. Department of Labor, Bureau of Labor Statistics. (2012). Retrieved from www .bis.gov.

Historical Context

Historical context is a qualitative approach to the analysis of media content, based on the premise that media texts often derive their significance from the events of the day.

The historical context approach to media literacy analysis can follow several lines of inquiry.

1. *A media presentation can provide valuable insight into the period in which it was produced.* To be sure, the primary goal of the journalist is to record occurrences that have political or social significance. However, news programming is not necessarily a complete and accurate record of historical events. Ian I. Mitroff and Warren Bennis (1989) contend that TV news presents information in isolation, without the historical context that provides meaning:

> With very few exceptions, most issues on network television news are presented in a completely historical context or no context whatsoever. Most news issues, especially local items, merely appear; they drop in from out of the blue. . . . The overall effect is one of dazzling confusion. Little or no attempt is made to present larger view in which the issues could be located in a coherent framework. (p.13)

Although a primary goal of the journalist is to record occurrences that have political or social significance, time and space limitations often prevent news reports from furnishing the historical context necessary for a comprehensive understanding of events. Instead, articles include only the most recent incident causing tension and potential strife. Rarely are viewers reminded of the conflict's origin or what past steps might have been taken to remedy the situation. In addition, they can conduct research to uncover needed information, while paying particular attention to the different media being used (i.e., books, magazines, Web sites).

To gain a thorough understanding of stories of this sort, students need to examine how much historical background is provided and whether this information adequately contributes to the sufficient knowledge of the subject matter. Thus, when examining news programming, useful questions include the following:

- How much historical background is provided?
- Does this information adequately contribute to the sufficient knowledge of the subject matter?

Entertainment programming and advertising are also influenced by current events, albeit in an indirect fashion. Consider that the 2010 primetime television lineup was a microcosm of the global economic crisis: The premise of an NBC sitcom titled *Outsourced*, for example, involved a young executive who was transferred to India after his midwestern novelty company moved its call center there. The setting of entertainment programming can also provide historical context. A 2010 police drama, *Detroit 1-8-7*, takes place in a city that has been particularly hard hit by the economic downturn.

Thus, the following questions can provide ways in which an understanding of historical events can promote analysis of media and media presentations: (1) When was the media production first presented? (2) What prior events led to the climate in which this media presentation was produced? (3) How did people react to the production when it was first presented? (4) How do people react to the production today? (5) How do you account for any differences in reactions?

2. *Conversely, an understanding of historical events can enrich the interpretation of a media presentation.* An ad for Dove liquid dish detergent that appeared in 2010, for example, featured baby ducklings and otters bathed in the detergent. However, this curious use of the product makes sense within the context of the events surrounding the release of the ad. April 2010 marked the date of the oil-rig disaster in the Gulf of Mexico, which was ruinous to the environment. Dove, which is normally used to clean dishes, was therefore promoted as a product that could clean the wildlife that had been doused in oil.

3. *Historical references embedded in a media presentation can provide insight into its themes and messages.*

4. *Popular media programming can anticipate historical events.* To illustrate, according to film critic A. O. Scott (2009), Iranian films released over the past 15 years forecast many of the issues facing contemporary Iran:

No national cinema is easily summarized, and movies are always an imperfect window on the world. But to watch, say, *The Apple* (1998), Ms. Makhmalbaf's first film; *The Circle* (2000), *Crimson Gold* (2003) and *Offside* (2006) by Mr. Panahi; the more tenderly sentimental films of Majid Majidi (including *The Color of Paradise* and *Baran*); and Bahman Ghobadi's tough, poetic films about Kurdistan—and this is a very partial list—is to encounter images and stories that add depth and meaning to the raw videos and tweets of recent weeks. You see class divisions, the cruelty of the state, the oppression of women and their ways of resisting it, traditions of generosity and hospitality, and above all a passion for argument.

5. *A media presentation can serve as a barometer of current attitudes toward historical events.* Traditionally, media programming has been a source of commentary on historical events. John Leland (2005) explains,

> In the 18th century, songwriters responded to current events by writing new lyrics to existing melodies. "Benjamin Franklin used to write broadside ballads every time a disaster struck," said Elijah Wald, a music historian, and sell the printed lyrics in the street that afternoon. This tradition of responding culturally to terrible events had almost been forgotten, Mr. Wald said, but in the wake of Hurricane Katrina, it may be making a comeback, with the obvious difference that, where Franklin would have sold a few song sheets to his fellow Philadelphians, the Internet allows artists today to reach the whole world.

6. *Popular media programming plays an active role in shaping historical events.*

7. *Historical context can provide insight into ways in which historical events can alter content.* To illustrate, in the summer of 2011, Marvel Studios and Paramount Pictures released *Captain America: The First Avenger*, a superhero film. However, in Russia, Ukraine, and South Korea, the film was altered, as the superhero's name was removed from the title. In Russia and Ukraine, this was a result of anti-American sentiment—a carryover from the Cold War. But in the case of ally South Korea, the title change was brought on by more recent foreign policy decisions by the United States. Reporter Brooks Barnes (2011) explains,

> Although [South Korea] is one of Hollywood's top-performing territories, resentment about the continued presence of the United States military runs deep. Marvel and Paramount worry that those feelings are particularly strong among younger South Koreans, the ones who powered "Iron Man 2" to $27 million in ticket sales in that country last year.

8. *Media presentations such as historical dramas may distort the facts or shift emphasis for dramatic purposes.* For instance, the historical events

in the epic film *Titanic* (1997) were presented as a backdrop to the romance between Jack Dawson (Leonardo DiCaprio) and Rose DeWitt Bukater (Kate Winslet). But Michael Parenti (1992) observes that, although docudramas are not intended as an historical record, the audience often believes that these programs present an accurate historical picture—sometimes with dangerous consequences:

> In the minds of many Americans, movie and television dramas are the final chapter of history, the most lasting impression they have of what the past was like, what little of it they may have been exposed to. For the most part, make-believe history is an insipid costume epic, a personalized affair, the plotting, strutting, and yearnings of court figures and state leaders. Tyrants become humanly likable as the social realities of their tyranny are ignored. The revolutionary populace is represented as tyrannical and irrational, while the sources of their anger and misery remain unexplained. Conflicts and wars just seem to happen, arising out of personal motives and ambitions. In these ways make-believe history reinforces the historical illiteracy fostered in the schools and in political life in general. (p. 68)

Thus, examining the historical events depicted in entertainment media presentations can serve as a useful springboard for additional research. Areas of investigation include the following line of questions: (1) Is the dramatization an accurate portrait of events? (2) Are the causes leading to the events in the presentation clear? (3) What were the consequences of the dramatized events?

9. *Tracing the evolution of a particular medium, genre, or presentation can provide insight into changes in cultural attitudes and concerns.* Analyzing the history of a genre of programming or individual media texts can provide insight into shifts in cultural attitudes and concerns. For instance, the nuclear family, as represented in 1950s television sit-coms such as *Father Knows Best* and *Leave It to Beaver*, has changed to keep in line with shifting cultural mores and values.

See also: Advertising—Media Literacy Analysis; Journalism

References

Barnes, B. (2011, July 3). "Soft-pedal Captain America Overseas? Hollywood Says No." *New York Times*. Retrieved from http://mediadecoder.blogs.nytimes.com/2011/07/03/soft-pedal-captain-america-overseas-hollywood-says-no

Leland, J. (2005, July 27). "Art Born of Outrage in the Internet Age." *New York Times*. Retrieved from http://www.nytimes.com/2005/09/25/weekinreview/25leland.html

Mitroff, I. A., & Bennis, W. (1989). *The Unreality Industry.* New York: Oxford University Press, 1989.

Parenti, M. (1992). *Make Believe Media.* New York: St. Martin's Press.

Scott, A. O. (2009, June 20). "Iran's Tensions, Foreshadowed in Its Cinema." *New York Times.* Retrieved from http://www.nytimes.com/2009/06/20/movies/20cinema.html

How to Take Notes in Media Analysis

The first step in media literacy analysis involves learning to take notes on media presentations. This process can be challenging. The student is writing in total darkness about what just occurred, as new information appears on screen. Indeed, this process even involves a modification in *posture*—from the reclining position that is typical of how we watch television at home to an upright position, leaning forward, in an attentive mode.

W. Andrew Collins's (1970) discussion of *explicit* and *implicit* content provides an excellent way to teach students how to take notes on media presentations. Collins employed these terms in his research on children's comprehension of media content.

Explicit content refers to the significant events and activities in the plot that are displayed through the visible action. Explicit content is the answer in response to the question, "What is the media presentation about?" The respondent then selects the most significant events in the story (otherwise, the answer would be as long as the film itself).

Implicit content refers to those elements of plot that remain under the surface:

- Motivation
- The relationship between events
- The relationship between characters
- Consequences

One effective way for students to learn to take notes on a media presentation is first, to record the explicit content of the narrative. For instance, when watching a film, note the significant events in a scene, including actions, dialogue, and striking production elements. Then go back to these notes and identify implicit content. What are the motives behind the events that have been recorded? What are the relationships between the events? What do the events reveal with respect to the relationship between the characters? And finally, what consequences to the events (if any) are depicted?

To illustrate, at the conclusion of the action/adventure film *Die Hard* (1988), Officer John McClane (Bruce Willis) has succeeded in foiling a terrorist plot. In the process, however, he has been involved in the killing of numerous characters and the destruction of a skyscraper in the heart of Los Angeles. However, examining the implicit content of the film reveals that there is no consequence to the on-screen violence. McLean simply gets into a cab with his wife, without filing a report or providing an explanation for the mayhem in which he was a central figure.

Some students prefer to use different colored highlighters to draw the connections between events and characters in the presentation.

This explicit–implicit dichotomy is also useful in the analysis of particular media and genres. For instance, in the analysis of news presentations, television is a medium that is better equipped to focus on *explicit* content (i.e., events, issues) than print. At the same time, newspaper accounts are better suited to examine the *implicit* content (i.e., motives, connections between events and people, and consequences) *behind* events or issues.

In light of the complexity of events, it is particularly critical to give some thought to implicit content when reading news articles. When examining a story, ask:

- Why did this event occur?
- What are the possible connections between events?
- What are the possible consequences of these events?
- Which questions does the story answer?
  ◦ Who?
  ◦ When?
  ◦ Where?
  ◦ How?
  ◦ Why?
- Have any of the above questions have been omitted? How does this omission affect your understanding of the story?
- Where would you find the answers to these unanswered questions?

Reference

Collins, W. A. (1970). "Learning of Media Content: A Developmental Study." *Child Development 41*, 1133–1142.

Iconographic Analysis

Iconographic analysis is a qualitative approach to media analysis that focuses on ways in which the connotative properties of images convey media messages.

In a world characterized by different languages and dialects, the use of images in media presentations can be a powerful communications vehicle, influencing how we think about our world. According to media scholar Bill Nichols (1981),

> [i]mages . . . contribute to our sense of who we are and to our everyday engagement with the world around us. What these signs never announce is that they are most fundamentally the signifiers of ideology. . . . After all, seeing is believing, and how we see ourselves and the world around us is often how we believe ourselves and the world to be. (p. 3)

Astute media communicators have learned to use the connotative properties of images to their advantage. The selection of images that appear in media presentations can have an enormous impact on the audience's response to a story. For instance, during the Gulf War, the pictures that appeared in American media were vastly different from the images displayed elsewhere in the world. American news outlets were reluctant to show pictures of civilian casualties; in contrast, the Arab media presented images depicting the harsh realities of the war. Nihad Awad, executive director of the Council on American-Islamic Relations, declared, "There are two wars. One that's shown around the world through the eyes of Arab and European networks and the other that Americans see through American networks" (Shesgreen, 2003).

However, images are ambiguous. Photographs often appear with no background information: Who the subjects are, and why they appear in the photo frequently goes unexplained. In addition, photos only capture an instant, which may not represent the reality occurring before and after the shot was taken.

The meaning of images is further restricted by the arbitrary boundary of the frame, which can either eliminate essential elements or distort their importance. Framing a photograph can isolate two figures in a crowd, setting up relationships that had not existed before.

Technical factors can also alter the reality captured by the camera:

- *The proximity of the camera* affects the treatment of the subject. For instance, a close-up photo is perceived as more intimate and revealing,

while a "long" shot provides more emphasis on the environment surrounding the subject.

- *Lighting* can influence the characterization of the subject; for instance,
  the gradation and placement of lights can make a subject appear dark
  and evil, or bright and angelic.
- *Digital manipulation* seamlessly affects the appearance of images, so
  that all of the laws of nature have been suspended.

Some images possess *universal* associative properties, generating a positive response among audiences, regardless of culture, gender, income, or
race. Other images have a *cultural* significance. For example, the American flag symbolizes the democratic traditions, principles, and history of the
United States. These images can furnish perspective into attitudes and preoccupations within a country. International media communicators should be
aware that images may convey unintended messages in other cultures and
may choose to substitute other images to achieve the intended purpose.

Images may also derive their meaning through *context*. For instance, fire
can symbolize either protection or destruction, depending on the surrounding
environment depicted in the presentation.

Imaging Techniques

The following types of image manipulation influence the meaning of the
media presentation:

- *Symbolic representations* are images that suggest another, broader
  meaning. For example, imagine a photograph of a male political candidate seated at his desk in his study. The bookshelves behind him, filled
  with volumes, convey the message that he is a learned man (although
  there is no evidence that he has read the books or that they are even his).
  This setting may be enhanced by a family photograph, which signals his
  position on family values (although, once again, there is no proof that
  he is a devoted family man or, indeed, if this is even *his* family).
- *Imagistic layering* occurs when two images, put together, form a third
  meaning. The fusion of two images operates on humans' *gestalt*, or
  predisposition to order, so that the audience naturally constructs a
  third, distinct meaning from the two disparate images (described by
  the equation A + B = C). This production technique enables a media
  communicator to comment on the relationship between objects and
  events. For example, ads commonly employ images of sexy women

Symbolic representations are images that suggest another, broader meaning. For instance, a photograph of a political candidate seated in a study filled with books conveys the message that the candidate is a learned person who is well qualified for public office. (Photo by Lisa Marcus)

with automobiles, which associates cars with sexual desire. Over time, transference occurs, so that the cars themselves are seen as sexy.

- *Metonymy* is the technique in which an image stands for a group of attributes. For example, in liquor and beer advertisements, the consumption of the product stands for fun, friends, youth, happiness, and fitness.
- *Masking images* present a worldview that reframes how we think about the worldview of the image. For instance, ads for gambling boats show everyday citizens hitting it rich, masking the reality that the only big winners are the owners of the casinos.

Infographics

Infographics refer to various pictorial (as opposed to photographic) representations that appear in the media. Infographics such as illustrations, logos, graphs, maps, typefaces, and political cartoons are used as companions to written language, drawing the viewer's attention to information for emphasis. In addition, infographics offer a way to communicate information despite problems posed by illiteracy. Infographics are particularly effective in inter-national communications, transcending language barriers.

Evidence of infographics predates written languages. Five thousand years ago, the Egyptians developed the first calendar that divided time into 365 days a year. They also drew maps of the Earth and charted events such as the flooding of the Nile River.

Infographics are particularly well suited for the presentation of certain kinds of information. For example, maps are the most effective means of orienting people with regard to location. According to James Glen Stovall (1997),

> The graphics pictured for readers . . . help explain the what, where, and why of the story in ways that traditional forms of conveying infor-mation could not. . . . Infographics can be used to explain and show why and how things occur. . . . You can photograph the effects of an earthquake. But can you show them an earthquake? When a major earthquake disrupted life in Northern California in October 1989, a number of newspapers tried to show readers how the earthquake occurred and moved through the ground. . . . They did this by creat-ing a graphic that led readers through the process of the earthquake. (pp. 3, 6)

However, there are limits to this form of communication. Infographics are not as precise as the written word and therefore can be easily distorted. Stovall (1997) makes the following recommendations regarding the construction and interpretation of infographics:

> Avoid graphics for the sake of graphics. Unless you can show an increase, decrease, or a significant trend, a graphic won't show much. . . . Don't repeat the story, add to it. (p. 30)
>
> The (media communicator) should always ask the questions, "What is the purpose of what I am doing?" and "What is necessary to accom-plish that purpose?" (p. 23)

A *logo* is a visual symbol of an organization, product, or ideology. A logo must be instantly recognizable, regardless of culture and language barriers. The design and production elements make a distinctive visual statement about the mission and character of the subject.

To illustrate, in 2002, Malayawata Steel Berhad announced that it was adopting a new corporate logo "to better reflect the company's current image and corporate culture":

Executive chairman Lim Kiam Lam said the symbol, which comprises a perfect circle and a geometrical square in its centre, signifies precision at the core management and operational levels. "Precision is the key essence which enables Malayawata to chart significant progress time after time," he said. Lim said the logotype, which consisted of two bars, reflected strength and resilience.

"The corporate blue denotes the will power to succeed—a personification of our commitment to excel in every aspect of our operations. It is also a symbol of integrity and far-sightedness. Orange represents a vibrant, competent workforce that embraces the spirit of teamwork; the embodiment of a strong corporate culture."

A logo can serve several functions:

- *Establish identity.* Corporate logos are designed to embody the essence of the company. To illustrate, the tourist divisions of various countries employ logos to establish their global identities. In 2002, Poland adopted a national logo in the form of a kite. According to Szymon Gutkowski, the logo connotes "youth, freedom, playfulness and hope in any language, any country." According to reporter Sarah Boxer, this logo also conveys another latent message. "The hope is that the kite will lift Poland up and let it float gently away from its past and toward the prosperity of Europe" (Boxer, 2002).
- *Convey information.* Logos provide a range of information, such as directions (e.g., street signs), warnings to the public, or visual notification of quality assurance.
- *Promote a positive emotional attitude toward the organization.* The affective (emotional) properties of visual communication are utilized to cultivate a positive attitude toward the organization.
- *Announce significant changes.* Logos are an effective way to draw attention to significant changes such as company mergers. For instance, when ING, the banking and insurance company of Holland, merged with Vysya Bank, the company came out with a new logo that incorporated visual elements of the Vysya and ING logos into a new design.
- *Conceal the mission of the organization.* On occasion, a logo may be employed to disguise the central focus of the organization. As an example, the process of irradiating food has come under considerable criticism by members of the scientific community, out of concern that the irradiation process interacts with pesticides found in foods to create

toxins like benzene and formaldehyde (Lee, 2003). In response to this negative publicity, the industry designed a logo resembling the logo of the U.S. Environmental Protection Agency (EPA). According to the Organic Consumers Association, this logo signals that irradiation is a natural, healthy process:

> People have a good feeling about the EPA, because it is supposed to be a watchdog for the people. People don't have a good feeling about irradiation, because it often uses radioactive materials, and it benefits meat and poultry packers and producers, not the consumer.
>   The EPA symbol appropriately shows water, the sun and a flower. The radura shows a flower in a broken circle, symbolizing the radiation. The radura distracts your attention from the fact that irradiation is mostly about 'sterilizing' feces-contaminated food, not about preserving flowers. (Organic Consumers Association, n.d.)

A *graph* is a chart or table that shows the relationship between two or more variable quantities. This numerical information is often presented along two axes, usually at right angles. However, graphic representations such as pie charts can make numerical data clear and understandable.

Stovall (1997) cites several keys that influence the effectiveness of graphs as a communications vehicle:

- Is information missing from the graphic?
- Is there really a correlation between the data being displayed? Are they comparable?
- Are the time intervals proper?
- Is the scale of the data in the graphics accurate? (p. 27)

Illustration refers to any sort of representational drawing. An illustration can show a sequence of events, to demonstrate how the parts of an event fit together. Furthermore, as Stovall points out, an illustration can move beyond the literal description of events, "articulat[ing] the story's underlying emotional element or theme" (p. 30).

The *typeface* employed in print can reinforce the essential message of the content. Each typeface has its own distinctive shape, design, and personality, characterized by the following:

- The thickness of the stroke making up the type
- The width of the characters

- The height of the characters (type size: up to 72 points)
- The face of the type (e.g., bold, italic)
- The amount of space *between* letters

The choice of typeface can also reinforce the function, or purpose of the message. For instance, the type employed in headlines is designed to attract immediate attention. Typeface can also comment on the information. For instance, bold typeface signals the importance of the information.

In addition, a variety of *fonts* are available, even in personal computers. A font refers to the style of the type. The choice of font can express an attitude toward the content (`serious` or **whimsical**) or give instructions to the reader (e.g., **pay attention to the information**).

Political Cartoons

Political cartoons are drawings that comment on world events, leaders, and ideologies. Christina Michelmore (2000) observes,

> Cartoons do not just illustrate the news. They are graphic editorials, and like all editorials they analyze and interpret a situation; they pass judgment. They tell readers what to think and how to feel about what is happening—amused, sympathetic, chagrined, angry, afraid. (p. 37)

Political cartoons, which rely predominantly on drawings, surmount the obstacles of illiteracy. Political cartoons often rely on *caricatures* of a person's appearance or behavior to make a point. A caricature is an illustration that exaggerates particular features or characteristics of the subject. But in the process, caricatures provide serious commentary on the people and issues being lampooned in the cartoon. Critical analysis of political cartoons focuses on the following questions:

- To what person(s) or issue is the political cartoon referring?
- What characteristics or qualities of the subject are being exaggerated in the caricature?
  - What messages are conveyed in the caricature?
  - What does caricature reveal about the cartoonists' attitudes toward the subject?
- What point of view is expressed through the situation and people in the political cartoon?

Examining contemporary political cartoons can be an effective way to gauge current global opinion on world events. During the height of the Iraq War, David L. Paletz declared:

If Americans want to understand the hostile feelings many people in the Arab/Muslim world have about the U.S., its leaders and their policies, they should take a hard look at the striking cartoons from the region. Political cartoons in Arab/Muslim newspapers draw a Moral equivalent between the war in Afghanistan and terror attacks, ridicule the United States for its incompetence in locating Osama bin Laden, and portray the U.S. as a powerful yet often blind or misled soldier. (Paletz, 2002)

The Internet has broadened the scope and audience for political cartoons. Political cartoons appear on numerous Web sites, including the Village Voice, Mother Jones, Salon.com, and Netzeitung.de, which are providing new arenas for political cartoonists. Some of these political cartoons are animated, with audio and video capabilities, which attracts younger audiences.

See also: International Communications, Media Literacy Approach; Mass-Mediated Reality; Production Analysis Approach

References

Boxer, S. (2002, December 1). "A New Poland, No Joke." *New York Times*. Retrieved from http://www.nytimes.com/2002/12/01/magazine/01PROCESS.html?pagewanted=all

Lee, T. (2003, January 13). "Schnucks Is the First in the Area to Offer Irradiated Meat." *St. Louis Post-Dispatch*. Retrieved from http://business.highbeam.com/435553/article-1G1-96397402/schnucks-first-area-offer-irradiated-meat

Malayawata Steel Berhad. Retrieved from http://www.eternalsolutions.com/client/mwata/index.html.

Michemore, C. (2000, Winter). "Old Pictures in New Frames: Images of Islam and Muslims in Post World War II American Political Cartoons." *Journal of American and Comparative Cultures*, *23* (4), 37–50.

Nichols, B. (1981). *Ideology and the Image*. Bloomington: Indiana University Press.

Organic Consumers Association. (n.d.). Retrieved from www.organicconsumers.org/Irrad/EPA-radura.cfm

Paletz, D. L. (2002). Quoted in "Post-September 11 Cartoons in Arab Media Skewer the United States, Article Says." Retrieved from http://today.duke.edu/2002/08/cartoons0802.html

Shesgreen, D. (2003, April 6). "World Press Is Showing Different, More Graphic War." *St. Louis Post-Dispatch*.

Stovall, J. G. (1997). *Infographics: A Journalist's Guide*. Boston: Allyn & Bacon.

Ideological Analysis

Ideological analysis is a qualitative approach that provides insight into ways in which the media *reflect*, *reinforce*, and *shape* ideological systems. *Ideology* refers to the system of beliefs or ideas that help determine the thinking and behavior of a culture. Ideology is integral to all aspects of media production, distribution, exchange, and consumption. Although ideology typically refers to a political orientation, cultural historian Raymond Williams (1995) observes that ideology may involve a "more general way of seeing the world, human nature, and relationships" (p. 118). However, even this expanded notion of ideology has political implications, containing assumptions about how the world should operate, who should oversee this world, and the proper and appropriate relationships among its inhabitants.

Ideological analysis has its roots in the discipline of *cultural studies*. The focus of cultural studies is not on aesthetic aspects of text, but rather what these texts reveal about social systems. One of the central tenants of cultural studies is that the media does not merely *reflect* or *reinforce* culture but in fact *shapes* thinking by promoting the dominant ideology of a culture through *cultural hegemony*; that is, the ability of the dominant classes to maintain economic and political control over the subordinate classes.

The dominant ideology frequently assumes a disarming "naturalness" within a text, which makes it particularly effective in promoting and reinforcing the prevailing ideology. These media presentations begin with unquestioned assumptions about the correctness of this order. As an example, in police dramas, basic assumptions about the origin and nature of crime and criminals are adopted by actors with whom we identify. Although a media program may be open to several interpretations, the text generally dictates a *preferred reading* that asks the audience to assume the role, perspective, and orientation of the primary figures, so that the sympathies of the audience are aligned with the values and beliefs of the dominant culture.

To illustrate, *consumer ideology* holds that success is defined in terms of material acquisition. Personal problems and metaphysical issues have been transformed into consumer needs. Are you lonely? Have money problems? Are you aging? These issues all find resolution through a prudent consumer purchase. In many media programs, social problems are resolved through consumerism rather than political action. By purchasing the right products, we can move into another social class (or at least maintain the illusion of upward mobility). The concept of the "citizen" has been replaced in the American vernacular by the label "consumer." We celebrate our democratic (or rather, capitalistic) system by participating in the market economy. When asked what Americans could do in response to the terrorist attacks of 9/11, President George W. Bush responded, "shop." Shopping was equated with freedom of movement, and dressing in style was equated with freedom of self-expression.

Ideological Approach to Media Literacy

The media have emerged as a principal means through which ideology is introduced and reinforced. As a product (and beneficiary) of the prevailing system, the media generally reflect the predominant ideology of a culture. One of the chief goals of the ideological approach to media analysis is *ideological detoxification*—that is, cultivating a healthy skepticism toward ideologically based explanations of the world conveyed through media presentations. This approach, then, moves beyond the description of a media production into a discussion of the values implicit within it, as well as whose interests are served by such ideas.

The ideological approach may not account for all media messages, but this perspective can provide considerable insight into the behaviors, attitudes, values, and preoccupations of media audiences and the culture.

Ideological analysis includes the following objectives:

- Becoming more sensitive to the impact of ideology on media content
- Examining media presentations as a way to identify the prevailing ideology of a culture
- Broadening the public's exposure to the unique experience and contributions of subcultures in society
- Identifying media presentations as a means of tracing ideological shifts within a culture

Lines of Inquiry

Ideological analysis consists of the following lines of inquiry.

Cumulative Messages

One way in which the dominant culture maintains its superior position is by presenting *cumulative messages* in media presentations that, collectively, reinforce the dominant ideology. Cumulative messages occur with such frequency over time that they form meanings that are independent of any individual production. These messages are reinforced through the countless hours of media programming that repeats the cultural script. Although there are a multitude of messages (indeed, conflicting cumulative messages may exist at the same time), the ultimate test of a cumulative message is its *universality*; that is, the degree to which an audience is able to recognize a cumulative message that is conveyed through a variety of media channels and programs.

These cumulative messages disclose the sources of power and authority in a culture, the class system, and hierarchy of values.

The following cumulative media messages provide insight into the belief system that defines American culture:

- *A world preoccupied with the self rather than the collective good.* In the narcissistic world of media programming, the *greater good* has been reduced to *individual satisfaction*. Ads declare that "you deserve a break today," urging the audience to indulge their own needs. A hierarchy of values is established in media programs, in which personal amusement is valued over societal well-being.
- *A world of immediate gratification.* In media programming, the solution to a problem is never far off. Advertising accelerates this push toward immediate gratification. Advertising measures its success by its ability to influence the consumer to buy their products as soon as possible. Some ads actually command the consumer to act and act quickly by using directive words such as "hurry" and "now." One clear media message is that change is swift, immediate, and dramatic.
- *A world that expects simple solutions to complex problems.* In America's market-driven media system, media communicators are compelled to present a world that is easy to identify and understand. Consequently, the world of entertainment programs and ads are populated by uncomplicated characters who represent a particular value or point of view in the story. Popular films and television programs generally deal in absolutes (e.g., Good vs. Evil, Right vs. Wrong).
- *A world operating according to a romantic ideal.* The romantic ideal presumes the existence of an ordered universe that is a microcosm of heaven. This world operates according to an absolute value system, consisting of *truth*, *beauty*, *justice*, *faith*, and *love*. These values are fixed and interchangeable. Thus, in this world, the heroines are beautiful, as a reflection of inner virtue. It is a just world, in which good always wins in the end. Faith is an integral part of the romantic ideal.

As Jiminy Cricket croons in Disney's *Pinocchio*, "When you wish upon a star your dreams come true." In other words, if you are deserving and believe hard enough in the romantic ideal, you will be rewarded.

- *The substance of style.* The media industry frequently co-opts the ideological significance behind a program, star, or genre for commercial purposes, leaving only the framework and style intact. By exploiting the image of a movement, the original ideology is lost. When Elvis Presley burst on the American scene in the 1950s, he was regarded as dangerous by influential members of the dominant (i.e., white, middle-class) culture. Elvis's hip gyrations and snarling lip emitted a sexuality that threatened the 1950s sexual mores. Furthermore, Elvis was firmly rooted in black culture; he was a white kid who sounded black. Consequently, the recording industry manufactured a series of clean-cut rock 'n' roll idols who maintained the image of Elvis, devoid of the ideological substance: Ricky Nelson, Fabian, Bobby Rydell. This pattern was repeated in the 1960s: The Beatles, who sang about revolution, led to the creation of the Monkeys, who warbled harmlessly about that last train to Clarksville. This depletion of meaning culminated in a 1995 TV spot, in which Ringo Starr teamed up with members of the Monkeys . . . as spokespersons for Pizza Hut. Substance has been reduced to pure image.

  The consumer culture co-opts people as well. Marilyn Monroe, Anna Nicole Smith, and Charlie Sheen are examples of people who were transformed into commodities. Athletes measure their success by their ability to land endorsement deals—paltry sums when compared to their astronomical salaries. Even as they walk off of the field, the Super Bowl victors cannot wait to capitalize on their success and fame, announcing, "I'm going to Disney World."

In like fashion, the media industry has co-opted grassroots political movements. For example, an ad for Alcatel Americas, a company that builds communications networks, was a thinly disguised adaptation of Martin Luther King's apocalyptic sermon. The commercial used footage of the 1963 "I Have a Dream" speech King delivered from the steps of the Lincoln Memorial. But in the commercial, the vast crowd was electronically removed, so that the commercial could make a point about the value of its communications devices: "Before you can inspire," says the voiceover, "you must first connect."

Columnist Leonard Pitts Jr. (2001) decried this "financial exploitation of King's legacy":

The sermon King preached from Lincoln's doorstep is worthy of reverence . . .

Unfortunately, that's a word the nation in general and Madison Avenue in particular can't spell. . . . Commercial culture seeps like dirty water into places it has never been, soiling even that which is worthy of reverence. Now, a man who once spoke to our highest faith and deepest fears speaks for a glorified phone company instead?

I don't think that's the dream he had in mind.

This ad reduced Dr. King's vision and, indeed, the civil rights movement, to a pitch for a phone company. Once again, ideology has been diverted, and style has triumphed over substance.

- *A hierarchal (rather than democratic) world.* Media programming reinforces a hierarchal class system through their depictions of rulers and those who serve. The model society depicted in popular media programs is far from democratic. Only the major characters play significant decision-making roles, leaving the supporting cast with no choice but to follow their leaders. The world depicted in the media is predominately populated by members of the dominant stratum. In contrast, members of subcultures often are presented as powerless, marginalized members of society. Thus, one of the chief measures of success in the world of entertainment programming is simply being a member of the dominant stratum.
- *A world that is satisfied with the status quo.* Media presentations instruct audiences about success through adherence to the system. More than merely selling a product, ads often sell a successful lifestyle. The young, attractive models are beneficiaries of the system who have found happiness through the acquisition of the product.

These cumulative messages contribute to an ideology of apathy, cynicism, and lack of connectedness, ultimately discouraging active participation in the community. This sensibility feeds into the ideology of the dominant culture, leaving major decisions in the hands of those currently holding positions of power.

I. Point of View

Examining *point of view* is a way of identifying the prevailing ideology of a media presentation. Point of view refers to the source of information—who tells the story. Point of view has an impact on how a story is told and what information is conveyed, including (a) who or what is important, (b) what is included and excluded, and (c) commentary on what is being presented. In that way, point of view influences the audience's attitudes toward the content. We are directed to see the world in a particular way and base our responses to characters on the point of view of the narrative.

The audience naturally assumes that information is being presented in a truthful, straightforward manner. However, the perspective of narrators (or reporters) may not be reliable, for a variety of reasons:

- Media communicators may have agendas or conflicts of interest that affect the presentation of media content.
- Media communicators may be influenced by their personal background, experiences, or belief systems.
- Media communicators may have an insufficient command of the information to prepare a thorough and balanced presentation.
- Media communicators may include inaccuracies by mistake.

Media presentations generally assume the point of view of members of the dominant culture. According to media scholar Michael Parenti (1992), historical dramas typically assume the point of view of the aristocracy. For example, *The Private Lives of Elizabeth and Essex* (1939), starring Bette Davis and Errol Flynn, takes a sympathetic view of the burdens of rule facing Queen Elizabeth. In another Flynn film, *The Adventures of Robin Hood* (1938), the revolt incited by the Robin's merry band is not intended to install democracy but rather to restore the rightful, benevolent ruler to the throne of England. Indeed, in the course of the film Robin Hood gently rebukes King Richard for having deserted his subjects to join the crusades, which necessitated that the lower classes (led by Robin) fight to restore him to the throne.

Even when the manifest (or surface) point of view offers an alternative perspective, the latent (under the surface) point of view often remains the dominant culture. To illustrate, children's programming appears to be presented from a kid's perspective. However, commercials for children feature actors who are slightly older than the target audience. Young audiences are influenced by how "cool" these performers are; consequently, they either "take their word" for the quality of the product or associate the positive qualities of the actors with the quality of the product. And ultimately, the "actual" media communicators—the producer, writer, and advertising executive—are typically white male adults whose interest in the audience extends only to profit margin. An interesting exercise, then, is to show a television ad and ask children who is *really* speaking—and why.

Oppositional interpretation is a related approach that furnishes perspective into the ideological point of view of a media presentation involves. Even though media presentations offer a *preferred reading*, all texts are open to alternative interpretations. In this approach, individuals assume the point of view of one of the secondary characters in the narrative.

These subordinate characters are often members of the underclass (e.g., African American, females, or Latinos). These characters literally play "supporting roles," serving the main characters who generally are members of the dominant culture. In this way, media presentations serve as microcosms of the social systems that operate in the world outside of these fictional narratives.

Conducting an oppositional interpretation can provide into the ideology of the media presentation, in several respects:

- Providing insight into the operation and impact of the dominant ideology presented in the text
- Enhancing the audiences' sensitivity to the ideology of subcultures that exists within the dominant culture
- Disclosing the dynamics between the dominant ideology and subcultures

An oppositional analysis follows the following line of questioning:

- Adopt the perspective of the members of the dominant culture presented in the media presentation:
  - What opportunities are available to you?
  - What advantages do you have?
  - What do you "get away with" in the story because of your position?
  - What conclusions can you draw from this analysis?
- Adopt the perspective of a member of the subordinate culture:
  - What could you accomplish as one of *these* characters?
  - What opportunities would be available to you?
  - What advantages would you have?
  - What could you "get away with" because of your position?
  - What conclusions can you draw from this analysis?

In this way, media presentations can be examined as microcosms of the social systems that operate in the world outside of these fictional narratives.

Consider *Gone with the Wind*, a film that presents an idealized vision of the antebellum South in which slaves and masters lived in harmony. In the film, the slaves regard the outbreak of the Civil War as an unwelcome disruption of their harmonious plantation life instead of an end to the institution of slavery.

The oppositional approach can furnish perspective into the operational ideology in newspaper articles as well, uncovering the myths and false suppositions in the ideology of the media presentation. The application of Oppositional Analysis consists of the following steps:

- Identify the existing dominant ideology in the presentation
- Rewrite the headline and "lead" (first) paragraph from an oppositional point of view

For example, in 2007, *New York Times* reporter Simon Romero wrote an article titled "Chávez Takes Over Foreign-Controlled Oil Projects in Venezuela." The article begins as follows:

SAN FELIPE, Venezuela, May 1—President Hugo Chávez on Tuesday seized control of the last remaining oil projects in Venezuela controlled by large American and European energy companies. The move to take over the projects, announced in January, is the centerpiece of recent actions aimed at consolidating his government's control over the economy. . . .

Venezuela's control over the oil-production projects, which are in the Orinoco region in the country's interior and worth an estimated $30 billion, will weaken companies like Exxon Mobil, Chevron and Conoco-Phillips in one of the world's most promising oil exploration regions.

Rewriting the article from the point of view of the native-born peasant class in Venezuela could be expressed thusly:

SAN FELIPE, Venezuela, May 1—President Hugo Chávez on Tuesday reclaimed the last remaining oil projects in Venezuela controlled by large American and European energy companies. . . .

Venezuela's control over the oil-production projects, which are in the Orinoco region in the country's interior and worth an estimated $30 billion, will strengthen the national oil industry, which distributes its profits among the nation's poor.

This exercise serves as an indication of how the mainstream media continues to reinforce the dominant culture. By assuming the perspective of the Venezuelan working-class natives, it becomes clear that the international oil companies have been the beneficiaries of the previous oil agreement, while and the indigenous natives were exploited in the previous oil agreement.

II. Worldview

A related line of inquiry focuses on the *visual field* that is encompassed by the gaze of the protagonist. This field of vision consists of a worldview that operates according to certain principles. Media presentations establish *who* and *what* are important within the worldview of the program. In adopting this worldview, the subordinate class willingly supports the continued preeminence of the dominant class.

The following questions related to worldview are useful in identifying the ideology of a media presentation:

- What culture or cultures populate this world?
  - What kinds of people populate this world?
  - What is the ideology of this culture?
- What do we know about the people who populate this world?
  - Are characters presented in a stereotypical manner?
  - What does this tell us about the cultural stereotype of this group?
- Does this world present an optimistic or pessimistic view of life?
  - Are the characters in the presentation happy?
  - Do the characters have a *chance* to be happy?
- Are people in control of their own destinies?
  - Is there a supernatural presence in this world?
  - Are the characters under the influence of other people?
- What hierarchy of values is in operation in this worldview?
  - What embedded values can be found in the production?
  - What values are embodied in the characters?
  - What values prevail through the resolution?
  - What does it mean to be a success in this world?
    - How does a person succeed in this world?
    - What kinds of behavior are rewarded in this world?

Frequently, the protagonist (and audience) sees an imperfect world, in which members of a subculture are the source of the problems in the story. This depiction serves as the ideological foundation of the media presentation—the need for restoration of order (as defined at the conclusion of the presentation).

III. Discourse Analysis

Another line of inquiry involves identifying the ideological meaning contained in discourse. Discourse is associated with the communications interactions of two or more participants. J. P. Gee (1996) elaborates,

Discourse . . . is composed of ways of talking, listening (often, too, reading and writing), acting, interacting, believing, valuing, and using tools and objects in particular settings at specific times, so as to display and recognize a particular social identity. Discourses create "social positions" (perspectives) from which people are "invited" (summoned) to speak, listen, act, read and write, think, feel, believe and value in certain characteristic, historically recognizable ways, combined with their own individual styles and creativity. (p. 128)

The unit of language employed in discourse is generally longer than a sentence. John Hartley (1994) explains,

Discourse analysis is concerned not only with complex utterances by one speaker, but more frequently with turn-taking interaction between two or more, and with the linguistic rules and conventions that are taken to be in play and governing such discourses in their given context. (p. 92)

Discourse features can influence an audience's ability to recall information, coloring the interpretation and facilitating the speed of processing information.

Discourse can be used to impose the dominant ideology on a culture in the following ways:

- *Masking.* Discourse can conceal class exploitation in a specific manner, to the extent that all trace of class domination is systematically absent from its language.
- *Displacement.* This occurs when emphasis is shifted from the sphere of production to the sphere of exchange of consumption.
- *Fragmentation.* Discourse identifies the audience not as members of a collective group but rather as individuals with no meaningful connection to others. The only group cohesion offered through discourse is a consumer identity.

IV. Narrative Analysis

Plot conflicts can be considered ideological oppositions, as represented by the characters in the program. In many narratives, the triumph of good over evil is dependent on the characters' adherence to the values and goals of dominant culture. Daniel Chandler (n.d.) notes that "The structure of the text works to position the reader to 'privilege one set of values and meanings over the other.' " Thus, heroes and heroines epitomize those qualities that society considers admirable and thus generally reflect the values of dominant culture.

Audience identification can also provide insight into the ideology of a narrative. The media text encourages the audience member to identify with the primary protagonists, who are the sources of power in the presentation. By imagining themselves in the role of the primary figure in the program, individuals gain insight into the sources of power and assumptions about what constitutes "the good life," within the context of the media presentation. Questions to consider include:

- As the lead character, what could you accomplish?
- What opportunities would be available to you?
- What advantages would you have? What could you "get away with"?

The conclusion of a narrative should be a logical extension of the ideology of the premise, characters, and worldview. In the 1930s, Hollywood's Motion Picture Production Code asserted that "no picture shall be produced that will lower the moral standards of those who see it. Hence the sympathy of the audience should never be thrown to the side of crime, wrongdoing, evil, or sin" (The Motion Picture Production Code of 1930).

Thus, the "Hollywood Ending" was characterized by tidy resolutions that reinforced the moral belief system, in which good prevails over evil.

Significantly however, the conclusion of many media programs are illogical, confused, or simply implausible when considered within the flow of the program. Given the ideology of the program, a happy ending requires the "divine" intervention of a scriptwriter and director. Although the main characters may be struggling throughout the course of the program (often because of flaws in the system), the resolution of the narrative finds them at peace. The triumph of the hero at the conclusion of the program, therefore, reinforces the ideology of the dominant culture. At the same time, villains are inevitably brought to justice—for their crime and, in a broader sense, for their transgressions against the system. A critical question, then, is: Given its premise, characters, and worldview, how *should* the film end?

V. Genre Analysis

A *genre* is a type, class, or category of artistic work, featuring a standardized narrative format, such as horror films, romances, science fiction, situation comedies, Westerns, and the evening news. Each genre is distinctive and readily identifiable, regardless of time or place of composition, author, or subject matter. Moreover, genre is not confined to one medium. For instance, at one time or another, superhero tales have appeared in print, on radio, on television, and in film.

Every genre contains patterns in plot, structure, characteristic conventions, or devices (such as horses, characters, and outfits found in Westerns), and stylistic similarities. Individual programs generally conform to a clear formula of the genre.

Examining the *shared ideological orientation* can provide insight into the ideology of a genre. Each genre operates according to a distinctive belief system, with respect to the following:

- What culture or cultures populate this world
- Definitions of success
- Whether people are in control of their own destinies

To illustrate, the ideology of the *action drama* is essentially conservative, in that the central focus of each program is a return to the status quo. The conventional plot operates according to the formula of Order/Chaos/Order. Initially, the world exists in a state of harmony. However, almost immediately some problem (i.e., a troublemaker or natural disaster) disrupts this initial tranquility. The remainder of the plot focuses on the restoration of order, which is achieved at the conclusion. Thus, this world is reactionary; it does not require change but changing *back*. Action dramas operate in a Darwinian environment, in which audience members value protection and security, often at the expense of an individual's civil liberties.

The ideology of *horror* genre focuses on primal issues of good and evil. One subgenre consists of stories in which evil originates *within* human beings. Film critic Robin Wood introduced the idea, rooted in psychoanalytic theory, that "scary movies provide a valuable window onto what our society 'represses or oppresses.' " The monster, he wrote, represents the marginalized, the sexually or politically subversive, the taboo. Furthermore, Wood contends that the first zombie in the 1968 classic "Night of the Living Dead" was a manifestation of family dysfunction (Zinoman, 2011).

But in addition, the horror genre conveys ideological messages about threats, or perceived threats, to the system. For instance, the economic uncertainty stemming from the economic recession of 2008 was accompanied by a wave of media programming featuring zombies. *Slasher movies* depict a world in which *we* are the monsters: human nature is bestial, wicked, and corrupt. In this Darwinian world, the weak (usually women characters) are preyed on and brutalized by the strong.

The *gangster* genre presents conflicting ideological messages, as reflected in the rise and fall of the protagonist. The beginning of the film typically focuses on the spectacular success of the young gangster, who epitomizes the American ideology of hard work, initiative, and free enterprise. But at a critical point in the narrative, the protagonist typically crosses a moral line and is punished for his violation of the social order. This stage of the plot sends the message that individuals must obey the law and conform to the system.

The *science fiction* genre offers commentaries on the present and future condition of society. One subgenre consists of invasion films, in which some foreign element threatens our current system. One subcategory consists of allegories that are set in the future but comment on present conditions. The genre of science fiction has long focused on this theme of a world in which the machines have taken over and punish human beings for their hubris of playing God, in the creation of these omnipotent computers. Another subgenre, *Utopian* science fiction programs, offer a glimpse into highly evolved civilizations that have transcended many of the limitations which plague contemporary earthlings These films extend hope to a world which has become corrupt and self-absorbed.

Other genres such as Westerns, quiz shows, situation comedies, reality shows, news programs, tabloid talk shows, spy programs, and sports programming also possess distinctive ideological orientations that send messages about what life is and what life ought to be. Examining the ideological underpinnings of these genres can provide insight into ways in which a genre shapes audiences' expectations and understanding and context.

See also: Audience Analysis; Cultural Context; Formulaic Analysis; Genre Study, Media Literacy Approach; Narratology

References

Chandler, D. (n.d.). "Semiotics for Beginners." Retrieved from http://www.aber .ac.uk/dge/semiotic.html

Dowd, M. (2011, August 2). "Washington Chain Saw Massacre," *New York Times.*

Gee, J. P. (1996). *Social Linguistics and Literacies: Ideology in Discourses.* London and Bristol, PA: Taylor & Francis.

Hartley, J. (1994). *Key Concepts in Communication and Cultural Studies.* London and New York: Routledge.

The Motion Picture Production Code of 1930 (The Hays Code). ArtsReformotion .com http://www.artsreformation.com/a001/hays-code.html

Parenti, M. (1992). *Make Believe Media.* New York: St. Martin's Press.

Pitts, L. Jr. (2001, April 5). "'I have a dream' . . . for Sale." *St. Louis Post-Dispatch*. Retrieved from www.stl.com

Romero, S. (2007, May 1). "Chávez Takes Over Foreign-Controlled Oil Projects in Venezuela." *New York Times*. Retrieved from http://www.nytimes.com/2007/05/02/news/02iht-web0502venez.5527473.html

Williams, R. (1995). *Keywords: A Vocabulary of Culture and Society*. London: Oxford University Press, p. 118.

Zinoman, J. (2011, July 16). "The Critique of Pure Horror." *New York Times*. Retrieved from http://www.nytimes.com/2011/07/17/opinion/sunday/17gray.html?pagewanted=all

Information Management Analysis

This managerial approach to media communications involves the construction and the dissemination of information within organizational and business settings. A familiarity with information management can provide insight into the identification and analysis of media messages, as well as the impact it has on the public.

Information management operates on the premise that information is a commodity that companies must use efficiently. To illustrate, IFC, a consulting firm in information and document management, promotes its services as follows:

> We live in a society where information is abundant. Having the "right" information is essential if your organization is to carry out its duties . . . (IFC is) designed to support the work of your organization by improving the management of the information and enabling a more effective and efficient exchange of information with external bodies. (IFC In Form Consult, 2012)

The key to delivering the message is consistency and repetition of the message. Thus, an effective information management plan is characterized by the following: (a) a carefully constructed message; (b) selection of the appropriate time, place, and method; and (c) a variety of media that converge on an audience from several avenues.

Information management strategies are applied in business, public relations, and political communications. Many kinds of information are employed in a corporate setting: internal, external, lateral, horizontal (i.e., top to bottom), interdepartmental (between departments), intradepartmental (within a department).

According to James Robertson (2005), common information management challenges include the following:

- Large number of disparate information management systems
- Little integration or coordination between information systems
- Range of legacy systems requiring upgrading or replacement
- Direct competition between information management systems
- No clear strategic direction for the overall technology environment
- Limited and patchy adoption of existing information systems by staff
- Poor quality of information, including lack of consistency, duplication, and out-of-date information
- Little recognition and support of information management by senior management
- Limited resources for deploying, managing, or improving information systems
- Lack of enterprise-wide definitions for information types and values (no corporate-wide taxonomy)
- Large number of diverse business needs and issues to be addressed
- Lack of clarity around broader organizational strategies and directions
- Difficulties in changing working practices and processes of staff
- Internal politics impacting on the ability to coordinate activities enterprise-wide

Information management professionals develop plans that enable their corporations to use information efficiently and effectively.

A comprehensive communication plan consists of the following stages:

- Conducting an assessment of current practices and policies
- Recommending new plans that will achieve the goals of the company
- Implementing new plans that will achieve the goals of the company
- Developing an assessment instrument to determine whether the new applications of information achieve the goals of the company

References

Consultants in Information and Document Management. Retrieved from http://dlm forum.typepad.com/Information_Management_Strategyv1.pdf

IFC In Form Consult: Corporate Information Management. (2012). "Services." Retrieved from http://www.inform-consult.com

Robertson, J. (2005, November 1). "10 Principles of Effective Information Management." Step Two Designs. Retrieved from http://www.steptwo.com.au/papers/kmc_effectiveim/index.html

Inquiry-Based Pedagogy, Media Literacy Education

Inquiry-based pedagogy refers to an educational philosophy employed in the discipline of media literacy in which teachers work collaboratively with students so that their personal encounters with the media enrich their learning experience. Elizabeth Thoman and Tessa Jolls (2004) explain, "Media literacy, grounded as it is in inquiry-based, process-oriented pedagogy, offers not a new subject to teach but rather a new way to teach and even more important, a new way to learn" (p. 21).

This educational philosophy owes much to the Brazilian educator Paulo Freire. In his seminal work, *Pedagogy of the Oppressed* (1968), Freire looked at classroom dynamics as a microcosm of power relations in society, making the point that the hierarchical nature of teacher–student relations often inhibits learning opportunities. Freire refers to this as the "banking model," in that the teacher simply makes "knowledge deposits" into the minds of the students.

This media education is democratic, challenging the typical hierarchical structure of our educational system. Unlike literature or history, which have specific and limited sets of primary materials, media is a discipline in which it is impossible for a teacher to be conversant with all of the significant newspaper articles, tweets, international television broadcasts, films, and Internet software. As a result, it is inevitable that students will be familiar with content with which teachers are unacquainted.

Consequently, under the inquiry-based system, the role of the teacher has shifted from *authority* to *designer*, *facilitator*, and *critic*. Educator Jackie Cossentino (2004) observes, "[These] attributes can lead to enhanced engagement and learning, build positive bonds with students and to not manage but moderate the classroom."

Media literacy is a process-oriented discipline that lends itself to an inquiry-based approach to education. Rather than directing students to a specific set of conclusions, media literacy equips students with strategies to analyze the media and media presentations. Canadian media literacy educator Chris Worsnop declares, "Media education teachers focus on respecting students' choices and decisions regardless of their orientation, provided those choices and decisions are well formed and properly supported" (Seeman, 2004).

This egalitarian education model can be a challenge to teachers who are used to being the unchallenged classroom authority. Another major problem facing teachers is being able to recognize their own biases. Reflecting on his classroom teaching experience, Chris Sperry (2010) admits,

> When I watch Fox News I can easily identify the ways in which the reports use language, facts, music and interviews to push their slanted position. But then I listen to *All Things Considered* and it sounds like pretty objective news. Their biases are harder for me to see. . . .
>
> I do not believe that it is possible, let alone desirable, to be free from bias as a teacher or as a human being. My belief in social justice and equality, like my commitment to listening to students, shape my teaching, and I do not apologize for this. I want my students to know and identify when I am operating from these biases. But one of my greatest goals in teaching adolescents is to get them to think rigorously and deeply and independently. . . . If I lead a decoding of a conservative news source but then I use a clip from a liberal source without decoding, or decode each with a different attitude or body language, I am giving a clear message about what sources are to be trusted and what sources are to be criticized. Pretty soon my students will be reacting to my values, not figuring out what they believe.
>
> I need to earn my students' trust that my primary goal is their independent thinking, not filling them up with my values. I do have clear positions that affect my teaching and my decoding. I choose what documents to bring in, what issues we will study, what questions to pose. This is a huge responsibility. I would not legitimize certain perspectives I see as racist or violent or offensive by bringing them into the classroom without being able to deal fully with these issues. Sometimes that means keeping them out of my classroom all together. But teaching is not persuading. The decoding that I do in the classroom must be open. (p. 97)

However, teachers can derive great benefit from tapping into the experiences of their students. Indeed, *listening* is one of the most important skills that a teacher of media literacy can possess. Sperry (2010) explains,

In order to understand (students') meaning-making I must learn to listen well, and I can't do that if I am always talking at them and trying to fill them up with my knowledge. . . . The only way we can truly understand the impact of our work is if we develop the skills and attitudes, the methodologies and materials that allow us as teachers to listen well to our students. This means listening for developmental capacities, listening for their cultural orientations, listening to their experiences of school and our classrooms, listening to how they understand and interpret the world. (p. 89)

Significantly, teachers who have adopted a participatory model of media education have reported many positive results. Kathleen Tyner examined a study conducted by Apple Classrooms of Tomorrow and found that "[Teachers] were personally working harder and longer hours, but enjoying their work more. They acted more as guides and less as lecturers" (in Dwyer, 1996: 90).

Postman and Weingartner (1969) have described ways in which Inquiry-based education has altered classroom dynamics:

- The teacher rarely tells students a personal opinion about a particular social or political issue;
- does not accept a single statement as an answer to a question;
- encourages student–student interaction as opposed to student–teacher interaction and generally avoids acting as a mediator or judging the quality of ideas expressed; and
- lessons develop from the responses of students and not from a previously determined "logical" structure.

One effective application of the Inquiry-based approach involves instructors asking the students to bring in their own examples of media presentations that illustrate the principles being discussed and then being prepared to share these examples with the class. The following are examples of classroom assignments based on this educational philosophy:

1. Assignment: Audience
   Bring to class two advertisements for the same product that are directed at different audiences (e.g., cigarette ads placed in *Ebony* vs. *Time* Magazine, or radio commercials playing on a country station vs. a pop station). Identify the audiences for the two ads.

Be prepared to discuss the following:
    a. Does the communications strategy of the ads differ? Explain.
    b. Does the style of the ads differ? Explain.
    c. Does the content of the ads differ? Explain.

2. Written Assignment: Journalism, 3 Pages

Conduct a media literacy analysis of print journalism, using selected keys to interpreting media messages. Note which keys you intend to use in your analysis.

Your analysis may focus on **one** of the following:
    a. One story in depth
    b. The layout of a single page
    c. An entire newspaper
    d. A comparison of two papers that appeared on the same day
    e. Magazines

3. Assignment: Advertising

Bring in an example of a print ad which contain **one** of the following:
    a. False and misleading ads
    b. Incomplete/distorted message
    c. The big promise
    d. Hyperbole
    e. Similie
    f. Parity statement
    g. Unfinished statement
    h. Qualifier words
    i. Illogical premise
    j. Extraneous inclusion

Be prepared to share your findings with the class.

In addition to bringing in their own media presentations *into* the classroom, students learn to apply the principles and concepts of media literacy to their experiences *outside* of the classroom. For example, being able to apply media literacy strategies can enrich a student's appreciation of a movie. As media literacy educator Paul Mihailidis explains,

Seeing education as "learning-centered" sheds light as to how learning in the classroom can go beyond the simple dissemination and retention of knowledge. If the teacher can successfully evoke critical understanding and active learning in students, they can begin to see the connections between the classroom and their larger social surroundings. (Mihailidis, 2009)

It should be noted that students sometimes report that, initially, media literacy education can detract from their simple enjoyment of media presentations. In this case, the best advice is simply . . . to *relax*. Students are often surprised (and delighted) to discover that they are able to "see" more as a result of having given so much thought to strategies of analysis. Furthermore, students can choose to refer to the tools of analysis for postpresentation reflection and discussion.

References

Cossentino, J. (2004). *Talking about a Revolution: The Languages of Educational Reform*. Albany: State University of New York Press.

Dwyer, D. C. (1996). *Changing the Conversation About Teaching, Learning & Technology: A Report on 10 years of ACOT Research*. Cupertino, CA: Apple Classrooms of Tomorrow.

Freire, P. (1968). *Pedagogy of the Oppressed*. New York: Continuum.

Mihailidis, M. (2009). "Student-Centered Educational Approach, Media Literacy Education Active Teacher/Student Engagement." Unpublished manuscript, University of Maryland.

Postman, N., & Weingartner, C. (1969). *Teaching as a Subversive Activity*. New York: Delacorte Press.

Seeman, N. (2004, January). "Beware the Media Police." *Fraser Forum*, (pp. 19–20).

Sperry, C. (2010). "The Epistemological Equation." *Journal of Media Literacy Education*, *1* (2), 89–98.

Thoman, E., & Jolls, T. (2004). "Media Literacy—A National Priority for a Changing World." *American Behavioral Scientist 48*, 18–29.

Institutional Analysis

Institutional analysis is an approach that analyzes media content as a product of institutional power. This qualitative approach examines how the structure of a media organization affects the processes of decision making, policy formation, and resource management; that, in turn, influences the selection, emphasis, and treatment of media content.

The Center for the Study of Institutions, Population and Environmental Change (n.d.) provides the following explanation:

Institutional analysis is that part of the social sciences which studies how institutions—i.e., structures and mechanisms of social order and cooperation governing the behavior of two or more individuals—behave and function according to both empirical rules (informal rules-in-use and norms) and also theoretical rules (formal rules and law).

This focus examines the characteristics of social institutions, rules of governance and behavior (both formal and informal), and external interactions; that is, how institutions work together to address cultural issues. As an example, a number of prestigious scholars, including Elinor Ostrom, Roy Gardner, and James Walker, have examined the role of institutions in the development of environmental policy. Institutions have been developed to protect against overexploitation of the environment. In an interdisciplinary approach to this topic, authors have explored empirically, theoretically, and experimentally the nature of such institutions and the way they come about. They consider the institutional and physical variables that affect the likelihood of successful external interrelations:

> Forests, irrigation systems, fisheries, groundwater basins, grazing lands, and the air we breathe are all examples of common-pool resources (CPRs). Because no one has property rights or control over such a resource, users of CPRs are frequently assumed to be caught in an inescapable dilemma—overexploitation of the resource, or what is commonly known as "the tragedy of the commons." . . . Understanding the conditions under which users of CPRs successfully develop and maintain effective institutions is critical to facilitating improved resource policies. (Ostrom et al., 2004; description of book at http://www.press. umich.edu/9745)

A media literacy approach to institutional analysis focuses attention on ways in which the parameters of the media industry affect content. Using interviews, participant observation, and the study of records, institutional analysis examines the scheme of power roles and their impact on decision making in the communications industry.

Canadian education specialist Jane Tallim explains, media literacy

> is the instinct to question what lies behind media productions—the motives, the money, the values and the ownership—and to be aware of how these factors influence content. (Media Awareness Network: wwwmedia-awareness.ca)

Media institutions may be analyzed in terms of the following elements.

- *Types of power roles or groups within the institution*: authorities, patrons, management, auxiliaries, colleagues, competitors, and publics
- *Types of leverage*: political, military, control over resources, control over personnel, access to specialized services, access to authorities
- *Functions of institution*: arbitration, regulation, set conditions for the supply and operation of funds, setting and supervising policies, set and overseeing standards

Media literacy pioneer Elizabeth Thoman (1993) observes that an examination of industry considerations can establish an agenda with regard to current public policy:

The stage of social, political, and economic analysis of mass media involves exploring deeper issues of who produces the media, and for what purpose. This inquiry can sometimes set the stage for various media advocacy efforts to challenge or redress public policies or corporate practices.

See also: Ownership Patterns, Media; Sectors, Media Literacy

References

The Center for the Study of Institutions, Population and Environmental Change. Indiana University. Retrieved from http://www.indiana.edu/~cipec

Ostrom, E., Gardner, R., & Walker, J. (2004). *Rules, Games, and Common-Pool Resources*. Ann Arbor: University of Michigan Press.

Tallim, J. "What Is Media Literacy?" Media Awareness Network. wwwmedia-aware ness.ca

Thoman, E. (1993, Spring). "Media Literacy: Educating for Today and Tomorrow." *Curriculum/Technology Quarterly, 2*. http://www.ascd.org/publications/ctq/spring 1993/Media-Literacy@-Educating-for-Today-and-Tomorrow.aspx

Integrated Approach to Media Literacy Education

One of the major debates among media literacy educators at the primary and secondary level involves the relative merits of "stand-alone" media literacy courses versus an "integrated pedagogical model" in which media literacy principles are incorporated into established disciplines. Advocates of the integrated approach use the analogy with foreign language instruction, pointing out that offering classes in Latin, French, or Chinese once or twice a week is not nearly as effective as becoming immersed in the language by traveling to a foreign country. The Integrated Approach is particularly useful in an environment in which teachers have little room in their curriculum to teach additional subjects because of required courses and standardized tests.

Some critics maintain that when media literacy is not the primary focus of attention, some critical principles may be overlooked. However, media literacy educator Frank Baker points out that as a critical thinking skill, media literacy can actually *enhance* the instruction of established disciplines:

> Media literacy education can be integrated into every area of current school curriculum. While worthy of concentrated time in the classroom, one of the benefits of media literacy education is that it can be applied to other subjects, doubling the benefit of the lesson. Media literacy promotes critical thinking skills that can be applied to all areas of study, including mathematics, history and geography; topics that may not be automatically associated with media literacy education. An example of a mathematics lesson would be to analyze statistics presented within the news, such as polls. An example of a historical lesson would be analyzing political cartoons from the last century. (Baker, n.d.)

A number of educators have successfully examined ways to incorporate media literacy into a range of established disciplines, including language arts, social studies, health sciences, and mathematics. Examples include the following:

- University of Wisconsin at Madison professor David Williamson Shaffer developed an online game that allows science students to act as journalists in investigating, developing, and creating stories for an online science newsmagazine, thus giving the students an opportunity to be "critical consumers of scientific information they encounter" (Hobbs, 1996: 2). The students are thus engaged in science vocabulary and concepts and applications of media literacy simultaneously.
- Misty Dawn Carmichael's (2007) dissertation focused on "Teaching Media Literacy in the Composition Classroom."
- Carlos Cortes declares that media literacy is essential to multicultural education: "Media can be used to stimulate students to consider multiple perspectives on current and historical multicultural dilemmas" (Hobbs, 1996).

This educational philosophy can also be extended to higher education. At Webster University (St. Louis, Missouri), traditional communications courses such as International Communications, Genre Studies, and Video Production are taught from a media literacy perspective.

See also: Curriculum Developments in Higher Education; Foundations of Media Literacy Education

References

Baker, F. (n.d.). Retrieved from http://www.ithaca.edu/looksharp/resources_12 principles.php; www.fbaker1346@aol.com)

Carmichael, M. D. (2007, May). "Teaching Media Literacy in the Composition Classroom: Are We There Yet?" PhD dissertation, Georgia State University.

Hobbs, R. (1996). "Expanding the Concept of Literacy." In R. Kubey (Ed.), *Media Literacy in the Information Age*. New York: Transaction Press.

International Communications, Media Literacy Approach

International communications is an established area of study within the discipline of media communications that can be approached from a media literacy perspective. International communications typically considers the histories and characteristics of media systems around the world. However, a media literacy approach to international communications also teaches students how to make sense of information being conveyed through the international channels of mass communications.

Global media presentations have become increasingly available to international audiences. However, universal *access* to the media should not be confused with media literacy, a field of study in which individuals develop the ability to analyze *media messages* (that is, the underlying themes or ideas contained in a media presentation). Columnist Thomas Friedman (2011) declares,

At its best, the Internet can educate more people faster than any media tool we've ever had. At its worst, it can make people dumber faster than any media tool we've ever had. The lie that 4,000 Jews were warned not to go into the World Trade Center on Sept. 11 was spread entirely over the Internet and is now thoroughly believed in the Muslim world. Because the Internet has an aura of "technology" surrounding it, the uneducated believe information from it even more. They don't realize that the Internet, at its ugliest, is just an open sewer: an electronic conduit for untreated, unfiltered information.

The following factors provide *context* that affects media content:
- Geographic Context
  - Does the *proximity* to neighboring countries affect its media coverage?
  - Does the *geopolitical* relationship between neighboring countries influence media coverage?
- Availability of Resources
  - How do the technical resources of a country affect its media system?
  - How do the natural resources of a country affect its media system?
  - How do the trained personnel of a country affect its media system?
- Ethnic Composition
  - What is the ethnic composition of the country?
  - Is the ethnic composition of the country homogenous or mixed?
  - In the case of a country with multi-ethnic composition, consider the following:
    - Does the media represent the dominant ethnic culture?
    - Are there media that express the perspective of other ethnic groups?
    - Are there tensions between the ethnic cultures that might affect the presentation and interpretation of content?
    - Are there ethnic references (e.g., words, humor, and culture) in media presentations that provide insight into media messages?
- Religious Composition
  - What religion(s) exist within the country?
  - Is one religion predominate within the culture (either officially or unofficially)?
    - If so, does this have an impact on the selection of stories, point of view, inclusion and omission of information, etc.?
    - Are there religious references (words, humor, and culture) in the media presentation that provides insight into media messages?

Media Literacy Strategies

A media literacy approach to international communications familiarizes students with a range of strategies with which to analyze and discuss international media messages. The following strategies are particularly useful in the analysis of media and media presentations in other cultures.

Media Communicator

The point of view of the media communicator may appear in the text through such production techniques as editing decisions, connotative words, and images.

The challenges of identifying the media communicator are compounded in the arena of global communications. The sheer number of reporters, editors, filmmakers, and webmasters makes it impossible to be familiar with all of their backgrounds, credentials, and orientations, as well as an acquaintance with the educational institutions where a foreign media communicator received his or her training. Although an article or television program often cites the sponsoring organization, there is rarely any accompanying information that provides information on who funds this organization, its mission, or orientation.

The following classroom exercises demonstrate the types of media analysis that can be conducted using the media communicator line of inquiry:

- Identify the media communicator(s), focusing on the following demographic information:
  - Nationality
  - Gender
  - Age
  - Income
  - Religion
  - Race/Ethnicity
  - Educational level
  - Affiliation of the media communicator
    - Who funds this organization?
    - What is the mission of the media organization?
    - Is the media organization national or international?
    - How does this affiliation affect the point of view of the media presentation?
  - Nature of expertise of the media communicator
    - Is this person qualified to speak authoritatively on the subject?
    - Does this person's contribution fall within his or her range of expertise?
    - What are the criteria for being considered an expert?
    - Do the criteria for being considered an expert vary in different countries?
- Point of view
  - Examine the word choice, images, and headlines in a media presentation as a way to detect a particular point of view of the media communicator.

      ∘ Compare media presentations from different countries. Does the comparison provide insight into the point of view of the media communicators?

Audience

The audience for a media presentation is influenced by cultural, economic, and historical factors, which, in turn, influences its response to media content.

Questions for students to consider in the analysis of audience include the following:

- What is the audience's interaction with the media?
- What medium is used most frequently?
- Does the audience seek particular media for certain kinds of information?
- Does audience behavior vary between certain segments of the population?

Cultural Context

Media communicators construct a complete world based on certain fundamental assumptions about how this world operates. Examining the *worldview* of a media presentation examines what kind of world is depicted in a media presentation (or series of media presentations) within a culture.

The following framework provides information about the worldview of a media presentation:

- What culture or cultures populate this world?
- Does this world present an optimistic or pessimistic view of life?
  - ∘ Are the characters in the presentation happy?
  - ∘ Do the characters have a chance to be happy?
- Are people in control of their own destinies?
  - ∘ Is there a supernatural presence in this world?
  - ∘ Are the characters under the influence of other people?
- What hierarchy of values is in operation in this worldview?
  - ∘ What embedded values can be found in the production?
  - ∘ What values are embodied in the characters?
  - ∘ What values prevail through the resolution?
- What does it mean to be a success in this world?
  - ∘ How does a person succeed in this world?
  - ∘ What kinds of behavior are rewarded in this world?

International Media Stereotypes. Most people form their acquaintance with members of other nationalities through media stereotypes. A stereotype is an oversimplified conception of a person, group, or event. Stereotyping is an associative process, based on a common set of assumptions; if there is no general consensus about a group, there can be no stereotype.

Stereotyping is a common coping mechanism. Even people who are victims of stereotyping in turn stereotype others. Thus, stereotyping serves as a kind of shorthand that enables us to make everyday decisions in our lives.

Some stereotypes are universal, transcending national boundaries. Other stereotypes are national, meaning that they have distinct meanings only for particular cultures. The following classroom exercises can furnish information with regard to international media stereotypes:

1. National stereotypes
   a. Are there historical or cultural contexts that account for these stereotypes?
   b. What characteristics define these stereotypes?
   c. Are the characteristics associated with national stereotypes similar to characteristics associated with groups in other countries?
   d. Are stereotypes more likely found in the program of one country?
   e. Compare stereotypical depictions of different nationalities (e.g., English, Germans, Swedes). Identify similarities, differences.
   f. How is your nationality depicted in international media presentations? Construct a stereotypical profile from foreign films, television programs, advertisements, or magazines.
2. Survey a sample of international media programs. Identify stereotypes of different groups.
   a. Identify the characteristics commonly associated with the group being depicted in the media.
   b. Does word choice reinforce stereotypes?
   c. Editing decisions—is information included in the media presentation that reinforces stereotypes?
   d. Connotative Images—do images appearing in the media presentation reinforce stereotypes?

Historical Context

Historical context is an approach that provides insight into the country of origin. The following framework forms the basis of media literacy analysis:

- Media presentations can provide insight into a country's historical background.
- Historical events can shape media content.

- An understanding of historical events can enrich the interpretation of a media presentation.
- Historical references embedded in a media presentation can provide insight into its themes and messages.
- Popular media programming can *anticipate* historical events.
- A media presentation can serve as a barometer of current attitudes toward historical events.
- Popular media programming plays an active role in shaping historical events.
- Popular media presentations can distort historical facts or shift their emphasis.
- Tracing the evolution of a particular medium, genre, or presentation can provide insight into changes in cultural attitudes and concerns.

Ownership Patterns

The ultimate the media communicator is the entity (individual, government, or corporation) that owns the media production company. The owners make decisions (or oversee the decisions) that affect the production and distribution of media messages.

There are four basic types of global media ownership systems, each of which exercises a distinct influence on the construction of media messages:

1. *State-Owned Media Systems.* In authoritarian countries such as China, Cuba, and North Korea, the media industry is controlled by the government. Under this system, the *function*, or purpose of the media is to exercise control over the populace.
2. *Public Ownership.* In this system, the media are owned by the public but operated by the government.
3. *Private Ownership.* In countries such as the United States, newspapers, magazines, radio stations, film studios, and television stations are privately owned—either by individuals or, increasingly, by large, multinational corporations. The primary function of the media under this system is to generate profit.
4. *Hybrid Media Ownership Systems.* As a byproduct of globalization, the privately owned ownership model has begun to gain entry into countries that had previously operated under other ownership models.

The emergence of transnational media conglomerates has an impact on the kinds of information that we receive in numerous ways, including:

- *Support of status quo.* As beneficiaries of the existing political and economic systems, media conglomerates resist changes that do not support their own financial interests.
- *Controlling access to content.* Transnational media corporations control both the production and distribution of media content. This merging of the content and carrier means that a transnational media conglomerate is able to control all phases of the media industry: production, distribution, and exhibition.
- *Programming as product.* Under the market-driven system, the primary purpose, or *function*, is to generate the maximum possible profit. Because of this bottom-line mentality, the quality of the productions can suffer.
- *Conflicts of interest.* These may arise when a media conglomerate covers stories in which the parent company has an interest.
- *Allocation of resources.* In large transnational media conglomerates, budgetary decisions are often made on the basis of the imperative to maximize profit.

Production Analysis

Production analysis examines ways in which the production elements (e.g., editing, color, lighting, and camera position) are used in the construction of media messages. In an international arena, production elements have assumed an increased importance as a way to transcend language barriers.

Production elements can have a universal meaning, which is rooted in human experience. However, production elements may also have culturally specific denotations. By understanding that production elements may convey unintended messages in another culture, a media communicator can make production choices that convey the desired message.

The following classroom exercises demonstrate the types of media analysis that can be conducted using the production elements line of inquiry:

1. Examine a body of work produced in a particular country, focusing on aesthetic style:
   a. Can you identify a national aesthetic style?
   b. Can you identify aesthetic influences from other countries/cultures/traditions (e.g., the influence of African music on American jazz)?
2. Examine an international media presentation, focusing on universal and culturally specific meanings:
   a. Identify universal meanings associated with production values in the presentation:

1) Where do they appear in the presentation?
2) When do they appear in the narrative?
3) What does the appearance of these universal production values reveal about the themes and messages in the presentation?

b. Identify culturally specific meanings associated with production values in the presentation:

1) Are there choices of production values that run counter to the meaning normally assigned to it in your culture?

3. Color
   a. Colors can evoke a wide range of emotional responses. Examine a sample of international media presentations, focusing on the affective properties of color:

   1) How does the color set the mood and tone of a production?
   2) What feelings are evoked by the use of colors?
   3) Do the colors convey meanings that correlate with or contrast with the content of the production?

   b. Conduct research on a particular country, focusing on the culture-specific meanings assigned to colors. Compare the uses of color to media presentations in your own country.

   c. Examine a sample of international media presentations, focusing on connotative properties of color. How does the use of color reinforce messages and themes in the presentations?

   1) Do the colors in the presentations convey particular messages and themes?

4. Editing
   a. Examine impact of editing decisions on the construction of meaning. Compare international media coverage of an issue. How do the following editing decisions affect the construction of meaning?

   1) Inclusion and omission
      a) Inclusion and omission of stories. Identify stories that appear in the media of some countries but not others. What accounts for this inclusion and omission?
      b) Inclusion and omission of Information in Stories. What information can you find in the media of one country that doesn't appear in another?

   2) Providing context
   3) Arrangement of information
   4) Selective emphasis—what aspects of a story are given prominence?

    b. Sustained coverage

        1) Trace the coverage of an issue in a sample of international news sources.

    a. Which stories receive sustained coverage?

    b. Do some stories receive sustained coverage in some national sources but not others?

        2) Piece together stories (e.g., environmental changes) that are covered sporadically in the newspaper. When seen collectively, what messages are being conveyed?

    c. Does this comparative analysis furnish perspective into the biases of a country's news?

    d. Does your analysis provide insight the prevailing attitudes in other cultures? Explain.

5. Word choice

    a. Analyze a sample of international presentations (print, broadcast, or Internet).

        1) What does word choice in the presentation reveal about a nation's

        2) Historical sensibility

        3) Political life

        4) Cultural sensibility

    b. Translation

        1) If you have skills in a foreign language, translate a newspaper article into your native tongue:

            a) Is the translation accurate?

            b) Does the translation affect the meaning the presentation?

6. Connotative image

    a. Analyze a sample of international presentations (print, broadcast, or Internet).

        1) What do the images in the presentation reveal about

            a) A nation's historical sensibility?

            b) A nation's political life?

            c) A nation's cultural sensibility?

    b. Analyze a sample of international media presentations dealing with the same topic, focusing on images.

        1) Identify universal images.

        2) Identify national images.

            a) Are images used in one country interpreted differently in your culture? Explain.

        b) Does the appearance of an image in the media furnish perspective into cultural attitudes, preoccupations, and myths?

    c. Examine several images, focusing on point of view:

        1) How do the images reflect the points of view of the productions?

        2) How do the images affect the interpretation of the audience?

        3) How do they alter the meaning of the presentation?

    d. Identify connotative images in the media presentation.

        1) What is the connotation of the image?

        2) Why was the image included in the media presentation?

7. Music

    a. What does a country's indigenous music reveal about its culture?

        1) History

        2) Religion

        3) Ethnic composition

    b. What do the lyrics of contemporary songs can furnish insight into the following:

        1) Current conditions in a country

        2) Attitudes toward issues

        3) Attitudes toward other countries

    c. Does the music in a media presentation fulfill one of the following *functions*?

        1) Influencing behaviors and attitudes

        2) Eliciting an affective response

        3) Punctuating the visuals

        4) Providing editorial comment

        5) Conveying narrative cues to the audience

    d. Examine how the use of music reinforces messages and themes in the media presentation.

Other qualitative media literacy strategies that are applicable to the study of international communications include the following:

- A *nonverbal approach* focuses on nonverbal communications as a strategy for discussing and interpreting media content.
- An *iconographic approach* to media analysis considers ways in which the connotative properties of images convey media messages.
- *Mythic analysis*—one way to account for the appeal of many media programs is that these stories are transmitting myths that provide insight into the culture in which they were produced.

- *Ideological analysis* provides insight into ways in which the media reflect, reinforce, and shape the system of beliefs that determines the thinking and behavior of a culture. Media presentations contain assumptions about how the world should operate, who should oversee this world, and the proper and appropriate relationships among its inhabitants.

Applied Areas of Analysis

International media literacy examines media formats such as journalism, advertising, and political communications and considers mass media issues, including violence in the media, media and children, and media and social change.

Journalism

The ready access to primary source material provides opportunities to compare the points of view of journalists, news organizations, and national perspectives. Media literacy students have the opportunity to compare the coverage of issues by news organizations throughout the globe, by focusing on the following:

- What information is included and omitted
- Connotative word choice and images
- Order of presentation
- Use of quotes
- Point of view

Online journalism also provides invaluable research opportunities for media literacy scholarship. Using digital databases, researchers can instantly record and track the number of times that a word appears in the media, providing insight into emerging areas of cultural interest and concern. In particular, social media provides immediate public response to historical and cultural events. Journalist Ben Zimmer (2011) notes that

Twitter is many things to many people, but lately it has been a gold mine for scholars in fields like linguistics, sociology and psychology who are looking for real-time language data to analyze. Twitter's appeal to researchers is its immediacy—and its immensity. Instead of relying on questionnaires and other laborious and time-consuming methods of data collection, social scientists can simply take advantage of Twitter's stream to eavesdrop on a virtually limitless array of language in action.

In addition, social media provide invaluable research data for *sentiment analysis*—public attitudes *toward* a subject. For instance, the death of Libyan ruler Colonel Muammar Qaddafi in October 2011 was followed by a dramatic increase in the frequency of word choice such as "good" and "wonderful" in Tweets by residents of the country.

Advertising

Some international advertising campaigns have a *universal* appeal. As an example, beer ads take advantage of the fact that everyone gets thirsty. Thus, regardless of culture, beer commercials emphasize the refreshing quality of the product. In contrast, other ads are *local*, which are effective only in a particular country or region.

The following classroom exercises demonstrate the types of media analysis that can be conducted in international advertising:

1. Examine a sample of ads, which have been produced for an international audience.
   a. Do the ads reflect a standardized or localized approach?
      - If an ad is localized, analyze how the communications strategy, style, and content have been adapted to the culture of the country.
      - Identify the values, attitudes, and preoccupations that are reflected in the ad. Do they conflict with the values, attitudes, and preoccupations of the country in which the ad appears? Explain.
2. Compare national ads, which have been produced for its domestic market.
   a. How are the following products advertised:
      - Alcohol
      - Tobacco
      - Computers
   b. What messages are conveyed about these products in different countries?
      - Compare ads that promote the same brand (e.g., Budweiser or IBM). What do the differences reveal about these countries?
3. Examine a sample of ads produced in one country.
   a. Who is the target audience?
   b. Identify affective appeals used in these ads.
   c. What is the worldview of the advertisements?

   d. What do the ads reveal about the country's cultural preoccupations, attitudes, values, behaviors, and myths?
   e. Can you identify a "national style" characteristic of ads produced within the country?
   f. Is there evidence of the influence of Western cultural values in the ads?
   g. In what ways do the following elements provide perspective into the cultural sensibility of a country?
      • Advertising theme
      • Slogan
      • Product attributes
      • Product packaging
      • Product name
4. Analyze a sample of national ads, focusing on the use of the following nonverbal elements.
   a. Do any nonverbal elements (e.g., gesture, posture, and facial expression) convey messages?
   b. Do any nonverbal elements appear incongruous? Could they have a cultural significance?
   c. Models/Performers
      • Describe the people who are being used to promote the product in the ad. What messages do these people convey with regard to images of success?
      • Do the models/performers provide insight into the target market? Explain.
      • Are celebrities used to promote the product? What messages are conveyed by the selection/presentation of these celebrities?
5. Select a country and conduct research on its advertising.
   a. How much advertising appears in the country?
      • What proportion of its advertising is produced and distributed within the country?
      • What proportion of its advertising is produced and distributed outside of the country?
   b. What kinds of products are advertised in the country?
   c. Are there national regulations on advertising?

Political Communications

International media literacy examines the impact of media on the political systems of different countries and furnishes a way to assess the political landscape of a nation. For instance, examining the *function*, or process, of the media provides insight into a country's political system. Thus, the function of the media consists of the following possibilities ranges from *informing* to *controlling* its citizens.

The following classroom exercises demonstrate the types of media analysis that can be conducted on international political communication:

Select a country and, using the following guidelines, describe its media system:

1. What is the political system of the country?
   a. Totalitarian
   b. Democratic
   c. Transitional
2. How does the country's political system affect the flow of information?
3. Conversely, how does a country's media system affect its political system?
4. Describe the regulation of information carried on the channels of mass communication.
   a. How does this country define freedom of the press?
   b. What kinds of information are permitted?
   c. What kinds of information are prohibited?

See also: Advertising—Media Literacy Analysis; Affective Response Analysis; Cultural Context; Function; Historical Context; Iconographic Analysis; Inquiry-Based Pedagogy, Media Literacy Education; International Communications, Media Literacy Approach; Journalism; Key Principles and Concepts, Media Literacy; Mass-Mediated Reality; Nonverbal Approach to Media Analysis; Ownership Patterns, Media; Political Communications, American; Production Analysis Approach

References

Friedman, T. (2011, December 13). "Global Village Idiot." *New York Times*.

Zimmer, B. (2011, October 29). "Twitterology: A New Science?" *New York Times*. Retrieved from http://www.nytimes.com/2011/10/30/opinion/sunday/twitterology-a-new-science.html

International Media Literacy

International media literacy is an area of study that examines the discipline of media literacy from an international perspective.

An international approach to media literacy includes the following areas of focus.

1. Shared Areas of Consensus

Although individual countries may have their own approaches to the discipline of media literacy, there are several points of *conceptual consensus*:

- *Media literacy is a critical thinking skill that is applied to the source of much of our information: the channels of mass communication.* Media literacy enhances individuals' ability to make sense of the information being conveyed through the media. Furthermore, media literacy students are able to transfer these critical thinking skills to established disciplines such as language arts and social studies.

- *Media literacy furnishes individuals with the tools to make independent choices with regard to (a) which media programming to select and (b) how to interpret the information that they receive through the channels of mass communication.* Despite efforts by media communicators to impose direct instruction (e.g., "Buy it today") or indirect messages ("Measures of success are . . ."), media literacy students learn to develop a critical distance from what they are watching, hearing, and reading.

- *The media are constructions of reality.* The Ontario Canada Ministry of Education states that media presentations present *versions* of reality. Although media programs may appear to be natural, they are in fact carefully crafted productions that have been produced to serve a range of objectives—from information to generating profit (Pungente, 1989).

- *The media are neutral channels of information* The media are simply channels of communications that can be used in either a positive or negative fashion. For instance, at the same time that digital media is promoting social change, this channel is also used to *obstruct* political movements. The factors that determine the impact of a media presentation, include (a) who is producing the presentation, (b) what is the function (or purpose) behind the production of the presentation; and (c) who is the intended audience.

- *Media literacy is apolitical.* Rather than promoting a particular interpretation of the media or media content, media literacy provides individuals with strategies that enable them to come up with carefully considered and well-documented interpretations. In that sense, media literacy educators don't teach their students *what* to think but, rather, *how* to think. Thus, in response to questions about the ideology of the discipline of media literacy, it can be argued that media literacy is *apolitical*. The interpretations of media content are based on the systematic application of media literacy strategies, as well as their ability to support their observations with concrete examples from the media "text" (e.g., film, television programs, Internet sites).

2. Assessing National Media Literacy Programs

Is there such a thing as a national media literacy program?

One of the major considerations in this area of study is the fundamental issue of *universal* verses *local* media literacy programs. Some aspects of media literacy programs have a universal applicability, whereas others are shaped by the distinctive characteristics of a particular culture. UK media literacy scholar Robin Blake (n.d.) explains,

> The promotion of media literacy across the globe shares many similarities. However, there are also important, if subtle, differences that influence the activities of media literacy practitioners and researchers in each country. To share research meaningfully across cultures and countries, these differences need to be explicitly identified, agreed upon, and understood.

Blake cites the following example of the distinctive nature of media literacy programs in the United Kingdom:

> In the case of the UK, in the social context, it is influenced by issues such as cultural heritage (a tradition of public service broadcasting), changing demographics (an aging population), and the place of media education in the curriculum. In the policy context it is influenced by political priorities and interventions, such as those aimed at shaping the workforce through investing in skills development, and shaping the market through initiatives. . . . And the drive to deliver government services online will have a significant impact on the need to promote the media literacy of those who will be affected most.

Questions to consider when comparing national media literacy programs include the following:

- Are there distinctive features that characterize a country's media literacy program?
- What distinguishes a particular country's media literacy program from others?
- Are there particular media literacy concepts and principles that characterize a country's media literacy program?

- Are there particular theoretical approaches to media literacy that characterize a country's media literacy program?
- What cultural, economic, and historical factors have contributed to shaping a country's media literacy program?
- How does a country's distinctive media system contribute to its media literacy program?
- Have specific individuals or organizations influenced the development of a country's media literacy program?
- What can one country learn by studying the media literacy program(s) of another country or culture?

3. Comparative Analysis

Comparative analysis can provide invaluable context for analysis of media literacy program(s) in one's country of origin. The comparison includes contextual elements that affect its media system, such the prevailing cultural, historical, political, economic, religious, and legal sensibilities of a country. Conversely, the study of national media systems can furnish perspective into a country's history, culture, political system, and economic structure.

Other points of analysis are specific to analysis of media systems, including the following:

- System(s) of ownership
- Levels of digital technology
- Media ethics
- The history of the development of the media systems
- Definitions of freedom of the press, privacy, and conflicts of interest

Comparative analysis also considers the *educational system* of a country and its impact on media literacy pedagogy. Questions to consider with regard to the educational system include:

- *What subjects are emphasized in the country's schools? What subjects are deemphasized in the country's schools?*
- *What is the schools' general approach to learning? How does this affect the presentation and interpretation of media messages?* To illustrate, in the Asian educational system, the objective has been to listen and absorb the information imparted by the instructor, as opposed to questioning the authority of the teacher. However, as Len Masterman (1980) has pointed out, media literacy does not work effectively in a hierarchical

system. Countries that include media and journalism curriculum in their schools are able to produce trained journalists and other media communicators who have learned to present information in a professional and insightful fashion.

• *How does the discipline of media literacy fit into a country's educational philosophy?* Canada, England, and Australia, for example, have histories of emphasizing media literacy throughout their school curricula
• *Are there approaches to media literacy education that characterize particular countries?*

4. International Collaborative Efforts

Media literacy organizations are establishing networks of media literacy scholars, producers, consumers, and students. For example, the mission of the International Media Literacy Network (n.d.) is to promote partnerships and collaborative projects:

> to exchange knowledge, creativity, experiences, projects, research, publications, events and materials with other Media Literacy organizations around the world. This makes the network the perfect place to meet international partners for your projects. . . . The Media Literacy Network will also organize worldwide sessions, congresses and master classes to facilitate members of the network in meeting, inspiring and supporting each other. Besides the meetings the network will also initiate new Media Literacy projects to share with you.

This nonprofit foundation has developed innovative media projects on topics such as Safe Internet, Digital Bullying, Sexualization of the Media, the Mobile Internet, Online Privacy, and Transmedia Storytelling.

Ofcom, the independent regulator and competition authority for the communications industries across Great Britain, discusses the value of partnerships on its Web site:

> Partnerships are a central part of fulfilling our Media Literacy duties. We have put media literacy clearly on the agenda of stakeholders—including policy makers, education, industry and the voluntary sector—providing leadership and stimulating debate, adding value to existing media literacy activity, catalysing new work, and promoting and directing people to advice and guidance on new communications technologies.

In addition, international media literacy organizations are now promoting collaborative media literacy scholarship. The ofcom.org Web site makes the following statement about international scholarship:

We need a vehicle for sharing findings, experience and expertise. That is why the International Media Literacy Research Forum (The Forum) was formed. The Forum was created by the partnership of Ofcom with the National Association for Media Literacy Education in the US, CAMEO from Canada, the Australian Communications and Media Authority, the New Zealand Broadcasting Standards Authority, and the Dublin Institute of Technology.

Robin Blake (n.d.) observes,

The overall aims of sharing research are to inform greater understanding by learning from the experience of others, to catalyze new approaches for research activity and, as a result, to improve the dissemination of research and the use of findings to inform practice by policy makers, regulators, and practitioners in the field.

To illustrate, the *International Journal of Learning and Media* is a peer-reviewed journal, featuring articles by media literacy scholars throughout the world. Volume 3, Issue 1 (Winter, 2011), for example, includes the following articles:

- "Blogging for Facilitating Understanding: A Study of Videogame Education," Jose Pablo Zagal & Amy S. Bruckman, pp. 7–27
- "The Personal and the Political: Social Networking in Manila," Larissa Hjorth & Michael Arnold, pp. 29–39
- "The Nirvana Effect: Tapping Video Games to Mediate Music Leaning and Interest," Kylie Peppler, Michael Downton, Eric Lindsay, & Kenneth Hay, pp. 41–59

Furthermore, teachers from different countries are now able to share lesson plans. As an example, in 2011, Project Look Sharp, a media literacy initiative of Ithaca College, produced *The Teacher's Guide to Media Literacy: Critical Thinking in a Multimedia World* (Scheibe, & Rogow, 2011), which provides a range of teaching materials (including lesson plans) for K–12 media literacy instructors. In addition, the Media Literacy Clearinghouse (http://www.frankwbaker.com) and Alliance of Civilizations (http://

www.aocmedialiteracy.org) are Web sites that make lesson plans available for teachers.

5. Anticipating Changes in the Media Landscape

We live in a world in which developments in one part of the world affect citizens in other regions. Media literacy advocates recognize the value of sharing information and anticipating changes in the media landscape. On its Web site, OfCom recognizes the importance of this function:

> Developments in Europe also have a direct or indirect bearing on media literacy promotion in the UK; examples include the European Commission's Communication on a European approach to media literacy in the digital environment (2007), its recent Recommendation, the Audio-Visual Media Services Directive and the Safer Internet 2009–2013 programme. Therefore as the promotion of media literacy moves up the policy agenda there is a growing need to maximise efforts to understand and share learning about emerging issues at a European and international level. We cooperate with European counterparts (particularly the European Commission), providing leadership and stimulating debate with stakeholders, and contribute at conferences and events throughout the UK, in Europe and beyond.

In the United Kingdom, for example, the growth of on-demand and time-shifted media consumption and the move of advertising revenue from broadcasting to the Internet is reshaping the media market. Robin Blake (n.d.) explains,

> The ongoing debate about regulation of the Internet is clearly going to impact on both society and industry. In the UK, the increasing move to "self-regulation" pushes more responsibility onto the other players, and increases the need for more education and public information campaigns.

6. Identifying the Most Effective Strategies with Which to Analyze and Discuss Media Messages

Media literacy equips individuals with a range of qualitative and quantitative approaches that provide insight into the themes and ideas contained in a media presentation.

Questions to ask with regard to methodology include the following:

- What qualitative and quantitative approaches are the most effective for the study of international media literacy analysis?
- What are the most effective approaches to media literacy analysis in particular countries?

See also: Foundations of Media Literacy Education; Historical Analysis, Media: Systems Approach; International Communications, Media Literacy Approach

References

Blake, R. (n.d.). "The International Media and Literacy Research." *International Journal of Learning and Media.* Retrieved from http://ijlm.net/news/international-media-and-literacy-research-forum.

International Media Literacy Network. Retrieved from http://www.medialiteracynetwork.org

Masterman, L. (1980). *Teaching about Television.* Basingstroke, UK: Macmillan.

Ofcom. http://www.ofcom.org.uk.

Pungente, J. (1989). Originally written for *Media Literacy Resource Guide: Intermediate and Senior Divisions.* Ontario, Canada: Ontario Ministry of Education.

Scheibe, C. L., & Rogow, F. (2011). *The Teacher's Guide to Media Literacy: Critical Thinking in a Multimedia World.* Thousand Oaks, CA: Corwin Press.

Introduction

The beginning of a media presentation is a key to deciphering media messages. The introduction of a film, television program, or Web page is often a microcosm of the media presentation, acquainting the audience with the primary characters, plot, and worldview of the media presentation. Thus, the introduction foreshadows what to expect in the course of a media presentation. The *title* of a media presentation often encapsulates the essential meaning of the media presentation and suggests thematic concerns addressed in the presentation. Even titles for film sequels, such as *Hangover II* (2011) and *Hangover Part III* (2014), announce that the audience should expect more of the same formulaic characters, action, and plot.

In the market-driven American media industry, newspaper headlines, advertising slogans, political mottos, and song and movie titles must generate interest in the presentation. To attract a sizeable audience, some titillating titles promise sex and violence.

Another strategy involves selecting titles that make exorbitant claims. Reporter Patricia Cohen (2009) provides the following example:

> Francis Fukuyama, an international political economist, hit the sweet spot with his influential 1992 post-cold-war treatise, "The End of History and the Last Man," which combined hyperbole with a seeming paradox. (Absent a supernova here, how could history end?)
>
> Soon publishers were handing us the end of prosperity and the end of poverty; the end of food, which perhaps was the inspiration for the end of overeating; the end of America, followed by the end of American exceptionalism; the end of religion, the end of the Jews (a novel), the end of faith as well as the end of materialism; the end of the present world, the end of your world and the end of the world as we know it; the end of empire, memory, education, free speech, oil, fashion and money; the end of lawyers? (given the question mark, apparently more uncertain than the end of the present world).

Thus, questions to ask with respect to the introduction of a media presentation include the following:

• What events constitute the introduction of the media presentation?
• What does the title of the presentation signify?
• Does the introduction foreshadow events and themes in the body of the production? If so, explain.

Journalism Analysis

In the *pyramid style* characteristic of American print journalism, the most essential information is positioned in the first paragraph of the story, providing answers to the following questions: *who*, *what*, *when, how*, and *why*. Indeed, in modern culture, the introduction has added significance, because the audience often only has time to skim the headline and lead paragraph.

Consequently, the introduction of a news article can furnish perspective into its point of view. As an example, compare the same story as presented in three publications on July 21, 2007:

St. Louis Post-Dispatch (Print version)
    "Bush Bars Some Tough Interrogation Methods," Deb Riechmann, The Associated Press

WASHINGTON—President George W. Bush signed an executive order Friday prohibiting cruel and inhuman treatment, including humiliation or denigration of religious beliefs, in the detention and interrogation of terrorism suspects.

New York Times
"Rules Lay Out C.I.A.'s Tactics in Questioning," Mark Mazzetti
The White House said Friday that it had given the Central Intelligence Agency approval to resume its use of some severe interrogation methods for questioning terrorism suspects in secret prisons overseas.

St. Louis Post-Dispatch (Online)
"Bush Revives CIA's Terror Interrogation Program, with Limits on 'Inhuman Practices'," Katherine Shrader, Associated Press Writer
President Bush breathed new life into the CIA terror interrogation program Friday in an executive order that would allow harsh questioning of suspects, limited in public only by a vaguely worded ban on cruel and inhuman treatment.

The headline of the first Associated Press version of the story (which was carried by the print version of the *St. Louis Post-Dispatch*) conveys the message that President George W. Bush assumed personal responsibility for restricting "tough" interrogation methods. The lead paragraph then spells out which "tough interrogation methods" he prohibited.

In the *New York Times*, the language to describe the program was concise and negative—the CIA could use "severe" interrogation methods in "secret prisons overseas." However, no personal responsibility was assigned to anyone—in the headline, the "Rules Lay Out C.I.A.'s Tactics," as though the rules had written themselves. Then in the lead paragraph, the "White House" was the subject of the first sentence, giving "approval" to the CIA. This *language collective* is a form of personification, which ascribes human qualities to a large, all-encompassing organization or entity (e.g., "the White House said . . ."). In reality, a building is incapable of giving permission. However, this misuse of language makes absolute claims, overlooking individual dissent or disagreement among people within the organization, and averts any personal responsibility. Thus, the latent message in this version of the story is continued secrecy.

The third version, also written by an Associated Press reporter, uses language associated with life to describe Bush's efforts (Bush "revives," Bush "breathed new life") to resuscitate the program, while employing words associated with death to describe the program ("harsh," "cruel and inhuman"). This creates an unnatural effect, which adds to the negative message.

On the surface, the use of the term *terror interrogation* describes the techniques employed to get information from terrorism suspects. However, pieced together, the term *terror suspects* rather than *terrorism suspects* can describe the feelings of terror aroused in the suspects, generated by the interrogation techniques.

These versions convey radically different impressions about the same event. Thus, as this analysis demonstrates, it is imperative that when reading newspaper articles, readers verify whether the lead paragraph indeed encapsulates the major thrust of the article.

Illogical Premise

A *premise* refers to the initial circumstances, situation, or assumption which serves as the point of origin in the narrative. A description of premise usually answers the question, "What is this program about?" Identifying the premise can furnish perspective into the unwritten assumptions behind an article.

According to Samuel Taylor Coleridge, our enjoyment of fiction is characterized by a *willing suspension of disbelief*, in which the audience willingly accepts the premise of the program, no matter how outlandish. For instance, it is easy to dismiss Mickey Mouse on the grounds that animals cannot talk, wear gloves, or own another animal (the dog Pluto) as a pet. However, this realistic assessment can spoil the audience's enjoyment of the cartoon.

Once an initial premise has been accepted, the remainder of the narrative generally progresses in a logical fashion. To illustrate, examine the following premise carefully:

> A scientist in a galaxy far from earth discovers that his planet faces imminent destruction. He does not have the time to save himself or his wife; however, he is able to construct a small rocket for his infant son. The rocket, carrying the boy, lifts off just before the planet explodes.
>
> The rocket finds its way to earth. Significantly, because of the earth's atmosphere, the boy has super powers; he can fly, has super strength and hearing, and never needs a haircut.

Once the audience has accepted this extraordinary premise for *Superman*, the remainder of the narrative proceeds naturally: the boy assumes an earthly identity, moves to the city, finds a job, and fights crime.

Although this decision to "suspend disbelief" generally pertains to entertainment programming (especially fantasy), the principle can also apply to other types of discourse as well.

Advertising frequently relies on an illogical premise to sell products. For instance, a TV ad depicts a pack of young women hunting down a young man, driven wild by his choice of Axe deodorant. Once this premise has been accepted, an ad can be very persuasive.

This principle also applies to political communications. Columnist William Safire presented the following example:

> In a Senate hearing room on Sept. 11 (2007), Gen. David Petraeus, commander of United States forces in Iraq, gave his promised report on progress in the war. Senator Hillary Rodham Clinton . . . told him, "I think that the reports that you provide to us really require the *willing suspension of disbelief.*" ("Suspension of Disbelief")

The use of the term *willing suspension of disbelief* suggests that the American public consciously decided to withhold their skepticism and accept the rosy premise of the report about the progress of the Iraq War. However, the reality is that the audience often accepts, *without question*, the premise of political communications, news stories, and advertising. However, the audience can, indeed, make a conscious decision whether or not to suspend their disbelief. If, at that point, they choose *not* to suspend their disbelief, they are in a position to examine the underlying assumptions behind the premise of the media presentation.

First Impressions

There are many clichés about the importance of making a good first impression. This truism applies to media presentations as well. In a book for scriptwriters, Christopher Vogler (1992) discusses the significance behind the initial entrance of the characters:

> Every actor likes to "make an entrance," an important part of building a character's relationship with the audience. . . . [The entrance of the hero] is a wonderful opportunity to speak volumes about his attitude, emotional state, background, strengths, and problems. The first action should be a model of the hero's characteristic attitude and the future problems or solutions that will result. (p. 104)

Because the media communicator pays particular attention to the first appearance of the main characters, the initial interaction with other characters, and the setting, the audience should focus on the meaning conveyed by this first impression as well.

As an example, James Bond films typically begin at the "climax" of another adventure. To illustrate, *Casino Royale* (2006) begins with Bond in full pursuit of an adversary. Although the reason for this chase is not explained, the pursuit tells the audience a good deal about James Bond. This introduction of the character is particularly noteworthy in that *Casino Royale* is the first Bond film with a new leading man, Daniel Craig.

Bond's nemesis is a remarkable physical specimen, who scales buildings and making spectacular leaps across a construction site that serves as an elaborate obstacle course. But Bond keeps up the chase, surmounting every barrier in his way. Bond's adversary finally makes it to a diplomatic sanctuary, seemingly beyond Bond's grasp. But disregarding conventional rules, Bond disarms those in the encampment and vanquishes his enemy. Thus, in this introductory scene, the audience has learned about Bond's physical stamina, relentlessness, resourcefulness, coolness under pressure, and disregard for convention—all of which will come in handy as the film "begins again" with a new adventure—at Casino Royale.

Although Vogler is making his observations about entertainment narratives, his observations about first impressions can be applied to other forms of media presentations as well, including political communications, journalism, and advertising. Consequently, critical analysis of *initial impressions* in a media presentation focuses on the following questions:

- What is the major character doing the first time we see him or her?
- What is he or she wearing?
- How do others react to him or her?
- What is the character's behavior the first time we see him or her?
- What is the character's attitude, emotional state, and goal at that moment?
- What do we learn about the character through this first impression?

See also: Formulaic Analysis; Narratology

References

Cohen, P. (2009). "Titlenomics, or Creating Best Sellers." *New York Times*. Retrieved from http://www.nytimes.com/2009/06/16/books/16titles.html?_r=0

Mazzetti, M. (2007, July 21). "Rules Lay Out C.I.A.'s Tactics in Questioning." *New York Times*. Retrieved from http://www.nytimes.com/2007/07/21/washington/21intel.html

Riechmann, D. (2007, July 21). "Bush Bars Some Tough Interrogation Methods." The Associated Press, in *St. Louis Post-Dispatch.* Retrieved from www.stltoday.com.

Safire, W. (2007, October 7). "Suspension of Disbelief." *New York Times.* Retrieved from http://www.nytimes.com/2007/10/07/magazine/07wwln-safire-t.html

Shrader, K. (2007, July 21). "Bush Revives CIA's Terror Interrogation Program." Associated Press.

Vogler, C. (1992). *The Writer's Journey.* Studio City, CA: Michael Wiese Productions.

Journalism

As a product of our economic system (as well as a significant player), the American newspaper industry has been in a state of crisis. Between 2008 and 2009, newspaper circulation decreased by more than 10 percent. The industry sold about 44 million copies a day—fewer than at any time since the 1940s. Many papers went out of business during this period, leaving vast regions without a newspaper with roots in their communities. Large media conglomerates such as the Tribune Company, which operates the *Chicago Tribune*, the *Los Angeles Times*, and six other daily papers filed for bankruptcy protection (Swensen & Schmidt, 2009).

Even profitable newspapers were in financial distress, saddled with the debt of its parent company. To illustrate, the *New York Times* was forced into severe austerity measures to contend with the financial losses of the Times Company, which had purchased a high-rise office building in New York City (Perez-Pena, 2009).

In response, newspapers have made drastic cuts in their operations, reducing spending by $1.6 billion a year (Hoyt, 2009). The most pressing cuts have come at the expense of personnel. Clark Hoyt, former ombudsman of the *New York Times*, cites the following examples:

> From *The Baltimore Sun*, down to 150 journalists from 400, to *The Los Angeles Times*, where a staff of more than 1,100 has been cut nearly in half, newsrooms are shrinking at an alarming rate. Last week alone, *The Wall Street Journal* announced it was closing its Boston bureau, and . . . the Associated Press may have to resort to layoffs to reduce its payroll by 10 percent by the end of the year. (Hoyt, 2009)

Comparative Media

Although the choice of media may have shifted, Americans spend about the same time keeping up on the news (just over an hour a day) as they did a decade ago (Lester, 2006). But thanks to innovations in media technology, individuals now have much more choice with regard to the channel through which the news is delivered—newspapers, radio, television, and the Internet, even cell phones.

The most radical decline with regard to the consumption of news is print media. In 2006, just over 40 percent of adults surveyed said they had read a newspaper, in print or online, the previous day, as opposed to 58 percent in 1994 (Lester, 2006).

However, local and community news remain big attractions for newspapers. Because of the concentration of media ownership, local news and information is often overlooked. But small, locally owned community newspapers remain a vital source of information.

Although television remains the most popular source of news, network news has been declining over the past three decades. In 2010, network news shows experienced continuing decline, with viewership down 3.4 percent from 2009 (Pew Research Center, 2011). In contrast, approximately 60 percent of U.S. residents get their news online, whereas only 1 in 50 did a decade ago (Internet and American Life Project, 2010).

The significance of this shift is that the audience is getting a different *kind* of news, depending on the medium they select. Every medium offers a distinctive way to present information. For instance, watching the news on television provides insight into the events as they unfold, whereas print journalism furnishes valuable background and context with regard to these events. Consequently, the best course of action is a *balanced media diet*, consulting different media to get a broader understanding of events.

Online Journalism

Digital media are the ultimate hybrid, combining print, still images, graphics, video, and audio to convey information. David Carr (2011a) describes how online articles rely on different media to tell their stories:

> "Lifted," by [Evan] Ratliff . . . is about an immense heist at a Swedish cash repository, weighed in at 13,000 words. But instead of opening with a long explanation of how it was done, the reader is dropped into the actual video taken by the security cameras. A helicopter comes into view; dark-clad men in ski masks send a ladder down through a skylight and then are seen carrying guns, and later, heavy bags of cash through the interior. The video ends, cue text, and the story is rolling.

Online journalism features distinctive characteristics that affect the ways in which information is presented and interpreted. For instance, less popular (although no less important) content such as book reviews has been omitted from online versions of newspapers such as the *New York Times* (Elliot, 2008).

Other distinctions of digital journalism include the following.

Audience-driven process. Online journalism adheres to the postmodern communication model in which the audience can circumvent traditional gatekeepers such as major news organizations. Readers decide what features (e.g., video or photos) they want to see, or hit a "hot link" to learn more about particular aspects of a story. Howard Kurtz observes, "The good news is that the average consumer can . . . choose from sources he trusts and enjoys rather than being spoon-fed by a handful of big corporations" (Kurtz, 2006: C01).

Depth of information. Online journalism has been characterized by a depth of coverage. Stories frequently contain links that take the reader to additional sources of information. David Carr (2011a) notes,

> David Grann's 16,000-word piece in *The New Yorker* about a possible wrongful execution in Texas generated almost 4.5 million page views, while a Twitter feed called LongReads has about 20,000 followers and a fast-growing Web site. A recent study by the folks at Read It Later, a service that helps a reader bookmark and save an article, demonstrated that many owners of the iPad are time-shifting longer articles for evening reading.

At the same time, however, online journalism sacrifices *breadth* of coverage. Individuals can fall victim to *cultural segregation*, becoming immersed in a few, selected areas of personal interest while remaining completely uninformed and disinterested in other cultural spheres. As a result, individuals know *more* and *more* about *less* and *less.* For example, fans of soccer may know everything about that sport but are unfamiliar with basketball or rugby. As a result, people no longer share points of commonality that are the foundation of cultural cohesion and community.

Verification Issues

Unlike print stories, online articles can be difficult to verify. Without citations and references, it can be difficult to authenticate the veracity of the information. In addition, the writer may use a pseudonym, and information about the background, expertise, and motives for contributing may not be available.

Rush to deadline. Without a specified deadline, there is constant pressure to publish information immediately, which affects media content in several respects. First, although the traditional protocol required that *two* sources confirm the veracity of information before publication in the newspaper, now it is acceptable to publish information with only *one* verification, which leads to mistakes. According to CNN anchor Aaron Brown, in the first moments of a crisis, sources are often wrong. "In the chaos of a breaking story all of us who have dealt with it, if we are honest with ourselves, have to ask ourselves: Are we sure? Because we all have been burnt, every one of us" (Brisbane, 2011).

Hyperlocal coverage. Sensing a vacuum in the local news market due to the closing of midsize and large newspapers, large Internet companies such as AOL, Google, and Yahoo, have embarked on a *hyperlocal* strategy, developing local networks. In some cases, online news publications pursue national stories from a local perspective. For instance, in 2009, MSNBC began an ongoing series about the impact of the economic recession on the city of Elkhart, Indiana. Jennifer Sizemore, editor in chief of MSNBC.com explained,

> The adage that all news is local is absolutely true It is coverage of a national story through the lens of one location, and includes tools and data that are relevant no matter where you live. . . . We're focused on the themes that are familiar to all Americans and using our reporting in Elkhart to deal with those universal issues. (Stelter, 2009)

In 2007, AOL set up a network, called Patch.com, that, by 2011, was already set up to cover local news in 800 towns, supported by local online advertising—gift shops, plumbers, regional hospitals, car dealers—which was expected to reach $15.9 billion in 2011 (Kopytoff, 2011).

Media Literacy Approaches

Media literacy offers the following lines of inquiry for the analysis of journalism content.

Point of View

The American press adheres to the principle of *objectivity*, in which journalists represent events precisely, without bias. The Society of Professional Journalists Code of Ethics (2012) declares:

> Good faith with the public is the foundation of all worthy journalism.
>   1. Truth is our ultimate goal.
>   2. Objectivity in reporting the news is another goal which serves as the mark of an experienced professional. It is a standard of

performance toward which we strive. We honor those who achieve it.

However, bias can be subtly introduced into reporting through a number of journalistic techniques, including the selection of images, construction of headlines, word choices, camera angles, and the inclusion (and omission) of information. In addition, the following journalistic persuasion techniques can, intentionally or unintentionally, affect the point of view of a story:

- *Presentation of opinion as fact:* a technique in which reporters inject opinion into a story disguised as fact.
- *Vague authority* refers to instances in which reporters cite undocumented or generalized groups to support a particular point of view.
- *One-person cross section:* a persuasion technique in which one person is used as a metaphor for a larger group—which may not be the case.
- *The designated spokesperson:* sometimes the press arbitrarily appoints a spokesperson who assumes a position of authority and leadership in relation to a particular issue or event. But whether these people actually enjoy the support of a broad constituency is open to question.
- *The slanted sample:* sampling the public for their response to issues and events is a common journalistic approach. However, this sample may be chosen in an arbitrary fashion and therefore is not representative of the public at large.
- *The "not available" ploy:* stories that include the statement that "the subject was unavailable for comment" implies that the subject was uncooperative, ducking the reporter, and had something to hide.
- *The passive catch-phrase:* sentences can be written in either the *active* or *passive* voice. In the active voice, the subject is explicitly responsible for the action (e.g., Bob threw the ball). But in the passive voice, the subject is the *receiver* of the action (e.g., the ball was thrown to Bob). The passive voice is particularly useful in describing an action in which the actor is unknown or can be used to deflect responsibility for the action, because it is unstated *who* initiated the action.
- *Selective quotes:* reporters can influence the meaning of a story by deciding *when* to use quotes, *whose* quotes to include, and *which parts* of the person's interview to extract into a quote.
- *Inaccurate paraphrase:* instead of directly quoting a subject, reporters sometimes opt to paraphrase what their subject said. However, a reporter's summary may not always be an accurate interpretation.

- *Biased interviewing strategies:* a reporter can slant a story through the type of questions he or she poses to subjects:
  - *Compliance as assertion:* reporters may come to an interview prepared with a point of view (and a quote) to include in an article and only be asking for the *consent* of the subject. In this case, reporters may phrase a question, "Would you agree that . . .?" "Would you say that . . .?" or "So what you are saying is . . ."
  - *Leading or loaded questions:* reporters ask questions that contain a false premise or are loaded with negative allegations or a false premise. An example would be, "Are you concerned that higher rates as proposed by the electric company might force many people to give up their service?" Any response to a question phrased like this (even a denial) legitimizes the position of the reporter.
  - *"Gotcha" questions:* In this practice, reporters' questions take the form of a pop quiz, the ostensible goal being to test the veracity of a subject's claims.
  - *Hypothetical question:* questions beginning with phrases such as "What would happen if . . .?" put the subject in a speculative position that is then presented as fact andcan catch the interviewee off-guard, so that he or she may offer an opinion that is not thoroughly considered.
  - *Either-or choices:* reporters offer a limited range of responses to their interviewees.

Regardless of intention, faithfulness to this ideal may not be feasible, for several reasons. This code assumes that an Absolute Truth exists and, moreover, that journalists are in a position to present this objective Truth, without distortion or personal bias. However, in this complex, subjective world, the truth may be difficult to identify. Indeed, a reporter's coverage of events may be influenced by his or her personal background, values, and knowledge of the topic. Ironically, the press is often the target of criticism for biased reporting from both liberals and conservatives, depending on the audience's particular version of the truth.

Indeed, in some cases, a journalist cannot avoid articulating a point of view. To illustrate, only a limited number of stories appear on the front page. But when editors move an article to page two, they are making a statement about the relative importance of a story. In like fashion, the "lead" (first) story in a newscast is generally considered the most important. However, only one story can appear at a time, so that even if several stories are considered equally important by the news director, only one story will be seen as "most important." Moreover, repeating the same word in a story (e.g., "he *said*, she *said*") is dull. However, substituting a synonym (e.g., "argued" rather than "said") can add a layer of meaning to a story.

Some scholars find this notion of objectivity in the press to be not only *unrealistic* but *undesirable*. According to this line of reasoning, American journalism has become trapped by modern ethic of objectivity, forcing the press to forego its responsibility as opinion leaders. The defining issue in American journalism, then, may not be *objectivity*, but rather *judgment, fairness, transparency,* and *perspective*:

- *Judgment.* Journalism is as much an art as it is a craft; that is, in the many individual cases that come across an editor's desk, the situations are complex. Editors and reporters must rely upon *news judgment*, based on journalistic principles and collective experience. However, at times, there may be disagreement, even among veteran journalists, about how to treat a story.
- *Fairness.* Do journalists strive to represent all sides of an issue? Byron Calame (2006), public editor of the *New York Times*, explains,

   Getting both sides of a story and sorting them out for readers is the basic job of newspaper reporters and editors. This is a key to creating a newspaper that is fair—both to readers and to the people and institutions that are the subjects of stories. Seeking comment from those written about, especially when they are put in an unfavorable light, is a particularly important aspect of fair coverage. It helps ensure that readers get the most complete and accurate view possible of a newsworthy development.

- *Transparency.* Being clear about the point of view of the publication, the reporter's perspective, and the background and motive of sources enables the audience to filter the information and make up their own minds about the topic.
- *Perspective.* In a world in which events often appear unconnected and consequences only appear over time, journalists have a responsibility to put these events into meaningful perspective. At the same time, however, the audience has the responsibility to challenge these assertions to make sure that journalists handle this charge responsibly.

Recognizing the fallacy of objectivity, media literacy calls for students to identify the point of view in a news story, so that they can filter this information and come to their own independent judgments about the information in news programming.

Function

American news channels, such as newspapers, magazines, radio, television, and the Internet, serve a variety of *functions*, or purposes, including *information*, *persuasion, agenda setting, disclosure*, and *entertainment*.

As a market-driven industry, profit is a major function of American news operations. Consequently, news programming increasingly presents *news as entertainment*. News producers tend to select stories that are dramatic, sensational, and that have an identifiable cast of characters and a clear narrative structure (with a beginning, middle, and conclusion).

But significantly, a majority of people surveyed thinks that the news is too sensationalized, stating that the press spent too much time reporting on the private lives of public officials (Roper Center, 2012). This would suggest that newspapers might be more successful if they were less driven by profit and instead concentrated on its role as a public service.

At times, the function of a story is unclear, leading to confusion on the part of the audience. After four months as *New York Times* public editor, Arthur S. Brisbane declared that the No. 1 challenge that the *Times* faces is the "blending of opinion with news":

> Although there is a distinct separation between the Editorial Page operation . . . and the news operation . . . , the news pages are laced with analytical and opinion pieces that work against the premise that the news is just the news. (Brisbane, 2011)

Questions to ask regarding function include the following:

* What is the purpose behind the presentation?
* Does the media communicator want you to think or behave in a particular way as a result of receiving the information?

Implicit Content

A news story may only represent an installment in a far larger story, which is still in the process of unfolding. Thus, although newspapers provide information on the day's events—the *who, what, when, where*, and *how* questions that are the hallmarks of journalism—they may not have the space to consider the broader *why* question. Moreover, the consequences of an event may not be readily apparent. For instance, it will be many years before the ramifications of global warming become fully evident.

In light of the complexity of events, it is particularly critical to give some thought to *implicit content* when reading articles. When reading a story, ask:

- Why did this event occur?
- What are the possible connections between people in the story?
- What are the possible connections between events?
- What are the possible consequences of these events?

News Literacy

News literacy is a discipline that focuses on the application of media literacy principles and strategies to the discipline of journalism. In 2008, Stony Brook University's School of Journalism established the News Literacy Project (NLP), an educational program in which professional journalists work with middle school and high school students to promote the critical analysis of journalism. The mission of the NLP (2012) is as follows:

> The project's primary aim is to teach students the critical thinking skills they need to be smarter and more frequent consumers and creators of credible information across all media and platforms. Students are learning how to distinguish verified information from raw messages, spin, gossip and opinion and are being encouraged to seek news and information that will make them well-informed citizens and voters.

The NLP curricula focuses on the following areas:

- Why news matters to young people
- What the First Amendment and a free media in a democracy mean
- How to identify reliable information

The material is presented through hands-on exercises, games, and videos, as well as the journalists sharing their professional experiences with the students.

See also: Business Models, Journalism; Digital Media Literacy; Function; International Communications, Media Literacy Approach; International Media Literacy; Introduction; Medium Theory; Nonverbal Approach to Media Analysis

References

Brisbane, A. (2011, January 9). "Hanging on as the Boundaries Shift." *New York Times*. Retrieved from http://www.nytimes.com/2011/01/09/opinion/09pubed.html

Brisbane, A. (2011, January 29). "Speed and Credibility." *New York Times*. Retrieved from http://www.nytimes.com/2011/01/30/opinion/30pubed.html

Calame, Byron (2006, November 5). "Listening to Both Sides in the Pursuit of Fairness." *New York Times*. Retrieved from http://www.nytimes.com/2006/11/05/opinion/05pubed.html.

Carr, D. (2011a, March 27). "Long-Form Journalism Finds a Home." *New York Times*. Retrieved from http://www.nytimes.com/2011/03/28/business/media/28carr.html

Carr, D. (2011b, September 11). "News Trends Tilt Toward Niche Sites." *New York Times*.

Elliot, S. (2008, December 9). "Next Year Is Looking Even Worse." *New York Times*. Retrieved from http://www.nytimes.com/2008/12/09/business/worldbusiness/09iht-09adco.18508223.html

Hoyt, C. (2009, November 1). "Recession, Revolution and a Leaner Times." *New York Times*. Retrieved from www.nytimes.com/2009/11/01/opinion/01pubed.html

Internet and American Life Project. (2011). Pew Research Center. Retrieved from http://www.pewinternet.org/Reports/2011/Internet-as-diversion/Report.aspx

Kopytoff, V. (2011, January 6). "AOL Bets on Hyperlocal News, Finding Progress Where Many Have Failed." *New York Times*. Retrieved from http://www.nytimes.com/2011/01/17/business/media/17local.html?pagewanted=all

Kurtz, H. (2006, March 13). "The Big News: Shrinking Reportage." *Washington Post,* p. C01.

Lester, W. (2006, July 30). "Growth of Online News Readers Levels Off." *Associated Press Online*. Retrieved from Retrieved September 2012 from http://www.ap.org

The News Literacy Project. (2012). About. Retrieved from http://www.thenewsliteracyproject.org/about

Perez-Pena, R. (2009, February 8). "Resilient Strategy for Times Despite Toll of a Recession." *New York Times*. Retrieved from http://www.nytimes.com/2009/02/09/business/media/09times.html?pagewanted=all

Pew Research Center. (2011). "State of the News Media 2011. An Annual Report on American Journalism." Retrieved from http://stateofthemedia.org

Roper Center. Retrieved September 2012 at http://newseum.org

Society of Professional Journalists Code of Ethics. (2012). Retrieved from http://www.spj.org/ethicscode.asp

Stelter, B. (2009, August 10). "News Site Keeps Focus on Town's Recession." *New York Times*. Retrieved from http://www.nytimes.com/2009/08/10/business/media/10elkhart.html

Swensen, D., & Schmidt, M. (2009, January 28). "News You Can Endow." *New York Times*. Retrieved from http://www.nytimes.com/2009/01/28/opinion/28swensen.html

Key Principles and Concepts, Media Literacy

The following media literacy terms, concepts, and principles are critical to an understanding of media literacy.

A *medium* is a channel of mass communications that enables people to communicate with large groups separated in time and space from the communicator. The principal media include print, photography, radio, film, television, and interactive media. Less obvious media may include clothing with advertising logos, billboards, and key chains. In some cases, determining whether a channel is a mass medium depends on its *function*. For example, using the computer to compose a letter or term paper would be categorized as *machine-assisted interpersonal communication*, whereas when going online, the computer would be classified as a *mass medium*.

Text refers to productions, programs, and publications produced through print, photography, film, radio, television, and interactive media. Media literacy analysis provides ways to interpret and discuss media texts, such as newspaper articles, Web pages, or a film.

Clutter is a term that applies to all of the media messages, competing media programming and visual images that are directed at the media consumer on a daily basis. The overwhelming nature of media clutter can make it difficult for audiences to focus on one particular text for a sustained period of time. For their part, media communicators are faced with the challenge of "breaking through the clutter," that is, making their presentation so distinct that it will attract the attention of the public. Consequently, news programs may opt for a sensationalized treatment of the day's events, films and television programs may rely on sex and violence, and rock bands may stretch the limits of convention.

Construct. As a verb, *to construct* refers to the process through which a media text is shaped and given meaning. Construct is subject to a variety of decisions and designed to keep the audience interested in the text. As a noun, a construct is a fictional or documentary text that appears to be "natural" or a "reflection of reality" but, in fact, represents only a version of reality (see "Key Concepts of Media Literacy," point 1, later in this entry).

Cumulative messages appear in the media with such frequency that they form new meanings, independent of any individual presentation. Cumulative messages appear in media presentations with regard to gender roles, definitions of success, violence, tobacco products, and racial and cultural stereotypes.

Neutrality of channel. By itself, a medium is simply a channel of communication and, consequently, is neither good nor evil. A number of factors determine the impact of a media presentation, including: (a) who is producing the presentation, (b) what is the function (or purpose) behind the production of the presentation, and (c) who is the intended audience.

Media messages. The underlying themes or ideas contained in a media presentation. There may be two layers of meaning: *manifest* and *latent* messages. Manifest messages are direct and clear to the audience. Latent messages are indirect and beneath the surface, and, consequently, escape our immediate attention. Latent messages may reinforce manifest messages or may suggest entirely different meanings. Latent messages can be conveyed through affective strategies, embedded values, production techniques, and cumulative messages.

Deconstruction refers to the *process* of media literacy analysis in which the audience identifies the elements that make up the construction of meaning within a text. Deconstruction originated as a strategy of critical analysis developed by French philosopher Jacques Derrida as a way of examining unquestioned metaphysical assumptions and internal contradictions in philosophical and literary language. Deconstructionists tend to focus on close readings of texts and how the texts refer to other texts, to uncover what is left out, ignored, or silenced by the text, and reveal the illogical and paradoxical aspects of the text.

A media presentation (e.g., film, newspaper) may be broken down into identifiable elements for purposes of analysis. By "taking apart" the reality constructed for us, we can begin to see how meaning is constructed.

The Key Concepts of Media Literacy (developed by the Association for Media Literacy at the Request of the Ontario Ministry of Education; Pungente, 1989)

1. All Media Are Constructions

This is arguably the most important concept. The media do not simply mirror external reality. Rather, they present carefully crafted constructions that reflect many decisions and are the result of many determining factors. Media literacy works toward deconstructing these constructions (i.e., taking them apart to show how they are made).

2. The Media Construct Versions of Reality

The media are responsible for the majority of the observations and experiences from which we build our personal understanding of the world and how it works. Much of our view of reality is based on media messages that have been pre-constructed and have attitudes, interpretations, and conclusions already built in. Thus the media, to a great extent, give us a sense of reality.

3. Audiences Negotiate Meaning in Media

If the media provide us with much of the material on which we build our picture of reality, each of us finds or "negotiates" meaning according to individual factors: personal needs and anxieties, the pleasures or troubles of the day, racial and sexual attitudes, family and cultural background, moral standpoint, and so forth.

4. Media Messages Have Commercial Implications

Media literacy aims to encourage awareness of how the media are influenced by commercial considerations and how they impinge on content, technique, and distribution. Most media production is a business and, as such, must make a profit. Questions of ownership and control are central: A relatively small number of individuals control what we watch, read, and hear in the media.

5. Media Messages Contain Ideological and Value Messages

All media products are advertising in some sense, proclaiming values and ways of life. The mainstream media convey, explicitly or implicitly, ideological messages about such issues as the nature of the good life and the virtue of consumerism, the role of women, the acceptance of authority, and unquestioning patriotism.

6. Media Messages Contain Social and Political Implications

The media have significant influence on politics and social change. Television can greatly influence the election of a national leader on the basis of image. The media involve us in concerns such as civil rights, famines in Africa, and the AIDS epidemic. They give us an intimate sense of national issues and global concerns, so that we have become McLuhan's Global Village.

7. Form and Content Are Closely Related in Media Messages

As Marshall McLuhan noted, each medium has its own grammar and codifies reality in its own particular way. Different media will report the same event but create different impressions and messages.

8. Each Medium Has a Unique Aesthetic Form

Just as we notice the pleasing rhythms of certain pieces of poetry or prose, we should also be able to enjoy the pleasing forms and effects of the media.

National Association for Media Literacy Education (NAMLE) Core Principles of Media Literacy Education (www.namle.net)

The purpose of media literacy education is to help individuals of all ages develop the habits of inquiry and skills of expression that they need to be critical thinkers, effective communicators and active citizens in today's world. NAMLE (2007) has set forth the following six core principles of media literacy education.

1. Media literacy education requires active inquiry and critical thinking about the messages we receive and create.
2. Media literacy education expands the concept of literacy (i.e., reading and writing) to include all forms of media.
3. Media literacy education builds and reinforces skills for learners of all ages. Like print literacy, those skills necessitate integrated, interactive, and repeated practice.
4. Media literacy education develops informed, reflective, and engaged participants essential for a democratic society.
5. Media literacy education recognizes that media are a part of culture and function as agents of socialization.
6. Media literacy education affirms that people use their individual skills, beliefs, and experiences to construct their own meanings from media messages.

See also: Audience Analysis; Cultural Context; Effects Theories, Media Literacy; Function; Sectors, Media Literacy

References

National Association for Media Literacy Education. (2007). "The Core Principles of Media Literacy Education." Retrieved from http://namle.net/wp-content/uploads/2013/01/CorePrinciples.pdf

Pungente, J. (1989). Originally written for *Media Literacy Resource Guide: Intermediate and Senior Divisions*. Ontario, Canada: Ontario Ministry of Education.

Labeling Theory

Labeling theory is a qualitative approach to the study of media content that considers the transmission and legitimation of labels in the mass media. It examines ways in which language is decoded by different audiences and traces the derivation, sources, and meanings associated with labels.

According to linguist Kenneth Burke, language *precedes* thought. That is, ideas and concepts do not "exist" until there are words to recall, categorize, and talk about them. In that regard, the use of language in the media affects how individuals think about the essential meaning of a concept.

In addition, word choice can influence attitudes toward events and phenomena. For instance, John Holdren, professor of Environmental Policy at the Kennedy School of Government at Harvard University, contends that *global warming* is a misleading term to describe environmental changes. Global warming is inaccurate in three respects:

1. It implies something that is mainly about temperature.
2. Global warming is a gradual phenomenon.
3. Global warming is a phenomenon that is uniform across the planet.

Instead of *global warming*, Holdren finds the term *global disruption* to be more accurate: "In fact, temperature is only one of the things that's changing it's sort of an index of the state of the climate. The whole climate is changing: the winds, the ocean currents, the storm patterns, snowpack, snowmelt, flooding, droughts—temperature is just a bit of it" ("Global Disruption," 2008).

Analyzing the word choice in a media presentation can provide insight into a media communicator's attitude toward the subject. To illustrate, the Israeli and Palestinian press use different synonyms to describe the conflict in the Middle East, reflecting their dramatically different points of view:

Israeli Press	**Palestinian Press**
Disputed Territories	The Occupied Territories
Suicide Bombers	Martyrs
Insurgents	Resistance Fighters
Pinpoint Preventive Operations	Assassination

Language also provides a means of attaining membership in subcultures. To illustrate, reporter Joe Holleman (2003) conducted research on the American hipster subculture by examining its distinctive slang. For instance terms that are unique to hipster culture include:

- *Bennie*: a hat
- *Berries*: dollars, money
- *Bronson*: beer (in honor of actor Charles Bronson)
- *To bust a Moby*: to dance

- *Frado*: ugly guy who thinks he's good looking
- *Hilfiger*: someone with no fashion sense

A number of extraneous factors influence the meaning of words, including sources of political and financial power within a culture. As an example, over the past decade, nearly all of the growth in the food industry has been tied to the organic foods niche market, accounting for yearly sales of approximately $12 billion (Warner, 2005). Coinciding with this financial windfall, there has been a vigorous debate with regard to the meaning ascribed to "organic" foods. The term *organic* has been defined as "a system of food production that promotes a natural, chemical-free approach to farming." However, organizations affiliated with the corporate food industry have successfully lobbied to broaden this definition, to include a range of chemicals and artificial materials under the label "organic." Since 2002, 38 artificial ingredients and industrial chemicals have been accepted as "organic," including boiler additives, disinfectants, and lubricants (Warner, 2005).

Language also reflects *shifts* in a culture. Tracing the application of labels can furnish perspective into cultural change. Former *New York Times* public editor Clark Hoyt (2010) explains:

Labels are more than descriptors. They are also weapons in our polarized political culture. Sharon Jarvis, an associate professor of communication studies at the University of Texas, has written extensively on political labels. She traced the path of "liberal" from something Harry Truman was proud to be to a term John Kerry seemed to run from. Republicans have been more successful at defending their labels and demonizing the other party's, she told me.

In addition, labels are often employed as tools to further political agendas. Clever politicians use word choice to deliberately obfuscate issues or mislead the public. To illustrate, political consultant Frank Luntz has recommended that the Republican Party adopt the term *scientific certainty* to influence voters' attitudes toward their environmental policy, the message being that "[n]o scientific certainty exists that human beings have contributed to worldwide climate change." An editorial in the *St. Louis Post-Dispatch* explains the rationale behind Luntz's recommendation:

Mr. Luntz is an accomplished practitioner of obfuscation. . . . As a matter of politics, Mr. Luntz's counsel was brilliant. The difference between "scientific certainty" and "scientific consensus" seems trivial

. . . [However], "Certainty" never exists in science. Even 350 years after it was first quantified, *gravity* remains a theory subject to revision. Still, there's no doubt what would happen if you stepped off the (St. Louis) Gateway Arch.

. . . The appeal for "sound science" allows corporations to raise the issue of scientific uncertainty, no matter how powerful or conclusive the evidence (of human influence on Climate Change). ("The Art of Obfuscation," 2005)

Thus, examining *function* (or purpose) can furnish perspective into the appearance of particular labels in media presentations. For instance, language is frequently used to soften the brutalities associated with warfare. Linguistics professor Robin Tolmach Lakoff (2004) has identified the following categories of labels that help defeat the enemy in wartime:

- *Impersonal Pronouns.* The Austrian ethologist Konrad Lorenz suggested that "the more clearly we see other members of our own species as individuals, the harder we find it to kill them . . . [Thus], an American soldier refers to an Iraqi prisoner as 'it.' A general speaks not of 'Iraqi fighters' but of 'the enemy.' A weapons manufacturer doesn't talk about people but about 'targets.'"
- *Nicknames.* If we give (the enemy) nicknames, we can see them as smaller, weaker and childlike—not worth taking seriously as fully human.
- *Demeaning Terms.* The names may refer to real or imagined cultural and physical differences that emphasize the ridiculous or the repugnant. So in various wars, the British called the French "Frogs." Germans have been called "Krauts," a reference to weird and smelly food. Although the specific terms change from war to war, from enemy to enemy, the purpose remains the same. Moreover, during World War II, the Germans were given demeaning names, in part to help overcome the invincible image of the German soldier.
- *Collective Nouns.* These encourage soldiers to see the enemy as an undifferentiated mass. American soldiers are trained to call those they are fighting against "the enemy." It is easier to kill an enemy than an Iraqi.

Language Categories

Connotative words refer to words that have associated meanings beyond their *denotative* (dictionary) definitions. A connotative word is universally understood and agreed on. For instance, the word *house* simply describes a structure. However, *home* conjures up a much richer visual picture: a family gathered around the hearth, children playing video games, and the smells of dinner wafting in from the kitchen.

Writers frequently employ synonyms to avoid repetition and liven up the prose. However, synonyms often possess different connotative meanings that affect the reader's understanding of a subject. Thus, the differences between synonyms are not simply cosmetic but reflect very significant nuances of meaning.

Euphemisms are inoffensive terms that temper, or soften, the meaning of an explicit, harsh, or distasteful idea or concept. The derivation of euphemism comes from the Greek word *euphonos*, or sweet voiced, suggesting that this discourse device can make harsh concepts or ideas "sweeter," or more palatable to the target audience.

For example, William Lutz (1996) cites the following examples of euphemisms used in war:

- *Preemptive counterattack*: an invasion where we strike first (p. 6)
- *Predawn vertical insertion*: we strike first, and when it's still dark (pp. 6–7)
- *Collateral damage*: civilian casualties (p. 176)
- *Aluminum transfer containers*: temporary coffins (p. 176)
- *Energetic disassemblies*: nuclear explosions (p. 258)
- *Radiation enhancement devices*: nuclear weapons (p. 190)

Advertisers frequently employ euphemisms to change public perceptions of products. For instance, the California fruit industry has changed the name *prunes* (with its digestive connotation) to *dried plums*.

Special-interest organizations often assume euphemistic titles to conceal their mission, ideology, and sponsorship. Jim Drinkard (1997) refers to this phenomenon as "astroturf," in that the names of these organizations suggest grassroots activism. For instance, the Information Council on the Environment, which sounds like a pro-environmental group, is actually an organization formed by the oil and coal lobbies to *discourage* the establishment of climate change policies. Other examples of other "astroturf" lobbying groups, whose names mask their financial backing and agenda, include:

- *The Center for Regulatory Effectiveness*: an organization supported by Philip Morris, with the goal of developing "the right criteria that will favorably evaluate and be applicable to secondhand smoke" ("The Art of Obfuscation," 2005).

- *Coalition for Energy and Economic Revitalization*: formed by a Roanoke, Virginia, public relations consultant, this organization is pushing for a new 115-mile power line for American Electrical Power Co., which is paying its expenses (Drinkard, 1997).
- *Coalition for Vehicle Choice*: in arguing against stricter auto-fuel economy standards, this group, financed by Detroit automakers, has cited police needs for large cruisers, the need for full-sized vans for the disabled, and the safety of big cars (Drinkard, 1997).
- *The Organic Trade Association*: An industry lobbying group that has proposed congressional legislation specifying that certain artificial ingredients could be used in organic food (Warner, 2005).

Politicians rely on euphemisms to present information that might be unfavorably received by the public. Thus, rather than using the word *hunger* to describe the 12 percent of Americans (35 million) who could not put food on their table at least part of the year, the U.S. Department of Agriculture now describes these people as experiencing *very low food security*.

Politicians also rely on euphemisms as a strategy to sell unpopular policies and programs. For example, as the gambling industry devised its campaign to legalize casinos throughout the United States, polls revealed that some people considered gambling to be immoral. Consequently, efforts to legalize casinos throughout the country met with less resistance when the name of the industry was changed from gambling to *gaming*.

Code words are terms that contain clear and distinct meaning for subgroups within the general audience. As an example, former president George W. Bush embedded code words into his speeches directed at general audiences to convey particular messages to his Evangelical supporters. Historian Bruce Lincoln (2004) explains,

As president, Bush has always been outspoken about his faith, letting evangelicals know he shares their values and vision for America. But he has also been careful. Aware that he must appeal to the center to secure reelection, he employs double-coded signals that veil much of his religious message from outsiders. Biblical references, allusions to hymns, and specialized vocabulary are keys to this communication.

Slang expressions are informal words or phrases that are more frequently used in conversation than in formal speech or writing. The appearance of slang expressions can provide insight into the lifestyle, developments, and preoccupations of a culture. For instance, reporter Douglas Quenqua (2009) observes that "there are now 2,500 words for 'drunk.' Soon there will be 3,500." The Internet has contributed to the organic nature of language. As Quenqua points out, "The life of slang is now shorter than ever, say linguists, and what was once a reliable code for identifying members of an in-group or subculture is losing some of its magic."

Neologisms refer to new words that have been created. In advertising, the look and sound of neologisms are designed to suggest the essence of the product. Some neologisms used in advertising combine terms. For instance, advertising agency BBDO came up with a new concept called *Procrealligence*, which combines three concepts: Pro (activity), Crea (creativity), and lligence (intelligence) to describe their distinctive approach to the advertising industry. As BBDO explains: "Procrealligence is the foundation of our positioning, our method for attaining the highest standard of 'work'" ("Killer Innovations: Re-blog," 2007).

Labeling Theory and Media Literacy

Given the impact of labels on the public's understanding of concepts, the choices that are made with respect to language require reflection and discussion on the part of media communicators. As Clark Hoyt (2010) observes, "The Times navigates a semantic minefield" with almost every story. Letters to the Editor from newspaper readers testify to the power of word choices in the construction of meaning. To illustrate, Nathan Dodell of Rockville, Maryland, charged that it was "tendentious and arrogant" for reporter Helene Cooper to use the word *settlements* four times in an article about the conflict between Israel and Palestine, when the Israeli prime minister, Benjamin Netanyahu, explicitly rejected the use of the term in relation to East Jerusalem. Dodell asked why the reporter didn't use a neutral term such as *housing construction*. Hoyt (2010) explained the impact of this choice on the construction of meaning:

> *Settlement* is a charged word in this context, because it suggests something less than permanent on someone else's land. Israel argues that all of Jerusalem is its undivided capital, a claim not recognized by the United States and most of the world.

Thus, the critical analysis of language focuses on the following questions:

- What type(s) of labels are used in the media presentation?
- What is the *function*, or purpose behind the inclusion of particular words?
- What messages are conveyed with respect to these choices?
- What do these choices reveal with respect to cultural attitudes and preoccupations?
- What do these choices reveal with respect to shifts in the culture?

See also: Political Communications, American

References

"The Art of Obfuscation." (2005, July 30). *St. Louis Post-Dispatch* (editorial). Retrieved from www.stltoday.com.

Drinkard, J. (1997, December 23). "Lobbying Groups Play Distracting Name Game." Associated Press in the *St. Louis Post-Dispatch*. www.stltoday.com.

"'Global Disruption' More Accurately Describes Climate Change, Not 'Global Warming.'" (2008, July 3). *DemocracyNow!* Retrieved from http://www.democracynow.org/2008/7/3/global_disruption_more_accurately_describes_climate

Holleman, J. (2003, January 30). "When You've Mastered the Hipster Look and Lingo, Buy a Round of Bronsons." *St. Louis Post-Dispatch*. Retrieved from http://www.stltoday.com

Hoyt, C. (2010, May 14). "Public Editor: Semantic Minefields." *New York Times*. Retrieved from http://www.nytimes.com/2010/05/16/opinion/16pubed.html?_r=0

"Killer Innovations: Re-blog." (2007, January). Retrieved from http://techtrend.com/blog/reblog/2007/01/neologisms_for_creativity_and.html.

Lakoff, R. T. (2004, May 18). "From Ancient Greece to Iraq, the Power of Words in Wartime." *New York Times*. Retrieved from http://www.nytimes.com

Lincoln, B. (2004, September 12). "How Bush Speaks in Religious Code." *Boston Globe*. Retrieved from http://www.bostonglobe.com

Lutz, W. (1996). *The New Doublespeak: Why No One Knows What Anyone Is Saying Anymore*. New York: HarperCollins.

Quenqua, D. (2009, August 23). "Dude, You Are So (Not) Obama." *New York Times*. Retrieved from http://www.nytimes.com

Safire, W. (2008, June 29). "Gaffe." *New York Times Magazine*. Retrieved from http://www.nytimes.com

Warner, M. (2005, November 1). "What Is Organic? Powerful Players Want Say. *New York Times*. Retrieved from http://www.nytimes.com

Mass-Mediated Reality

Mass-mediated reality refers to the influence of the media on the construction and perception of reality. Mass-mediated reality is a multilayered topic that requires considerable attention. This entry suggests a few of the ways in which the media influence how we see the world, other people, and ultimately, ourselves.

Canada's Association for Media Literacy first declared that one of the major principles of media literacy is that all media are *constructions* (or versions) of reality:

> The media do not simply mirror external reality. Rather, they present carefully crafted constructions that reflect many decisions and are the result of many determining factors. Media literacy works toward deconstructing these constructions (i.e., taking them apart to show how they are made). (*Media Literacy Resource Guide*, 1989)

In its ability to instantaneously preserve a moment of time in space, a media image creates the illusion of *verisimilitude*, or lifelike quality. We must remember, however, that the media can capture only a brief instant, without the context that gives it meaning. A skilled filmmaker/videographer can establish a "preferred reading" that dictates the "reality" that the audience experiences through the selection and arrangement of the subject matter. For instance, in a close-up shot, one person takes up the entire frame, so that it appears that the subject is alone. However, as the photographer pulls away to a wide-angle shot, the subject may suddenly be surrounded by a large crowd of people.

Furthermore, the very *presence* of the media often affects what is being recorded. Subjects often act differently when they know that they are being photographed.

Media presentations operate according to a different concept of time. On the most literal level, the media has altered the way in which we spend our time. Reading the paper during breakfast, listening to the radio in the car, and watching television every evening provide a personal sense of order for the individual. A sudden absence of media (the morning paper not being delivered, for example) is accompanied by a feeling of disorientation—the upset of routine. Media, then, serve as an important constant in our lives, which are characterized by change. Discrete periods of time have long been defined by particular media presentations: the Colgate Radio Hour, Monday Night Football, Super Sunday, a week's World Series, and finally, a two-week block every four years devoted to Olympic telecasts.

Production choices often dictate the nature of the "reality" that the media captures. For instance, the framing of a photograph determines what is communicated with the image. Thus, a close-up photo (small inset) conveys the message that the subject is alone. However, the full shot reveals that the subject is part of a crowd of people. (Photo by Lisa Marcus)

The advent of the instant replay has also revolutionized our conception of time by heightening attention on "the moment." Significant plays are frozen and replayed in slow motion to capture every nuance of a play.

In the construction of media presentations, economy is essential, both in terms of the audiences' attention span and the exorbitant costs of media production. Through editing techniques, the audience is presented only with "meaningful minutes" as defined by the media communicator. Editing techniques involve decisions with regard to what to include and what to omit. Thus, in a film an entire day or lifetime of a character can be condensed into two hours. The audience must therefore simultaneously exist within two time frames; the time frame constructed within the narrative and the actual chronological time in which the presentation occurs.

Other media presentations piece together moments in time, based on thematic concerns of the narrative. For instance, a film may linger over particular events in the life of the protagonist, looking at the development of a hero and skipping over other "unimportant" moments. In like fashion, a romance only includes those scenes that touch on the relationship between the hero and heroine. For instance, in *Something's Gotta Give* (2003), starring Jack Nicholson and Diane Keaton, the main characters are successful professionals in their fields; however, the film rarely shows them actually working—except those moments when the romance interrupts their work activities.

The flashback is a production technique that signifies that the story is moving back in time. *Parallel editing* (also known as *crosscutting*) is another production technique that manipulates our conception of time. In this technique, two separate actions are edited together back to back, which signals that the two events are occurring at the same time.

In addition, the characters (or the actors, who become identified with the characters) appear real—due, in large measure, to the amount of time that the audience spends with their favorite characters. This illusion is also reinforced by the process of *Intertextuality*, in which characters assume a reality that transcends a particular programming.

- *Horizontal intertextuality* provides a sense of authenticity as characters appear across different programming. To illustrate, the 2013 film release *Star Trek into Darkness* is a *prequel* that focuses on the early, formative years of the crew of the spaceship *Enterprise*. The narrative focuses on the formation of the relationships between the primary characters and provides hints about the character traits that have made the characters readily identifiable and endearing to loyal fans.
- *Vertical intertextuality* occurs when characters appear in both primary and secondary programming, such as celebrity commercials, political events, tabloid journalism, or blogs.

But at the same time, the characters that appear in the media transcend time and space. These screen immortals remain eternally young. To illustrate, in *Raiders of the Lost Ark* (1981), Harrison Ford appears as a 39-year-old man—whether we watch the film today or 10 years hence. Indeed, digital enhancement enables media communicators to "animate" these stars, by synchronizing the speech and movements of actors from the stockpile of old footage and incorporating them into new productions. Thus, a 2012 sequel to *Raiders of the Lost Ark* could again feature the young Harrison Ford of the initial film, while costarring the 70-year-old Ford as his own grandfather.

Media Literacy Strategies

Media literacy strategies offer systematic ways to examine and discuss the topic of mass-mediated reality. For instance, *de-identification* is a technique that focuses attention on the limits of media identification. Although film, television, and the other media may appear to reflect the experience of the audience, the media construct a reality that is impossible to emulate in real life. Through editing, the media communicator presents selected moments that make the world depicted in the media appear exciting. The addition of a musical score makes even pedestrian acts like crossing the street appear dramatic. Special effects and stunt specialists enable characters to perform astonishing acts of strength and daring. And because the action is scripted, our heroes and heroines never miss a line, accidentally spill their food, or die in the middle of the story.

Moreover, through the use of makeup, editing, lighting, and digital manipulation, actors always look perfect. The members of the audience cannot possibly measure up to these idealized figures.

Indeed, actress Isabella Rossellini, age 45 at the time of the interview, was asked about the secret of her unlined looks, captured on the cover of *Vogue* magazine:

> Well, you can't go by the photo. Because obviously, the photo is an enhanced version of me, you know. It generally takes hours of makeup and fantastic lighting, a great photographer. So I don't think I look as good in life as in my photos. (Sumner, 1997)

Ironically, even the stars themselves cannot measure up to their own idealized standard of beauty.

Thus, examining these production and performance elements can provide insight into how efforts to identify with media characters can create unrealistic expectations on the part of the audience. Questions to ask with regard to *de-identification* include the following:

- In what ways does the media presentation construct a reality that is different from your everyday experience?
- What production elements are used to construct this reality?
- Are the actions of the characters unrealistic?

Willing Suspension of Disbelief. When watching entertainment programs, the audience willingly accepts the premise of the program, no matter how outlandish. This *suspension of disbelief* enables us to believe that mice can talk and penguins can dance. Once the initial premise has been accepted, the remainder of the narrative progresses in a logical fashion.

In some cases, the audience accepts, without question, a premise with ideological overtones. For example, the premise of police shows such as *Homicide* assumes the following: (a) that we live in a dangerous world, (b) that the predators who pose a threat to the dominant culture are members of lower classes and African Americans, (c) that the heroes instinctively know who is innocent and who is guilty, and (d) what is needed is a strong, undeterred authoritarian presence to remedy these problems. The reactionary political ideology behind this premise, in which civil liberties are sacrificed in the name of law and order, is made to look like an appealing option in this turbulent world.

Advertising frequently relies on an *illogical premise* to sell products. Once its premise has been accepted, an ad can be very persuasive. For instance, a television commercial begins with a shot of a door with the words "The Ponds Institute" etched on the glass. The door swings open, and the audience is thrust into the midst of a group of people in lab coats walking purposefully as they conduct their business. A voiceover announces that "Here at the Ponds Institute, we are concerned with combating the effects of aging on the skin." This scenario instills us with confidence in Ponds products. Upon reflection, however, several questions arise regarding the premise:

- Where is the Ponds Institute located?
- Can you get a degree from the Ponds Institute?
- Is it located near the Sassoon Academy?
- What kind of research is conducted at the Ponds Institute?
- What kind of methodology is employed in its research?
- Can the public obtain a copy of the results of the research?

It must be noted that the suspension of disbelief is a *choice* that is made by audience members. Thus, as individuals watch a film, see an ad, or read the newspaper, they can question the underlying assumptions behind the premise of the presentation and make a conscious decision whether or not to suspend their disbelief.

Further Areas of Discussion

Additional areas of discussion with regard to the topic of mass-mediated reality include the following:

- Impact of the media on conceptions of space
- Alternate realities (digitally enhanced reality)
- Media as reflection of reality
- Genre
  - Reality television
  - Genres (e.g., historical dramas and science fiction) as a reflection of the public's fascination with the past and the future
- Media distortions of reality

See also: Digital Media Literacy; Introduction

References

Media Literacy Resource Guide: Intermediate and Senior Divisions. (1989). Ontario, Canada: Ontario Ministry of Education.

Sumner, J. (1997, July 16). "Isabella Rossellini—Without Makeup." *St. Louis Post-Dispatch.* Retrieved from www.stltoday.com

Media and Social Change

The media have been criticized at various times both for taking too active a role in promoting social change and obstructing needed societal change. However, the media merely provide a channel through which communicators can reach their audience. The media's role with regard to social change is determined by the following factors:

- The intentions of the communicator
- The predilections of the audience
- The capabilities of the medium

Popular media programming can have a *prosocial impact* by bringing issues to public attention that had been the source of private shame. For instance, over her illustrious career, Oprah Winfrey has brought public attention to a number of issues that viewers had heretofore suffered in private, such as date rape, spousal abuse, and international child prostitution rings.

Social media such as Facebook and Twitter are particularly well suited as tools for social activism:

- 11 percent of Internet users have become online political activists (defined as users who have posted their own commentary to a newsgroup, Web site or blog, or posted or forwarded someone else's commentary, video or audio recordings) (Silverblatt, 2007: 38).

- 97 percent of political advocacy groups are using at least one social media platform to communicate with stakeholders (Cordasco, 2010).
- During one six-week period in 2011, an aggregate total of 1,474 tweets and 656 posts concerning congressional legislation were recorded (Cordasco, 2010).

The Internet provides individuals with the tools to organize grassroots social causes. To illustrate, in 2011, Noah Fradin, a high school senior, set up a Web site that promoted charitable giving through everyday purchases. Fradin set up CherryCard.org, a Web page, in which anyone who visits the site is given 25 cents to spend for a cause. According to reporter Amy Wallace (2011), the Internet start-up works as follows:

> Participating retailers will hand out business-card-size vouchers to their customers after a purchase. "Redeem this card at CherryCard.org to give $0.25 to the cause of your choice," reads a typical card, which is printed with a code. Later, after a consumer logs in to the CherryCard site via Facebook and types in that code, the card's monetary value is deposited in their account, which they can draw upon to give to charities (which are not charged to be listed on the site).
>
> Mr. Fradin believes CherryCard can be financed out of retailers' marketing budgets because it identifies them as socially conscious enterprises. Their logo will appear on the CherryCard site and will pop up on consumers' Facebook pages when they donate.

In addition, social media are uniquely structured to facilitate the process of *shared intentionality*—that is, the ability to form a plan with others for accomplishing a joint endeavor—that distinguishes humans from other species (Wade, 2011). To illustrate, social media such as Facebook, Twitter, and location-based services such as Foursquare have revolutionized the way in which epidemiologists discover and track the spread of disease. In 2011, a global team of "computational epidemiologists," who use unconventional data sources to help predict disease outbreaks, used Facebook to gather information leading to the diagnosis of the sudden appearance of legionellosis disease throughout the globe. Dr. Taha Kass-Hout, deputy director for information science at the Centers for Disease Control and Prevention (CDC), explains, "Given that the next severe acute respiratory syndrome (SARS) probably can travel at the speed of an airliner from continent to continent in a matter of hours, it just makes perfect sense to adapt the speed and flexibility of social networking to disease surveillance" (Garrity, 2011). By the time that Los Angeles County health authorities and the federal CDC began their formal investigation, a global community of "computational epidemiologists" had already made their own diagnosis and had posted a Wikipedia entry about the outbreak of the disease.

In another example, Professor John Brownstein and Clark Freifeld, a software designer, designed HealthMap, which tracks the occurrences of diseases by searching the Web for disease reports from local news articles, witness accounts, blogs, Twitter, and official reports from the CDC and World Health Organization.

The 2011 democratic revolution that swept throughout the Middle East and northern Africa is a striking illustration of the impact of social media on global social movements. In Egypt, a group of young, Internet-savvy activists called for protests against the rule of President Hosni Mubarak, urging sympathizers to converge on the central Liberation Square at Friday prayer before marching together toward the square. This message, which spread virally, resulted in more than 100,000 people pouring into the streets of the capital. The impact of this demonstration reverberated across the country. Novelist Mansoura Ez-Eldin (2011), who participated in the demonstrations in Egypt, observed,

> In the blink of an eye, the Twitter and Facebook generation had successfully rallied hundreds of thousands to its cause, across the nation. Most of them were young people who had not been politically active, and did not belong to the traditional circles of the political opposition. The Muslim Brotherhood is not behind this popular revolution, as the regime claims. Those who began it and organized it are seething in anger at police cruelty and the repression and torture meted out by the Hosni Mubarak regime.

In this virtual approach to social activism, social movements are less reliant on the personalities of their leaders than on the traditional face-to-face organizing efforts. Indeed, during the upheaval in Egypt, the leaders were difficult to identify.

> In the tableau of revolution that Tahrir Square has become, the very passions that have inspired the protests here were countered Monday by a question that could determine whether President Hosni Mubarak

relinquishes nearly 30 years in power: Who will speak for people who have never had a voice?

Some protesters said they did not need leadership for an uprising that was about sweeping away the old order. Others wondered whether anyone could articulate the frustrations of a generation that, as events rapidly unfolded Monday night, was closer than ever before to forcing Mr. Mubarak's fall. "We don't want [Mohamed] ElBaradei or the Muslim Brotherhood, and we don't want the ruling party," said Mohammed Nagi, a 30-year-old protester. "You feel like everyone is walking on his own, speaking for himself, because there's no group that represents us."

The fact that the movement lacks, in the words of one activist, "clear structure and clear leadership," has helped it captivate the Arab world, which has greeted it with a mix of exhilaration and romanticism. (Shadid, 2011)

Online activists operate within the Digital Communications model, in which individuals circumvent both the established government officials and the traditional opposition leaders. (See entry Communication Models.) One of the chants voiced by the crowd was "No to the [Muslim] Brotherhood, no to the parties." One of the banners read, "A revolution of the people, not the parties" (Shadid, 2011).

Young people have become a driving force behind recent social movements. David D. Kirkpatrick and Mona El-Naggar (2011) assembled the following profile of the young leaders of the movement to topple Egyptian president Hosni Mubarak:

They were born roughly around the time that President Hosni Mubarak first came to power, most earned degrees from their country's top universities and all have spent their adult lives bridling at the restrictions of the Egyptian police state—some undergoing repeated arrests and torture for the cause.

Media as Impediment to Social Change

As mentioned earlier, digital media is merely a channel that can be used in a variety of ways. Thus, at the same time that the media promote social change, these channels of mass communication can also *impede* political movements. In 2011, for example, as protests in support of democratic revolutions was sweeping the Middle East and Africa, government officials in Zimbabwe monitored television news coverage of protests in their country against President Robert Mugabe and then arrested the dissidents.

Media activists and governments often engage in a contest of *media ping-pong*, which consists of the following steps:

- Media activists use media technology to elude repressive government regulations.
- The government then institutes new technological measures to clamp down on dissidents.
- In response, the activists implement new technological strategies that circumvent the new government measures.
- The government then institutes new technological measures to clamp down on dissidents.
- The activists then implement new technological strategies that circumvent these government measures.
- And so on.

National Public Radio reporter Deborah Amos (2011) provides the following example of how Syrian social activists used media technology to evade the repressive measures of the government:

Social media activist Rami Nakhle, 27, is on the run—he changes his numbers often and doesn't give out his address. In Syria, he is a wanted cyberactivist. He fled to Lebanon ahead of a prison sentence. . . . Nakhle's site is now a hub for protest pictures, eyewitness accounts and the names of the dead documented by human rights groups—a network of activists who know and trust each other. . . . He downloads a live stream of cell phone videos for uploads to YouTube. Syria has banned almost all international media, but Nahkle says, so far, Syria's social media network can beat the ban with technology.

"We are playing two roles: first, to spread the news, then to influence the street. We are not leading at all, but we're trying to influence. . . . We have, like, thousands and thousands of youth. It's like a national brainstorming, really. It's like, they are creative and every idea just will get picked up by many, many, many small groups. . . . Now, we have the . . . anti-dictator tools. What is the dictator tools? Their propaganda, their secret police—they still have the same old tools and we are . . . developing our tools, day after day after day."

But as reporter Jennifer Preston points out, within one month the Syrian government had countered the strategies of the dissidents:

> Human right advocates warned that the government could use Facebook to closely monitor regime criticism and ferret out dissidents as nearby countries erupted in revolt. Security officials are moving on multiple fronts—demanding dissidents turn over their Facebook passwords and switching off the 3G mobile network at times, sharply limiting the ability of dissidents to upload videos of protests to YouTube. . . . Supporters of President Bashar al-Assad, calling themselves the Syrian Electronic Army, are using the same tools to try to discredit dissidents. . . . [In addition], the Syrian government is turning off electricity and telephone service in neighborhoods with the most unrest, activists say.

However, once again, social activists came up with strategies to circumvent the moves of the government. The Syrian activists then began sharing passwords with friends so that if they were arrested, their friends could delete incriminating evidence from their Facebook pages.

Media Literacy Strategies

Worldview

In the aftermath of the social upheaval in Arab States in 2011, commentators pointed out that the chief opponents to the totalitarian regimes were young advocates of democracy; the Islamic fundamentalist groups like al-Qaeda or the Muslim Brotherhood played only a minor role in the conflict. Reporter David D. Kirkpatrick (2011) observed, "Most of the group are liberals or leftists, and all, including the (Muslim) Brotherhood members among them, say they aspire to a Western-style constitutional democracy where civic institutions are stronger than individuals."

One way to account for this phenomenon is to consider the *worldview* of social media, which is *democratic*. This worldview is made up of one virtual nation that transcends traditional boundaries. According to reporter Michael Slackman (2011),

> Young people interviewed across the region echoed the same ideas, tactics and motivations that set off revolutions in Egypt and Tunisia. In Morocco and Jordan, monarchs have already offered concessions, fueling excitement and hope.

Moreover, in this virtual world, there is no hierarchy; one person has as much right to be on the Internet as anyone else. Indeed, women are not subjugated in this digital world. Slackman (2011) observes,

> Ramsey Tesdell, 27, who was leading the discussion, said that social media allowed young women in the village to bypass the men—fathers, brothers, husbands—who circumscribed their worlds and their ability to communicate. They cannot go to the park unaccompanied and meet friends, but they can join a chat room or send instant messages. "In a lot of ways, it has taken the power away from the traditional powerful leaders, especially older men," Mr. Tesdell said.

Given the amount of time that they spend in this virtual world, it is not surprising that its citizens wish to replicate its democratic worldview in the "real" world.

See also: Communication Models; Cultural Context; Digital Media Literacy; Sectors, Media Literacy; Social Networking

References

Amos, D. (2011, April 22). "Syria." National Public Radio, Morning Edition. www .npr.org.

Bronwyn Garrity, B. (2011, June 13). "More Expedient, Direct than Traditional Scientific Approach." *New York Times.* www.nytimes.com

Cordasco, P. (2010, July 13). "Vast Majority of Leading U.S. Political Advocacy Groups Are Using at Least One Social Media Platform to Connect and Organize Stakeholders, Study Finds." *Business Wire.* Retrieved from http://www.business wire.com/portal/site/home/permalink/?ndmViewId=news_view&newsId=20100 713006744&newsLang=en

Ez-Eldin, M. (2011, January 30). "Date With a Revolution." *New York Times.* Retrieved from http://www.nytimes.com/2011/01/31/opinion/31eldin.html?pagewanted=all

Kirkpatrick, D. D. (2011, February 9). "Wired and Shrewd, Young Egyptians Guide Revolt." *New York Times.* Retrieved from http://www.nytimes.com/2011/02/10/ world/middleeast/10youth.html?pagewanted=all&_r=0

Kirkpatrick, D. D., & El-Naggar, M. (2011, January 30). "Protest's Old Guard Falls in Behind the Young." *New York Times.* Retrieved from http://www.nytimes .com/2011/01/31/world/middleeast/31opposition.html?pagewanted=all

Preston, J. (2011, May 22). "Seeking to Disrupt Protesters, Syria Cracks Down on Social Media." *New York Times.* Retrieved from http://www.nytimes.com/ 2011/05/23/world/middleeast/23facebook.html

Shadid, A. (2011, January 31). "In Crowd's Euphoria, No Clear Leadership Emerges." *New York Times*. Retrieved from http://www.nytimes.com/2011/02/01/world/middleeast/01square.html?pagewanted=all

Silverblatt, A. (2007). *Media Literacy: Keys to Interpreting Media Messages* (3rd ed.). Westport: Praeger Publishing.

Slackman, M. (2011, March 17). "Bullets Stall Youthful Push for Arab Spring." *New York Times*. Retrieved from http://www.nytimes.com/2011/03/18/world/middleeast/18youth.html?pagewanted=all

Wade, N. (2011, March 14). "Supremacy of a Social Network." *New York Times*. Retrieved from http://www.nytimes.com/2011/03/15/science/15humans.html?pagewanted=all

Wallace, A. (2011, April 16). "Serving a Cause, 25 Cents at a Time." *New York Times*. Retrieved from http://www.nytimes.com/2011/04/17/business/17proto.html

Media Math

Events, people, or positions on issues may be distorted in the press, operating on the principle of media math. To adhere to the notion of *objectivity*, media communicators strive to give equal exposure to differing points of view, regardless of the amount of support for these perspectives. As a result, the *same* event, as presented in the media, can feel like *separate* incidents. For example, the overwhelming coverage of the 2008 Virginia Tech massacre conveyed the cumulative message that there were dozens of attacks on the college campus.

An excellent example of an application of media math can be found in the coverage of climate change in U.S. newspapers and magazines. The United Nations Framework Convention on Climate Change defines this phenomenon as "a change of climate which is attributed directly or indirectly to human activity that alters the composition of the global atmosphere and which is in addition to natural climate variability observed over comparable time periods" (United Nations, 2009).

By an overwhelming margin, the scientific community supports the notion that human beings have contributed to climate change. A 2009 study found that 82 percent of the scientists surveyed believe that human activity has been a significant factor in the phenomenon of climate change ("Scientists Agree," 2009). It should be noted that this survey, published in the *Science News*, was carefully crafted for accuracy: 3,146 Earth scientists throughout the world were surveyed, and all of the scientists who were contacted were listed in the 2007 edition of the American Geological Institute's Directory of Geoscience Departments.

In contrast, only 5 percent of the scientific community believes that human activity does *not* contribute to greenhouse warming; the rest are unsure. Moreover, since 1991, the last major survey of American climate scientists, belief in human-induced warming has more than *doubled* (Lichter, 2008).

Despite this overwhelming consensus, reporters frequently devote a disproportionate amount of space to the alternate point of view, in the name of "fairness." As an example, on August 14, 2010, the *New York Times* published an article, "In Weather Chaos, a Case for Global Warming," that examines the issue of possible connections between extreme weather incidents and climate change. The article, written by Justin Gillis, consisted of 1,297 words. Within the article, the amount of space dedicated to scientists holding the position that human beings play a direct role in climate change (through the manufacturing of carbon dioxide) is *292* words. In contrast, the amount of space dedicated to scientists holding the position that human beings play no role in climate change is *126* words:

- "If you ask me as a person, do I think the Russian heat wave has to do with climate change, the answer is yes," said Gavin Schmidt, a climate researcher with NASA in New York. "If you ask me as a scientist whether I have proved it, the answer is no—at least not yet."
- Climate-change skeptics dispute such statistical arguments, contending that climatologists do not know enough about long-range patterns to draw definitive links between global warming and weather extremes. They cite events like the heat and drought of the 1930s as evidence that extreme weather is nothing new. Those were indeed dire heat waves, contributing to the Dust Bowl, which dislocated millions of Americans and changed the population structure of the United States. (Gillis, 2010)

In sum, the amount of space dedicated to scientists denying a human role in climate change amounted to 43 percent of the space devoted to scientists supporting the "human factor" position. Thus, from a media math perspective, although only 18 percent of scientists deny that humans play a role, the amount of space dedicated to this position in the article (i.e., "Media Math") leaves readers with the impression that 43 percent of the scientific community opposes the position that human technology is responsible for climate change.

This media coverage conveys the message that there is a genuine "debate" in the scientific community over whether CO_2 emissions are driving global warming, contributing to a discrepancy between the views of the scientific community and the public perception of climate change. Significantly, a 2010 poll reveals that only 58 percent of the American public thinks human activity contributes to global warming. Naomi Oreskes, a history of science professor at the University of California at San Diego, declares that the media coverage of climate change has allowed people to think that global warming is a "fad" that could "go away" in a few years, much like the unfounded scare over the pesticide Alar in the late 1980s.

The scientific community recognizes that this principle of media math has undermined their effort to address the issue. Rick Piltz, a former senior associate in the federal government's Climate Change Science Policy office said, "Right now, the global warming denial machine has influence way outside of its merit." Oreskes has pointed out that although there is an "overwhelming [scientific] consensus (on global warming) when it gets translated to the general public [by the media], it comes across as 'uncertainty' or 'they don't know what's going on." Many scientists criticize the media for giving too much attention to global warming "denialists," as they have dubbed them. Oreskes faulted reporters for continually quoting well-known global warming skeptics such as Fred Singer, noting some were discredited years ago for denying the link between chlorofluorocarbons and the destruction of the ozone layer. "Why should these people be considered credible when we know the history of their activities?" she asked (Hansen, 2006).

The following approach provides a useful way to determine the impression of the significance of an event:

- Obtain statistical information on the frequency of these incidents, compared with the amount of media coverage.
- Multiply the number of times a single event is reported in the media; this results in its *media frequency*—that is, how many times an event *appears* to occur.
- Compare the two sets of data.

Thus, in the case of the University of Virginia shooting, if seen five times in an hour, the media coverage leaves the impression that five separate incidents occurred.

A variation of this notion of media math can be found in broadcast journalism, referring to the number of times in which a particular story is repeated on television news programming. Thus, one way to assess the coverage of a topic or incident in television news programming involves asking the following questions:

- How many times do they repeat a story in a 24-hour news cycle?
- How much time do they devote to a story within a news program?
- How many stories on the topic do they provide (relative to other news items)?
- How many times do they break in with news updates—even when there isn't much new to report?

See also: Journalism

References

Gillis, J. (2010, August 14). "In Weather Chaos, a Case for Global Warming." *New York Times*. Retrieved from http://www.nytimes.com/2010/08/15/science/earth/15climate.html?pagewanted=all

Hansen, B. (2006, July 31). "Panel Faults Media for Playing Up 'Debate' over Global Warming." Inside Energy with Federal Lands. Retrieved from http://www.platts.com

Lichter, S. R. (2008, April 24). "Climate Scientists Agree on Warming, Disagree on Dangers, and Don't Trust the Media's Coverage of Climate Change ." *STATS*. Retrieved from http://stats.org/stories/2008/global_warming_survey_apr23_08.html

"Scientists Agree Human-Induced Global Warming Is Real, Survey Says." (2009, January 21). *ScienceDaily*. Retrieved from http://www.sciencedaily.com/releases/2009/01/090119210532.htm

United Nations. (2009). "The United Nations Framework Convention on Climate Change." http://unfccc.int/2860.php

Media Production Approach, Media Literacy Education

Media production adds a distinctive and important approach to media literacy education. Students are introduced to media literacy principles through hands-on experience.

Since the mid-1950s, Alan Bloom's *Taxonomy of Learning* has served as a means through which educators systematically assess the effectiveness of their teaching strategies. Over time, Bloom's taxonomy has changed to reflect many of the changes in education. Most recently, and at the top of the higher order thinking skills sits the verb *to create*. In this model, the process of constructing media presentations such as film, video, blogs, and audio podcasts provides opportunities to apply the principles of media literacy (Churches, 2008).

Media educators have developed curricula in which students are introduced to media literacy principles through hands-on experience in the layout of newspapers, animated films, documentaries, short films, television newscasts, and advertising campaigns.

Advocates of this approach emphasize that this is not a media production course designed to educate professional photographers, videographers, and the like. Instead, the goal is to increase students' theoretical understanding of the media through the production process. A familiarity with production elements such as editing, color, lighting, shape, movement, scale, relative position, angle, connotative words, connotative images, and audio can help individuals develop a critical understanding of the *process* of media production. As they produce a media program, the media production team learns to identify its audience, including their background and interests. In addition, they must define the goals and objectives of the project—what they want to accomplish, and what messages they wish to convey. Another content area is *preproduction*, including research, legal issues, budgeting, and casting. Finally, hands-on production enables students to recognize narrative conventions as they appear in media presentations. In the process of creating media presentations, students become aware of why TV dramas and news stories are presented in a particular way.

However, teachers of video production attest that students who have been exposed to this production approach to introductory video production create projects that are superior to the class exercises that employ the traditional approach to video production. Instead of simply asking students to demonstrate an understanding of different production techniques, this approach to the study of video helps students understand the messages conveyed by their production choices. For example, in an Introduction to Video Production class, a unit on camera angle includes an exercise in which students select camera angles that make the subject's point of view appear "legitimate." The students then use the camera angle that tilts up (literally "looking up to" the subject).

In addition, media production analysis fulfills the following educational objectives:

- *Developing aesthetic appreciation.* Hands-on production introduces students to conventions—that is, formulaic ways of setting up and shooting stories. This experience enables students to recognize these formulas in mainstream media presentations. In the process, students become aware of why TV dramas, news, newspaper stories are presented in a certain way. At the same time, hands-on production provides opportunities for students to experiment, to move beyond these conventions.

- *Understanding the process of media production.* While producing a media program, the production team must identify its audience, including their background and interests. In addition, they must define the goals and objectives of the project—what do they want to accomplish, and what messages do they wish to convey. A script must be developed which combines clear visuals and narration.
- Other considerations include preproduction planning, including research, legal issues, budgeting, and casting.
- *Developing social skills.* Media production is a collaborative enterprise in which the success of a project is dependent on the ability of the crew to work together. The production team must develop a close working relationship defined by mutual respect, a sense of compromise, and problem-solving skills.

In addition, the media production approach works toward the goal of improving the media industry by preparing practitioners who combine technical skill with an understanding of the responsibilities of the media communicator.

A related application of the production analysis approach involves the use of *authentic media texts* in the classroom, which enables students to see how media messages are constructed in actual media "texts." Media literacy educator Frank Baker provides the following examples of ways in which authentic texts can be used in the study of advertising:

- An elementary school educator might begin by asking her students to identify and be aware of signs. A billboard can be presented as one type of sign—and thus students begin to be aware that signs are ads and use colors, words, and images to get attention.
- A middle-grade teacher might have her students engage in a semester-long survey of their environment, identifying where ads are located, including at home and at school. Students could use digital cameras to photograph the ads, making note of locations, demographics, and persuasion techniques.
- Using magazines found at school or at home, students could conduct a "content analysis," noting which products are pitched and who is being targeted.

- Students might watch episodes of AMC's *Mad Men* to get a feel for how ad agencies pitched campaigns in the 1960s.
- An advertising professional could serve as a guest speaker to dispel some of the myths portrayed in the *Mad Men* series.
- Students might research how a particular product or political candidate was marketed in the past, noting similarities and the differences to current practices.
- Students could bring in examples of ads, focusing on the analysis of word choice, images, layout, inferred and subtext messages. She might then have them create their own ads, using online tools (e.g., Glogster or VoiceThread) or by simply using construction paper and markers (Baker, n.d.).

See Also: Affective Response Analysis; Audience Analysis; Dialectical Analysis; Iconographic Analysis; Ideological Analysis; Integrated Approach to Media Literacy Education; Key Principles and Concepts, Media Literacy; Production Analysis Approach

References

Baker, F. (n.d.). Media Literacy Clearinghouse. http://www.frankwbaker.com

Churches, A. (2008, April 1). "Bloom's Taxonomy Blooms Digitally." *Technology & Learning Magazine*. Retrieved from http://www.techlearning.com/article/8670

Zettl, H. (1998). "Media Aesthetics: Contextual Media Aesthetics as the Basis for Media Literacy," *Journal of Communication* (Winter 1998), 81–94.

Medium Theory

Medium theory holds that each medium is defined by a set of distinctive characteristics that influences its ability to present certain types of information. The effective media communicator takes advantage of the unique properties of each medium to convey media messages. For instance, radio obviously cannot employ visuals in transmitting information. However, the radio producer can appeal to the imagination of the listener through creative use of words and sounds. The media communicator must decide which medium can best accommodate the message and use the "language" of that medium to reach the intended audience.

Considerations in assessing the distinctive characteristics of a medium include the following:

- The *senses* involved in receiving information affect people's ability to assimilate certain kinds of information, as well as the ways in which they respond to the content
- The *pace* of the presentation refers to the rhythm or rate at which information should be assimilated.
- The *environment*, or physical surroundings, in which the medium is presented affect how an individual comprehends and responds to a media presentation.
- *Dissemination patterns* refer to (a) the amount of time it takes for information to be conveyed through a particular medium and (b) the route that it takes to get to the public.

Certain types of information may be more effectively presented through one medium than another. These characteristics have an impact on the appropriate selection of a medium for the presentation of content. For example, newspapers lend themselves to the detailed presentation of contextual information and discussion of complex issues, but television is unparalleled in the presentation of *events*. Thus, an understanding of medium theory enables the audience to make appropriate decisions with regard to the appropriate medium to use, given the kind of information being presented.

As an example, *data visualization* is a subset of graphic communications that makes statistical information comprehensible. Professor Ben Shneiderman observes, "The purpose of visualization is insight, not pictures" (Singer, 2011). For instance, Gapminder, a nonprofit group based in Stockholm, uses data visualization techniques to educate the public about global disparities in health and wealth. Reporter Natasha Singer (2011) explains:

Visual analytics play off the idea that the brain is more attracted to and able to process dynamic images than long lists of numbers. . . . Hit the play button and an animated graphic, called Gapminder World, shows a constellation of brightly colored bubbles, each representing a different country, bouncing along over two centuries. Without ever having to view yawn-inducing numbers on gross domestic product per capita, you can watch some countries, like the United States, rapidly growing healthier and wealthier before your eyes while smaller bubbles, for countries like Congo, rise on the life expectancy axis even as they dip on the income line.

The medium theory holds that each medium offers a distinctive way to present information. Thus, the audience is getting a different kind of news, depending on whether they rely on print, radio, television, or the Internet. Consequently, the best course of action is a balanced media diet, in which individuals use media in combination to benefit from the unique characteristics of each medium. (Photo by Lisa Marcus)

In the 1990s, Shneiderman developed the process of "tree mapping," which uses interlocking rectangles to represent different kinds of information, like revenue or geographic region. According to Jim Bartoo, the chief executive of the software company Hive Group, tree mapping is an intuitive human process: "It's the ability of the human brain to pick out size and color. Information visualization suddenly starts answering questions that you didn't know you had" (Singer, 2011).

In addition, data visualization can be applied to social media as a research tool that detects societal patterns and trends. For example, in 2009, Stamen Design, a technology and design studio in San Francisco, created a live visualization of Twitter traffic during the MTV Video Music awards. This presentation consisted of an animated graphic that displayed which celebrities were dominating Twitter talk during the program. Floating bubbles, in the image of a star, expanded or contracted, depending on the amount of Twitter activity about a celebrity at that moment.

Thus, one of the principles of media literacy involves the value of a balanced media diet, in which consumers of media use media in *combination* to take advantage of the distinctive attributes of each medium. As discussed earlier, the stories selected for broadcast news are unparalleled at showing events as they unfold. In contrast, print stories contain essential detail and context. Consequently, using *both* media provides the audience with a more comprehensive understanding of the news event.

In addition, medium theory considers the relative impact of each channel of mass communication on its intended audience by influencing the *strategy*, *style*, and *content* of the media presentation. To illustrate, at times, the immediacy of the e-mail format makes e-mail correspondence appear rude. As a result, reporter Marci Alboher recommends the following changes with regard to these communication elements:

- *Communications strategy* (the approach, or purpose behind, a communications activity):
  - *Don't use e-mail when another medium makes more sense.* Use e-mail only when it's the best method. In many work cultures (like Yahoo!), instant messaging is popular for quick conversations and sending links back and forth. If you know a colleague is on the road a lot and more likely to see a text message than an e-mail, then use text messaging. If you know someone is at her desk and might not check an e-mail about a meeting change in half an hour, the old-fashioned land line might be the best choice.
  - *Answer questions inline.* When someone sends an e-mail asking several questions, train yourself to reply inline, inserting your answers directly beneath each question.
  - *Change the subject line every time you start a new conversation.* The e-mail subject line should tell the reader what the message is about. So if an e-mail strand about "next Thursday's meeting" suddenly morphs into a discussion about "Mary's retirement party," consider changing the subject line. Having descriptive subject lines helps people quickly scan their inbox to decide which messages to read first and also helps when searching for a message after a conversation has ended.
  - *Use the cc function sparingly.* Try to cc only those who need to know and avoid cc-ing long lists of people unless it is important that everyone know who else received a message. Certainly don't use the cc function if you don't want people on the list to know the names of the other people receiving the same message.

- ○ *Ask whether people prefer attachments or inline pasting.* Many people dislike receiving attachments, but it's good to ask someone's preference if you're going to be sending documents back and forth. Consider tools that allow two people to share and work on a document together rather than attachments.
  - ○ *Avoid shared e-mail addresses.* Do not share an e-mail with a spouse or partner (either professional or business e-mails).
- *Style* (the approach to a presentation that reflects the individuality of the communicator):
  - ○ *Don't get the last word in.* There is usually no reason to cap off a long exchange with a final "thank you" (and certainly, "you're welcome"). An e-mail conversation has to end at some point.
  - ○ *Keep it brief.* When was the last time you read a work-related e-mail and wished it was longer?
  - ○ *Give up cutesy handles.* Try to stay as close to your name or a shorthand for your name as possible. "Purtygrl" might be just fine for your online dating life, but give it up when you're corresponding about work matters.
- *Content* (the choice of information that is included in a presentation):
  - ○ *Use personal e-mail for personal correspondence.* This includes job searching.
  - ○ *Say no to chain letters and jokes.* The rare, forwarded e-mail may evoke a smile or a warm feeling, but they are mostly irritating. (Alboher, 2009)

Today, television has merged with computers and, as a result, has been transformed into an *information appliance*. Sree Kotay, chief software architect for Comcast, is enthusiastic about "all the interactive tasks that developers have started to imagine, especially combining text, graphics and video from cable channels and the Internet. And the next generation will go further" (Hansell, 2009).

Individual audience members are now able to add applications, or *apps*, to give each digital device its own unique, distinctive character. As of 2009, independent developers have written more than 65,000 apps for televisions (Hansell, 2009). As a result, it is not simply each *medium* that is unique but every individual television set is defined by a set of distinctive characteristics—apps—that, in turn, influence the presentation of information.

Examples of apps that individuals can select to micro-personalize their television/computer hybrid include the following:

- FiOS, the Facebook application, enables people to see photos on their television screens that have been shared by their friends.
- Echostar has introduced a box with a full Internet browser that can play video from nearly any site on the Web.
- AT&T's U-verse service offers an interactive version of the Professional Golfers Association golf tournament that enables viewers to switch between cameras aimed at different parts of the course.
- Comcast, Time Warner Cable, and most of the other major cable companies are making available an enhanced TV binary interchange format software that presents caller ID information on the TV screen when the phone rings.
- Other apps provide information and photographs related to the programs they watch and the actors in them. (Hansell, 2009)

Finally, medium theory involves understanding the capabilities and limits of media systems. As an example, although Twitter can promote global democratic movements, the structure of this social medium can also discourage critical thinking. The Arab Spring movement of 2011 is directly attributable to the immediate and interactive characteristics of this medium. However, like Newspeak, the language employed in the totalitarian society in George Orwell's futuristic novel *1984*, Twitter is a reductive language: only 140 characters are allowed in a single tweet. Orwell's comments about the impact of Newspeak on thought may also be applicable to Twitter, in the following respects:

- *Ideas are reduced to literal meaning.* There is no space to examine the implications of meaning.
- *No context to information is provided.* There is no room to discuss ideas within a historical or cultural context.
- *Language assumes a neutral tenor.* The use of abbreviations eliminates the emotional connotation of content.

As an example, MSNBC anchor Rachel Maddow questioned how a complex issue such as the Middle East can be addressed in such a constricted format: "The Israeli government is trying to explain a conflict that people write books about, a conflict that newspaper writers struggle to explain in 2,000 words, in 140 characters at a time" (Cohen, 2009).

See also: Historical Analysis, Media: Systems Approach; Media and Social Change

References

Alboher, M. (2009, June 28). "How to Improve Your Email Etiquette." Working the New Economy. Retrieved from http://shine.yahoo.com/channel/life/how-to -improve-your-email-etiquette-481584

Cohen, N. (2009, January 4). "The Toughest Q's Answered in the Briefest Tweets." *New York Times*. Retrieved from http://www.nytimes.com/2009/01/04/ weekinreview/04cohen.html

Hansell, S. (2009, September 7). "Like Apple, TV Explores Must-Have Applications." *New York Times*. Retrieved from http://www.nytimes.com/2009/09/07/ business/07cable.html?pagewanted=all

Singer, S. (2011, April 2). "When the Data Struts Its Stuff." *New York Times*. Retrieved from http://www.nytimes.com/2011/04/03/business/03stream.html

Memetic Approach, Media Literacy Analysis

The memetic approach to media analysis offers strategies for discussing and interpreting media content. This is an example of a *disparate approach to media analysis* in which the principles of another discipline are applied to the interpretation of media content.

A *meme* is a term that was originally used to describe a biological process involving the transmission of genes. Over time, this concept has been applied to the transmission of culture from one mind to another, through the channels of mass communication. In general, memes are clearly identifiable: The identical story is repeated through the various channels of mass communication.

A memetic approach to media analysis examines the construction and recurrence of memes: What makes certain stories "stick" in the media? Examples of contemporary memes include the following:

- Obama is not "American"—he is a Muslim and/or is not an American citizen.
- 9/11 was a conspiracy orchestrated by the U.S. government.
- The 2010 Health Care Bill included "death panels" that would eliminate the elderly.

Professor Jure Leskovec and Stanford PhD candidate Jaewon Yang have conducted research that successfully predicts how widely a story will travel. The researchers can predict, with 75 percent accuracy, the following patterns that are applicable to the understanding of memes:

- How a story's popularity will rise and fall
- The volume of attention that a story will receive
- The pattern by which it will spread
- The way that stories are shared online (Naone, 2011)

A number of factors influence the duration of a meme: the content of the story itself, the popularity of the site of origin, and the nature of the community of readers at which it's aimed. In addition, the medium (or media) in which the story initially appears affects its longevity. Leskovec explains, "By looking at when particular types of media get involved, you can see different patterns arise. For example, if a blog breaks a story, the pattern tends to be different than when a story is broken by a traditional news media" (Naone, 2011). The timing of additional input by social media is also a major factor in determining the longevity of a story. Reporter Naone (2011) explains,

> The point at which blogs get involved in a story . . . is a major factor in determining its longevity. For example, even if traditional media focus on a story for a brief time, blog discussion can keep it in the public eye longer.

The research provides additional information that can be applied to the study of memes:

- Furnishing perspective into how information travels online
- Determining the influence of writers or bloggers by showing how their content appears and how it is shared
- Helping sites manage their content (For example, this information could help online editors to decide how long to give a story a prominent place on its front page)

But although memes are commonly held beliefs, they may or may not be *true*. Sam Wang and Sandra Aamodt (2008) explain,

> False beliefs are everywhere. Eighteen percent of Americans think the sun revolves around the earth, one poll has found. Thus it seems slightly less egregious that, according to another poll, 10 percent of us think that Senator Barack Obama, a Christian, is instead a Muslim.

In addition to the repetition of the identical story, there are several other categories of memes.

Metaphorical Memes

On the surface, a meme may appear to be simply a diversion from the pressing issues of the day. However, a meme often derives its significance as a symbol of larger issues. Thus, rather than dismissing these recurring stories as trivial, we should pay *more* attention to them. It can therefore be useful to consider the meme's larger significance, in order to determine what, exactly, the meme "represents."

To illustrate, stories about CEOs' salaries and bonuses have become a constant drumbeat in the media. John Paulson, a hedge fund manager in New York City, made $4.9 billion in 2010, equivalent to the per capita income of 184,000 Americans (Kristof, 2011). Another recurring story involves the extravagant lifestyles of these CEOs, such as the story of the chief executives of the three biggest American automakers flying to Washington on their private jets to ask Congress for an enormous amount of bailout money. But although the amount of money that these CEOs received amounted to millions of dollars, this outlay of funds were hardly the reason that their corporations had failed. The significance behind this persistent meme is that it serves as a metaphor of the greed and conspicuous consumption that contributed to the hemorrhaging of the global market-driven economy. Sheryl Gary Stolberg (2009) explains,

> What these stories share is a simple and clear narrative that captures the public imagination by tapping into some . . . existing perception—"a proxy for a bigger concern," in the words of Ed Gillespie, former counselor to [former President George W.] Bush. If that concern runs deep enough, the side issue becomes the main issue.
>
> Thus did the A.I.G. bonuses become a symbol of long-simmering taxpayer resentment over Wall Street bailouts, and economic inequity in general, raising essential questions about fairness and personal responsibility.

Cultural Memes

Cultural memes are stories that provide insight into cultural values, behaviors, preoccupations, and myths. To illustrate, political memes reflect an anti-intellectual climate that is part of the populist tradition in the United States. Reporter John Harwood (2009) observes,

> George Wallace attacked "pointy-headed intellectuals who couldn't park their bicycle straight." Richard M. Nixon contrasted the "silent majority" of Middle America with unruly protesters, whom his vice

president, Spiro T. Agnew, condemned as "an effete corps of impudent snobs." Crusading against government excess, Reagan, as a candidate, lampooned a "Chicago welfare queen" who received benefits under multiple identities. George Bush used the rapist Willie Horton to cast Democrats as soft on crime.

Thematic Memes

Thematic memes are stories that, on the surface, do not appear to be related. However, considering these stories as aspects of a single theme puts the appearance of these stories into perspective.

To illustrate, a number of apparently unrelated stories involving President Barak Obama routinely crop up in the media:

- Obama is Muslim
- Obama is not a U.S. citizen
- Obama is a socialist
- Obama is gay

Although the specifics of these stories differ, they share a thematic narrative: *Obama is a foreigner.*

These stories tie into a body of research revealing that most Americans associate "Americans" and Caucasians. Columnist Nicholas Kristof (2008) observes,

> One study found that although people realize that [Chinese-American actress] Lucy Liu is American and that Kate Winslet is British, their minds automatically process an Asian face as foreign and a white face as American—hence this title in an academic journal: "Is Kate Winslet More American Than Lucy Liu?"

This manifestation of social bias is a mechanism that is common to the human species—even groups that are targets of racial discrimination, such as Latinos and Asian Americans.

During the 2008 presidential campaign, researchers found that subjects subconsciously considered candidate Barack Obama to be *less American* than either Hillary Clinton or John McCain (Kristof, 2008). Thus, the recurrence of these thematic memes—that Obama is Muslim, an illegal alien, or a socialist—are tied to racial attitudes, in which people who are perceived as different—even when they belong to the same culture—are regarded as outsiders.

Affective Memes

Affective memes occur when seemingly unrelated stories are all expressions of a particular primal emotion. Some memes strike an emotional chord in the audience. Wang and Aamodt (2008) explain,

> Ideas can spread by emotional selection, rather than by their factual merits, encouraging the persistence of falsehoods about Coke—or about a presidential candidate.

Although the specific stories change, the underlying emotion behind these stories remains. To illustrate, consider the following headlines:

- "Arkansas Suspects Had Rage Toward Government," *New York Times*, May 23, 2010
- "Tea Party Lights Fuse for Rebellion on Right," *New York Times*, February 16, 2010
- "Birthright Madness: Anti-immigrant Sentiment at Fever Pitch," *Arizona Sentinel*, September 14, 2010
- "ObamaCare Slur Hurled in Budget Talks," *Miami Herald*, April 27, 2011

All of these stories share an underlying anger, stemming from *fear of change*. Columnist Frank Rich (2010) explains,

> But the explanation is plain: the health care bill is not the main source of this anger and never has been. It's merely a handy excuse. The real source of the over-the-top rage of 2010 is the same kind of national existential reordering that roiled America in 1964. . . . The conjunction of a black president and a female speaker of the House—topped off by a wise Latina on the Supreme Court and a powerful gay Congressional committee chairman—would sow fears of disenfranchisement among a dwindling and threatened minority in the country no matter what policies were in play. When you hear demonstrators chant the slogan "Take our country back!," these are the people they want to take the country back from.

Thus, a goal of media communications is, often, to make messages emotional: "For people to take action, they have to *care*" (Heath & Heath, 2007:168).

The following strategies are useful in the construction of Affective messages:

- *Personalize the message.* "Vivid details boost the credibility of a message. You don't give to 'African poverty,' you sponsor a specific child" (Heath & Heath, 2007, pp. 137, 168).
- *Identify the primal emotions behind behaviors & attitudes.* Construct messages around these emotions.
- *Construct messages around the attitudes of the audience.* For instance, in the construction of memes about smoking, advertisements exploit the emotions behind the attitudes of the young target audience—vanity, need for acceptance, and a sense of rebellion.

Imagistic Memes

An image can also function as a meme, transcending time periods and individual media presentations. To illustrate, an iconic image of Che Guevara, captured in a 1960 photograph taken by the Cuban photographer Alberto Díaz Gutiérrez (also known as Korda), has long resonated with the public as a romantic symbol of revolution.

> Red and black posters based on Korda's photograph became symbols of the resistance movement during the 1968 student protests in Paris, and they surfaced, too, in America, where the revolutionary was embraced by both the Black Power movement and by hippies and antiwar activists. . . . For many, Che has become a generic symbol of the underdog, the idealist, the iconoclast, the man willing to die for a cause . . . Che is embraced in Latin America and the Middle East and by antiglobalization protestors as "a die-hard foe of yanqui imperialism"; in Hong Kong as a symbol of rebellion against the authoritarianism of the Beijing government; and in the United States by immigrant activists, demanding "the right to inclusion, to be considered part of the American Dream." (Kakutani, 2009)

In like fashion, Shepard Fairey's campaign photograph of Barak Obama has emerged as an imagistic meme, symbolizing hope. The photograph, which depicts Obama on a red, white, and blue field, has appeared on numerous popular culture artifacts, including posters, coffee mugs, and T-shirts. The image has so transcended its original purpose that in 2011, the National Portrait Gallery in Washington, DC, added the poster to its collection.

Questions to ask regarding *imagistic memes* include:

- Why is this image sustained in the media?
- What message(s) are conveyed by the image?
- Have new meanings become associated with the image?
- What does this explain with regard to cultural attitudes, values, and preoccupations?

Lines of Inquiry

The memetic approach to media literacy analysis can follow several lines of inquiry:

1. Identifying the Characteristics of Memes

What are the shared characteristics of memes? Identifying these characteristics can accomplish the following:

1. Lead to the recognition of memetic messages in the media
2. Provide insight into why certain stories remain embedded in the public consciousness
3. In the case of media communicators, being able to construct memes

Memes share the following characteristics:

- *Unexpected elements.* A successful meme must attract the attention of the audience. The public is drawn to sensational, extraordinary, and shocking stories, which accounts for memes that involve conspiracy theories, gossip, and sexual escapades. Memes may also introduce surprising "facts," plot twists, and unexpected conclusions (often known as "O. Henry endings," after the author). Chip and Dan Heath explain,

  > Surprise makes us want to find an answer—to resolve the question of why we were surprised—and big surprises call for big answers. If we want to motivate people to pay attention, we should seize the power of big surprises. (Heath & Heath, 2007: 69)

In addition, many memes revolve around mysteries or puzzles stories that arouse the audience's curiosity. Memetic news stories present the audience with situations that have unknown resolutions: *What will happen*? And *Was I right*?

- *Stories focusing on various threats to the environment*
  - *Personalized and intentional threats.* According to columnist Nicholas Kristof (2009), humans are particularly sensitive to information that affects them: "Like gazelles, we are instinctively and obsessively on the lookout for predators and enemies."
  - *Threats to system of morality.* Professor Daniel Gilbert explains that "people are incensed about flag burning, or about what kind of sex people have in private, even though that doesn't really affect the rest of us. Yet where we have a real threat to our well-being, like global warming, it doesn't ring alarm bells" (Kristof, 2009).
  - *Imminent threats.* The more immediate a threat is, the more real it appears to be. Kristof (2009) observes, "We yawn at a slow melting of the glaciers, while if they shrank overnight we might take to the streets."
- *Simplicity.* Memetic stories share a *"profound compactness"* (Heath & Heath, 2007: 52) that can easily be recalled by the audience. Significantly, these simple messages often touch on the complex experience and memories of the audience. The Heaths observe, "You use flags. You tap the existing memory terrain of your audience. You use what's already there" (p. 52). The Heaths cite Biblical proverbs as examples of stories that are profound and yet memorable in their simplicity.
- *Concrete content.* According to the Heaths (2007), constructing specific stories is, perhaps, the most effective way to create memorable, enduring memes (p. 120). "Concrete memes consist of specific people doing specific things. Abstraction makes it harder to understand an idea and remember it. Abstraction also makes it harder to coordinate our activities with others, who may interpret the abstraction in very different ways" (p. 100). "On the other hand, concreteness is a way of mobilizing and focusing your brain" (p. 120). Thus, concrete language helps people, "especially novices," understand new concepts (p. 104).

  However, memes often move from concrete to abstract thought. The ultimate appeal of a story often stems from the abstract level of meaning. For instance, the enduring story of the leaking of CIA agent Valerie Plane's identity during the George W. Bush administration was ultimately a story about the abuse of power.
- *Credibility of stories.* The ability to inspire or trust is key to the perpetuation of memetic stories. Credibility can come from several sources:
  - An *authority figure*, whose expertise, credentials, or demeanor lend legitimacy to a story
  - A respected *organization* (e.g., Harvard)

- *Engaging narrative.* Memetic stories often adhere to the entertainment sensibility of storytelling. These stories are often characterized by identifiable characters and a clear and memorable storyline. For instance, a meme like the "outing" of CIA operative Valerie Plane Wilson has a clear narrative structure (beginning, middle, and end), a gripping cast of characters, and sense of drama.
- *Repetition* facilitates the recall of memes. Sam Wang and Sandra Aamodt (2008) cite a study that demonstrates the role of repetition in the development of memes:

> A group of Stanford students was exposed repeatedly to an unsubstantiated claim taken from a Web site that Coca-Cola is an effective paint thinner. Students who read the statement five times were nearly one-third more likely than those who read it only twice to attribute it to *Consumer Reports* (rather than *The National Enquirer*, their other choice), giving it a gloss of credibility.

In addition, repetition contributes to a sense of a meme's legitimacy; when individuals hear a story frequently enough, they tend to believe that it is true. In American politics, one campaign strategy calls for candidates to call attention to the misstatements of their opponents. However, the danger of this strategy is that repeating a false rumor can inadvertently *reinforce* the message (Wang & Aamodt, 2008).

2. Tracing the Origin and Evolution of Memetic Stories

As is the case with many rumors, identifying the "voice" behind a meme (i.e., an individual or organization) can be a difficult task. Storing and transmitting memes actually has a neuroscientific explanation, tied to a phenomenon called *source amnesia*. Political media strategists have learned to exploit source amnesia to spread misinformation. Wang and Aamodt (2008) continue, "This phenomenon can lead people to forget whether a statement is true. Even when a lie is presented with a disclaimer, people often later remember it as true."

Identifying the source of a meme can provide insight into the *motives* behind the creation of the story. Even if it is impossible to identify the exact author of a meme, tracing the development of a meme can furnish perspective into the meaning behind the story. To illustrate, the meme about extravagant purchases by people in power that has reemerged with news of exorbitant CEO bonuses is rooted in 19th-century American populism. John Harwood (2009) explains, "Anger over economic change spawned the Populist Party after the Gilded Age in the late 19th century. Championing rural America, the party accused East Coast elites of dividing the country into 'tramps and millionaires.' Likewise, Franklin D. Roosevelt attacked 'the economic royalists' during the Great Depression. 'They are unanimous in their hate for me,' Roosevelt said, 'and I welcome their hatred' " (Harwood, 2009).

3. Examining the Influence of the Media in the Formation and Perpetuation of Memetic Stories

This line of inquiry examines the influence of the media on the formation and perpetuation of memes. The distinctive features of interactive media are conducive to keeping stories in the public consciousness. Journalist Virginia Heffernan (2009) asks,

> How do big ideas spread on the Internet, and how are they changed in the process? . . . As a fan of intensely specific forms of communication—blogs, memoirs, reality TV—I don't believe that any idea exists apart from its mode of dissemination. But I also know that ideas that seem especially big and irresistible are usually so elegantly integrated with particular communication technologies that it's hard to conceive of them separately. Could Rush Limbaugh's patriotic anti-elitism have coalesced anywhere but on AM radio? Could "family values" have emerged without Christian TV?

Interactive media are particularly effective in keeping stories alive about conditions in oppressive regimes and efforts to effect social change. To illustrate, during the summer of 2009, citizens of Iran protested vigorously in response to questionable presidential election results. The Iranian government imposed severe restrictions on news coverage, expelling the BBC's correspondent in Tehran and detaining *Newsweek*'s correspondent. But despite these repressive steps, citizens used digital technology to keep the civil protests alive on both a national and international stage. Videos shot on cellphones were distributed over YouTube and were then carried by mainstream television news outlets. In addition, individuals sent messages, using Twitter.

Videos posted on Web sites kept the spirit of the protests alive when, otherwise, the repressive tactics of the Iranian government would have killed the movement. One video, which recorded millions of hits on YouTube (Stelter, 2010), showed Neda, a young student, shot to death as she demonstrated in the street. A Facebook memorial page was been set up for the young woman, with the inscription: "In memory of Neda—the fallen ANGEL of Freedom."

A reformist candidate, Mehdi Karoubi, referred to her as a martyr who did not "have a weapon in her soft hands or a grenade in her pocket but became a victim by thugs who are supported by a horrifying security apparatus" (Fathi & Slackman, 2009).

4. Industry Considerations

One way to account for the appearance of a meme is, simply, that it is profitable to keep the story alive. Any programming that attracts an audience is advantageous to media corporations. Indeed, in the 1930s, radio personalities Jack Benny and Fred Allen concocted a "feud," exchanging insults on their programs. This faux argument attracted huge audiences to both shows.

In addition, a meme can also be an antidote to a "slow news day." When a meme appears in the media, it can be useful to see what else is going on in the news that day.

5. Oppositional Line of Inquiry

Another useful line of inquiry is to consider the opposite scenario: Why *doesn't* a story stick in the media? And what does this reveal with regard to cultural attitudes, values, behaviors, preoccupations, and myths?

To illustrate, in response to a recent election legalizing same-sex marriage in Vermont and Iowa, a video, titled *Marriage Gathering Storm*, was distributed on YouTube in April 2009. Produced by a conservative group called the National Organization for Marriage, the video comprised comments by a diverse group of people denouncing homosexuality as a threat to American culture.

According to *New York Times* columnist Frank Rich, the lack of resonance signaled that homosexuality is no longer a divisive issue in the United States and that its citizens have moved beyond those politicians who have used this social issue to marshal support in elections. According to a 2009 *New York Times*/CBS News poll, 42 percent of all respondents said they supported same-sex marriage, compared with 22 percent in March 2004 (Nagourney, 2009). Reporter Adam Nagourney (2009) observes that "for a lot of these Americans, same-sex marriage is not something they spend a lot of time worrying about, or even thinking about." Moreover, Nagourney points out that younger viewers are even less moved by this social issue:

> Consider this: In the latest *New York Times*/CBS News poll, released (on April 27, 2009), 31 percent of respondents over the age of 40 said they supported same-sex marriage. By contrast, 57 percent under age 40 said they supported it, a 26-point difference. Among the older respondents,

35 percent said they opposed any legal recognition of same-sex couples, be it marriage or civil unions. Among the younger crowd, just 19 percent held that view. . . . It simply does not appear to have the resonance with younger voters that it does with older ones.

Consequently, the public needs to pay attention to stories that *don't* linger in the public consciousness.

6. Genric Memes

One useful line of inquiry involves examining the appearance of memes in particular genres, such as advertising, news, or entertainment stories. For instance, one major arena for memes is *political communications*. According to sociologist Francesca Polletta, brief, emotionally charged narratives can travel through a population faster than any virus and infect the political landscape: "Any story that is short and powerful and throws into relief exactly the sort of issues people are thinking about at the moment they're making a decision can have enormous impact" (Carey, 2008).

Political media strategists are practiced in the art of capitalizing on memes to promote their agenda. Columnist Paul Krugman (2008) provides the following examples of political memes designed to discredit opponents:

Al Gore never claimed that he invented the Internet. Howard Dean didn't scream. Hillary Clinton didn't say she was staying in the race because Barack Obama might be assassinated. And Wesley Clark didn't impugn John McCain's military service. . . . Again and again we've had media firestorms over supposedly revealing incidents that never actually took place.

Political memes take full advantage of the characteristics of the Internet. For instance, it is common for rumors to be floated on Internet sites and social media, forcing hurried denials and gaining life in the court of public opinion. Noam Cohen (2008) explains,

an example from the Drudge Report is instructive about how false news—in effect, reputational short-selling—spreads. On Friday, Sept. 5, Drudge Report hailed an exclusive about the newly nominated Republican vice-presidential candidate: "Oprah Balks at Hosting Sarah Palin; Staff Divided."

Oprah Winfrey later that day released a statement denying the report. But it was in the news enough for Tom Brokaw of NBC's "Meet the

Press," to introduce the subject to the Democratic vice-presidential nominee Joe Biden: "Do you think that some people will see that as an elitist position, that in some ways Democrats may be afraid of her, Sarah Palin?"

See also: Digital Media Literacy; Political Communications, American

References

Carey, B. (2008, January 13). "The Crying Game, and the Political Herd." *New York Times*. Retrieved from http://www.nytimes.com/2008/01/13/weekinreview/13carey.html

Cohen, N. (2008, October 13). "Spinning a Web of Lies at Digital Speed." *New York Times*. Retrieved from http://www.nytimes.com/2008/10/13/business/media/13link.html

Fathi, N., & Slackman, M. (2009, June 22). "Unrest in Iran Sharply Deepens Rift Among Clerics." *New York Times*. Retrieved from http://www.nytimes.com/2009/06/22/world/middleeast/22iran.html?pagewanted=all

Harwood, J. (2009, March 23). "For Populism, a Return to Economic Roots." *New York Times*. Retrieved from http://www.nytimes.com

Heath, C., & Heath, D. (2007). *Made to Stick*. New York: Random House.

Heffernan, V. (2009, August 23). "The Feminist Hawks." *New York Times Magazine*. Retrieved from http://www.nytimes.com/2009/08/23/magazine/23FOB-medium-t.html

Kakutani, M. (2009, April 21). "Brand Che: Revolutionary as Marketer's Dream." *New York Times*. Retrieved from http://www.nytimes.com/2009/04/21/books/21kaku.html?pagewanted=all

Kristof, N. D. (2008, October 30). "What? Me Biased?" *New York Times*. Retrieved from http://www.nytimes.com/2008/10/30/opinion/30kristof.html

Kristof, N. D. (2009, July 2). "When Our Brains Short-Circuit." *New York Times*. Retrieved from http://www.nytimes.com/2009/07/02/opinion/02kristof.html

Kristof, N. D. (2011, July 6). "Taxes and Billionaires." *New York Times*. Retrieved from http://www.nytimes.com/2011/07/07/opinion/07kristof.html

Krugman, P. (2008, July 4). "Rove's Third Term." *New York Times*. Retrieved from http://www.nytimes.com/2008/07/04/opinion/04krugman.html

Nagourney, A. (2009, April 29). "Same-Sex Marriage Holds Peril for G.O.P." *New York Times*. Retrieved from http://www.nytimes.com/2009/04/29/us/politics/29memo.html

Naone, E. (2011, January 14). "Will You Tweet This? New Analysis Could Help Predict How Stories Will Be Shared." *Technology Review*. http://www.technologyreview.com/news/422404/will-you-tweet-this/

Rich, F. (2010, March 28). "The Rage Is Not About Health Care." *New York Times*. Retrieved from http://www.nytimes.com/2010/03/28/opinion/28rich.html

Stelter, B. (2010, February 22). "Honoring Citizen Journalists." *New York Times*. Retrieved from http://www.nytimes.com/2010/02/22/business/media/22polk.html

Stolberg, S .G. (2009, March 22). "The Art of Political Distraction." *New York Times*. Retrieved from http://www.nytimes.com/2009/03/22/weekinreview/22stolberg .html?pagewanted=all

Wang S., & Aamodt, S. (2008, June 27). "Your Brain Lies to You." *New York Times*. Retrieved from http://www.nytimes.com/2008/06/29/opinion/29iht-ed wang.1.14069662.html

Mythic Analysis

Mythic analysis is a qualitative approach that addresses the question, why do audiences watch the same media programs repeatedly? One way to account for the appeal of many media programs—no matter how redundant they may seem—is that these stories are transmitting myths that tell us about ourselves and our cultures.

A myth is any real or fictitious story, recurring theme, or character type that gives expression to deep, commonly felt emotions. In the most general sense, myths may be distinguished from simple narratives, in that they appeal to the consciousness of a people by putting human beings in touch with elemental feelings associated with the experience of being human. Joseph Campbell (1988) explains,

> What human beings have in common is revealed in myths. Myths are stories of our search through the ages for truth, for meaning, for significance. We all need to tell our story and to understand our story. We all need to understand death and to cope with death, and we all need help in our passages from birth to life and then to death. We need for life to signify, to touch the eternal, to understand the mysterious, to find out who we are.

Myths often focus on the *deep truth* of human experience. In the process of telling stories about themselves and their world, media communicators tap into a wellspring of universal mythic concerns. Thus, human beings do not *invent* myths; they *discover* them as part of our universal unconscious.

Myths may be grouped into three general areas: *nature myths*, *historical myths*, and *metaphysical myths*.

- In the prescientific age, *nature myths* provided explanations for natural events, including meteorological, astronomical, terrestrial, chemical, and biological phenomena.
- *Historical myths* chronicle significant events and rulers of previous civilizations.
- *Metaphysical myths* explore the elemental part of the human experience: creation, birth, death, divine presence, good and evil, and afterlife.

A mythic approach can help make media content accessible in the following ways:

- To identify the *mythic functions* of media programming
- To provide perspective on media content as a *retelling* of traditional myths
- To identify *mythic elements* in media programs (and the meanings behind these elements) as a way to approach critical analysis of a narrative
- To identify *cultural myths* in media programs that furnish perspective into that culture

Function

Myths fulfill a range of *functions*, or purposes, which now are also served by media programming: to inspire awe, to facilitate self-actualization, to exalt, to provide meaning, to instruct, to provide order, to promote social conformity, and as social ritual.

Media and the Transmission of Traditional Myth

Many contemporary media programs are modifications, variations, or extensions of traditional myths. Recent traditional myths that have appeared in film include *Troy* (2007) and *Thor* (2010). Indeed, the story of Thor, Norse god of thunder, has been retold on screen 21 times since 1973, originating in six countries.

Media programming may also feature traditional mythic characters that have been updated in the media. The warriors of professional wrestling capture the attention and adulation of the public because, in many respects, they represent a modern adaptation of mythic heroes such as Hercules.

Ways to address the appearance of traditional myths and mythic characters in the media include the following:

- Examining ways in which modern adaptations depart from the original myth (The modern versions can provide insight into contemporary cultures.)
- Comparing and contrasting traditional myths as they have been adapted by various societies to reveal essential differences between cultures
- Examining why a traditional myth appears at a particular time
- Considering what adaptations signify with regard to cultural attitudes, beliefs, values, and preoccupations

Mythic Elements in Media Presentations

Mythic elements such as mythic *plots, themes, characters, motifs*, and *images* frequently appear in media presentations. Recognizing these mythic elements in media presentations can be a useful way to uncover meaning in a media presentation. Myth scholar Henry Murray (1960) maintains that "[Mythic elements are] very commonly sufficient to bring the complete mythic event to the consciousness of those who are familiar with it."

Mythic Plots

A *plot* is a planned series of events in a narrative, progressing through a struggle of opposing forces to a climax and a conclusion. A plot is not simply recorded action but consists of carefully selected elements.

A finite number of mythic plots have been retold countless times, from antiquity to contemporary films, comics, and video games. Examples of mythic plots include the following:

- The Quest
- The Death and Resurrection plot
- The Imminent Annihilation plot
- Adam and Eve plots
- Faustian plots (a man's pact with the devil)
- Prometheus plots (human beings' hubris—pretensions to deities)
- David and Goliath plots (the underdog)
- Revenge plots

Mythic Themes

A *theme* is an abstract idea that is given expression or representation in a narrative. Mythic themes raise issues pertaining to the human condition, as well as human beings' unique relationship to the universe. These mythic themes correspond to what Rollo May (1991) has identified as a series of *existential crises* that accompany the stages of human development:

- *Birth.* Many myths focus on the miracle and mystery of birth. Myths often feature a hero whose birth has extraordinary significance (e.g., Jesus, Moses). These myths reflect human beings' efforts to assign meaning to this seemingly random act of nature. A cosmic variation of this stage consists of myths that attempt to explain or account for essential questions about creation and the order of the universe.
- *Infancy.* This stage originates in young children between the ages of five and six, when they first become aware that human beings are born of union between man and woman. One theme related to the stage of awakening is the Oedipal longing, named after the famous Greek myth. Sigmund Freud interpreted this myth from a sexual perspective—the son's desire to eliminate his rival (father) and possess his mother. However, Carl Jung applies a spiritual interpretation to the Oedipus myth, focusing on the image of the mother as the source of life. Within this context, the Oedipus myth responds to humans' growing awareness about their inevitable separation from the protected womb of the mother. Although this separation is a part of life, this step is, at the same time, a form of death, as the individual can never again recapture the same sense of safety and connectedness to the source of life.

  This existential crisis is also reflected in stories in which characters must let go of loved ones as they pass away. For instance, in Disney's *Bambi* (1942), the young deer and his mother are trapped by hunters and are forced to flee. In her efforts to save her son, Bambi's mother is killed. Once he has reached safety, Bambi (and the audience) become aware of the tragedy and mourn the loss.

  A derivative story involves characters who must bid farewell forever, which is a form of death-in-life. In *E.T.* (1982), the extraterrestrial's return home meant that he would be separated forever from Elliott, his new Earth buddy. The emotional moment of E.T.'s departure signaled a form of death—as defined by a final separation. A third variation of this theme involves tales of abandonment, in which a character is deserted and must cope with feelings of rejection and isolation.

  According to Murray (1960), the following additional thematic concerns are associated with this stage of awakening:
  - A statement of need and helplessness in a perilous or hostile environment and the wish for an omnipotent, omniscient, and benevolent protector, provider, and director

- ○ Narcissism and the wish to be omnipotent and superior to others (psychic source of countless self-glorification and heroic myths)
- ○ The wish to obtain a *graphic* explanation of birth
- ○ Dread of temptation and punishment (psychic source of numerous images of demonic (satanic) tempters, threatening indignant deities, and myths of crime and punishment (e.g., Sodom and Gomorrah; the Deluge)
- ○ Collective motivations, such as fear of starvation and a consequent decline of social and regal vigor in a barren, dry environment leading to ardent wishes for the revival of fertility and of vigor (psychic source of the important death and resurrection myth) (pp. 316–317)

- *Adolescence.* These mythic themes originate in adolescents' need to assert their independence as part of the process of establishing their own identity. Fundamental to the stage of adolescence is the drive to test *taboos*, or limits that have been imposed on human beings, either by nature or society. The desire to break away from one's earthly existence is expressed in the Icarus myth, in which young Icarus and his father, Daedalus, flew, having constructed wings made of feathers glued with wax. Despite his father's warning, Icarus became intoxicated with his new powers of flight and soared too close to the sun; in the process, the heat melted the wax, and Icarus plunged into the sea and drowned.

  This existential crisis is reflected in stories of revolt or rebellion against the established order (parents, society, and the gods). Many popular films of the 1950s such as *Rebel without a Cause* with James Dean and *The Wild One* starring Marlon Brando focused on this existential crisis. These actors became cultural mythic icons, epitomizing teenage angst and rebellion. Although Dean and Brando were defying their parents or social institutions (police or school) in their films, the act of rebellion itself was ultimately the source of meaning in the films. At one point in *The Wild One*, an adult asked Brando, "What are you rebelling against?" Brando replied coolly, "What have you got?"

  One common adolescent thematic issue appearing in both myth and media is the role of fate versus free choice. Classic myths like Odysseus raise questions about whether human beings are independent entities who control their own destinies, or if they are merely players who act out a script that has been written for them. In many media programs, the protagonists carve out their own destiny in the face of a society that has already prescribed their futures. This empowerment theme underlies many advertisements that suggest that their products are key to overcoming our human limitations.

Another theme connected to the crisis of adolescence is *love and romance*. Many classic myths, including those of Aphrodite, Cupid, and Psyche, deal with the beauty and transcendent power of love, as well as its many complications—jealousy, loss of trust, and rejection. Film and television programs place a heavy emphasis on the travails of love and romance—responding to the strong adolescent market, as well as the adolescent sensibilities in adults.

- *Adulthood.* The crisis of adulthood involves the ultimate acceptance of human limitations (or taboos). The Greek myth of Prometheus offers a classic example of this theme. As the gods distributed the gifts of life to the creatures of Earth, humans were left out. Consequently, human beings lacked the strength, swiftness, and protection (fur or feathers) of other animals. Prometheus, a Titan, took pity and stole fire from the gods to give to humans. In doing so, Prometheus brought civilization to humans. However, Zeus punished this tragic hero, chaining him to a rock. Prometheus was doomed to suffer like the humans he befriended; for while he could see beyond his chains, he was confined forever.

- *Death.* In this stage, human beings come to terms with their own mortality. According to Freud, human beings are both terrified and fascinated by death. A common advertising strategy involves positioning the product as a form of security. For example, sales for car phones jumped dramatically when ads began promoting the product as a security device.

  Another theme rooted in this stage of life occurs as human beings finally embrace their mortality. *Star Trek*'s Mr. Spock epitomizes this theme. Half Vulcan and half human, Spock is strongly attracted to his mortal side, which connects him to a wellspring of feelings that originate in the impermanence of human beings.

Mythic Figures

Mythic figures appear throughout media presentations. Recognizing the mythic antecedents and mythic aspect of these characters can furnish perspective into a media presentation.

Sometimes mythic figures are transplanted directly from classic myth. For example, a television ad for BMW depicts a race between a winged figure and an automobile. Although the ad makes no effort to identify the character, the wings on his hat are a clear reference to the Roman god Mercury, who, as Jupiter's messenger, is associated with swiftness. Added to the mythic context of the ad, the race takes place in an ancient, Roman-looking coliseum.

This allusion reinforces the ad's message about the speed and agility of the BMW, which easily wins the race against Mercury.

The inclusion of this mythic reference in the commercial serves to educate those uninitiated members of the audience. The audience learns to associate the winged figure with swiftness without formally knowing anything about Greek mythology.

In addition, characters appearing in media presentations may reflect *mythic archetypes*. According to psychologist Carl Jung, an archetype is a projection of humans' collective or universal unconscious. In its simplest terms, an archetype corresponds to the different aspects of the psyche. All archetypes, taken together, make up the self. The balance, or relationship between the archetypes determines the personality of an individual. The goal of Jungian psychology is to work toward the proper "constellation" of all of the archetypes to achieve a balanced personality.

Over the ages, these archetypes, or aspects of self, have been externalized in the form of mythic characters. In the same way, archetypes are also found in media presentations as projections of Jung's universal self. These archetypes may assume many forms, or *archetypal images*, which are decided by the culture and the individual storyteller. Thus, Odysseus and Rocky are both archetypal images of the hero archetype.

The *hero archetype* epitomizes the best in human character and achievement. The hero archetype offers an opportunity for the audience to get in touch with their own heroic attributes.

Joseph Campbell (1988) has identified several types of archetypal hero:

- *Hero as warrior.* Myths often extol the hero's strength, athleticism, and power. However, in some myths (e.g., David and Goliath), the hero is overmatched physically but prevails due to heroic intangibles: courage, quick-wittedness, or faith.
- The adventures of the warrior symbolize the inner conflicts confronting all humans. For example, Campbell interprets myths in which medieval knights slay dragons as "Slaying the dragon in me: slaying monsters is slaying the dark things."
- *Hero as lover.* The hero and heroine also may distinguish themselves as paragons of love. Examples of young tragic love include the Greek myth of Pyramus and Thisbe and Shakespeare's Romeo and Juliet.
- *Hero as world redeemer.* This mythic hero is a crusader who resists injustice and oppression. These heroes inspire others through their idealism and selfless commitment to a cause—even at the cost of their own lives.

- *The reluctant hero.* At times, the hero is a reluctant agent who requires the assistance of a mentor to act. In *The Matrix* trilogy of films (1999–2003), Morpheus acts as a mentor for Neo. He chooses and guides the young man, who at first doubts that he is "the one," as Morpheus insists.

The *villain* is another mythical archetype. Evil is externalized in both mythic tales and media presentations, appearing in people, animals, inanimate objects, and metaphysical beings such as devils and witches. In this sense, the villain is a projection of the audience member's own impure or weak impulses. This externalization of evil enables people to distance themselves from these very complex and disturbing impulses within themselves. Moreover, villains are the embodiment of the corruption and sterility of society, and of life itself, and are associated with winter, darkness, confusion, sterility, moribund life, and old age

Villains fall into the following general categories:

- *Usurpers* seize the power, position, or rights of another, by force and without legal right or authority.
- *Criminals* intentionally break the law or regulations for personal gain.
- *Violators* disregard the wishes or preferences of an individual to violate another individual. This can involve either physical violence (e.g., assault or rape) or emotional violence.
- *Betrayers* breach a confidence, are disloyal, or deceive another.
- *Corrupters* are guilty of spiritual villainy. They are immoral, dishonest, and depraved and can contaminate others by seducing them to betray their own principles.

The *mentor* archetype represents those aspects of self that are in supreme authority. This superior master and teacher is an ideal figure, the embodiment of order and rationality. Author Christopher Vogler (1992) points out that in the course of the hero's journey, the mentor provides support, motivation, inspiration, and guidance:

The relationship between hero and Mentor is one of the most common themes in mythology, and one of the richest in its symbolic value. It stands for the bond between parent and child, teacher and student, doctor and patient, god and man. The Mentor may appear as a wise old wizard (*Star Wars*), a tough drill sergeant (*Officer and a Gentleman*), or a grizzled old boxing coach (*Rocky*). (p. 21)

The mentor often expresses the central theme or insight of the narrative. At a pivotal moment in the narrative, the mentor expresses a revelation, prophesy, or counsel that the hero (and audience) should heed. The hero's success is determined by his or her ability to absorb and apply the counsel of the mentor during the course of the narrative.

Threshold guardians are figures who attempt to block the path of the heroes and challenge their powers. These mythic figures appear at decisive moments in a narrative, when the main characters are faced with crucial choices. Threshold guardians can appear as henchmen, bodyguards, gunslingers, mercenaries, guards, doormen, or lieutenants of the chief antagonist.

Threshold guardians also may be well-intentioned supporters who are opposed to the hero making changes. In this sense, the threshold guardian represents our own uncertainties as we contend with change. Vogler (1992) explains,

> These Guardians may represent the ordinary obstacles we all face in the world around us: bad weather, bad luck, prejudice, oppression, or hostile people. But on a deeper psychological level they stand for our internal demons: the neuroses, emotional scars, vices, dependencies, and self-limitations that hold back our growth and progress. (p. 64)

The *herald* brings a challenge to the hero and announces the coming of significant changes. In Greek mythology, Hermes was the messenger god, who was charged with dispatching messages from Zeus. Heralds may appear in the form of dreams, visions, oracles, or foreshadowing devices. The herald also may signal the *need* for change. Vogler (1992) notes, "Something deep inside us knows when we are ready to change and sends us a messenger" (p. 70).

The *victim* is deficient, either morally, physically, or emotionally, and frequently is in need of protection by an outside agent—either a hero or divine intervention. This mythic figure is a projection of the weaknesses of human beings. A variation of this archetype is the character who has been victimized by forces outside of his or her control, such as fate or injustice. Female characters frequently are cast in the role of victim in media programs, reflecting cultural attitudes with respect to the female gender.

The *divine child (Puer Aeternus)* corresponds to the infantile side of self. Myths featuring a child as hero include Hercules, Moses, and Chandragupta (the founder of the Hindu Maurya dynasty). These characters are marked as special at birth, symbolizing the nobility and divinity of human beings. The divine child appears prominently in contemporary media presentations, reinforcing the American cultural myth that celebrates youth culture. Contemporary media programming suggests that the American culture prizes this side of self. In the horror and science fiction genres, it is the children who are able to see the supernatural forces that are beyond the comprehension of adults.

Shapeshifters are mythic characters who change during the course of a narrative. Vogler (1992) explains, "Shapeshifters change their appearance or mood, and are difficult for the hero and audience to pin down. They may mislead the hero or keep him/her guessing, and their loyalty or sincerity is often in question" (p. 75).

Shapeshifters may appear as wizards, witches, and ogres, who have the ability to alter their appearance through disguises or physical transformation. These mythic figures may also assume *emotional masks* that hide their true natures or motives.

Mythic Motifs

A *motif* is a recurring idea, symbol, or incident employed in narratives. Recognizing these mythic motifs can enrich one's understanding and appreciation of media presentations

To illustrate, the *personification* motif occurs when objects, plants, animals, and gods are given human features, emotions, personalities, and speech. Thus, cartoon figures like Mickey Mouse or Barney assume human characteristics. Even when they cannot speak, animals like Flipper and Lassie possess human intelligence and emotions. By making nonhumans act in human ways, audiences are better able to understand the motives and sensibilities of the world at large. In addition, this motif establishes a comfortable distance that enables myths to comment on human issues and concerns. For instance, in *Arctic Tale*, the animals are forced to contend with the effects of global warming—an environmental danger that affects the entire animal kingdom—including human beings.

Magic is a mythic motif that admits the audience into an extraordinary world of possibilities that transcend natural laws, logic, and human limitation. As Sir James George Frazer (1959) notes, magic functions as a form of *wish fulfillment* in mythic tales: "A dramatic representation of the natural processes which (human beings) wish to facilitate; for it is a familiar tenet of magic that you can produce any desired effect by merely imitating it" (pp. 171–172).

Magicians such as Merlin are *shamans*—mystics who use their magical powers to see into the future and influence events to promote the welfare of the human community. However, magic also has a darker side; villains employ magic to achieve their own self-serving ends or to wreck havoc on the heroes.

Occasionally, "average" humans like Pandora and young Harry Potter attempt to use magic. Being human, they are not equipped to control this power and, consequently, threaten the natural order.

Magic is a common motif in media programming as well. One reason that magic is prevalent in media presentations is simply because film and television *can* produce the illusion of magic. Indeed, futuristic technology often assumes the visage of magic wands. For example, in *Star Trek*, the crew would "magically" disappear as they were beamed from one locale to another.

Prophesy is a mythic motif in which predictions foreshadow the events of the story. In classic myths, prophesies take place through an oracle—a shrine at which prophecies are made known. These oracles are divine in origin and therefore are considered reliable sources of information. However, prophecies are often enigmatic statements or allegories; the exact meaning behind the prophecy only becomes clear as the story unfolds. In media presentations, an oracle may assume more pedestrian forms, such as a letter or mysterious stranger who provides a clue about upcoming events in the story.

In addition, the introduction of media programs often foreshadows what will be covered. In newspapers, the headline and lead paragraph provide a summary of the article. The introduction often also serves as a microcosm of the story, establishing the premise, as well as specifying the setting, characters, and situation. The body of the narrative, then, is the fulfillment of the "prophecy" presented at the beginning.

Production elements may also serve as a form of prophesy, foreshadowing events in the narrative. For instance, in *Jaws* (1975), the music recurs throughout the film, signaling that danger is lurking under the surface.

Mythic Symbols

Mythic symbols operate as a language that provides clues and cues for the audience. According to psychoanalytic theory, mythic symbols originate within the human imagination, as a manifestation of the collective unconscious, and thus have a shared meaning for the audience. In myths and media presentations, the exact meaning of mythic symbols is often determined by *context*.

Mythic symbols commonly found in both myths and media presentation include the following:

- *Fire* may represent evil, as illustrated in the fires of hell. However, fire also can symbolize knowledge, power, and enlightenment. In the Greek

Reflected images in myths are symbols, revealing a character's internal essence or desires. This mythic symbol is also commonly found in media presentations. (Photo by Lisa Marcus)

myth of Prometheus, fire was the element that distinguished humans from other animals. Fire also can be a defense against forces of evil (witches) or predators (animals).

- As a primal element, *water* is associated with birth, as well as purification. However, water also can symbolize death and rebirth. Baptism is a ritual in which a person undergoes spiritual regeneration by being immersed in water. Examples from myths include Catholic Holy Water and the biblical story of Noah and the flood.

- The *circle* has a mystical quality, representing the endless, cyclical conception of time (e.g., the zodiac and clock faces). This shape has direction and is complete; as a result, it is associated with endlessness and wholeness. In many cultures, the circle is a symbol of the sun and, as a result, signifies warmth and life.

  However, although the circle joins people and things together, it also *separates*, setting objects apart. Stonehenge and Avebury are examples of ancient use of the circle to mark the boundary of a sacred area. Similarly, a Babylonian rite involved laying a circle of flour around a person's sickbed to keep demons away.

- A *reflected surface* such as a mirror often reveals an individual's unexplored Self or inner secrets, furnishing knowledge not yet known or revealed. An example of this symbol is the evil queen's looking glass in *Snow White*, which discloses the truth about the queen's "ugly" nature—a truth that the queen cannot admit to herself.

  In other myths, people look in the mirror and see a reflection of their deepest dreams and desires. People look in the mirror and see a reflection of their deepest dreams.

Cultural Mythology

Cultural myths are a series of beliefs that are tied to self-concept; how a people or group sees itself. Every culture develops its own set of myths that expresses its distinctive character. Consequently, examining cultural myths can provide insight into the attitudes and preoccupations that define a society.

Examining cultural myths tells stories about the history of the culture. For instance, through countless hours of watching Westerns on film and television, international audiences have become acquainted with the California gold rush, the stand at the Alamo, the battle of the Little Big Horn, and the gunfight at the O.K. Corral. Even if these stories are not factually accurate, they contribute to the myth about the settling of the American West.

Over time, cultural myths assume a *mythic reality* as people buy into it. The danger presented by mythic realities is that people sometimes make decisions on the basis of these myths.

Cultural myths play a fundamental role in an individual's socialization by telling stories that reinforce the prevailing societal standards of success and failure. In many media programs, the triumph of good over evil is dependent on the characters' adherence to cultural values and goals.

American culture has a rich tradition of cultural myths, reinforced and perpetuated through the media:

- The *New World myth* stems from the "discovery" of America by Europeans in the fifteenth century. The New World became a symbol of innocence and hope, in contrast to the tired civilization of western Europe. As the new "chosen people," Americans regard themselves as the standard-bearers of a new civilization.

- *Manifest Destiny*, a political policy originating in the 19th century, held that the United States was the guardian of the Western Hemisphere and had both the right and the duty to expand throughout the North American continent. Today, the American news media reinforce this myth of manifest destiny. The amount of international coverage in newspapers and television is minuscule, and the majority international coverage focuses on allies of the United States or international news items that directly affect America.
- *The Mythic Frontier* is also an extension of the New World myth. As settlers spread west in the 19th century, America offered the prospect of a fresh beginning. Having shed the vestiges of civilization, man was free of corruption. This myth is rooted in the democratic ideal; instead of status being determined by social class, success was based on an individual's innate qualities—courage, imagination, determination, honesty, and integrity. The myth of the frontier was also associated with abundance and opportunity.
- *The Myth of the Old West.* As depicted in countless novels, films, and radio and television programs, the mythic west generally was set between 1865 (the end of the American Civil War) and 1890. In the face of the significant changes in American culture, the myth of the frontier has remained constant. The western myth has been incorporated into other genres, such as science fiction (the starship *Enterprise* exploring the "last frontier") and police programs.
- *The Horatio Alger Myth* has become emblematic of the American Dream. Horatio Alger was an author of juvenile fiction about young boys who achieved success through hard work and perseverance. The Horatio Alger myth contains an optimistic message about achieving success by following the American Dream. It celebrates the fundamental democratic principle of America—not that everyone will be successful but that everyone has a *chance* to make it in America (no matter how great the odds).

The heroes of cultural mythology embody the highest aims and ideals of a society. When a culture is constant, so are its cultural heroes. Thus, although the individual performers change, the essential type remains the same. For example, John Wayne, Arnold Schwarzenegger, and the Rock are generational representatives of the *rugged individualist* cultural hero, who epitomizes the virility, self-sufficiency, and independence of the American male.

But as cultures evolve, different heroes emerge to fit the times. Father Andrew Greeley (1962) contrasts the elections of Dwight Eisenhower in

1952 and 1956 with John Kennedy's victory in 1960: "In the early 1950s, the American people needed a father god to reassure them. They were provided with one. In the early 1960s . . . the people needed a young warrior god who would lead them to victories in the face of new challenges" (p. 82). Thus, examining cultural myths can disclose *shifts* in societal attitudes, behaviors, values, and preoccupations.

Recognizing *cultural symbols* can enrich the audience's understanding of media messages. Examples of cultural symbols include the following:

- *Small-town America* is a place that is characterized by "family values" such as honesty, loyalty, and volunteerism. In the myth of small town America, the nuclear family is the source of strength and identity of its citizens. A classic example of this cultural symbol is Bedford Falls, the small town in Frank Capra's *It's a Wonderful Life* (1946). This mythical town is equated with the simple life, defined by order and permanence in contrast with the complexity and chaos characteristic of urban life.
- *Guns* symbolize power, masculinity, and control. As a result, a person who wields this weapon is dangerous, violent, and virile. On the surface, the National Rifle Association's campaign over gun rights is founded on constitutional issues. However, at heart, defense of "gun rights" is based on the gun as a symbol of the American character.

Thus, critical analysis of cultural myths focuses on the following questions:

- What do these cultural myths reveal about the predominant values, concerns, and preoccupations within the culture?
- What do the cultural myths reveal about shifts within the culture?
- Are new cultural myths being created and conveyed through the media? Explain.
- Does the media presentation contain any of the following?
  - Cultural mythic themes
  - Cultural mythic figures
  - Cultural mythic symbols

See also: Dream Theory Approach to Media Analysis; Genre Study; Media Literacy Approach

References

Campbell, J., with Moyers, B. (1988). *The Power of Myth*. New York: Doubleday.

Frazer, J. G. (1959). *The New Golden Bough*. Edited, with Notes and Foreword by Theodor H. Gaster. New York: S. G. Phillips.

Greeley, A. (1962, December-January). "Myths, Symbols, and Rituals in the Modern World." *The Critic 22* (3).

Jung, C. (1959). *The Archetypes and the Collective Unconscious*. Translated by R. F. C. Hull (Bollingen Series XX). New York: Pantheon Books.

May, R. (1991). *The Cry for Myth*. New York: W. W. Norton.

Murray, H. A. (1960). "The Possible Nature of a 'Mythology' to Come." In *Myth and Mythmaking*. New York: George Braziller.

Vogler, C. (1992). *The Writer's Journey*. Studio City, CA: Michael Wiese Productions.

Narratology

Narratology is the study of narrative form and structure in a media presentation. As applied to media analysis, this critical framework focuses on the narrative elements that convey meaning in the construction of media presentations. According to literary critic Roland Barthes, every narrative is interwoven with "codes" that provide layers of meaning to the interpretation of the text. Barthes observes that, together, these codes function like a "weaving of voices" (Felluga, 2003: 20). This approach does not focus on individual texts but instead on patterns that characterize narrative elements. Narratology, then, involves identifying the structural patterns in a media presentation that convey meaning. Some of the narrative elements include the following.

Unifying Structure

Vladimir Propp's *morphological analysis* is useful in identifying the unifying structure in a genre. A morphology focuses on the structures—the systems, relations, and forms—that make meaning in a narrative and examines the structural patterns that characterize these texts. No single item in such a system has meaning except as an integral part of a set of structural connections.

Propp dissected the fairy tale, divesting it of its individual embellishments to identify its skeletal formula. He then traced the sequence of elements in a story to identify the basic structure common to this genre. Propp found that the number of structural elements, or *functions*, in the fairy tale is limited and complete. Despite the distinctive embellishments of individual stories, the essential structure of genres is uniform, reflecting a constant set of questions, issues, and concerns.

This morphological approach can also be applied to the study of popular genres, as presented in media programming. To illustrate, applying the morphological approach to courtroom dramas, the essential structure is as follows:

I. Introduction
    A. Background—justice system
    B. A crime is committed
        1. The truthfulness/veracity of the account of the crime is established
        2. The guilty party is identified
        3. The innocence of the defendant is established
II. The defendant is apprehended
    A. The defendant confesses guilt to his or her lawyers
    B. The defendant confesses his or her innocence to their lawyers
III. The jury selection process
IV. The development of the defense team's strategies
V. The defense attorney's tactics in court
VI. The prosecutors' tactics in court
VII. The verdict is rendered
    A. The jury deliberates behind closed doors
    B. The defendant admits his or her guilt under cross-examination

This morphology accounts for the basic structural elements found across the genre, while allowing for individual embellishments. Thus, a series that falls within this genre, such as *Perry Mason* or *Law and Order* permits considerable variation within the narrative. Moreover, each episode *within* the series contains its own specific nuances. Thus, the criminal and the nature of the crime in *Law and Order* vary each week.

Beyond any differences in specific detail, a slight manipulation of the formula drastically alters the narrative. As an example, some structural elements may be eliminated from a series (or episode), while the order of the other functions remains the same. For instance, in *Law and Order*, only Elements 1 and 2 listed under "A crime is committed" (IB) typically are employed:

I. Introduction
    A. Background—justice system

    B. A crime is committed

       1. The truthfulness/veracity of the account of the crime is established

       2. The guilty party is identified

Element B3, *The innocence of the defendant is established,* has been removed.

Because 3C is left out of this construct, *Law and Order* operates from the point of view of the prosecutor. Unlike the American legal system of justice, in which defendants are innocent until proven guilty, the audience *knows* who is guilty under this structural framework. Consequently, any efforts by the defense to protect the civil liberties of their clients would be perceived by the audience as a *deterrent* to justice.

In contrast, *Perry Mason* always operated without B1 and B2 and, instead, employed variation B3:

I. Introduction

    A. Background—justice system

    B. A crime is committed

    C. The innocence of the defendant is established

In this configuration, the series is presented from the point of view of the *defendant*; the audience doesn't know who perpetuated the crime, but they do know that Perry Mason's client is innocent.

In addition, the sequence of a tale can be rearranged; *interpolated* elements can be inserted in the middle of a tale, complicating the plot. As an example, in the film *My Cousin Vinny* (1992), the courtroom sequence is repeated several times, as follows:

    IV. The development of the defense team's strategies

     V. The defense attorney's tactics in court

    VI. The prosecutors' tactics in court

     V. The defense attorney's tactics in court

    VI. The prosecutors' tactics in court

     V. The defense attorney's tactics in court

The plot of the film involves the miscues of novice attorney Vincent Gambini (Joe Pesci) as he attempts to defend his clients, who have been accused of murder. The repeated sequence demonstrates Vinny's growth as an attorney, as he quickly learns proper deportment in the courtroom and begins to apply his considerable argumentative strengths to his clients' advantage.

Finally, reversing the order in which functions appear creates wide plot variations. For instance, in *My Cousin Vinny*, if Element 2 (*The defendant is apprehended*) had appeared *before* Element I *(Background)*, the audience would no longer have been a witness to the crime that established the innocence of Vinny's clients. Consequently, the dramatic emphasis would have shifted to discovering whether Vinny's clients were innocent or guilty, as opposed to the actual focus of the narrative—whether Vinny can successfully defend his innocent clients.

Plot

A *plot* is a planned series of events in a narrative, progressing through a struggle of opposing forces to a climax and a conclusion.

To keep the stories fresh, media communicators rely on contemporary issues, trends, and points of interest. As a result, the collective plots of a genre serve as a barometer of cultural attitudes, values, trends, and preoccupations. To illustrate, consider the following plot summaries of the soap opera *Days of Our Lives* that aired during the week of January 3–11, 2011 (from soap operacentral.com):

Jennifer seemed impressed with Ben's dedication to his patients, unaware that the organs he received were courtesy of his arrangement with Warden Jane and the premature death of prison inmates. Bo and Hope enlisted help from their old friend Leo while they were on the run from the Feds. Brady and Kate put their plan in motion to get rid of Vivian. Rafe encouraged Sami to try to deal with E.J. and Nicole until Johnny and Sydney returned home to them. Sami told E.J. that his marriage to Nicole would never work. Johnny ran away from home, right into Rafe and Sami's arms. Stephanie and Nathan returned to Salem after learning of Caroline's stroke. Daniel asked Chloe and Parker to move out, and then asked Victor to open his heart and provide financial support for Parker. Melanie and Nathan had a bittersweet reunion. Philip was livid when he learned that Stephanie had known that he was Parker's biological father and hadn't told him. Philip asked Melanie to forgive him, but she wanted no part of him or their marriage. Philip comforted a devastated Chloe and promised that he would be there for Parker. The captain of the Kiriakis corporate jet forced Vivian and Gus to parachute from the plane to tropical places unknown. As Stephanie prepared for her wedding day, Nathan learned that she had lied to him from day one about Parker's paternity.

Again, a major theme that emerges in these storylines is contending with *change*. In the world of the soap opera, extraordinary things happen to ordinary people. Consequently, soap opera characters strive to establish some degree of equilibrium in this rapidly changing world.

In addition, soap opera plots typically focus on relationships. In the capsule summary above, couples are engaged in romantic quests for true love. Soap operas include all of the stages of a romance: the blissful beginning, trouble in paradise, and resolution. A cumulative message that emerges from these plots is that happiness is fleeting.

Beyond romantic love, soap opera plots reinforce the value of relationships, particularly issues around children. Significantly, a number of plots deal with the separation of mothers and children (through death or abduction), despite the efforts of the women to hold on to their children.

In addition, secondary stories, called *subplots*, are frequently interwoven into narratives. Subplots may appear to be unrelated; however, because the characters operate within the same worldview, subplots often comment on different aspects of the same thematic concerns. Consequently, identifying thematic connections between subplots can furnish perspective into the cumulative messages contained in a program.

For instance, in the worldview of soap operas, numerous subplots deal with the issue of *identity*: "lost" relatives, cases of amnesia, and inheritance issues.

At times, subplots are *latent*—that is, not formally introduced but often of considerable interest to the audience. In both the British and American versions of the television sit-com *The Office*, for example, the romance between Dawn/Pam and Tim/Jim was an unspoken but central element of the plot.

The following questions can provide insight into messages conveyed by subplots:

- Identify the subplots that make up the program. What themes do these subplots share?
- What cumulative messages are conveyed by these subplots?
- Are there any *latent* subplots not formally acknowledged but of more interest to the audience than the manifest plot?

Setting

The *setting* is the physical background against which the action of a narrative takes place. The elements that make up a setting include:

- The geographic location (including its topography and scenery)
- The physical arrangement of the location such as the windows and doors of a room
- The time or period in which the action takes place.

The setting can furnish perspective into the worldview of a media program or genre. As an example, in the horror genre, the setting contributes to an atmosphere of gloom and terror. The gothic castles are filled with secret panels and underground catacombs—secret places that symbolizes the dark, dangerous, and evil worldview characteristic of the genre.

See also: Autobiographical Analysis; Genre Study, Media Literacy Approach; Mass-Mediated Reality

References

Days of Our Lives, January 3–7, 2011. Soapcentral.com/days. Retrieved from http://www.soapcentral.com/days/archives.php?year=2011

Felluga, D. (2003). *Barthes and Narratology*. Retrieved from http://www.wsp.krakow.pl/nkja/literature/theory/barthes_and_narratology.htm

Nonverbal Approach to Media Analysis

The nonverbal approach to media analysis is a qualitative approach to media analysis that focuses on nonverbal communications as a strategy for discussing and interpreting media content. This is an example of a *disparate approach to media analysis* in which the principles of another discipline are applied to the analysis of media content.

Nonverbal communication is a surprisingly sophisticated and efficient system for sending and receiving information:

- Subtle and implicit information is conveyed through nonverbal channels in a few seconds or even a fraction of a second (Rosenthal et al., 1979).
- People are quite accurate in decoding these brief instances of nonverbal communication (Burns & Belier, 1973; Ekman, Sorenson, & Friesen, 1969; Izard, 1977).
- Specific nonverbal behaviors accompany certain feelings (Ekman, Friesen, & Ellsworth, 1972).
- Nonverbal cues are especially adept at communicating information about emotions and mood (Ekman, Friesen, & Ellsworth, 1972).

However, as with verbal communication, there is always the possibility of misunderstandings. Although analysis can detect patterns of nonverbal behaviors, it cannot identify the *intention* behind these behaviors. But although the nonverbal approach may not always be definitive, it can be a useful springboard for further analysis.

Some nonverbal gestures have a universal meaning. To illustrate, the palm punch, in which the fist of one hand is punched rhythmically several times against the palm of the other, is an angry gesture that has a primal, symbolic significance across cultures. Other universal gestures include the chin stroke (pensiveness, concentration) and the chest beat (strength, power).

But in addition, the culture to which a person belongs can influence the meanings ascribed to nonverbal communications behaviors. In a study of 40 countries, nonverbal scholar Desmond Morris (n.d.) identified 20 common hand gestures that had a distinctive meaning in different cultures. To illustrate, in Thailand, people move their fingers back and forth with the palm down to signal another person to approach, whereas in the United States, people beckon someone by holding the palm up and moving the fingers toward their body.

Focusing on the *function* of nonverbal communication can provide clues and cues into cultural meanings. For instance, different cultures have their own versions of *openness gestures* (such as unbuttoning coats, uncrossing legs, or moving toward the edge of the chair) that convey a sense of self-confidence. In contrast, fidgeting, tugging at clothing, and playing with objects are all *nervousness gestures* found in different cultures. Thus, different cultures often have their own distinctive nonverbal behaviors that are expressions of the following communications functions:

- Clarification
- Persuasion
- Facilitating the communication process
- Expression of emotion
- Expression of intimacy
- Social control

Nonverbal Communication Approach to Media Analysis

Although nonverbal communication behavior generally has been linked to the study of interpersonal communication, it is applicable to the critical analysis of mass communications as well. The nonverbal analysis approach to media literacy analysis can follow the following lines of inquiry:

1. Nonverbal communications analysis provides insight into the ways in which nonverbal communication behaviors reinforce verbal messages in media presentations.

In visual media (photographs, film, and television), actors employ nonverbal behaviors such as body posture, accents, or subtle facial expressions and eye movements to establish themes and reinforce messages. People in the public eye, such as political figures, high-profile corporate executives, and broadcast journalists have been trained to develop their *presentational* skills as part of an overall "impression management" strategy.

A person's immediate nonverbal responses are often a barometer of his or her genuine feelings; however, these reactions are quickly replaced by a calculated response. Consequently, it can be useful to focus attention on an individual's immediate nonverbal reactions.

Nonverbal behaviors fall into the following categories.

Facial expressions are a reliable source of emotional information. According to psychology professor Dr. Paul Ekman, seven basic human emotions have very clear facial signals—anger, sadness, fear, surprise, disgust, contempt, and happiness. In addition, the face can reveal evaluative judgments (e.g., pain, pleasure, superiority, determination, surprise, attention, and bewilderment), the degree of interest or disinterest in the subject, and levels of understanding. (Foreman, 2003)

Some facial signals to be alert for include the following:

- Raised eyebrows indicate surprise
- A set jaw reveals anger, determination, tension, resolve, or decision
- A chin retraction is a protective action or a signal that something is scary or frightening
- Flared nostrils express anger
- A nose wrinkle signifies dislike, disapproval, or disgust

People tend to attribute positive characteristics to individuals who smile, such as intelligence, a good personality, and being a "pleasant person" (Pearson et al., 1994). Smiling also assumes gender-based meanings. Women tend to smile more often than men, perhaps reflecting a desire to please as a subordinate member of society. However, because smiling can be a social construction for women, their behavior may be scripted (i.e., covering other emotions) and, consequently, more difficult to interpret.

Facial responses are often culture centered as well. In China, people are conditioned by their culture to remain stoical, as a way, literally, to "save face." In many Mediterranean cultures, inhabitants exaggerate their facial expressions to convey emotions.

Eye contact is another nonverbal signal. A person's gaze offers a range of communication options: (a) establishing eye contact, (b) avoiding eye contact, (c) looking down, (d) shifting eyes, (e) squinting, (f) staring straight ahead, and (g) closing eyes (Porter & Samovar, 1995: 194). According to communications scholar Dale Leathers (1997: 42), the eyes serve the following communication functions:

- Indicating degree of attentiveness, interest, and arousal
- Influencing attitude, change, and persuasion
- Regulating interaction
- Communicating emotions
- Defining power and status
- Assuming a central role in impression management

A culture can dictate the permissible amount of eye contact among its people. In the United States, people are regarded as honest if they "look you straight in the eye," whereas in Japan, extended eye contact is considered a sign of disrespect.

Posture refers to a stance or positioning of the body or body part. Postures communicate a range of personal information about a communicator's character. An upright posture communicates a message of confidence and integrity, whereas a slumping posture conveys a sense of cowardice, meekness, sadness, or depression (Hargrave, 1995). Having good posture—standing tall—is an indication of empowerment, authority, and rank in society.

Examining posture in media presentations can provide insight into the relative positions of power and authority in society. In Japan, females often stand in a "cant" position, in which the head or body is bowed. The latent message of this body language is deference, submission, and subordination. In Germany and Sweden, however, slouching is a sign of rudeness, sloppiness, and incompetence.

Posture also can indicate the speaker's attitude toward the audience. Leaning toward a person expresses a positive position, while slumping conveys a sense of disrespect. In Turkey, putting your hands in your pockets is a sign of insolence.

Proxemic communication refers to the way that space configurations convey meaning. The use of space falls into three distinct categories:

- *Personal space* comprises the area we maintain between ourselves and others. The boundaries of personal space may be culturally determined.

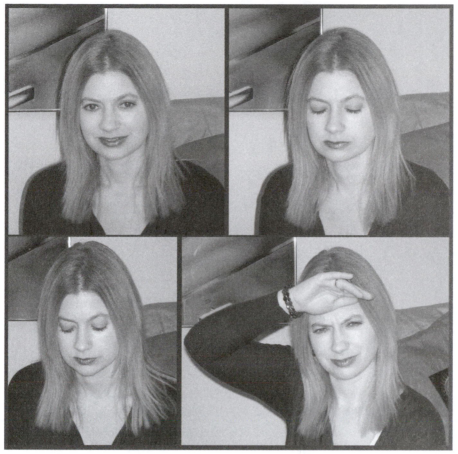

Observing degrees of eye contact such as direct, eyes closed, downward gaze, and squinting can be instrumental in the analysis of nonverbal communication. Cultural norms can alter meanings. For example, in Western culture, a direct gaze conveys the message that the audience member is being attentive. But in Asian cultures, a direct gaze may be regarded as rude. (Photo by Lisa Marcus)

Members of Arab nations typically stand closer when conversing than do Europeans. In addition, the boundaries of personal space also vary *within* a culture. For instance, in the United States, women tend to stand closer together than men.

- *Group formation* refers to where people are positioned in relation to one another. The arrangement of people within a group indicates status. In America, people at the head of the table are in control; in contrast, the individual seated to the left of the head of the table often has the least status in the group. In Japan, the most important person sits at one end of the rectangular table, with those nearest in rank at the right and left of this senior position. The lowest in class is nearest to the door and the opposite end of the table from the person with the most authority. Group formation also signals whether the assemblage of people forms an open or closed society (Leathers, 1997: 77–78). People standing in a closed formation are excluding others, whereas groups in an open formation are more inclusive.

- *Tactile communication*, or touch, can signal support, reassurance, intimacy, sexual interest, anger, or exhilaration. Some cultures are more inclined toward touching as a form of communication. Examples of these *high-contact* cultures include Arab, Latin American, and southern European countries. Low-contact cultures include northern European and North American countries.

Touching behaviors can reinforce verbal content or convey independent messages. For instance, politicians have mastered the art of holding a handshake for an instant longer than is normally expected, sending a message of personal regard, intimacy, and trust. In addition, touching violations can be an assertion of power and control by high-status individuals.

Costumes can assume cultural significance, signifying a person's affiliations within a culture, such as police uniforms, as well as indications of status. In addition, clothing can convey specific cultural messages. Consider the following example:

A Washington State agriculture official who was touring China a few years ago handed out bright green baseball caps at every stop without noticing that none of the men would put them on or that all the women were giggling.

Finally, a Chinese-American in the delegation took the man aside and informed him that "to wear a green hat" is the Chinese symbol of a cuckold. (Smith, 2002)

Vocalic communication refers to the quality of the voice, which can convey messages that are independent of the actual words that are spoken. Voice quality can transmit a wide range of information about the speaker's educational level, class, cultural orientation, and nationality. Psychologist Richard Wiseman declares that vocality can be a more accurate barometer of the communicator's intention than eye contact or gestures: "If you want to find out if a politician's lying . . . you're better turning away or shutting your eyes and just concentrating on the sound track" (1995).

Other vocalic elements include dialect, tonal quality, inflection, speed of delivery, accent, volume, tone, pitch, rate, duration, laughter, and . . . silence.

2. Nonverbal communications analysis identifies ways in which media communicators use "scripted" nonverbal strategies to create a particular image or impression.

Media figures carefully orchestrate their nonverbal behaviors to make their verbal messages more convincing. People who are interviewed on-camera often follow a "script" devised by impression formation managers. These professionals carefully choreograph the nonverbal behaviors of their clients to make their verbal messages more convincing. As an example, in 2007, Senator Larry Craig (R-Idaho) was arrested for sexual misconduct in the restroom of the Minneapolis airport. Craig then held a news conference to announce his innocence. As he approached the podium, he was holding hands with his wife, Suzanne. Asked about this carefully scripted nonverbal behavior, students in Art Silverblatt's media literacy class responded that the gesture sent nonverbal messages declaring Craig's innocence. Holding hands is "wholesome," a "romantic and platonic gesture which counterbalances the more sordid sexual aspects of the accusation." In addition, holding Craig's hand is "both a physical and emotional expression of support by Craig's wife."

3. Nonverbal communications analysis furnishes individuals with tools to detect "unscripted" behaviors that are at variance with the verbal message.

People who are interviewed on-camera often are unable to express their true feelings verbally. However, their nonverbal behaviors may disclose their actual thoughts and feelings. For instance, in 2007, Democrat Hillary Clinton, running in the New Hampshire presidential primary election, was asked by a prospective voter how she managed to persevere, despite all of the hardships involved in running for president. Obviously fatigued, Clinton responded with what appeared to be a spontaneous display of emotional nonverbal behavior. With tears welling up in her eyes, Clinton replied in a shaky voice that although her task was difficult, she cared about the country and didn't want it to "go backward." Clinton's win in New Hampshire defied the polls, which had predicted that Barak Obama would win by a wide margin. Postelection polls confirmed that a significant number of voters were influenced by this genuine nonverbal expression to change their vote to Clinton.

4. Nonverbal communications provide insight into the character and disposition of the media communicator.

Independent of the content, nonverbal behavior such as posture, body type, or dress sends messages about the speaker's self-image, competence, confidence, and trustworthiness.

5. Nonverbal communications analysis provides insight into the role of nonverbal communication cues in the depiction of media stereotypes.

Media communicators rely on nonverbal communications cues in presenting stereotypes in programs. For instance, body type plays a role in the casting of parts in films. Characters with athletic frames (mesomorphic body types) are often cast as the heroic figures: highly confident, task-oriented, energetic, talkative, aggressive, and dominant. People with heavy builds (endomorphic body types) are frequently cast as characters who are lazy, warm-hearted, sympathetic, good-natured, passive, and sloppy. Finally, characters with thin, fragile frames (ectomorphic body types) often play the role of characters who are tense, fussy, critical, suspicious, tense, nervous, pessimistic, anxious, self-conscious, and reticent.

References

Burns, K. L., & Beier, E. G. (1973). "Significance of Vocal and Visual Channels in the Decoding of Emotional Meaning." *Journal of Communication 23*, 118–130.

Ekman, P., Sorenson, R., & Friesen, W. V. (1969, April 4). "Pan-Cultural Elements in Facial Displays of Emotion." *Science*, New Series, 164, No. 3875, pp. 86-88.

Ekman, P., Friesen, W. V., & Ellsworth, R. (1972). *Emotion in the Human Face*. New York: Pergamon.

Foreman, J. (2003, August 5). "A Conversation with Paul Ekman; The 43 Facial Muscles That Reveal Even the Most Fleeting Emotions." *New York Times*, Section F; p. 5.

Hargrave, J. (1995). *Let Me See Your Body Talk*. Dubuque, IA: Kendall/Hunt.

Izard, Carroll E., *The Face of Emotion*. Century Psychology Series. Appleton-Century-Crofts, 1971.

Leathers, D. G. (1997). *Successful Nonverbal Communication: Principles and Applications* (3rd ed.). Boston: Allyn and Bacon.

Morris, D. (n.d.). *Gypsy Journal—The Review of Related Literatures*. Retrieved from http://www.gypsyjournal.com/Chapter.asp?ChapterID=1693

Pearson, J. C., West, R. L., & Turner, L. (1994). *Gender Communication*. Dubuque, IA: Brown and Benchmark.

Porter, R. E., & Samovar, L. A. (1995). *Communication Between Cultures* (2nd ed.). Belmont, CA: Wadsworth.

"Read or Listen, But Don't Look; Eyes Will Lie, Says TV Researcher." (1995, February 2). *St. Louis Post-Dispatch*, p. 2A.

Rosenthal, R., Hall, J., DiMatteo, M. R., Rogers, R., & Archer, D. (1979). *Sensitivity to Nonverbal Communication: The PONS Test*. Baltimore, MD: Johns Hopkins University Press.

Smith, C. S. (2002). "Beware of Cross-Cultural Faux Pas in China." *New York Times*.

Williams, A. (2004). "Live From Miami, a Style Showdown." *New York Times*. http://www.nytimes.com/2004/09/26/fashion/26DEBA.html

Wiseman, R. "Read of Listen, But Don't Look, Says TV Researcher." Contributors: Ap. St. Louis Post-Dispatch, 1995. Pp. 2.

Ownership Patterns, Media

The ownership patterns of the media industry influence both *what* information appears in the media and *how* it is presented. There are three basic global media ownership systems, each of which exercises a distinctive influence on the construction of media messages:

- State Ownership
- Public Ownership
- Private Media Ownership

State-owned System

State-owned media systems make up a sizable portion of the worldwide media operations. According to the United Nations' 2002 Human Development Report, 29 percent of the world's largest newspapers are state owned (Phillips, n.d.).

In authoritarian countries such as China, Cuba, and North Korea, the media are considered instruments of the state. Television programs, radio shows, films, and newspapers, as well as books and magazines, are produced and distributed under the close supervision of the government.

The news information agencies belong to the state. News and editorial functions are performed by government officials who are committed to its goals and practices. As government employees, these editors, reporters, anchors, and TV producers are subject to state labor laws.

Under this system, the primary function of the media is to promote the agenda of the government. State-owned media systems control access to sensitive topics, including religious materials, political dissent, and pornography. Consequently, media presentations furnish useful perspective into the official government position on issues. But in addition, digital technology (particularly social media) can express alternative points of view within a country.

Public Media

In countries such as Sweden, the Netherlands, and Kazakstan, the media are owned by the public but operated by the government. The operating costs of newspapers, television stations, and radio stations are generated through public taxes. Because of this system of public financing, regulations and policies are designed to guarantee a diversity of sources of information. For instance, Swedish law stipulates that at least two newspapers must be published in every town, reflecting differing points of view.

Under this system of ownership, writers, editors, and media technicians are civil servants who maintain a degree of autonomy from whatever political administration happens to be in office. Furthermore, because the money to produce programs and pay salaries is generated by public financing, media producers are insulated from market pressures and produce thoughtful and quality programming, free of pressures from advertisers and the audience. But at the same time, this system can promote an environment in which programming reflects only the narrow concerns and interests of these media communicators, ignoring the interests, concerns, and preferences of the audience.

Private Ownership

In capitalistic countries such as the United States, the majority of newspapers, magazines, radio stations, film studios, and television stations are privately owned—either by individuals or, increasingly, by large, multinational corporations. Under this market-driven system, a primary *function*, or purpose, is to generate the maximum possible profit for the owners (or stakeholders).

Over time, the number of media companies has decreased as large corporations have absorbed the small, family-owned media companies. In 1981, 46 corporations owned or controlled the majority of media outlets in the United States. However, as of 2012, that number had shrunk to eight corporations: Time/Warner, Disney, Vivendi Universal, Viacom, Sony, the News Corporation, Comcast, General Electric, and Bertelsmann. This ownership model fits F. M. Sherer and D. Ross's (1990) definition of an *oligopoly*:

> Oligopoly refers to an industry characterized by a few mutually interdependent firms, with relatively similar shares, producing either a homogeneous product (a perfect oligopoly) or heterogeneous products (an imperfect oligopoly). Under such a market structure, the industry leader often sets the price.

Hybrid Model

Many countries operate according to a hybrid ownership model, made up of different ownership systems. For instance, in Great Britain, the newspapers are privately owned, whereas BBC radio and television stations are state-run. And although the vast majority of U.S. media are privately owned, National Public Radio and Public Television are state-run media systems.

Impact of Media Ownership on Content

The market-driven media system in the United States can have a significant impact on media content, in several respects.

Homogeneity of Content. Because of the concentration of ownership, the content that we receive through the media is controlled by a very few corporations. Media outlets that are owned by a megacorporation are characterized by a uniform style, content, and operating philosophy. As an example, in 2011, Clear Channel Communications, the largest radio station operator in the United States, operating about 850 stations in the United States and employing 12,000 people, fired hundreds of local DJs. The local shows were replaced by one national program, with breaks for local traffic and weather updates. As a result, Clear Channel is spared the production cost of hiring a host, producer, and engineer. But unfortunately, the radio listeners are also denied programming presented from a local perspective.

Tony Lynn, one of the few local DJs retained, observed,

> I guess it all comes down to the bottom line, and as a small business owner, I understand that. But on the other hand, sometimes it's more than just a few dollars more. Radio is an intimate medium and that's what's being ignored. Listeners develop a special bond with the on-air personalities, and in the long run that proves beneficial for both the station and the advertisers. (Stelter, 2011)

Support of Status Quo. The conglomerates that own media companies are beneficiaries of the existing political and economic systems. As a result, although media companies may call for some refinements within the existing system, they cannot be counted upon to press for any radical overhaul of structure or policy. The reason? The media ownership is never going to advocate their own overthrow. As Ben Bagdikian declares, "The lords of the global village have their own political agenda. All resist economic changes that do not support their own financial interests" (1997). For example, one avenue for political campaign reform calls for television, as a guardian of the public airwaves, making free airtime available for political ads. Needless to say, the media conglomerates do not support this idea.

Programming as Product. In this market-driven media system, media presentations are thought of as products, like shoes or showerheads, to be manufactured and sold. Conglomerates purchase media holdings as sources of cash flow to support other enterprises within the corporate empire. This economic imperative has had a dramatic impact on the content of media presentations. To illustrate, during the quarterly ratings period known as the "sweeps," local television stations commonly feature weeklong "news" stories on provocative topics such as wrestling, prostitution, and breast implants in hopes of attracting the largest possible audience.

Conflicts of Interest. These may arise when a media conglomerate covers stories in which the parent company has an interest. In some cases, the executives of these wealthy and influential media conglomerates may have ties to the political establishment, creating conflicts of interest that can affect their presentation of information. In 2011, for example, Rupert Murdoch's media empire, NewsCorp, was embroiled in a scandal that began over revelations about illegal phone hacking by one of his tabloid newspapers, *The News of the World.* Reporter Nick Davies of the *Guardian* newspaper in London, whose investigative stories first got the attention of the public, found that of the 45 employees of the press office of Scotland Yard, 10 were former employees of *News of the World.* According to Davies (2011),

> If you see this in context, the reality of life in this country for some decades has been: you can't run a government and you can't run a police force unless you are on close, friendly terms with the Murdoch organization. So, there are all sorts of connections between the Metropolitan Police, Scotland Yard—that's biggest police force in the country—and News International, which owns Murdoch's newspapers in this country. And so, the fact that ex-journalists were being employed by their press office is part of that picture. But there's a whole set of connections.
>
> And to me, what's so revealing about this story is what—the sequence is this, you see? You have *News of the World* journalists going out there breaking the law, routinely, and they're allowed to get away with it. . . . Of all the evidence that they collected during that inquiry, they didn't properly investigate, because they didn't want to get into a fight with that powerful organization [the Murdochs]. And then, you see the seriousness of that, that they were exempted from normal law enforcement just because they're so powerful. Really, really wrong.

Moreover, as part of the coverage of the scandal, information came to light about the extraordinarily close ties between the Murdoch family and members of the British government, including Prime Minister David Cameron. Reporter John F. Burns (2011) observed,

> Mr. Cameron's aides released a (calendar) of his meetings with executives and editors of News International. The (calendar) shed light on what Mr. Cameron acknowledged last week was the 'cozy and comfortable' world in which politicians, the press and the police in Britain have functioned for decades, one he said had to yield to much greater public scrutiny.

On occasion, owners have intervened directly in editorial decisions when the issues affected their political interests.

> Two former senior news executives . . . said at a parliamentary hearing that they had informed James Murdoch, chief of News Corporation's European and Asian operations (and son of Chairman of the Board Rupert Murdoch), at a 15-minute meeting in London in 2008 that the hacking of voice mail as a reporting tool went beyond the work by a lone "rogue" reporter and a private investigator that the company had acknowledged at the time. The men said they had conveyed that message as part of a plan to win Mr. Murdoch's backing for a record $1.4 million settlement that bound a hacking victim to silence about his case. (Burns & Cowell, 2011)

In an article tracing developments in the Murdoch scandal, *New York Times* journalists John F. Burns and Alan Cowell (2011) reported that far from being a passive victim of the illegal activities of a lone underling, the testimony alleges that "Murdoch was shown an e-mail in which a junior reporter quoted from transcripts of three hacked voice mail messages, indicating a broader pattern of illegal intercepts" and that "Murdoch's approval of the record $1.4 million settlement with Gordon Taylor, chief of an organization representing Britain's professional soccer players, was . . . an effort to buy Mr. Taylor's silence and prevent the scandal from spreading."

Cross-promotion. Media programs sometimes serve the function of promoting other holdings within the corporate empire. As an example, in March 2009, Robert Thomson, editor of *The Wall Street Journal*, wrote a memo directing *Journal* reporters to send their breaking news first to Dow Jones Newswires, a business news "wire" service also owned by parent company

NewsCorp. Thomson's memo declared, "Henceforth, all Journal reporters will be judged, in significant part, by whether they break news for the Newswires." Newswires is a smaller operation than its more highly regarded competitors Thomson Reuters and Bloomberg. Consequently, according to reporter Richard Perez-Pena, "Dow Jones executives see *The Journal* as a way to make the Newswires more competitive" (2009).

Reliance on Formula. Because the economic bottom line is paramount, the media industry is increasingly reluctant to take programming risks. Reporter Bill Carter (1998) explains,

> Though there is near uniform agreement that only shows with truly original concepts seem to be connecting with viewers, an unwillingness to take risks often derails ideas before they are even tried, several executives said.

To illustrate, film studios only produce movies with formulaic plots, sequels and "bankable" stars. As Rick Lyman and Laura M. Holson (2002) point out,

> Gradually over several years . . . the prestige studio movies . . . have all but disappeared from the holiday schedule. In their place, with a few notable exceptions, come more and more sequels, remakes, spinoffs and other risk-averse, mass-market fare driven by the need for fast dollars.

Influence of Advertisers. Because of this corporate sensibility, U.S. media companies are inordinately sensitive to the objections and concerns of the primary sources of revenue—advertisers.

To illustrate, reporter Blythe Bernhard (2011) discusses the merging of ads and editorial content in the field of medicine:

> Hospitals have long competed for patients by advertising in television commercials and newspaper ads. Increasingly, the ads can blend into news as economic pressures in the health care and media industries have created partnerships that some say cross the ethical line separating marketing and journalism.

Ownership and the Digital Domain

The Internet represents a significant battleground with regard to ownership. Digital media is a democratic channel of communication that thus far has resisted central ownership. Former Supreme Court Justice Paul Stevens praised the "democratic forum" of the Internet, which he described as "the most mass participatory medium yet invented, . . . as diverse as human thought" (*St. Louis Post-Dispatch*, 1997).

The principle of *Net Neutrality* asserts that all Internet communication should be distributed without prejudice to volume or content. However, major Internet service providers (ISP) such as AT&T, MCI, and Charter contend that they should have the right to "prioritize" the information that is distributed through their networks. The criteria for this multi-tiered system would be based on commercial considerations. Cable and telephone companies want to sell specialized services that would speed some content to users more quickly for a fee. The highest priority would be for those conducting business directly with these companies.

Civil liberties organizations such as www.savetheInternet.com and the Electronic Frontier Foundation argue that allowing an Internet service provider to favor some content amounts to a violation of free speech and the potential for unfair competitive advantage. Without Net Neutrality, an ISP could block or limit data transfer from certain sites.

In April 2010, a federal appeals court ruled that the Federal Communications Commission (FCC) lacked the authority to penalize Comcast, an Internet service provider, for secretly blocking traffic on its network (Corbin, 2010). The court maintained that the FCC could not require that an Internet service provider refrain from blocking or slowing down some content or applications, or giving favor to others.

In response to this 2010 court decision, Internet service and content providers Google and Verizon negotiated an agreement in which Verizon would speed some online content provided by Google to consumers more quickly in exchange. Journalist Edward Wyatt (2010) explains,

> Such an agreement could overthrow a once-sacred tenet of Internet policy known as net neutrality, in which no form of content is favored over another. In its place, consumers could soon see a new, tiered system, which, like cable television, imposes higher costs for premium levels of service.

> But critics charge that this plan contains some significant loopholes.

> Without adequate regulation, Internet access companies could exercise too much control over what their customers can do online, or how quickly they can gain access to certain content. They could charge

companies for faster access to consumers, hurting smaller players and innovation. (Miller & Miguel Helft, 2010)

Reporter Brian Stelter (2010) adds,

The rules] allow for "reasonable network management" by broadband providers. And they would discourage but not expressly forbid something called 'paid prioritization,' which would allow a media or technology company to pay the provider for faster transmission of data, potentially creating an uneven playing field.

In addition, the agreement stipulated that wireless would be exempted from net neutrality rules. However, critics express concern that if this were the case, Verizon could devote fewer resources to upgrading its network or get paid by Web companies for delivering content over the wireless network. According to Stelter,

Notably, the rules are watered down for wireless Net providers like AT&T and Verizon, which would be prohibited from blocking Web sites, but not from blocking applications or services unless those applications directly compete with providers' voice and video products, like Skype.

However, not all digital media providers endorse the dismantling of net neutrality. Many content providers, including Amazon, eBay, and Skype either prefer no favoritism on the Internet or they want to be sure that if a pay system exists, all content providers have the opportunity to pay for faster service.

In December 2010, the FCC passed rules that would create two classes of Internet access: one for fixed-line providers and the other for the wireless Net. These first binding network neutrality rules would prevent fixed-line broadband providers like Comcast and Qwest from blocking access to sites and applications. At the same time, however, wireless companies would have more latitude with regard to limiting access to services and applications. Citing the wireless proposal, Senator Al Franken warned that these rules were effectively sanctioning discrimination on the mobile Net:

Maybe you like Google Maps. Well, tough. If the F.C.C. passes this weak rule, Verizon will be able to cut off access to the Google Maps app on your phone and force you to use their own mapping program,

Verizon Navigator, even if it is not as good. And even if they charge money, when Google Maps is free. If corporations are allowed to prioritize content on the Internet, or they are allowed to block applications you access on your iPhone, there is nothing to prevent those same corporations from censoring political speech. (Stelter, 2010)

In November 2011, the FCC filed a revised set of "open Internet" rules, scheduled to go into effect on November 20. The new rules are designed to prevent fixed broadband providers (cable, fiber, and DSL) from blocking access to sites and applications. However, reporter Nate Anderson (2011) observes that these rules are different for wireless providers, in the following respects:

First, *transparency*: fixed and mobile broadband providers must disclose the network management practices, performance characteristics, and commercial terms of their broadband services. Second, *no blocking*: fixed broadband providers may not block lawful content, applications, services, or non-harmful devices; mobile broadband providers may not block lawful websites, or block applications that compete with their voice or video telephony services. Third, *no unreasonable discrimination:* fixed broadband providers may not unreasonably discriminate in transmitting lawful network traffic.
    Mobile networks still have broad leeway to discriminate and throttle and even block certain apps, though some of the most obviously objectionable activities are forbidden. (italics in original)

When a draft of the rules came out in December, roughly 80 grassroots organizations signed an open letter avowing their disapproval, complaining that the rules "leave wireless users vulnerable to application blocking and discrimination," use "unnecessarily broad definitions," and claiming that specialized services "would create a pay-for-play platform that would destroy today's level playing field" (Kessler, 2011).

Beyond the specifics of these "Open Internet Rules," the FCC has raised some serious questions about its purview. Wyatt (2010) explains,

The F.C.C. has proposed meanwhile, favors a level playing field, but it cannot impose one as long as its authority over broadband is in legal doubt. It has proposed a solution that would reclassify broadband Internet service under the Communications Act from its current designation as an "information service," a lightly regulated designation, to a "telecommunications service," a category that, like telephone service, is subject to stricter regulation. The F.C.C. has said that it does not want to impose strict regulation on Internet service and rates, but seeks only the authority to enforce broadband privacy and guarantee equal access. It also wants to use federal money to subsidize broadband service for rural areas.

Net neutrality remains a major issue that is still a matter of contention. Hogan Lovells, former member of the FCC, declared, "We're in the third inning of net neutrality. From here it's going to leave the FCC and move to the courts with some oversight in Congress" (Corbin, 2010).

One solace with regard to the possible abolition of Net Neutrality can be found in the principle of *media ping pong*, which holds that when government or corporate entities impose repressive regulations, activists implement new technological strategies that circumvent the regulations. In the case of net neutrality, activists could simply construct a new Internet that focuses on ideas rather than commerce (perhaps modeled after the Intranet found in many colleges and universities).

See also: Business Models, Journalism; Function; Media and Social Change

References

Anderson, A. (2011). "US net neutrality rules finalized, in effect November 20." Retrieved from http://arstechnica.com/tech-policy/news/2011/09/us-net-neutrality-rules-finalized-in-effect-november-20.ars

Bagdikian, B. (1997). *The Media Monopoly* (5th ed.). Boston: Beacon Press.

Bernhard, B. (2011, March 31). "TV-Hospital News Raises Questions About Ethics." *St. Louis Post-Dispatch*. Retrieved from http://www.stltoday.com/lifestyles/health-med-fit/fitness/tv-hospital-news-coverage-raises-questions-about-ethics/article_a31697ec-b6c1-50ad-967f-e727aee792b7.html

Burns, J. F. (2011, July 16). "A Day of Apologies for the Murdochs, and of New Questions for Cameron." *New York Times*. Retrieved from http://www.nytimes.com/2011/07/17/world/europe/17britain.html

Burns, J. F., & Cowell, A. (2011, September 6). "Murdoch Son's Testimony on Hacking Is Challenged by 2 Former Executives." *New York Times*. Retrieved from http://www.nytimes.com/2011/09/07/world/europe/07hacking.html?pagewanted=all

Carter, B. (1998, November 22). "Shrinking Network TV Audiences Set Off Alarm and Reassessment." *New York Times*. Retrieved from http://www.nytimes.com/1998/11/22/us/shrinking-network-tv-audiences-set-off-alarm-and-reassessment.html?pagewanted=all&src=pm

Corbin, K. (2010, December 30). "Net Neutrality 2011: What Storms May Come." Internet News.com. Retrieved from http://www.internetnews.com/government/article.php/3918831/Net+Neutrality+2011+What+Storms+May+Come.htm

Davies, N. (2011, July 24). Interview with Amy Goodman. *DemocracyNow!* www.democracynow.org.

Editorial. (1997, December 17). *St. Louis Post-Dispatch*, p. B6.

Kessler, S. (2011, September 23). "New Net Neutrality Rules Become Official." Retrieved from http://mashable.com/2011/09/23/net-neutrality-rules-become-official/

Lyman, R., & Holson, L. M. (2002, November 24). "Holidays Turn into Hollywood's Hot Season." *New York Times*. Retrieved from http://www.nytimes.com/2002/11/24/us/holidays-turn-into-hollywood-s-hot-season.html?pagewanted=all&src=pm

Miller, C. C., & Helft, M. (2010, August 15). "Google Plan with Verizon Disillusions Some Allies." *New York Times*. Retrieved from http://www.nytimes.com/2010/08/16/technology/16google.html?pagewanted=all

Perez-Pena, R. (2009, March 23). "Wall Street Journal Is Told to Feed Newswires." *New York Times*. Retrieved from http://www.nytimes.com/2009/03/23/business/media/23wsj.html

Phillips, P. (2003). "The Importance of Independent News Sources for Freedom and Democracy." Retrieved from www.projectcensored.org

Sherer, F. M., & Ross, D. (1990). *Industrial Market Structure and Economic Performance* (3rd ed.). Boston: Houghton Mifflin, 1990.

Stelter, B. (2011, October 27). "Clear Channel Cuts D.J.'s Across the Country." *New York Times*. Retrieved from http://mediadecoder.blogs.nytimes.com/2011/10/27/clear-channel-cuts-d-j-s-across-the-country/

Stelter, B. (2010, December 20). "F.C.C. Is Set to Regulate Net Access." *New York Times*. Retrieved from http://www.nytimes.com/2010/12/21/business/media/21fcc.html

St. Louis Post-Dispatch. (December 17, 1997). P. B6.

Wyatt, E. (2010, August 4). "Google and Verizon Near Deal on Pay Tiers for Web." *New York Times*. Retrieved from http://www.nytimes.com/2010/08/05/technology/05secret.html?pagewanted=all

Political Communications, American

The mass media have transformed the American political landscape. Modern politicians must use the media to present themselves and their positions. During the 2012 election season in the United States, more than $6 billion was spent, with most of the funds being used for the production and distribution of information in the media (Ludwig, 2012).

Once in office, elected officials must continue to raise money for reelection. As a result, American politicians split their time between fund raising and their legislative duties.

The relationship between politicians and the media can best be described as *reciprocal*. Some of the *functions*, or purposes, of the media's coverage of politics include the following:

* The media inform the public about the political life of the nation.
* The media provide public exposure for politicians.
* The media influence public attitudes toward politicians and issues.
* The media serve a government watchdog.
* The media rely on politicians for daily programming content and as a major source of revenue.
* The media frequently support the agenda of the government.

At the same time, politicians use the media for a range of functions:

* Protecting their positions of power
* Shaping public opinion

In today's mass-mediated environment, how something is communicated—style—can overwhelm the content. Politicians have learned to manipulate public attitudes and behaviors. Media literacy can be an important democratic instrument that empowers individuals to make independent choices, based upon a critical awareness of the information they receive through the media. Consequently, media literacy enables individuals to recognize how the mass media can discourage debate, conceal information, and mislead the public.

The media have influenced the American political process in the following ways.

Candidate selection. In the media age, candidates must come across as dynamic, charismatic, trustworthy, competent, and likable. According to political consultant Bill Carrick, the subtle style cues of gesture, posture, syntax, and tone of voice account for as much as 75 percent of a viewer's judgment about the electability of a candidate (Silverblatt, 2007: 136). To illustrate, during the 2012 presidential primary in Iowa, voters were asked by the *New York Times* for the reasons behind their selection of a Republican candidate. Answers by citizens included:

* Supporting Ron Paul because of his "high-pitched squirrelly voice." (Jonathan Gabhart, supporting Ron Paul)

- Mitt Romney's voice "drives me crazy. . . . When he's on TV or on a commercial, I put it on mute." (Rose Williams, voting against Romney)
- Jon M. Huntsman's gestures—"He comes across as a preacher, and I just want to take his hands and tie them behind his back because he's always pleading." (Eva Dunn, voting against Huntsman)

Significantly, Michael Dee of West Des Moines acknowledges the role of the media in candidate selection: "Personality does matter because this person is going to be on TV all the time as president" (Barbaro & Parker, 2011).

Media consultants coach politicians on phrasing, intonations, facial expression, eye contact, and body language, often relying on "electronic response" mechanisms to measure viewers' reactions to politicians' nonverbal cues (Silverblatt, 2007: 138). Media consultants also employ focus groups to gauge the public response to the most minute detail of a politician's appearance.

Media scrutiny. A candidate must be able to withstand the relentless scrutiny of the press. After initially promoting a candidate, the media almost immediately begin to delve into the private lives of these same politicians. Unfortunately, this media scrutiny limits the pool of potential candidates. It is safe to say that few people would feel comfortable permitting the press to comb through their pasts. In the process, this media scrutiny magnifies the human flaws of these candidates and undermines public confidence in politicians. Moreover, it can be argued that this media scrutiny inhibits the ability of elected officials to govern effectively. Politicians must monitor every action and reaction to maintain the desired image they wish to project and prevent any damage to this image.

During the 2012 U.S. presidential election, for example, Republican candidate Mitt Romney attended a fundraiser where he gave an informal address. Surrounded by supporters, Romney felt comfortable sharing some of his more private thoughts during his talk, including the comment that 47 percent of the population could be described as *takers* who enjoyed a lifelong dependency on the government. This comment created a backlash that played a role in Romney's defeat.

Campaign finance. In the early stages of a campaign, the amount of money raised by candidates has become a major criterion to measure the viability of a political candidate. The fundraising totals of the candidates are tracked closely by the press, with the "winner" designated as the frontrunner. Indeed, courting big donors is now regarded as the equivalent of an "invisible primary," with the winner assuming the lead position going into the actual primary election.

Special interest groups expect favorable treatment from a candidate who they have supported financially. This pressure sometimes forces politicians to take positions that they otherwise wouldn't adopt. And in some cases, these special interests play a direct role in the drafting of legislation—a right not afforded to average citizens.

- *Lobbyists* are often former government officials who use their connections to gain access to politicians on behalf of particular industries, such as oil and gas. Although these representatives are only authorized to provide information to politicians, their influence often exceeds this purely consultative role.
- *Political action committees* (PACs). The Federal Election Campaign Act of 1971 (FECA), amended in 1974 and 1976, permits corporations, labor unions, and religious organizations to support political candidates through the formation of PACs—a "separate segregated fund" within a company or as a self-sustaining, though related, organization. In 2010, the Supreme Court's ruling in the *Citizens United v. Federal Election Commission* case created a new category of "Super PACs" that permitted unlimited contributions from individuals, unions, and corporations (both for profit and not-for-profit) for the purpose of making independent expenditures.

Individual donors, who represent a narrow segment of American society, share a common political agenda. Columnist Bob Herbert (1998) explains,

I doubt that many people are aware of just how elite and homogeneous the donor class is. It's a tiny group—just one-quarter of 1 percent of the population—and it is not representative of the rest of the nation. But its money buys plenty of access. These major donors share a common political agenda. They on balance oppose national health insurance, additional anti-poverty spending, and reductions in defense spending, but back gay rights and free trade. They are fairly evenly divided on environmental protection and affirmative action.

Given the financial pressures of the political system, it is nearly impossible for politicians to avoid financial entanglements that can compromise the performance of their duties. Political candidates are required by law to disclose the sources of their contributions. It can, therefore, be extremely worthwhile to scrutinize this information, focusing on the following information:

- How much money has each individual/organization donated to the candidate?
- What industries do they represent?
- Is there any record of policy positions in these areas?

The rise of the media consultant. Where candidates used to solicit the support of the party machine, they now scramble for the services of a top media consultant. Top media consulting firms can command a fee of more than $1 million for a single political campaign.

The primary responsibility of the media consultant is to coordinate political ads and unpaid media coverage. However, the media consultant has branched out into all phases of a campaign, including media creation and promotion, direct-mail fund raising, and participation in the formulation of campaign strategies. Candidates often defer to the judgment of the consultant—not only on campaign strategy but on political issues as well.

Media consultants are advertising specialists who borrow heavily from traditional advertising techniques to "sell" their candidates to the public. Ironically, media consultant Bob Goodman laments that packaging a human being has distinct drawbacks:

> You can't put a candidate completely in a new package. You can take his polyester off and put him in a decent-looking suit. You have him blow dry his hair. You can teach him how to keep his eye on the camera. You can try to inspire certain attributes. But you don't have the complete freedom that you do when you're dealing with a bar of soap. (Sabato, 1981: 144)

Indeed, media consultant Vincent Breglio explains that "the extent to which a candidate is manageable" is a prime consideration when selecting his clients—an alarming criterion for a national leader (Sabato, 1981: 38).

The influence of the polls. Despite their influence, polls may not be a comprehensive or accurate barometer of public opinion, for several reasons:

- Only the *results* of polls are generally made public, so that vital information about the polling sample is omitted. For example, an important consideration in the assessment of a poll is the probability that the sample of respondents will actually vote. Polls that use the *general population* as its sample are the least reliable. Other polls that use a sample of *registered voters* are considered more accurate; however, about

10 percent who say they're registered really are not. The most accurate sample consists of *likely voters* (Worthington, 2004).

- Some demographic groups are not adequately represented in polls because of the way in which interviews are conducted. For example, during the 2012 presidential election, the polling sample was limited to people using "land lines," thereby missing a large proportion of young adults, who relied exclusively on cell phones.
- The sample selected for the poll may also reflect a cultural bias. For instance, most national polls in the United States are conducted only in English. As a result, the opinions of the Spanish-speaking population are underrepresented.
- Many polls only capture the mood of the moment that it was conducted. As a result, results may be subject to drastic swings as new events and information shape public opinion.
- Polls often overlook the depth of conviction on the part of the voters— in other words, how strongly those polled feel about the issue or candidate they favor.
- The wording of the poll also has an impact on its results.

Thus, critical analysis of polls focus on the following questions:

- How old is the poll?
- What is the size of the sample?
- Who sponsored the poll? Polls paid for by news organizations use safeguards not used by parties in the quick polls that candidates and parties use to guide strategy ("Experts Guide Voters," 1992).
- Is the poll state or national? State polls are often a few days older than national polls. Consequently, national polls can detect last-minute trends ("Experts Guide Voters," 1992).
- What is the margin of error in the poll? Because polls ask a sample of the population, the numbers can only approximate the tabulation of the entire target population. Statisticians are able to compute a reasonable "margin of error" for each poll, based on its sample size and methodology. If a poll has a 3 percentage point margin of error, the totals are likely to fall within plus or minus three percentage points— a six point swing. In this case, if a poll reports that a Republican candidate is ahead by two percentage points, the Republican could be ahead as much as five percentage points, or behind by one percentage point.

Obsolete Political Processes

In this media age, a number of established features of the American political system are no longer viable:

- *The Primary System.* The primary system for nominating party candidates was devised in a less sophisticated media era, when politicians could only gain access to voters by traveling around the country and declaring their positions on issues of regional interests and concern. This was also the only means by which the local citizens could hear what the candidates had to say.

    Today, thanks to extensive media coverage, state primaries receive national exposure. As a result, candidates can no longer regionalize their messages but are forced to repeat the same menu of positions on national issues at each stop. As a result, candidates must resort to attack ads and peppy slogans to give their campaigns a fresh and dynamic appearance.

    In addition, because of the national focus on state primaries, the initial contest in New Hampshire assumes an exaggerated importance. The winners of this primary actually receive few delegates However, the winners of these contests are anointed as the frontrunners by the media. In 2008, after the traditional opening primaries in Iowa and New Hampshire in January, 29 states, including California and New York, moved their primaries up to February 5.

- *Electoral College.* In the United States, candidates are not elected by a direct vote of citizens. Instead, elections work according to an Electoral College system, in which voters choose a slate of electors, who select the president and vice president. These electors are not obligated to vote for the slate chosen by his or her state's voters. Consequently, in the case of a closely contested nomination process during the party's convention, the slate may be released from its "official" selection.

    The Electoral College system was devised at a time in which collecting and tabulating votes throughout the nation would have been unwieldy. Transportation Secretary Ray LaHood stated that the Electoral College "is merely a relic of times past, running counter to the democratic process" ("Lawmaker," 1997). However, the media age offers the opportunity for a quick and precise national tabulation of votes.

- *Political Conventions.* Historically, political conventions were gatherings in which a political party's slate of candidates were selected.

However, in the modern political arena, these decisions are reached long before the convention. Instead, the convention has become strictly a media event, filled with scripted speeches, video sound bites, and rehearsed celebrations, and designed to generate momentum for the upcoming campaign.

In addition, digital technology has altered the relationship between politicians and their constituents. In January 2007, Senator Barack Obama announced his exploratory committee for president in a high-resolution video on his Web site. He also used MySpace and Facebook to reach nearly 250,000 young people during the first two months of 2007 (Hochberg, 2007). In 2006, 15 percent of Americans said that they received *most* of their political information online—double the number of the previous midterm election in 2002. Increasingly, candidates are turning to the Internet as a means of connecting with the voters. In the course of the 2012 presidential election, 34 percent of Obama's funding comprised donations of $200 or less, much of it from online donations (Ludwig, 2012).

But as with any channel, the Internet can be used to mislead voters. One example is the use of "link bombs" to discredit candidates. This occurs when opponents engineer a flood of Web links and cross-links to unfavorable content. As a result, negative articles about the candidate are posted at the top of the search rankings.

Information Management

Once in office, politicians must learn to use the media to govern effectively. The Reagan administration was the first to adopt an Information Management approach to governance. David Gergen, director of communications under both Ronald Reagan and Bill Clinton, explains:

> For one of the first times I'm aware of [the Reagan administration], molded a communications strategy around a legislative strategy. We very carefully thought through what were the legislative goals we were trying to achieve, and then formulated a communications strategy which supported them. (Hertsgaard, 1988: 108)

Each Friday, the administrative team discussed upcoming events from an information management perspective. The communications team would prepare its message with an eye on its potential effect on the audience, with the goal of controlling the agenda. As one participant commented, the dominant questions were "What are we going to do today to enhance the image of the president?" and "What do we want the press to cover today, and how?" (Hertsgaard, 1988: 35).

The Reagan Information Management plan consisted of the following strategies:

- *Consider the broader implications of the story.* The communications team looked at stories from the following perspective: How does information support (or threaten) the goals of the administration?
- *Respond promptly.* The Reagan team was poised to react swiftly to news stories. The communications team then framed a position that downplayed negative aspects of the story.
- *Act with unanimity.* Once an official line was decided on, it was important that the position be presented with consistency.
- *Manage the flow of information.* Recognizing that the news media depends on government as a primary news source, the Reagan team made available information that they wanted conveyed and simply withheld information that they weren't prepared to discuss. As Sam Donaldson observed, "So our options are, do nothing or do it their way" (Hertsgaard, 1988: 27).
- *Limit reporters' access.* Limiting access to the president reduced the chances that the administration would lose control of its agenda. It was vital, however, that Reagan maintain the *image* of accessibility. Thus, the president was often in view of the cameras but conveniently out of earshot (e.g., photo opportunities and boarding noisy helicopters).
- *Speak in one voice.* All administration officials presented a unified, official message. Consequently, it was imperative that the Reagan team remained discreet and loyal. This in part accounts for the Reagan administration's obsession with leaks within the administration.
- *Make it easy on the press.* The Reagan communications team provided the media with prepackaged information (which, of course, presented their perspective on events). The working assumption was that the press was inherently lazy and would accept the administration's version of news if it made their jobs easier. As Deputy Chief of Staff Michael Deaver explained, "If you didn't have anything, they'd go *find* something" (Hertsgaard, 1988: 52).
- *Mislead when necessary.* The Reagan team engaged in a "disinformation" strategy, in which they deliberately released false information to achieve political goals. For instance, in 1986, the press discovered administration memos confirming that the Reagan administration had

released disinformation about Muammar Gadhafi to destabilize the Libyan government (Weinraub, 1986).

Media Literacy Strategies

Political communications and cultural myths. Many political ads capitalize on our cultural self-image—not what we are, necessarily, but how we see ourselves, what we'd *like* to be.

- *Mythic Past.* Ads featuring a nostalgic look backward at mythic America have an enormous appeal, particularly during times of cultural stress. This appeal is designed to project the legacy of the past onto the future. Politicians talk about the values of small-town America. These ads present a worldview in which voters are empowered; we can make a difference. Our leaders ask for *our* support. Ideals like freedom, hope, and goodness are central to this world of possibilities.
- *The American Dream.* This myth offers the promise of opportunity for the individual, in which success comes to the deserving through hard work and faith in the system.
- *The Romantic Ideal.* Political spots offer a worldview filled with the promise of a better future. Reagan's famous "Morning in America" ads maintained that America's best days were ahead.
- *The Mythic Frontier.* This concept emerged in America in the 19th century, as the settlers spread west. As columnist Maureen Dowd (2006) has observed, modern political rhetoric has drawn from this cultural myth: "After 9/11, Americans had responded to bellicosity, drawn to the image, as old as the Western frontier myth, of the strong father protecting the home from invaders."

Explicit content. Examining the explicit content of political communications is a useful way to uncover fallacies, inconsistencies, and attempts to obfuscate issues or mislead the public. The following rhetorical techniques found in political communications influence how the public responds to issues and candidates:

- *Using selective facts.* In political communications, facts may be used selectively, distorted, or omitted entirely. In the face of a bewildering array of information, facts become meaningless. Truth has thus been reduced to a matter of *faith*—whose facts the public chooses to believe.

- *Misrepresenting* a person's position and presenting it in a form that people will reject.
- *Taking an opponent's words out of context.* Campaign teams routinely comb through comments of their opponents to find comments that can be damaging when taken out of context.
- *Bold assertions* are terms that are employed when politicians make pronouncements without sufficient evidence. Eleanor MacLean (1981) cautions, "Words like 'unquestionably' and 'indisputably' should be looked at very closely, as should such expressions as 'But the truth' is or 'The fact is'. . . . Can such statements be proven?"
- *Evading the question.* In formats such as debates and press conferences, a reporter has only one opportunity to ask a question, with no follow-up opportunity. This enables politicians to evade the question or respond with a nonanswer—that is, a response that does not properly address the question.
- *Downplaying the evidence.* When faced with incriminating evidence, one approach is to minimize its importance by downplaying potentially damaging evidence.
- *Attacking the person, not the argument.* This technique is often used to circumvent the reasoning behind an opponent's position. Much of the focus on character attacks is an effort to discredit the political positions of the opponent.
- *Qualifier.* Words or phrases that qualify, or modify, the meaning of the sentence subtly introduce doubt in a statement. To illustrate, in January 2005, the U.S. military mistakenly dropped a 500-pound bomb on a house outside the northern city of Mosul, Iraq, killing 14 people, including 7 children. The United States issued the following statement: "The house was not the intended target for the air strike. . . . Multi-National Force Iraq deeply regrets the loss of *possibly* [emphasis added] innocent lives." The use of the qualifier undermines the apology by raising doubts about the guilt of those killed in the attack (Wadhams, 2005).
- *Hasty generalizations.* This refers to a technique in which people make assertions based on only a few unrepresentative samplings, arguing that what may be true in one or more specific instances holds true for all cases. MacLean (1981) provides an example:

    If someone says, "Both Bill and Terry were on the first string basketball team; therefore both their younger brothers will probably also be stars," this person has jumped to a conclusion. The generalization is based on only two examples. Besides, human beings are too complex to be reduced to many generalizations: they often differ as much within a family as not. (p. 84)

Affective Response

Many media messages delivered by politicians are designed to touch the emotions of the average citizen. Formal media rituals, such as the inauguration, press conferences, and the State of the Union Address, are designed o inspire feelings of awe and respect for the members of the government.

In like fashion, political advertising is designed to elicit an emotional response from the voters as a way of shaping their attitudes and voting behaviors. Political ads may be directed at a range of *positive* emotions:

- *Reassurance* appeals promote a sense of confidence about the present. As media consultant Roger Ailes observes, "The candidate who makes the public most secure will win" (Silverblatt, 2007: 86).
- *Patriotic* ads reinforce our faith in our way of life and inspire a sense of pride in who we are.
- Ads for candidates are often designed to inspire *hope* in the audience. Listening to a speech by George W. Bush in February 2000, Ellen Goodman commented, " I counted the word 'hope' until I ran out of fingers" (Goodman, 2000: 87).

Political campaigns may also tap into a wellspring of *negative* emotions, including anger, frustrations, and dissatisfactions. Fear is another powerful emotion used by both political parties. Political ads tap into a range of common fears:

- *Fear of change.* Ads can exploit voters' anxiety about the future. Ads promoting the reelection of an incumbent convey the message that even if the voter wasn't satisfied with the elected official's overall performance, at least he or she was a known commodity.
- *Disenchantment with status quo.* Voting for a change can be an empowering act for the electorate—particularly when they are dissatisfied with current conditions. Even if the politicians are not responsible for a situation, the voters can derive some satisfaction from "throwing the bums out."
- *Fear of differences.* These ads may play on the basic mistrust of differences in American culture. As author George Orwell pointed out in *1984*, an enemy is a useful political device, providing a target for anger and a way of uniting the country. Ads with racist overtones play on this mistrust of difference.

- *Mistrust of politicians.* One constant political theme is based on the notion that whoever is in office is corrupt.

Production elements convey distinct messages about politicians and the political system:

- *Scale.* In American politics, height is often associated with power and authority.
- *Movement* suggests a sense of direction, purpose, and leadership. This might explain why political ads depict the politicians walking in the woods, busily engaged in legislation, and interacting with citizens.
- *Proximity of the camera* can promote feelings of familiarity and trust with the audience. Close-up shots of the candidates create the illusion that we know the candidate well, and inspire public confidence, suggesting that they have nothing to hide.
- *Angle.* Shooting up at a politician evokes feelings of respect and competence.
- *Word choice* can be an effective way to gauge the political ideology of the communicator. In addition, examining the *frequency* with which particular words in the media appear can furnish perspective into the themes that the communications team has decided to emphasize.

See also: Information Management Analysis; Nonverbal Approach to Media Analysis; Production Analysis Approach; Rhetorical Analysis

References

Barbaro, M., & Parker, A. (2011, December 30). "Voters Examining Candidates, Often to a Fault." *New York Times,* A1.

Dowd, M. (2006, November 11). "Drapes of Wrath." *New York Times.* Retrieved from http://www.nytimes.com/2006/11/11/opinion/11dowd.html

"Experts Guide Voters on Weighting Polls." (1992, October 30). *St. Louis Post-Dispatch*, 4C.

Goodman, E. (2000, February 3). "Passionate Conservatism: 1 Compassionate Conservatism." *St. Louis Post-Dispatch.* Retrieved from http://www.stltoday.com

Herbert, B. (1998, July 19). "The Donor Class." *New York Times.* Retrieved from http://www.nytimes.com/1998/07/19/opinion/in-america-the-donor-class.html?scp=1&sq=Herbert,%20Bob.%20(1998,%20July%2019).%20The%20Donor%20Class&st=cse

Hertsgaard, M. (1988). *On Bended Knee.* New York: Farrar, Straus & Giroux.

Hochberg, A. (2007, February 19). "Obama, Clinton Vie for Black Support in S.C." National Public Radio. Retrieved from http://www.npr.org/templates/story/story.php?storyId=7489278

Ifill, G. (2003, November 10). "Money and Politics; Online News Hour." *NewsHour with Jim Lehrer Transcript*. Retrieved from www.pbs.org/newshour/bb/politics/july-dec03/dean_11-10.html

"Lawmaker Calls Electoral College 'Relic'." (1997, September 7). *St. Louis Post-Dispatch*, 5E.

Ludwig, M. (2012, November 6). "Big Money Breakdown: Why 2012 Is the Most Expensive Election Ever." *Truthout*. Retrieved from http://truth-out.org/news/item/12561-big-money-breakdown-why-2012-is-the-most-expensive-election-ever

MacLean, E. (1981). *Between the Lines*. Montreal: Black Rose Books.

Sabato, L. (1981). *The Rise of the Political Consultants*. New York: Basic Books.

Seelye, K. Q. (2008, April 14). "Blogger Is Surprised by Uproar over Obama Story, but Not Bitter." *New York Times*. Retrieved from http://www.nytimes.com/2008/04/14/us/politics/14web-seelye.html?pagewanted=all

Silverblatt, A. (2007). *Media Literacy: Keys to Interpreting Media Messages* (3rd ed.). Westport, CT: Praeger Publishers.

Wadhams, N. (2005, January 9). "Mistaken Airstrike Kills at Least 5; U.S. Acknowledges Bombing Wrong Building." *Washington Post*. Retrieved from www.washingtonpost.com

Weinraub, B. (1986, October 4). " 'Disinformation' Risks Reagan's Credibility." *St. Louis Post-Dispatch*, 1B.

Worthington, R.L. (2004, November 2). "The Polemics of Polls." St. Louis Post-Dispatch. www.stltoday.com.

Production Analysis Approach

Production analysis is an approach to media literacy focusing on the use of production elements in the construction of media messages as a way to develop a critical understanding of media. The production analysis approach consists of three lines of inquiry.

The first line of inquiry is based on the supposition that production choices employed in the construction of media presentations convey distinct messages. The production choices made by media communicators (e.g., what to include or omit, camera angle, and selection of images) reinforce the manifest message of the media communicator or convey independent messages. For instance, the "shaky-cam" camera technique commonly employed in television commercials has an amateur appearance, conveying the impression that the program is authentic and spontaneous, so that the audience should believe what they see. Advertisers hope that the stylistic messages of authenticity will be transferred to the product.

At the same time, media production analysis reinforces the media literacy principle that *media is a construction of reality*. Through the examination of production choices (e.g., what to include or omit, word choice, and selection of images), students learn for themselves how stylistic considerations reinforce the manifest message of the media communicator. Production choices therefore affect how audience members respond to a media presentation.

A second line of inquiry is based on *contextual media aesthetics*, a line of inquiry developed by media scholar Herbert Zettl. Media aesthetics—standards of beauty applied to production elements—establish a *context* that influences an individual's responses to media presentations. To illustrate, the violent style found throughout media programming represents an aesthetic code that is as powerful as the violent content in a media presentation. Zettl (1998) explains,

> It is of little surprise, therefore, that even "media-literate" observers, while watching a hockey game with their children, might become concerned about promoting violence only when the game becomes especially rough or when the players begin to fight. However, they may not have noticed the perceptual violence of a series of quick zooms and high-volume sounds in the preceding cartoon of frolicking birds in a park. (p. 3)
>
> . . . Television violence should now include aesthetic criteria, which may well reveal that aesthetic violence in an otherwise tranquil scene may be more damaging to the viewer than a fistfight between the good guys and the bad guys. (p. 84)

Contextual aesthetics focuses on ways in which an individual's responses to media messages are influenced by production elements such as lighting, color, camera position, and editing. In addition, contextual aesthetics examines how these production elements interact with one another in the construction of media messages.

Aesthetic context affects the *cognitive mapping* processes in individuals—ways in which individuals access, store, and recall information. As applied to the comprehension of media content, cognitive mapping establishes a *preferred reading* that dictates how an audience member responds to a media presentation. Zettl (1998) provides the following example:

> Imagine, for a moment, a scene in which we see a fifth grader alone in his room, doing homework despite the rather late hour. Soft music comes from the small radio on his table. Most likely, we will perceive

the scene as rather peaceful and tranquil. We might admire the young student for having the discipline to get the assignment done before going to bed. We all know that it was the soft music that set the tone, the context by which we judged all other aesthetic elements as contributing to the tranquility of the scene: the warm, low-key lighting with its prominent shadows, the red accent of one of the books, and the comforting smile of the stuffed lion sitting on the book shelf. (p. 88)

Zettl has introduced a four-tiered hierarchical media literacy model, based on contextual media aesthetics, which is designed to facilitate decoding and encoding of media messages:

- *Level 1* consists of basic production elements such as lighting, editing, and camera proximity and their aesthetic fields. Thus, this first level focuses on the cues that these production elements convey to the audience.
- *Level 2* focuses on the impact of aesthetic and associative contexts of production elements and how these production elements are structured for specific purposes.

    Zettl (1998) provides the following example of how a child is influenced by the aesthetic context of a television commercial for cereal:

    After popping out of [a] cereal box, a little toy car transforms immediately into a hot sports car. The high-revolution engine sounds accompany the morphing sequence even before the red racer hurls toward the television screen. When the child finally succeeds in persuading Mom to buy the cereal, the high-powered sports car turns out to be only three inches long and promptly breaks when she tries to extract the toy through the sticky cereal.

    The bright (highly saturated) red color and the engine sounds set the high-energy context. The fast movement of the car toward the screen creates an additional high-energy vector and a plausible change to a big car. (p. 6)

- *Level 3* focuses on cognitive maps (described above), as well as the critical analysis of genres.
- *Level 4* addresses the issue of contextual media aesthetics as it applies to qualitative and quantitative approaches to media literacy analysis that analyze the messages being conveyed through media content. However, as Zettl (1998) notes,

Even this level is no longer divorced from contextual media aesthetics and its influence on the encoding and decoding of content messages. After all, it is not just content alone or form alone that shapes our media experience, but the synthesis of both. (p. 85)

A third line of inquiry involving a production approach to media literacy analysis involves the psychological principle of *cognitive fluency*. Cognitive fluency is a psychological principle in which individuals prefer to think about things that are easy, as opposed to those that are difficult—particularly in situations in which they are called on to evaluate information. Psychologist Adam Alter explains,

Every purchase you make, every interaction you have, every judgment you make can be put along a continuum from fluent to disfluent. If you can understand how fluency influences judgment, you can understand many, many, many different kinds of judgments better than we do at the moment. (Bennett, 2010)

Studies demonstrate that the ease with which an individual processes media content can affect how he/she responds to information:

- When subjects were exposed to a series of nonsense words or abstract geometric patterns, they expressed a preference for material that had been presented multiple times and therefore felt familiar (Bennett, 2010).
- Individuals thought that familiar faces, animals, or objects were more attractive than things that were unfamiliar (Bennett, 2010).
- People tend to answer a questionnaire less honestly if it appears in a font that is difficult to read than if it is more legible.
- When presenting people with written descriptions of moral transgressions, increasing the contrast between text and background to make it easier to read the description made people more forgiving (Bennett, 2010).

Thus, the *style* of a media presentation—putting information into rhymes, avoiding jargon that is difficult to pronounce, and employing visually friendly fonts—can affect the audience's receptivity to the message. The easier and more welcoming and positive the style of the presentation, as reflected in the production choices of performers and colors, the more inclined people are to accept the content. In addition, there is a correlation between how easy it is to "read" the message and how positively the audience feels about the media communicator (Bennett, 2010).

A study conducted by Piotr Winkielman and others found a correlation between a person's mood and the desire for fluency. Winkielman found that unhappy people were most responsive to familiar, "fluent" presentations. In contrast, happy people are less reliant on familiar, fluent stimuli than sad people:

> When we're unhappy, we seek out stability and a sense of safety; when we're happy, we're more open to the unfamiliar. Fluent things are familiar, but also boring and comfortable. Disfluency is intriguing and novel. Sometimes you like comfort food, like when you're sick. And usually you want to try something new when you're more comfortable. (Bennett, 2010)

Applying the principle of cognitive fluency can provide insight into the construction of media messages. To illustrate, the 2010 Super Bowl ads, which appeared in the midst of a tough economic climate, were populated by familiar faces: Don Rickles for Teleflora, Abe Vigoda and Betty White for Snickers, Chevy Chase and Beverly D'Angelo for HomeAway, Lance Armstrong for Michelob Ultra, Charles Barkley for Taco Bell, Brett Favre for Hyundai, Kool and the Gang for Honda, and Bill Withers for the Dante's Inferno video game. Even old, familiar childhood toys sock monkey and a teddy bear sold a new generation of kid products. Reporter Stuart Elliott (2010) commented on the effectiveness of nostalgia and familiar messages in these Super Bowl ads:

> The salutes on Sunday to bygone eras reached a peak perhaps not seen since the last time Fonzie said "Ayyyy" on "Happy Days." The reason is, of course, the economy and the belief along Madison Avenue that tough times call for familiarity rather than risks. . . . Sigh. It may take an economic recovery, even a boom, for Super Bowl advertisers to start taking chances again.

See also: Audience Analysis; Media Production Approach, Media Literacy Education

References

Bennett, D. (2010, January 31). "Easy=True." *Boston Globe*. Retrieved from http://www.boston.com/bostonglobe/ideas/articles/2010/01/31/easy__true/

Elliott, S. (2010, February 8). "In Super Bowl Commercials, the Nostalgia Bowl." *New York Times*. Retrieved from http://www.nytimes.com/2010/02/08/business/media/08adco.html

Zettl, H. (1998, Winter). "Media Aesthetics: Contextual Media Aesthetics as the Basis for Media Literacy." *Journal of Communication 48*, 81–95.

Rhetorical Analysis

Rhetorical analysis refers to certain linguistic techniques applied to media presentations to influence target audiences. *Rhetoric* refers to the use of language designed to influence the attitudes and behaviors of the target audience. Aristotle declared that rhetoric is "the ability, in each particular case, to see the available means of persuasion" (Ramage & Bean, 1998).

To illustrate, consider the following examples of a *polysyndeton*, a rhetorical device involving the repetition of conjunctions, which is often found in literature. Consider the following passage from John Milton's epic poem, "Paradise Lost":

[He] *pursues his way, / And swims, or sinks, or wades, or creeps, or flies*. (Shawcross, 1971)

Behold, the Lord maketh the earth empty, and maketh it waste, and turneth it upside down, and scattereth abroad the inhabitants thereof. And it shall be, as with the people, so with the priest; as with the servant, so with his master; as with the maid, so with her mistress; as with the buyer, so with the seller; as with the lender, so with the borrower; as with the taker of usury, so with the giver of usury to him. (Isaiah 24:1–2)

The syntactical repetition establishes a dramatic rhythm that establishes connections and patterns between the various elements in the sentence. Robert A. Harris (2009) observes,

The rhetorical effect of polysyndeton . . . [is] a feeling of multiplicity, energetic enumeration, and building up. . . . The multiple conjunctions of the polysyndetic structure call attention to themselves and therefore add the effect of persistence or intensity or emphasis to the other effects of multiplicity. The repeated use of "nor" or "or" emphasizes alternatives.

Some rhetorical devices, like polysyndetons, have become outmoded, along with the literary formats in which they appear. At the same time, new rhetorical techniques have been devised to influence audiences. In addition, the evolution of different media systems (e.g., the Internet) and applications (e.g., journalism and advertising) have broadened the uses of rhetorical devices.

Recognizing these rhetorical devices empowers individuals to form independent judgments about the appearance of these devices in the media. Richard Paul and Linda Elder (2004), authors of *The Thinker's Guide to Fallacies: The Art of Mental Trickery and Manipulation,* observe,

> The [public's] goal should be to recognize fallacies for what they are—the dirty tricks of those who want to gain an advantage. You will withstand their impact more effectively when you know these fallacies inside and out. When you are inoculated against fallacies, your response to them is transformed. You ask key questions. You probe behind the masks, the fronts, the fostered images, the impressive pomp and ceremony. You take charge of your own mind and emotions. You become [increasingly] your own person. (p. 34)

Certain rhetorical devices, detailed below, are characteristic of particular media applications.

Advertising

When a product is indistinguishable from other brands on the market (or is harmful to the public), advertisers rely on the following rhetorical devices to sway the public.

A *syllogism* is a subtle line of reasoning that seems true but is actually false or deceptive. For example, a magazine ad for California Almonds has the slogan, "California Almonds: A Tasty Snack & Nutritional Feast." The copy of the ad presents the following logic:

1. Roasted almonds are tasty.
2. Roasted almonds are healthy.
3. So, "Whenever the urge to snack comes out, make sure California almonds are in." The ad suddenly shifts from promoting the *product* (almonds) to a particular *brand* (California Almonds). The question to be asked, then, is: Even if you believe the first part of this syllogism, couldn't you then buy another brand of almonds?

The Big Promise involves making a claim that is far beyond the capacity of the product. As an example, Axe deodorant emerged as the top-selling brand in less than four years by promising to help men attract more women. An ad on the Axe Web site presents a mob of bikini-clad women charging madly toward the beach, until they come upon a man who is spraying himself with Axe deodorant. The ad slogan suggests a cause–effect relationship between the deodorant and attracting women: "Spray More. Get More. The Axe Effect."

Although advertisers would argue that this rhetorical device is intended simply as a figure of speech, some customers interpret the Big Promise literally. In 1997, a man sued Anheuser-Busch for false advertising, claiming that the implicit promises of success with women did not come true for him, causing physical and mental injury and emotional distress ("Examples of 'Crazy' Cases," 1997).

Thus, a critical analysis of the big promise focuses on the following questions:

- What promises does the ad make with regard to the product?
- Which promises can the product reasonably keep?
- Which promises are beyond the capabilities of the product?

Hyperbole is a part of the American storytelling tradition, which relies on exaggeration or absurd overstatement to make a point. In a country of seemingly limitless resources, Americans magnify events and locations for emphasis and dramatic effect. Examples include George Washington's coin toss across the Delaware River and tales of legendary lumberjack, Paul Bunyon, and his blue ox, Babe. This literary device also capitalizes on the American competitive spirit. Everything we do (or own) must be the best. However, advertising sometimes makes claims (e.g., "Milwaukee's finest beer") that, in fact, are merely statements of opinion.

A *simile* is a literary device that refers to a direct comparison between two things; such comparisons are introduced by *like* or *as*. According to William Lutz (1989), similes are employed "whenever advertisers want you to stop thinking about the product and start thinking about something bigger, better, or more attractive than the product." For instance, a wine that claims "It's like taking a trip to France" is designed to induce the consumer into romantic reverie about Paris instead of thinking about the taste of the wine.

Parity statements refer to ads that are worded in a way that suggests that a product is unique, when what the ad is *actually* stating is that the product is indistinguishable from its competition. For example, author Rick Berkoff (1981) points out that the Personna Double II slogan ("There is no finer razor made. Period.") could be rephrased as follows: "Personna Double II: It's no better than its competition. Period."

Unfinished statements make implied claims that advertisers are unable to stand behind. Instead, they leave it to the consumer to complete the statement. Lutz (1989) provides the following examples:

- Batteries that "last *up to* twice as long." (Twice as long as what?)
- "You can be sure if it's Westinghouse." (Just exactly what we can be sure of is never explained.)
- "Magnavox gives you more." (This slogan never details what you get more of.)

Qualifier words impose conditions that undermine the claims of the ad. Phrases such as "some restrictions apply" are quickly flashed on the TV screen or are uttered with inhuman rapidity by the announcer, suggesting that this information is inconsequential. In print ads, warnings are placed away from the normal field of vision. In addition, the backgrounds of the ads blend in with the qualifier words.

Political Communications

Politicians rely heavily on the following rhetorical devices to promote their policies and candidates.

Spin is a rhetorical strategy in which communicators present their particular interpretation, or "spin," on a story to influence how information is presented, reported, and received by the public. The objectives of spin control are to (a) establish the agenda (what is important about the event or issue), (b) influence the public's attitudes toward the event or issue, and (c) in cases of negative news, to deflect responsibility for the event or issue in another direction.

As a result, one should assume that much of the information that is released to the public has been "massaged" by media professionals to support the agenda that they represent. For example, media consultants and political cronies typically circulate among the press after presidential debates, announcing that their candidate has "won" the event. Paul and Elder (2004) observe,

The critical consumer expects the media to put spin on all articles of news in keeping with the prejudices of the audience they "serve." He must consider alternate ways of looking at the issues in the news media, alternative ways of thinking about what is being presented, what is most significant about it, and how it is best represented. (p. 34)

Redirection is a rhetorical technique in which a media communicator uses language that shifts the audience's attention from a problematic issue to a more innocuous or acceptable subject. An example can be found in the ad campaign for Nike, the ubiquitous shoe empire. In the early 1990s, Nike moved its manufacturing operations from the United States to countries in Asia as a cost-saving measure. The labor abuses for the company have been well documented. As an example, the chemical solvent toluene was measured at levels of between 6 and 177 times the amount allowed by Vietnamese law. Consequently, 77 percent of the workers suffered from respiratory problems caused by prolonged exposure to this chemical (McKissack, 1997).

However, the advertising campaign for Nike substitutes an altogether different message of control and empowerment: *Just do it*. Nike's ideology has been redirected back onto itself, so that it promotes empowerment even while it continues its unfair labor practices abroad.

Misrepresenting a person's position and presenting it in a form that people will reject. In 2009, the Democrat-sponsored health care legislation included language directing Medicare to cover a voluntary discussion with a doctor once every five years about living wills, power of attorney, and end-of-life treatment preferences. Significantly, the majority of congressional Republicans supported similar provisions for terminally ill elderly patients in the 2003 prescription drug bill. But then Betsy McCaughey, former lieutenant governor of New York, mischaracterized these end-of-life provisions in the health care legislation, claiming that mandatory counseling session would tell people how (and when) to end their lives. Two days later, this deceit found its way into Republican politicians' statements. House Republican leader John Boehner declared, "This provision may start us down a treacherous path toward government-encouraged euthanasia if enacted into law" (Blumenauer, 2009). Former Governor Sarah Palin then coined the term *death panels* on her Facebook page to describe this provision. A significant portion of the public believed these allegations—quite naturally, given the stature of the politicians raising the charges—and as a result, supported the Republican position.

Take your opponent's words out of context. In this rhetorical technique, political campaign staffs find comments by the opponent that can be damaging when taken out of context. For example, during the 2012 presidential election, Republican hopeful Mitt Romney released a campaign ad consisting of a clip of President Barak Obama giving an address, declaring, "If we keep talking about the economy, we're going to lose."

Left out was the context for Mr. Obama's comment, which he made during the 2008 presidential election—he was talking about his opponent, Senator

John McCain of Arizona. What Mr. Obama said was, "Senator McCain's campaign actually said, and I quote, 'If we keep talking about the economy, we're going to lose.' "

Three-Card Monte. The three-card monte is a sophisticated rhetorical technique, used in the following way:

- The media communicator makes a false statement.
- He then qualifies it by admitting its falsehood.
- He then reiterates the first statement, reinforcing the idea in the minds of the public.

As an example, columnist Paul Krugman (2005) points out that the George W. Bush administration employed this rhetorical technique as part of its Iraq War strategy, linking terrorism and the Iraq War:

Speeches about Iraq invariably included references to 9/11, leading much of the public to believe that invading Iraq somehow meant taking the war to the terrorists. When pressed, war supporters would admit that they lacked evidence of any significant links between Iraq and Al Qaeda, let alone any Iraqi role in 9/11—yet in the next sentence it would be 9/11 and Saddam, together again.

Shifting the burden of proof. This legalistic sounding term refers to when a party in a dispute has the responsibility to prove what he or she asserts. This concept is also tied to the notion of whether a person is presumed innocent or guilty. A prime example of shifting the burden of proof occurred during the 2008 presidential campaign when Republican candidate John McCain submitted an article to the *New York Times* in response to an editorial written by his opponent, Barak Obama. McCain criticized Mr. Obama for his lack of specificity with regard to his plan for Iraq: "I am dismayed that he never talks about winning the war—only of ending it," Mr. McCain wrote.

However, the Editorial Department of the *New York Times* asked Senator McCain for revisions before they would consent to publishing the article. As *New York Times* reporter Kate Phillips explained, "McCain criticized Obama for lack of specifics, but refused to provide his own specifics" (Snow, 2002).

Scapegoating is a psychological process in which people blame others for their own deficiencies or problems. The group targeted for scapegoating generally consists of people who are powerless or those who have been the object of prejudice or derision.

During the 2008 presidential election, both candidates had their own scapegoats to blame for their own limitations. For instance, in an article in which he had been put on the defensive, Republican John McCain lashed out at trial lawyers:

> [Obama] also criticized Mr. McCain over his opposition to legislative action to help bring wages of women up to those of men. The McCain campaign fired back, saying the legislation to do so would have been a boon to *trial lawyers*, who have supported Mr. Obama's campaign. (Cooper, 2008)

Shifting the argument. Media communicators have learned to change their rationale for a policy if the given reason falls flat. The success of this reconstruction of reality relies on (a) the limited attention span of the audience, (b) the convincing nature of the media communicator, and (c) media support. To illustrate, the rationale for going to war in Iraq shifted several times during the course of the war:

- Iraq possessed "weapons of mass destruction."
- Saddam was complicit in the terrorist attack of 9/11.
- Saddam was an evil man who gassed his own people.
- The war would bring democracy to Iraq.

Substitute fact for truth. Political rhetoric often confuses the public by presenting isolated facts as truth. For example, during the 2010 midterm elections, a common campaign theme of Republicans was that the 2009 health care bill contained a $500 billion Medicare "cut" that decreased benefits for Medicare recipients. But in fact, the law stipulates that guaranteed Medicare benefits won't be reduced. The "cut" to which the Republicans referred involved *reducing the future growth* of Medicare spending over the next 10 years by about 7 percent. Indeed, the legislation adds some *new* benefits, such as improved coverage for medications (Henig, Novak, & Jackson, 2010).

In the face of this bewildering array of information, facts become meaningless. Truth has been reduced to a matter of *faith*—whose facts to believe.

Spurious evidence refers to cases in which a politician cites evidence in support of a position; however, this proof does not actually support the point being made. To illustrate, during the 2010 midterm election in Wisconsin, Republican Reid Ribble claimed, "I lost my health insurance and doctor because of Obamacare." But research by Bill Adair of PolitiFact.com revealed that Ribble's insurance company actually had planned to get out of the health insurance business years before this piece of legislation was passed (Adair, 2010).

Counterfeit sources. Television ads for political candidates often "prove" their charges by flashing information about the source on screen. However, this sometimes only provides the *appearance* of validity. Bill Adair (2010) of PolitiFact.com conducted research and found the following:

> In many ads, small white letters flash on the screen showing the date of a newspaper story or a congressional vote. Those citations are supposed to back up the claim, but we have often found they were only tangentially related or provided little evidence.

Evasive rhetorical techniques. The following rhetorical techniques are designed to avoid difficult or embarrassing questions.

- *Jokes:* answering a hard question with a joke that deflects the query.
- *Diversions:* providing such long and detailed answers that the speaker manages to avoid the thrust of the question.
- *Talking in Vague Generalities:* Paul and Elder (2004) explain, "It is hard to prove people wrong when they can't be pinned down. So instead of focusing on particulars, manipulators talk in the most-vague terms they can get away with" (p. 34).
- *Ignoring the Main Point.* Politicians typically appear in venues in which their statements go unchallenged, such as debates or press conferences in which the journalist asks only one question. As a result, they can simply ignore the question and provide an answer to a different topic.

See also: Advertising—Media Literacy Analysis; Journalism; Political Communications, American

References

Adair, B. (2010, October 28). PolitiFact.com. Retrieved October 2011.

Berkoff, R. (1981). "Can You Separate the Sizzle from the Steak?" In G. Rodman (Ed.), *Mass Media Issues*. Chicago: SRA.

Blumenauer, E. (2009, November 15). "My Near Death Panel Experience." *New York Times*. Retrieved from http://www.nytimes.com/2009/11/15/opinion/15blumenauer.html?pagewanted=all

Cooper, M. (2008, June 24). "McCain Proposes a $300 Million Prize for a Next-Generation Car Battery." *New York Times*. Retrieved from http://www.nytimes.com/2008/06/24/us/politics/24campaign.html

"Examples of 'Crazy' Cases." (1997, December 3). *West News*, p. 7.

Harris, R. A. (2009, December 24). *A Handbook of Rhetorical Devices.* Retrieved from http://virtualsalt.com/rhetoric.html

Henig, J. Novak, V., & Jackson, B. (2010, October 26). "Whoppers of Campaign 2010: The Biggest Falsehoods of the Midterm Elections." *New York Times.* www.nytimes.com.

Krugman, P. (2005, February 18). "Three-Card Maestro." *New York Times*, A23.

Lutz, W. (1989). *Doublespeak.* New York: Harper and Row.

McKissack, F., Jr. (1997, November 21). "Nike Memo Details Abuses in Asian Factory." *St. Louis Post-Dispatch*, p. C19.

Paul, R., & Elder, L. (2004). *The Thinker's Guide to Fallacies: The Art of Mental Trickery and Manipulation.* Tomales, CA: The Foundation for Critical Thinking (www.criticalthinking.org).

Ramage, J. D., & Bean, J. C. (1998). "A General Summary of Aristotle's Appeals." In *Writing Arguments* (4th ed.), pp. 81–82. Needham Heights, MA: Allyn & Bacon.

Shawcross, John T. *The Complete Poetry of John Milton.* Garden City, New York: Anchor Books, Doubleday and Company, Inc. Revised Edition, 1971. Pp. 252–253.

Snow, D. A. and C. L. Phillips. "United Nations: Human Development Report." New York: United Nations/Oxford Press, 2002.

Scenario Development Approach to Media Analysis

Scenario development is a qualitative approach to media analysis that promotes reflection and discussion of media content by positing a number of possible "scenarios," based on certain assumptions, predetermined elements, and uncertainties. The scenario development approach is an example of a *disparate approach to media analysis* in which the principles of another discipline are applied to the interpretation of media content.

Scenario development was designed as a tool for thinking about options in the face of uncertainty and creating better strategies as a result. Scenarios are stories that present possible futures, based on present conditions and circumstances. The test of a good scenario is not whether it ultimately portrays the future accurately—whether it really "comes true"—but whether it enables an organization to learn and adapt to changing circumstances.

Scenarios provide a platform from which to envision new implications, opportunities, and challenges that would not have been visible otherwise. Peter Schwartz has identified the following characteristics of scenarios:

- Scenarios are a set of powerful stories about how the future might unfold in ways relevant to your organization or issue.
- You are thinking out loud and speculating, not making an argument requiring high burdens of proof.
- But an even more important result is a greater sense of the context in which your organization operates today and the contexts in which it may operate in the future.
- The scenario thinking process can be used on its own for setting strategic direction, catalyzing bold action, accelerating collaborative learning, or alignment and visioning. (quoted in Scearce, Fulton & Global, 2004: 23)

Scenario development was established after World War II as a method for military planning but soon was adapted as a business analysis tool. Juergen H. Daum notes (2001),

The U.S. Air Force tried to imagine what its opponents might do, and to prepare alternative strategies. In the 1960s, Herman Kahn, who had been part of the Air Force effort, refined scenarios as a tool for business prognostication. . . . Scenarios reached a new dimension in the early 1970s, with the work of Pierre Wack, who was a planner in the London offices of Royal Dutch/Shell in a newly formed department called Group Planning. Pierre Wack and other planners were looking for events that might affect the price of oil. And they found several significant events that have been in the air. . . . So to operate in an uncertain world, managers need to be able to question their assumptions about the way the world works, so that they could see the world more clearly. The purpose of scenario planning therefore is, to help managers to change their view of reality, to match it up more closely with reality as it is, and reality as it is going to be. The end result, however, is not an accurate picture of tomorrow, but better decisions about the future. (pp. 2–4)

According to author and consultant Diane Scearce (Scearce, Fulton, & Global, 2004), scenario development enables planners to see *the big picture*—the ability to look beyond immediate demands and peering far enough into the future to see new possibilities, asking "What if?" (p. 29). This exercise is used by organizations to stretch thinking, clarify choices, and create additional options before settling on a strategic plan, articulating a vision, or crafting a theory of change. Consequently, the scenario thinking process can help organizations develop robust pictures of future success and strategies to move toward a desired future.

Scenario development also promotes looking at the world from multiple points of view. Scearce (Scearce, Fulton & Global, 2004) explains,

> The introduction of multiple perspectives—diverse voices that will shed new light on your strategic challenge—helps you better understand your own assumptions about the future, as well as the assumptions of others. . . . [Multiple perspectives] exposes you to new ideas that will inform your own perspective. . . . The result is . . . you see new threats and opportunities that you otherwise may have missed. (p. 15)

Process—Scenario Development

The process of scenario development begins by clarifying the decision to be made or the issue to be explored. Reporter Lawrence Wilkinson (1995) explains,

> Scenario planning begins by identifying the focal issue or decision. There are an infinite number of stories that we could tell about the future; our purpose is to tell those that matter, that lead to better decisions. So we begin the process by agreeing on the issue that we want to address. Sometimes the question is rather broad (What's the future of the former Soviet Union?); sometimes, it's pretty specific (Should we introduce a new operating system?). Either way, the point is to agree on the issue(s) that will be used as a test of relevance as we go through the rest of the scenario-making process.

Scenario development is designed around a *matrix*—a continuum of possible scenarios ranging between two extremes. A matrix consists of two driving forces laid out on an axis (an arrow pointing in two directions) with end points that describe two possible alternative outcomes, then crossing the two axes to create a matrix with four quadrants (see chart). Each quadrant should describe a possible scenario.

Chris Ertel, Dianne Scearce, and Katherine Fulton provide the following explanation of the matrix procedure, using the scenario of health care as an example:

> There are a number of different approaches to developing a scenario set. The most common is to picture your critical uncertainties on two axes that frame the poles of what seems possible in your time frame. For instance, a group working in health care might cross an uncertainty about the financial and regulatory environment with an uncertainty

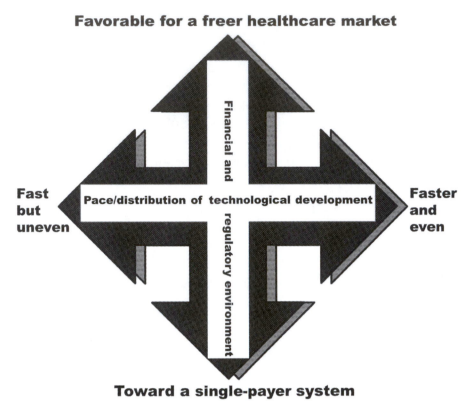

Scenario development is a qualitative approach to media analysis that promotes reflection and discussion of media content by positing "scenarios," based on certain assumptions and predetermined elements. Scenario development is designed around a matrix, in which two crossed axes create four quadrants, each representing a possible scenario. Media presentations offer an alternative to the use of the matrix in scenario development. (Graphic by Lisa Marcus)

about the pace and distribution of technological development to create a scenario matrix. Try to envision the four scenarios created by this matrix. What if the financial and regulatory environments are favorable toward a freer market in health care, and technology develops and spreads at a fast and even pace? This could be a world with a highly automated and efficient infrastructure for managing and administering health care with broad array of choice and a relatively weak safety net. As you try to envision each of the four possible scenarios, ask yourself: Do the combined critical uncertainties produce believable and useful stories of the future? The scenarios should represent a range of alternative futures, not simply a best, worst, and most likely world. (Ertel, Searce, & Fulton, and the Global Business Network community, 2004)

After considering the four possible scenarios, ask:

- Do the combined critical uncertainties produce believable and useful stories of the future? The scenarios should represent a range of alternative futures, not simply a best, worst, and most likely world.
- Use the scenarios to test current strategies. Would they work in all these worlds that you can imagine, or do they work best in only one of two of them?

Assumptions

After developing a set of plausible scenarios, the next step involves identifying the *underlying assumptions* that form the basis of individual scenarios. How, then, do different assumptions result in alternate narratives? Diane Sceare explains,

> Stories . . . resonate in some ways with what people already know and leads them from that to question their assumptions of how they see the world. (p.15)

Analysis of fundamental assumptions focuses on the following questions:

- What are the significant assumptions that are the foundation of a scenario?
- How have these assumptions contributed to the success (or failure) of the scenario? Explain.
- Would revising particular assumptions improve the scenario? Explain.
- Compare/contrast the fundamental assumptions that comprise different scenarios

Andrew Blau (2004: 57) adds these points of analysis regarding assumptions:

- Are your current strategies built on assumptions about the future that you now see as possible but not inevitable?
- If so, what are your alternatives in case the future you have been betting on is not what happens? And are there things you are doing now that wouldn't make sense in some or all of the worlds you have imagined?

Leading Indicators

Tracking *leading indicators* reveals whether a particular scenario is beginning to come to pass. Leading indicators are signs of potentially significant change—events to watch for that indicate which scenario (or combination of scenarios) is actually unfolding. These indicators can be subtle. Scearce provides the following example:

> A leading indicator may be something obvious like the passing of a debated piece of legislation, or it may be a subtle sign of a larger societal shift, like a rise in volunteerism. If the leading indicators are selected carefully and imaginatively, they will serve as powerful signals that you need to adapt your strategy to the changing environment. As leading indicators are identified, strategies can be put in place to respond to the emerging reality. (Scearce & Fulton, 2004: 34)

The effective use of *leading indicators* consists of the following steps: (a) identifying leading indicators, (b) monitoring these leading indicators as a way to track shifts in the environment, and (c) adjusting strategy accordingly.

According to Scearce, it is worthwhile to "look for small changes upstream that will lead to major shifts downstream":

> Pierre Wack, who pioneered the use of scenarios in the corporate world in the early 1970s, often told the story of how the flooding of the plains in northern India could have been anticipated by watching the amount of glacial run-off at the mouth of the Ganges River high up in the Himalayas. Similarly, U.S. state budget shortfalls of 2003 would have come as no surprise if you had looked "upstream" and seen the budgetary reallocations that were inevitable after the terrorist attacks on September 11, 2001. (p. 23)

Media Presentations as Scenarios

Media presentations offer an alternative to the use of the matrix in the process of scenario development. Like scenarios, media presentations offer depictions of the future or an alternative present—a world different from our own, but with recognizable links to the real world, based on certain characteristics of the present. As Arie de Geus, one of the pioneers of scenario thinking, has observed,

> Scenarios are stories. They are works of art, rather than scientific analysis. The reliability of (their content) is less important than the types of conversations and decisions they spark. (Scearce & Fulton, 2004: 30)

Peter Schwartz adds,

> A scenario planner is like an author or a scriptwriter (sic). The planner
> considers the converging forces in the plots and attempts to understand
> how and why they might intersect. From that analysis and understand-
> ing, coherent pictures of alternative futures are constructed. These are
> the scenarios. (Blyth & Young, 1994: 2)

In his definition of scenarios, Ivan Klinec (2004) identifies characteristics
that also typify media presentations:

- Scenarios are stories.
- Scenarios are maps of the future.
- Scenarios are mental maps.
- Scenarios are narratives.
- Scenarios are pictures.
- Scenarios are models.
- Scenarios are sets of indicators.
- Scenarios are tools.
- Scenarios are art.

Functions

A number of *functions*, or purposes, are served by both scenarios and media
presentations. One of the major functions of scenario development is preparing individuals to contend with *change*. Indeed, scenario development was
first established as a strategy that would enable organizations to prepare for
the future. Thus, a scenario/plot is an attempt to answer the following set of
questions related to change:

- What issues related to *change* does the media presentation express?
- What are the major forces of change affecting the scenario, and how
  should the (affected populations) prepare to face these changes?
- How might things change?
- How can we adapt to these changes?

In like fashion, many media presentations provide an arena in which
change can be envisioned and actualized. For instance, the science fiction
genre focuses on visions of the future or an alternate present. Consequently,
a useful line of inquiry begins by identifying forces of change in the narrative

that have an impact on the characters, such as *technology*, *politics/ideology*, and *environment*. These forces are combined in different ways to create a set of diverse stories about how the future could unfold.

Thus, narratives serve as scenarios that comment on issues related to *change*:

- What changes are depicted in the narrative?
- What accounts for these changes?
- What issues related to change does the media presentation express?
- What messages are conveyed in the media presentation with regard to how individuals can adapt to these changes?

The Business Council of Australia (2004), for example, created several scenarios for Australia in 2025.

This scenario explores the consequences of a breakdown in trust between people and institutions. It is a story of reform fatigue and complacency. Australia's capacity to grow is undermined by a loss of faith in institutions. This leads to a lack of long-term, targeted investment and reform, resulting in economic decline and social crises. A re-examination of the nation's political structures ensues. In this world, global prosperity is no guarantee of prosperity for Australia. Efficient and effective government and trust between people and institutions are critical to building the nation's capacity.

An example of a media presentation that comments on issues of change in Australia can be found in the *Mad Max* film trilogy (1979–1985). This trio of films was directed by George Miller and launched the career of Mel Gibson. Two critiques of the film by fans that appear on the Internet Movie Database Web site (IMDb; www.imdb.com) comment on the bleak worldview of the films as a result of contemporary decisions, such as the national energy policy:

[*Mad Max*] is set in the near future of a bleak, dystopian and impoverished Australia that is facing a breakdown of civil order primarily due to widespread oil shortages. (This is not explained in this film but in the sequel, *Mad Max 2: The Road Warrior*.) Central to the plot is a poorly funded national police unit called the Main Force Patrol (MFP), which struggles to protect the Outback's few remaining townspeople from violent motorcycle gangs. The MFP's "top pursuit man" is a young police officer, Max Rockatansky (Mel Gibson), badge number MFP4073.

Thus, critical analysis of a media-presentation-as-scenario can address the following lines of inquiry:

- As a platform to explore a topic of common interest to a large group. As a "visioning" vehicle that raises awareness around a desired future or strategic direction and as a way to consider the *big picture*. "Scenario planning can serve as an exercise to stretch thinking, clarify choices, and create additional options before settling on a strategic plan, articulating a vision, or crafting a theory of change" (Scearse & Fulton, 2004).
- As a tool for setting strategic direction. Media presentations can identify those factors in the present that lead to a clearly determined future. Like the film *The Terminator*—coming from the future (scenario) back to the present.
- Consider the assumptions that make up the foundation of these scenarios. Blyth and Young (1994) explain, "Scenario planning forces people to examine their deeply held assumptions and to think through what they would do if the future turns out to be quite different from what they expected."
- As a means of tracking shifts in the environment, as a microcosm of larger societal changes.
- As a means of identifying visions of success, as well as strategies to move toward this successful future.
- As a means of promoting social action. According to Scearse (2004), scenario development is a way to "rehearse" responses to possible futures: "Ask yourself: "What if this scenario is the future? What actions would I take today to prepare? Are there significantly different implications in each scenario?" (p. 30).

See also: Function

References

Blau, A. (2004). *Deep Focus.* San Francisco, CA: National Alliance for Media Arts and Culture.

Blyth, I. M., & Young, R. (1994). "Scenario Analysis—A Tool for Making Decisions for the Future." *Evaluation Journal of Australasia*, 6 (1).

Business Council of Australia. (2004). *Aspire Australia 2025*. Retrieved from http://www.bca.com.au/Content/94498.aspx

Daum, J. H. (2001, September 8). "How scenario planning can significantly reduce strategic risks and boost value in the innovation value chain." *The New Economy Analyst Report*. Retrieved from http://www.juergendaum.com/news/09_08_2001.htm

Klinec, I. (2004, September 16–18). "Strategic Thinking in the Information Age and the Art of Scenario Designing." Institute for Forecasting, Slovak Academy of Sciences. Retrieved from http://www.futurologia.sk/strategicthinking.ppt

Scearce, D., Fulton, K., & the Global Business Network community. (2004, July). "What If? The Art of Scenario Thinking for Nonprofits."

Schwartz, P. (1996). *The Art of the Long View*. New York: Currency Doubleday.

Wilkinson, L. (1995, September). "How to Build Scenarios." *Wired* (Scenarios 1.01 Special Edition). Retrieved from http://www.wired.com/wired/scenarios/build.html

Search Engine Optimization

Some of the articles on the Internet that appear to have an informational or entertainment function are actually designed to generate advertising profits through a strategy called Search Engine Optimization (SEO). Internet ad companies place these articles with the purpose of generating "hits" (i.e., the number of times that people access the article), thereby raising their client's profile on search engine lists—and their online advertising rates.

Thanks to the Internet, masses of people have become adept at conducting research without realizing it. As an example, an individual interested in taking a vacation in Mexico may go online and call up a search engine (quite often Google). After typing in the words "Mexico" AND "Resort," a list of vacation spots in Mexico appear. The order in which the sites appear on the Google list conveys messages about the sites; the sites at the top of the list are considered the most important and legitimate. Consequently, Internet ad companies produce these articles with the purpose of generating "hits" on key words and links, thereby raising their client's profile on search engine lists.

Consequently, the order of appearance on a search engine list has enormous financial implications. Daniel Ruby (cited in Segal, 2011) cites the following illustration:

> As an example, the Keyword Estimator at Google puts the number of searches for "dresses" in the United States at 11.1 million a month, an average based on 12 months of data. So for "dresses" alone, the number one (*sic*) Google site may have been attracting roughly 3.8 million visits every month . . . 34 percent of Google's traffic went to the number one result, about twice the percentage that went to number two.

Thus, companies strive to make it to the top of the list. The ways in which an individual or organization will "optimize" the chances that a person conducting a computer search will find them is known as SEO.

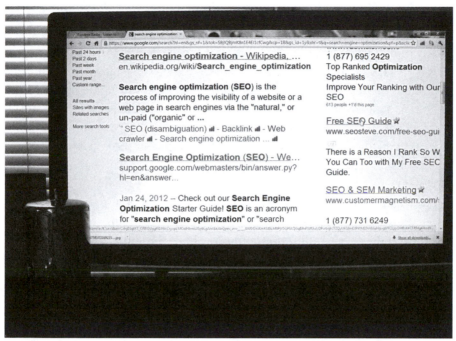

The order in which items appear on search engine sites like Google is determined by a complex set of mathematical algorithms. Search Engine Optimization is the process in which keywords are placed in articles and code on Web sites as a way to boost a company/product in search result listings. (Photo by Lisa Marcus)

In some cases, the hierarchy of a site is a result of *white hat optimization*, which simply means that the site at the top is an uncontested authority in the field. However, other rankings may be a result of "black hat" optimization, what reporter David Segal (2011) refers to as "the dark art of raising the profile of a Web site with methods that Google considers tantamount to cheating."

For example, Google maintains a confidential set of criteria that determines its ranking of sites. Google's algorithm takes into account more than 200 "signals," which the company will not discuss (Chace, 2011). However, two criteria that are evident are *keywords* and *links*. As a result, a thriving cottage industry of *content farms* has emerged in which individuals are paid to write articles that are loaded with keywords and links to boost the ranking of their client on Google. The content farm receives a fee each time that a keyword or link is activated.

To illustrate, J. C. Penny has been heavily involved in this "black hat" practice of planting keywords and links in online postings. Segal explains,

2,015 pages with phrases like "casual dresses," "evening dresses," "little black dress," or "cocktail dress." Click on any of these phrases on any of these 2,015 pages, and you are bounced directly to the main page for dresses on JCPenney.com. Some of the 2,015 pages are on sites related, at least nominally, to clothing. But most are not. The phrase "black dresses" and a Penney link were tacked to the bottom of a site called nuclear.engineeringaddict.com. "Evening dresses" appeared on a site called casino-focus.com. "Cocktail dresses" showed up on bulgariapropertyportal.com. "Casual dresses" was on a site called elistof banks.com. "Semi-formal dresses" was pasted, rather incongruously, on usclettermen.org. There are links to JCPenney.com's dresses page on sites about diseases, cameras, cars, dogs, aluminum sheets, travel, snoring, diamond drills, bathroom tiles, hotel furniture, online games, commodities, fishing, Adobe Flash, glass shower doors, jokes, and dentists—and the list goes on.

Certain clues and cues signal that material on the Internet is part of an SEO strategy:

- Instructional articles lend themselves to search engine optimization. Reporter Zoe Chace (2011) observes, " 'How-to' sites are very desirable to advertisers, for one simple reason: The content doesn't have an expiration date. It stays fresh. . . . [In addition] the material is thin, with a minimum of research." However, as Chace notes, "You can tell that whoever was writing it was trying to finish it as quickly as possible in order to get the tiny amounts of money they're making for doing these stories."
- Look for repetition of keywords.
- Follow the links.
  ○ Do they all go to the same site?
  ○ Do they connect with a site that is unrelated to the subject of the article?
- Most important, consider the *function,* or purpose behind the appearance of the article on the Internet. Although the manifest function may be information or entertainment, the latent function is to generate profit.

See also: Digital Media Literacy; Function

References

Chace, Z. (2011, April 22). "Web's 'Content Farms' Grow Audiences for Ads." NPR Morning Edition. Retrieved from http://www.npr.org/2011/04/21/135514220/webs-content-farms-grow-audiences-for-ads

Segal, D. (2011, February 12). "The Dirty Little Secrets of Search." *New York Times*. www.nytimes.com

Sectors, Media Literacy

Media literacy is a broad-based movement, originating from a number of different perspectives: education, professional, and public policy community-based, and media arts.

Education Sector

Media literacy as an academic discipline began with the film, TV, and visual communications movement in the 1930s. Educators began to recognize that nonprint media employed unique visual and aural language frameworks to encoded information. The ability to read the "text" of a motion picture, television program, advertisement, or photograph, for example, became important in expanding the definition of literacy.

Canadian media literacy scholar John Pungente (1989) identified nine key factors for the successful implementation of media literacy educational programs:

1. Media education must be a grassroots program, and teachers need to take a major initiative in lobbying for this important dimension in the curriculum.
2. Educational authorities must support such programs by mandating the teaching of media studies within the curriculum, establishing programs and guidelines.
3. Faculties of education must hire staff capable of training teachers in this area; they must also be prepared to offer special courses in media education.
4. In-service training at the school district level must be an integral part of program implementation.
5. School districts need consultative staff members who can work with teachers developing media studies programs and establish communication networks.
6. Suitable textbooks and audiovisual materials must be readily available.
7. Support organizations must be established for the purposes of workshops, conferences, dissemination of newsletters, and the development of curriculum units.

8. There should be appropriate education instruments developed, geared to the special characteristics of media students.

9. Because media education involves such a diversity of skills and expertise, there must be a collaboration between teachers, parents, researchers, and media professionals.

Professional Sector

Organizations established by the newspaper, film, and television industries have developed programs designed to promote critical understanding of content. The professional media sector can be a powerful and effective voice for media literacy outreach, lending valuable expertise and legitimacy to media literacy programs.

Organizations of media professionals with interests in media literacy include, for example, Creating Critical Viewers, Newspaper Association of America Foundation, Show Coalition, and Taos Film Festival. In some cases, media professionals work in partnership with educational institutions, community groups, or media literacy organizations.

Public Policy Sector

The public policy sector refers to the wing of the media literacy movement designed to democratize the communications environment. The discipline of media literacy focuses attention on the impact of ownership and regulations on media content. Consequently, organizations have been formed to analyze the political and economic impact of the established media system and identify strategies to implement change. In some cases, public policy organizations work in partnership with educational institutions, community organizations, or media literacy associations to promote changes in media policies. Some areas of attention include the following:

- Intellectual property and copyright
- Net neutrality
- Campaign finance laws
- Antitrust legislation to break up the media oligopolies
- Free expression policies
- Reviewing Federal Communications Commission mandates and policies
- Regulations to preserve individual rights in the digital landscape
- Legislation to broaden and diversify media ownership

Public policy organizations involved in media literacy activities include the Center for Digital Democracy, Free Press, Electronic Privacy Information Center, and Center for Digital Government.

Community-Based Sector

The community-based sector plays a significant role in supporting communities through its local media. Community media outlets solidify a community by celebrating the distinctive aspects of a culture. As an example, WWOZ, the community radio station in New Orleans, is one of the most popular radio stations in the region. In August 2011, John Goldstein, musician and former resident of New Orleans, observed, "Anybody who appreciates Louisiana culture listens to the station" (pers. comm.). The station promotes activities, broadcasts live events, and sponsors the annual Jazz Festival. Programs also feature New Orleans music and musicians.

In addition, many community media have established media literacy programs in their communities. These outreach efforts originate with community groups, religious organizations, public access groups, and privately funded organizations targeting audiences that typically are not the focus of academic institutions. For instance, in St. Louis, the community radio station, KDHX, has developed media literacy educational outreach programs for schools and church programs.

Media Arts Sector

Media arts programs can promote media literacy through both production and critical analysis. The production of independent video productions can provide insight into the construction of meaning through the process of creating media. In addition, creating videos can encourage self-discovery and growth through artistic expression. Analysis of independent media arts videos can provide insight into cultural perspectives and issues rarely addressed in mainstream media.

Media arts organizations include 911 Media Arts Center, L.A. Freeway, Minnesota Center for Arts Education, Arch City Chronicle, National Alliance for Media Education, and VID KID CO.

See also: Careers, Media Literacy; Marieli Rowe, "On the Genesis of Media Literacy in the United States" (Thread 2); Kathleen Tyner, "The Role of Media Literacy in the Media Arts" (Thread 2)

Reference

Pungente, J. (1989). Originally written for *Media Literacy Resource Guide: Intermediate and Senior Divisions.* Ontario, Canada: Ontario Ministry of Education.

Significant Developments, U.S. Media Literacy Education

Media literacy educator Frank Baker has identified the following significant developments in the discipline of media literacy in the United States.

1919 The Society for Visual Education, Inc. (SVE) is established as a for-profit educational publisher dedicated to the use of new technologies in teaching. In 1919, the technology is the 35mm motion picture. (http://dssmhi1.fas.harvard.edu/emuseumdev/code/emuseum)

1921 *Visual Education* journal first published by the SVE, the group of educators who built alliances with new entrepreneurs selling film projectors and equipment to schools. Articles written by classroom teachers demonstrated the design of lesson plans designed to give practice in English composition, to develop standards by which to judge motion pictures and to promote appreciation for the technique of the motion picture as contrasted from the play and the story. (http://www.xtimeline.com/timeline/History-of-Media-Literacy)

1922 Motion Picture Producers and Distributors of America in charge of administering the Hayes Code film censorship system.

1929–1932 Payne Fund Studies, early research into effect of movies on children's behavior.

1929 *Motion Pictures in the Classroom; An Experiment to Measure the Value of Motion Pictures as Supplementary Aids in Regular Classroom Instruction* is published by Houghton Mifflin.

1930 Motion Picture Production Code is created, spelling out acceptable and unacceptable content for motion pictures.

1935 American Association of University Women (AAUW) based in Madison, Wisconsin, begins a monthly newsletter, *Better Broadcast News.*

1942 The *Good Listening* newsletter debuts in Madison, Wisconsin.

1949 The Fairness Doctrine is enacted by the Federal Communications Commission.

1951 *The Mechanical Bride*, Marshall McLuhan's book about advertising, is published.

1953 American Council for Better Broadcasts (ACBB) forms in Madison, Wisconsin.

1954 National Council of Teachers of English (NCTE) establishes The Committee for the Study of Television, Radio and Film.

ACBB holds its first annual conference in Columbus, OH.

English Language Arts—Films for Classroom Use handbook is distributed nationwide.

1955 The phrase *media literacy* is first used in an issue of the ACBB's regular newsletter. (http://www.xtimeline.com/timeline/History-of-Media -Literacy)

1957 Vance Packard authors *The Hidden Persuaders.*

1958 CBS broadcast journalist Edward R. Murrow, in a speech to the Radio TV News Directors, declares: "This instrument [television] can teach, it can illuminate; yes, and it can even inspire. But it can do so only to the extent that humans are determined to use it to those ends. Otherwise it is merely wires and lights in a box." (http://dssmhi1.fas.harvard.edu)

1960 John Kennedy and Richard Nixon meet in the first of three "live" televised debates.

The Impact of Educational Television is written by researcher Wilbur Schramm.

1961 *Television and the Teaching of English* by Neil Postman is published.

Television in the Lives of Our Children, edited by Wilbur Schramm, is published.

Newton Minow labels television "a vast wasteland." (http://www.xtime-line.com)

1962 Historian Daniel Boorstin writes *The Image: A Guide to Pseudo-events in America.*

1964 *Understanding Media* by Marshall McLuhan is published.

A UNESCO (United Nations Educational, Scientific, and Cultural Organization) meeting in Norway lays the framework for "critical viewing skills" education.

A U.S. Senate committee holds hearing on television programming and youth.

1965 The National Council on Teachers of English (NCTE) publishes *The Motion Picture and the Teaching of English.* (http://www.ncte.org/positions/statements/composewithnonprint)

1966 Broadcast historian Erik Barnouw publishes the first (*A Tower of Babel*) of three books about American broadcasting history (*A Golden Web*, 1968; *The Image Empire*, 1970).

1967 *The Medium Is the Message: An Inventory of Effects* by Marshall McLuhan is published.

Researcher George Gerbner starts Cultural Indicators Research Project.

1968 Action for Children's Television (ACT) is formed to improve the quality of children's television.

Joe McGinniss's *The Selling of the President* is published.

1969 Sesame Street educational TV series starts on PBS stations.

The Center for Understanding Media is formed in New York City.

The first visual literacy conference is held in Rochester, New York.

Accuracy in Media (AIM) is founded.

1970 FCC Commissioner Nicholas Johnson authors *How to Talk Back to Your Television Set.*

NCTE passes Resolution on Media Literacy. (http://wwwdev.ncte.org/positions/statements/medialiteracy)

1971 The final TV commercial for cigarettes is broadcast. (www.frankwbaker.com/tobacco_on_television.htm)

Exploring Television: An Inquiry/Discovery Program is published by Loyola University Press.

Glencoe Press publishes *The Celluloid Literature.*

1972 McDougal-Littel publishes *Coping with the Mass Media.*

US Surgeon General forms an Advisory Committee on Television and Violence and issues a report.

1973 NCTE passes resolution "on preparing students with skill for evaluating media."

John Berger's book *Ways of Seeing* is first published in the United States as a companion to the BBC's "visual literacy" TV series of the same name.

The Center for Understanding Media, in collaboration with the American Library Association, publishes *Films Kids Like*.

McDougal-Little publishes *Coping with Television.*

1974 FCC issues Children's TV Report and Policy Statement.

"The Language of Advertising Claims," by Jeffrey Schrank, is published in the March issue of *Media and Methods* magazine.

TV Action Book by Jeffrey Schrank is published by McDougal-Littel.

1975 A Ford Foundation report recognizes the need for mass media education in America's schools.

The NCTE Passes Resolution on Teaching Media Literacy. *(*http://content dm.lib.byu.edu/ETD/image/etd3105.pdf)

Understanding Mass Media textbook is published.

1977 The first issue of *Media & Values* magazine is published by the Center for Media & Values, based in Los Angeles.

Marie Winn's book *The Plug-in Drug* is published.

1978 United States Office of Education (USOE) funds four seed projects for elementary and secondary teachers to teach students critical viewing skills.

Wisconsin Senator William Proxmire quashes critical viewing TV curricula by awarding it a "Golden Fleece" (for wasteful federal spending) (see pp. 3–4, http://utpjournals.metapress.com/content/hr904662v17p3807/full text.pdf).

Doing the Media is published by The Center for Understanding Media.

The Association for Media Literacy is founded—the first comprehensive organization for media literacy teachers in Canada.

1979 The NCTE publishes *The New Literacy: The Language of Film and Television.*

The NCTE establishes its Commission on Media.

How to Treat TV with TLC, The ACT Guide to Children's Television is published.

1980 *Teaching About Television* by Len Masterman published.

Inside Television: A Guide to Critical Viewing is published by WGBH (Boston) and the Far West Laboratory for Education Research and Development.

Critical Television Viewing: A Language Skills Work-a-Text is produced by WNET/Thirteen (New York) and published by Cambridge The Basic Skills Company.

1982 The United Nations Grunwald Declaration on Media Education is enacted. (http://www.unesco.org/education/pdf/MEDIA_E.PDF)

"We must prepare young people for living in a world of powerful images, words and sounds" (UNESCO, 1982).

The U.S. Surgeon General issues a report on TV and violence (10-year anniversary of the original report).

1983 The American Council for Better Broadcasts becomes the National Telemedia Council.

Ogilvy on Advertising is published by adman David Ogilvy.

1984 *Mind and Media: The Effects of Television, Video Games, and Computers* is published.

1985 Neil Postman writes *Amusing Ourselves to Death.*

Teaching the Media by Len Masterman is published.

1986 Fairness & Accuracy In Reporting (FAIR) is founded in New York City.

1988 *Mass Media & Popular Culture*, a Canadian textbook authored by Barry Duncan, is published by Harcourt, Brace, Jovanovich, Canada.

The National Endowment for the Arts (NEA) report *Toward Civilization* says "learning the vocabularies of the arts, including the media arts, is an essential tool for understanding, and perhaps one day communicating, in the medium of television."

The Assembly on Media Arts, part of the National Council of Teachers of English (NCTE) actively publishes a newsletter called "Media Matters" for more than 10 years. The newsletter includes news about media literacy projects, book and film reviews, interviews with experts, and lesson plans.

1989 Ontario Ministry of Education publishes its influential *Media Literacy Resource Guide.*

Bill Moyers: The Public Mind series airs on PBS, and includes programs titled "Consuming Images" and "Illusions of News"

The Center for Media & Values becomes the Center for Media Literacy.

1990 The First North American Media Education Conference, held in Guelph, Ontario, is sponsored by the Association for Media Literacy with the help of the Jesuit Communication.

George Gerbner launches the Cultural Environmental Movement.

Cable in the Classroom magazine is launched; media literacy education is a major focus.

HBO broadcasts the first of three "Buy Me That" programs, coproduced with Consumers Reports Television.

The Children's Television Act is enacted by the U.S. Congress.

1991 *Media & You: An Elementary Media Literacy Curriculum* is published.

Literacy in the Television Age is published.

1992 National Alliance for Media Education (NAME) is formed in Austin, Texas.

The Aspen Institute Leadership Forum on Media Literacy meets and issues a report on media literacy including this succinct definition: "the ability to access, analyze, evaluate and communicate."

How to Watch TV News, is published, coauthored by Neil Postman and Steve Powers.

Visual Messages: Integrating Images into Instruction, authored by David Considine and Jane Healey, is published by Teacher Ideas Press.

The NCTE publishes *Reading the Movies.*

1993 Harvard University hosts the first U.S. Media Literacy Teaching Institute.

The New Mexico Media Literacy Project is formed.

1994 *Screening Images: Ideas for Media Education* by Chris M. Worsnop is published.

Tuning in to Media: Literacy for the Information Age, a documentary hosted by Renee Hobbs and featuring other media educators, is released.

Visual Literacy in the Digital Age, a compendium of essays, is published by the International Visual Literacy Association (IVLA).

The "Taking Charge of Your TV" initiative is started by *Cable in the Classroom*, the National Cable Television Association (now the National Cable & Telecommunications Association), and the National PTA.

1995 Appalachian State University (Boone, NC) hosts the first annual media literacy conference in the United States.

Time Warner Cable and The Learning Channel coproduce education curriculum: "Know TV—Changing What, Why, and How You Watch."

Media Virus: Hidden Agendas in Popular Culture by Douglas Rushkoff is published.

1996 U.S. Telecommunications Act is signed into law.

NCTE/IRA Standards for English Language Arts recommend visual literacy: "Teaching students how to interpret and create visual texts . . . is another essential component of the ELA curriculum." http://www.ncte.org

NCTE passes Resolution on Viewing and Visually Representing as Forms of Literacy (http://www.ncte.org/positions/statements/visualformofliteracy).

Second annual National Media Education Conference is held in Los Angeles.

Harvard University hosts first annual Media & American Democracy Institute for social studies educators.

PBS airs teleconference and documentary, both titled *Media Literacy: The New Basic*.

The National Communication Association (NCA) develops standards for media literacy in K–12 education.

Annenberg Public Policy Center sponsors first Conference on Children and Television (later called Children & Media).

1997 First television content ratings system goes into effect.

The Partnership for Media Education (PME) is created.

The Texas teaching standards for English language arts include media literacy as represented by "viewing/representing."

The NCTE publishes *Reel Conversations: Reading Films with Young Adults.*

Scanning Television videotape series and accompanying curriculum is released by Face-to-Face Media and Harcourt Brace Canada.

The Media Education Foundation releases video *Killing Screens: Media and the Culture of Violence*, featuring researcher George Gerbner.

1998 Robert Kubey writes his essay "Obstacles to the Development of Media Literacy Education in the United States."

Renee Hobbs writes her essay "The Seven Great Debates in the Media Literacy Movement."

Kathleen Tyner authors *Literacy in a Digital World: Teaching and Learning in the Age of Information.*

The third annual National Media Ed Conference is held in Colorado Springs, Colorado.

In the late 1990s, recognizing the growing influence of media and of students' need to "read" media messages, Mid-Continent Research For Education and Learning (McRel) adds two new strands to their national Language Arts standards:

#9: Uses viewing skills and strategies to understand and interpret visual media.

#10: Understands the characteristics and components of the media. (Source: http://www.medialit.org/pdf/mlk/02_5KQ_ClassroomGuide .pdf, p. 11)

1999 Partnership for Media Education sponsors National Media Education Conference (NMEC) in St. Paul, Minnesota.

The first U.S. graduate program in media literacy is established at Appalachian State University, Boone, North Carolina.

The Op-ed "Has Media Education Found a Curricula Foothold?" published in *Education Week*, provides status of media literacy in state teaching standards.

Sex on TV: A Biennial Report to the Kaiser Family Foundation is published. (http://www.kff.org/entmedia/Media-Literacy.cfm)

2000 The "Summit 2000: Children, Youth and the Media: Beyond the Millennium" conference, held in Toronto, Canada, brings together media educators, media producers, and more.

South-Western Educational Publishing produces *Media Matters: Critical Thinking in the Information Age.*

Alliance for a Media Literate America (now known as the National Association of Media Literacy Education) defines media literacy as: "[empowering] people to be both critical thinkers and creative producers of an increasingly wide range of messages using image, language, and sound. It is the skillful application of literacy skills to media and technology messages. As communication technologies transform society, they impact our understanding of ourselves, our communities, and our diverse cultures, making media literacy an essential life skill for the 21st century." (http://namle.net/publications/media-literacy-definitions)

Assignment: Media Literacy curriculum created by Renee Hobbs for Maryland State Department of Education in partnership with Discovery Communications.

Handbook of Children and the Media, summarizing research known to date, is written by Yale University researchers Jerome Singer and Dorothy Singer.

The U.S. Department of Education and National Endowment for the Arts distribute $990,000 in grants to projects in eight states to "help young people better understand and interpret the artistic content of electronic media images—including those that contain violence."

2001 The AMLA sponsors the National Media Education Conference (NMEC), in Austin, Texas.

PBS broadcasts a FRONTLINE documentary *Merchants of Cool* hosted by Douglas Rushkoff.

Sex on TV 2, a report issued by the Kaiser Family Foundation, is published. (http://www.kff.org/entmedia/Media-Literacy.cfm)

The Action Coalition for Media Education (ACME) is formed.

Court TV airs *Mind over Media: Voices from the Middle School*.

2002 "Critically Thinking about Media" report is issued by *Cable in the Classroom* (http://www.ciconline.org/thinkingcritically)

2003 The NCTE issues position statement "Composing with Nonprint." (http://www.ncte.org/positions/statements/composewithnonprint)

NMEC annual conference held in Baltimore, MD.

National Board of Professional Teaching Standards (Adolescent and Young Adult, English Language Arts standards) recognizes the importance of media and visual literacy.

University of Connecticut hosts first annual Northeast Media Literacy Conference.

Sex on TV 3: TV Sex Is Getting Safer is released by Kaiser Family Foundation. (http://www.kff.org)

Media Literacy: Key Facts is released by the Kaiser Family Foundation. (http://www.kff.org)

FactCheck.org Web site is launched, sponsored by Annenberg Public Policy Center.

2004 "Navigating the Children's Media Landscape—A Parent's and Caregiver's Guide" authored by the American Institutes for Research and released by Cable in the Classroom, is released. (http://www.ciconline.org/parentsguide)

The National Council of Teachers of English publishes *Great Films and How to Teach Them*. (http://www.ncte.org)

PBS broadcasts the FRONTLINE documentary *The Persuaders* hosted by Douglas Rushkoff.

2005 First "Leaders in Learning" awards are given by the National Cable TV Association and National PTA; media literacy is one of the award categories.

Generation M: Media in the Lives of 8–18-Year-Olds survey is released by the Kaiser Family Foundation. (Retrieved at http://kff.org/other/event/generation-m-media-in-the-lives-of)

The *Sex on TV 4* study is released by the Kaiser Family Foundation. (http://kff.org/other/event/sex-on-tv-4/)

2006 College Board's Standards for College Success (in English Language Arts/Media Literacy standards) recognize media literacy education:

> "To be successful in college and in the workplace and to participate effectively in a global society, students are expected to understand the nature of media; to interpret, analyze, and evaluate the media messages they encounter daily; and to create media that express a point of view and influence others. These skills are relevant to all subject areas, where students may be asked to evaluate media coverage of research, trends, and issues."

"The Teen Media Juggling Act: The Implications of Media Multitasking Among American Youth" report is issued by the Kaiser Family Foundation. (http://www.kff.org/entmedia/Media-Literacy.cfm)

Action Coalition for Media Education (ACME) holds a conference in Burlington, Vermont. (http://www.acmecoalition.org/acme_summit_2006)

The NCTE publishes John Golden's *Reading the Reel World: Teaching Documentaries and Other Nonfiction Texts.* (http://www.ncte.org)

2007 *Fact Finders: Media Literacy* is the first media literacy book series for elementary students published by Capstone Press.

The NCTE publishes *Lesson Plans for Creating Media-Rich Classrooms.*

The Cost of Copyright Confusion for Media Educators is published by American University, Washington, DC.

2008 The NCTE releases its Position Statement: New Century Curriculum.

2009 The first online issue of *The Journal of Media Literacy* is published by NAMLE.

The K–12 Horizon Report (http://www.nmc.org/horizon) declares the no. 1 critical challenge for schools in the 21st century is "a growing need for formal instruction in key new skills, including information literacy, visual literacy, and technological literacy."

2010 *Generation M2: Media in the Lives of 8- to 18-Year-Olds* study is released by the Kaiser Family Foundation. (http://kff.org/other/event/generation-m2-media-in-the-lives-of)

References

Action Coalition for Media Education. (2006). Retrieved from http://www.acme coalition.org/acme_summit_2006.

Baker, F. Tobacco on Television. (Accessed on July 1, 2012). Retrieved from www .frankwbaker.com/tobacco_on_television.htm

Cable in the Classroom. (Accessed on July 1, 2012). Retrieved from http://www .ciconline.or

Curriculum Standards, National Council of Teachers of English. (Accessed on July 1, 2012). Retrieved from http://www.ncte.org/about/over/standards/110846.htm

Department of the History of Science, Harvard University. (Accessed on July 1, 2012). Retrieved from http://dssmhi1.fas.harvard.edu/emuseumdev/code/emuseum.

Encyclopedia.com. (Accessed on July 1, 2012). Retrieved from http://www.encyclo pedia.com

Grunwald Declaration on Media Education. (1982). Retrieved from http://www .unesco.org/education/pdf/MEDIA_E.PDF

The Henry J. Kaiser Family Foundation. (Accessed on July 1, 2012). Retrieved from http://www.kff.org/entmedia/Media-Literacy.cfm

National Association for Media Literacy Education. (Accessed on July 1, 2012). Retrieved from http://namle.net/publications/media-literacy-definitions

Navigating the Children's Media Landscape: A Parent's and Caregiver's Guide. Prepared for Cable in the Classroom. (Accessed on July 1, 2012). Retrieved from http://www.ciconline.org/parentsguide

Position Statements, National Council on Teachers of English. (1965). Retrieved from http://www.ncte.org/positions/statements/composewithnonprint

Singularity

Media literacy analysis can furnish perspective into the transformative impact of digital media technology on human culture. This vision of the future, in which digital technologies will assume a pivotal role, is called *singularity*.

Media visionary Kim Gordon (pers. comm., 2011) has identified five possible scenarios of the future:

- *Luddite scenario*, in which we begin destroying technology. Although this is hypothetically possible, this is the least likely scenario. Humans have never gone in this direction, no matter how negatively technological change has been perceived.
- *Terminator scenario*, in which the machines rise up in revolt against the human race. In this scenario, humans have lost control of machines. An advanced generation of computers develops subsequent incarnations

of computers that are beyond the capability of humankind. However, as becomes apparent in the Singularity scenario, it is more likely that humans will become the machines. Consequently, there will be no need for machines to rebel.

- *Status quo.* In this scenario, everything remains the same. However, this is an utter impossibility for the human race.
- *Extinction.* Unfortunately extinction of the human race is a distinct possibility. According to this scenario, humans will have damaged the environment so badly that humans cannot survive. A variation of this scenario is that humans develop a deadly virus that we cannot contain.
- *Singularity* refers to a futuristic scenario characterized by an intelligence explosion, brought about largely by digital technology.

Visionary pioneer Ray Kurzweil (2006) describes singularity as a *community*, in which technology will change society in unimaginable ways. Reporter Lev Grossman (2011) explains,

> The Singularity isn't just an idea. It attracts people, and those people feel a bond with one another. Together they form a movement, a subculture. . . . Once you decide to take the Singularity seriously, you will find that you have become part of a small but intense and globally distributed hive of like-minded thinkers known as Singularitarians.

The worldview of the singularity community is defined by the following characteristics:

- *Questioning conventional thinking.* Grossman (2011) declares, "Singularitarians . . . have little interest in the conventional wisdom about anything." Gordon (pers. comm., 2011) observes that now, the world is currently defined by limits—mostly as a result of its own mindset:

> The problems that we face are no longer technological but those of human nature. The limitations currently confounding humankind are largely self-imposed. As an example, our dependence of fossil fuels could be resolved, if we devoted all of our resources and attention to the issue. The system of limits is self-imposed (e.g., fossil fuels). If we devoted all of our resources to alternative energy, this problem would be entirely resolved in five years. Besides solar and wind power, research in photosynthesis simulation is being conducted, which will unleash all of the energy that is produced by the growth of plant life.

- *Belief in a world of possibilities.* However, Gordon, notes that singularity is chiefly distinguished by a *postscarcity* era, in which the humans have transcended their largely self-imposed limitations:

> Heretofore, discussions about the virtual world have resembled science fiction stories. However, we are now at the cusp of a limitless era, in which science fiction is becoming our reality. In a postscarcity era, we have sufficient significant technological answers to our problems—energy, food, education becomes cheap, if not free. Resources (what is thought of as scarce today) becomes bountiful. We're finally at a place that anything we can dream of, we can build. Machines are cheap enough. Bandwidth is cheap enough. Software is mature enough. And communication technology is robust enough that the imagination is, literally, the limit.

The singularity world is characterized by the *springboard effect*, in which ideas spawn better ideas. As an example, one of the instruments of technological change is the principle of *augmented reality*, in which a virtual overlay imposes a "new" reality on the world that we currently experience. Augmented reality software is already available, for use with mobile devices such iPhones. Thus, an individual activates the camera feature in the cell phone and aims at a desired location; the camera then superimposes information about the environment. For instance, by pointing the device at a church, historical and cultural information would appear over the image of the edifice.

The springboard effect is driven by two factors. The first is the communications revolution, in which ideas are broadly shared and expanded on by those involved in the conversation. The second factor consists of technological innovations, which opens an application to new possibilities. For instance, Metaio, a software company, has developed Junaio, the next generation of augmented reality, that is able to create a "new," *integrated reality*. Reporter Christopher Mims (2011) explains,

> Most "real world" augmented reality is primitive, at best. Applications like Layar and "rich storytelling" new media startup TagWhat produce software that can overlay, on your smartphone's camera view, interesting information about places and objects around you, but that's about it. Their interfaces are relatively static, relying on "tags" or pop-ups to provide information, rather than truly integrating their augmented reality with the real thing.

Metaio overlays augmented reality on top of real reality. Junaio (the app) is using a mere phone to: analyze a scene, interpret the distance to objects and the orientation of the phone in 6 dimensions, and project images on top of what it sees—*all in real time*.

. . . This, in short, is what *real* augmented reality looks like. And when it arrives—in conjunction with displays that fit into eyeglasses, which need to improve significantly before they can be used for this application—it will transform our lives as much as PCs and smartphones have, if not more.

From there, the springboard effect challenges conventional thinking, by beginning with the question, *"What If . . .?"* For instance, using the *augmented reality* discussion, the original idea and technology could *springboard* into new potential applications:

○ *What if* you could alter your environment, to enhance your reality?
  • What if you could look at the interior of a house through an "augmented real estate" lens? Augmented reality could preview how you would like to wallpaper your house.
  • What if you could alter your environment to match the Arcadian names in subdivisions (e.g., Babbling Brook Lane)?
○ *What if* the wallpaper changed every so often? Could the overlay device be a pair of augmented reality glasses? Or *what if* the wallpaper changed itself?
○ *What if* this process moved from a cell phone to your human optic nerve, so that the reality that is constructed becomes part of your worldview?

• *Control*. Singularitarians believe that technology enables people to assume control of the evolutionary process. As Grossman (2011) points out, the technology-driven 21st century has already experienced surprising rates of development:

The more you read about the Singularity, the more you start to see it peeking out at you, coyly, from unexpected directions. Five years ago we didn't have 600 million humans carrying out their social lives over a single electronic network. Now we have Facebook. Five years ago you didn't see people double-checking what they were saying and where they were going, even as they were saying it and going there, using handheld network-enabled digital prosthetics. Now we have iPhones. Is it an unimaginable step to take the iPhones out of our hands and put them into our skulls?

According to Kurzweil (2006), the human species will intersect with digital technology to arrive at a new, accelerated stage of evolution in 2045. Grossman (2011) explains,

> There's no reason to think computers would stop getting more powerful. They would keep on developing until they were far more intelligent than we are. Their rate of development would also continue to increase, because they would take over their own development from their slower-thinking human creators. Imagine a computer scientist that was itself a super-intelligent computer. It would work incredibly quickly. It could draw on huge amounts of data effortlessly.

Reporter Ashlee Vance (2010) adds,

> At that point, the Singularity holds, human beings and machines will so effortlessly and elegantly merge that poor health, the ravages of old age and even death itself will all be things of the past.

Singularity is characterized as a period of *exponential* growth, as opposed to the *linear* growth that defines human evolution. Kurzweil predicts that technological progress in the 21st century will be 1,000 times greater than that of the previous century. At that point, exact predictions are impossible, as the future will be shaped largely by powerful computers that exceed humans' ability to forecast possibilities.

But although the exact nature of these exponential changes remains unclear, what *is* known is that singularity will have an impact on a range of human experience:

º *Biological Singularity*. Technology is accelerating both the range and scope of biological projects. Examples include:
  - *The manufacturing of artificial life.* In May 2010, Synthetic Genomics created a bacterial genome from scratch. J. Craig Venter, a pioneer in the human genome industry, hailed the work of his company as "the first self-replicating species we've had on the planet whose parent is a computer" (Vance, 2010).
  - *The extension of human life.* As Grossman (2011) explains, "Biological boundaries that most people think of as permanent and inevitable, Singularitarians see as merely intractable but solvable problems. Death is one of them." Indeed, Singularitarian Peter H. Diamandis, 49, has announced plans to live to the age of 700 (Vance, 2010).
  - *Genetic engineering.* Genetic engineering techniques can serve a range of purposes, such as growing meat in factories rather than

harvesting it from dead animals. According to biologist Andrew Hessel, "I know in 10 years it will be a junior-high project to build a bacteria. This is what happens when we get control over the code of life. We are just on the cusp of that" (Vance, 2010).

o *Medical Singularity.* Medical technology has improved so rapidly that the expected human life span has increased by more than one year per year (Vance, 2010). Sonia Arrison, a founder of Singularity University declares: "One day we will wake up and say, 'Wow, we can regenerate a new liver' " (Vance, 2010).

As an example, Omneuron, a life sciences company, is developing technology that, using noninvasive methods, will allow patients, physicians, researchers, and subjects to visualize and control the functioning of the brain. The company is also exploring applications of functional brain imaging, so that "there can be some quantification of people's levels of depression and pain" (Vance, 2010).

o *Environmental Singularity.* An increasing number of companies are now dedicated to the cultivation of environmentally friendly, renewable energy sources. As an example, Kurzweil and Google cofounder Larry Page, created a renewable-energy plan for the National Academy of Engineering, advising clients that solar power will soon meet all of the world's energy needs. Companies are developing tools that will prevent environmental catastrophes, such as steering hurricanes away from populated areas (Vance, 2010).

Another avenue for energy production is through *human-powered systems*, so that an individual could be his or her own self-contained power supply. Nike is reportedly putting electrical piston systems in the heels of running shoes to convert human energy into a mechanical transportation system.

o *Economic Singularity.* Futurists predict that agriculture and industry will be the arenas of future economic singularities, stimulated by digital technologies. Ashlee Vance (2010) provides the following example:

> Devin Fidler . . . is in the midst of securing funding for a company that will build a portable machine that squirts out a cement-like goop that allows builders to erect an entire house, layer by layer. Such technology could almost eliminate labor costs and bring better housing to low-income areas.

The next stage of economic growth may also be a by-product of other "singularities" such as the environmental and biotech industries.

Economist and visionary Robin Hanson (2008) has predicted that the next economic singularity could increase economic growth between 60 and 250 times.

Ethics

Media literacy is a critical thinking skill that considers the impact of media technologies on individuals and society. Within this context, this discipline considers the ethical implications of this singularity world. Grossman (2011) raises the following ethical questions related to singularity:

- Is a computer conscious, the way a human being is? Or would it just be an extremely sophisticated but essentially mechanical automaton without the mysterious spark of consciousness—a machine with no ghost in it? And how would we know?
- Even if you grant that the singularity is plausible, you're still staring at a thicket of unanswerable questions. If I can scan my consciousness into a computer, am I still me? What are the geopolitics and the socioeconomics of the singularity? Who decides who gets to be immortal? Who draws the line between sentient and nonsentient? And as we approach immortality, omniscience, and omnipotence, will our lives still have meaning? By beating death, will we have lost our essential humanity?
- Underlying the practical challenges are a host of philosophical ones. Suppose we did create a computer that talked and acted in a way that was indistinguishable from a human being—in other words, a computer that could pass the Turing test. (Very loosely speaking, such a computer would be able to pass as human in a blind test.)

Singularity University

Singularity University was established in 2009, with a the following mission:

To assemble, educate and inspire a cadre of leaders who strive to understand and facilitate the development of exponentially advancing technologies to address humanity's grand challenges. (http://singularityu .org)

Funded by Google, Autodesk, ePlanet Ventures, and a group of technology industry leaders, Singularity University is based at NASA's Ames Research Center in Mountain View, California.

The interdisciplinary curriculum emphasizes convergence among different disciplines and technologies:

- Technology Tracks
  - Artificial Intelligence (AI) and Robotics
  - Nanotechnology
  - Networks and Computing Systems
  - Biotechnology and Bioinformatics
  - Medicine and Neuroscience
- Resource Tracks
  - Futures Studies and Forecasting Policy
  - Law and Ethics Finance
  - Economics and Entrepreneurship
- Application Tracks
  - Energy and Ecological Systems
  - Space and Physical Sciences

See also: Cultural Context; Digital Media Literacy; Scenario Development Approach to Media Analysis

References

Grossman, L. (2011, February 10). "2045: The Year Man Becomes Immortal." *Time Magazine*. Retrieved from http://www.time.com/time/magazine/article/0,9171,2048299,00.html

Hanson, R. (2008, September 11). "Economics of the Singularity." *IEEE Spectrum Special Report: The Singularity*. Retrieved from http://spectrum.ieee.org/robotics/robotics-software/economics-of-the-singularity

Kurzweil, R. (2006). *Singularity Is Near*. New York: Penguin.

Mims, C. (2011, August 10). "German Firm Metaio Demonstrates Real Augmented Reality." *Technology Review*. Retrieved from http://www.technologyreview.com/blog/mimssbits/27073/?nlid=nldly&nld=2011-08-11

Singularity University Mission. (2012). Retrieved from http://singularityu.org/about/overview

Vance, A. (2010, June 11). "Merely Human? That's So Yesterday," *New York Times*. Retrieved from http://www.nytimes.com/2010/06/13/business/13sing.html

Social Networking

Social networking refers to the use of mobile media technologies and software to create an ongoing, interactive personal network. Social media such as

Facebook and Twitter have swiftly emerged as an integral part of mainstream culture:

- As of 2010, access to mobile networks was available to 90 percent of the world population.
- Half of Americans have profiles on social networking sites.

Social media have redefined the nature of personal relationships in American culture. For many younger people, *high involvement* interpersonal relationships have been replaced by the *low involvement* "friends" characteristic of social media. But although some critics point to the superficial nature of these "friends," others note that social media teach young children about the value of cultivating social networks. According to social anthropologists, this ability to form communities is fundamental to humans' evolutionary development. Reporter Nicholas Wade (2011) explains,

> The two principal traits that underlie the human evolutionary success are the unusual ability of nonrelatives to cooperate—in almost all other species, only closely related individuals will help each other—and social learning, the ability to copy and learn from what others are doing. A large social network can generate knowledge and adopt innovations far more easily than a cluster of small, hostile groups constantly at war with each other, the default state of chimpanzee society.

At the same time, social media can be a source of emotional disturbances among its teenage audience. Pediatrician Dr. Gwenn O'Keeffe uses the term "Facebook depression" to refer to troubled teens who obsess over online sites (Tanner, 2011). According to O'Keeffe, there are unique aspects of Facebook that can make it a particularly tough social landscape to navigate for kids already dealing with poor self-esteem, including *cyberbullying*. The American Academy of Pediatrics social media guidelines state that online harassment "can cause profound psychosocial outcomes," including suicide (Tanner, 2011).

However, social media are simply a channel of communication, which can be used in a positive or negative fashion. Reporter Lindsey Tanner explains,

> Researchers disagree on whether it's simply an extension of depression some kids feel in other circumstances, or a distinct condition linked with using the online site. Indeed, using Facebook can enhance feelings of social connectedness among well-adjusted kids, and have the

opposite effect on those prone to depression. Dr. Megan Moreno said, "Parents shouldn't get the idea that using Facebook 'is going to somehow infect their kids with depression.'" (Tanner, 2011)

Given how pervasive Facebook and Twitter have become, social networking is being used in a variety of environments. For instance, educational institutions have begun using Facebook as a recruitment vehicle. In addition, restaurants, which rely on repeat customers, are using social media to maintain a loyal customer base. Elizabeth Olson (2011) explains,

> Restaurants and bars thrive on repeat business, but customers increasingly expect more than just good service, food and drinks. They want to be engaged and entertained, and some food establishments are turning to location-based social media to help keep customers happy and loyal.

For instance, Buffalo Wild Wings, a national restaurant chain that features casual dining and televised sports, has launched a media campaign called "Home Court Advantage," involving games and contests. Jeremy Burke, brand manager for Buffalo Wild Wings explained, "We are looking for social engagement. We want them to be able to tell others what they liked—a beer, a garlic flavor. Our goal is to build frequency. . . [As a result of the social media promotion], some 1,300 people checked in during a four-hour period" (Olson, 2011).

Social media have also played an important role in the American political landscape. Facebook has quickly become a feature of local, state, and national campaigns in the United States. During the 2008 presidential campaign, Barack Obama's Facebook network grew to more than 2 million "friends" and served as a solid platform to reach new and undecided voters.

In addition, governments are now employing social media as part of their propaganda campaigns. In 2011, the *Guardian* newspaper of London reported that the United States had developed an "online persona management service" that enabled the military to develop 10 false online personas at once. These identities can be employed to influence conversations through blogs, Facebook posts, and tweets to reflect the government agenda. A military spokesperson said that "foreign audiences would be targeted, as it would be illegal to use the technology on U.S. citizens" (*DemocracyNow!*, 2011).

See also: Media and Social Change; Political Communications, American

References

DemocracyNow! March 18, 2011.

Olson, E. (2011, January 19). "Restaurants Reach Out to Customers with Social Media." *New York Times*. Retrieved from http://www.nytimes.com/2011/01/20/business/media/20adco.html?_r=0.

Tanner, L. (2011, March 28). "Docs Warn About Facebook Use and Teen Depression." Associated Press. Retrieved from http://www.huffingtonpost.com/2011/03/28/facebook-depression-2011_n_841282.html

Wade, N. (2011, March 14). "Supremacy of a Social Network." *New York Times*. Retrieved from http://www.nytimes.com/2011/03/15/science/15humans.html?pagewanted=all&_r=0

Socratic Approach, Media Literacy

The Socratic approach is adapted from a method of inquiry developed by the ancient Greek philosopher Socrates. This qualitative approach to media literacy analysis enables individuals to identify the implicit assumptions behind the messages in many media presentations. This is an example of a *disparate approach to media analysis*, in which the principles of another discipline are applied to the interpretation of media content.

An individual's willingness to challenge established ways of thinking is often inhibited by the pressure to conform to the conventions of society. In addition, the widespread acceptance of prevailing opinions often reinforces the impression that conventional views must be correct and legitimate. Author Alain de Botton (2000) observes,

> Our will to doubt can be . . . sapped by an internal sense that societal conventions must have a sound basis, even if we are not sure exactly what this might be, because they have been adhered to by a great many people for a long time. It seems implausible that our society could be gravely mistaken in its beliefs and at the same time that we would be alone in noticing the fact. We stifle our doubts and follow the flock because we cannot conceive of ourselves as pioneers of hitherto unknown, difficult truths. (p. 13)

Moreover, conventional ideas generally are considered matters of common sense and, consequently, often go unquestioned. Thus, at one time, ideas such as slavery and human sacrifice were customary in ancient cultures. These practices are now considered aberrant and objectionable.

Characteristics of the Socratic Method

The Socratic approach to the analysis of media programming offers an approach for detecting illogical assumptions, beliefs, and values. The Socratic method is *skeptical*, beginning with Socrates' real or professed ignorance of the truth of the matter under discussion. de Botton (2000) explains, "This is the Socratic irony which seemed to some of his listeners an insincere pretense, but which was undoubtedly an expression of Socrates' genuine intellectual humility. . . . Socrates' doubt and assumed ignorance is an indispensable first step in the pursuit of knowledge" (pp. 14–15).

In addition, the Socratic method is *empirical* and *inductive* because abstract principles are examined within the context of specific circumstances. Socrates always tested definitions by recourse to common experience and to general usages. Thus, a definition is tested by drawing out its implications and deducing its consequences.

The Socratic method of inquiry consists of the following steps:

- Focusing attention on a statement that is confidently described as common sense.
- Imagining for a moment that, despite the confidence of the person proposing it, the statement is false. Search for situations or contexts where the statement would not be true.
- If an exception is found, the definition must be false or at least imprecise.
- The initial statement must then be revised to take the exception into account.

    De Botton provides the following example of the Socratic method as applied to a common definition of *success* in Western culture: *Being successful requires money.*
    - Search for situations or contexts where the statement would not be true.
        - Could one ever be without money but still be successful?
        - Could one ever be without money and be successful?
    - If an exception is found, the definition must be false or at least imprecise.
        - It is possible to have money and be unsuccessful.
        - It is possible to be poor and successful.
    - The initial statement then must be modified to take the exception into account, as follows:

        People who have money can be described as successful only if they have acquired it in a virtuous way, and some people with no money can be successful where they have lived through situations where it was impossible to be virtuous and make money. (de Botton, 2000: 14)

Adapting the Socratic approach to the analysis of media programming offers an approach for detecting illogical assumptions, beliefs, and values that are embedded in a media presentation. Consequently, this qualitative approach is particularly effective when applied to media presentations that operate on assumptions, such as advertisements and political communications.

As an example, consider the following television commercial advertising Dr. Pepper, a popular soft drink:

A handsome young man struts down a city street. He is wearing a sleeveless tee shirt, displaying a trendy tattoo on each shoulder. The young man glances behind him; following his gaze, the camera spies two young woman admiring him. The camera again shifts to the young man, who is drinking from a can of Dr. Pepper. The camera then shifts to a shot of a third young woman who clasps her hand to her breast, seemingly breathless at the sight of the protagonist. The next shot catches the reaction of a male doorman, who is visibly impressed by our Dr. Pepper drinker. These visuals are accompanied by the following jingle:

  Lucy, Phoebe, and Sarah Jane,
  All the little ladies driving me insane
  Got me on a leash, Mary Lou in vain
  Leading me around on a ball and chain.

The camera then tilts downward, revealing that the protagonist is a dog walker who has a full complement of canines on leashes. As he rounds the corner, he becomes entangled with an attractive young woman who is also walking a cadre of dogs. This disaster nearly causes the protagonist to spill his soft drink. However, in the last shot, the two are walking down the street together, in sync with the last line of the jingle: "Dr. Pepper—you make the world taste better."

The Socratic approach calls for (a) identifying the implicit assumptions behind the ad and (b) questioning the viability of these suppositions:

- *Being admired by others (most particularly, by members of the opposite sex) is a matter of ultimate importance.*

- ○ Is the young man's happiness dependent on the approval of others?
- ○ Would the young man be unhappy if he wasn't the center of attention?
- *Attractive people are admired, accepted, and considered important.*
  - ○ Is it possible for a person who is not physically attractive to be admired, accepted, and considered important?
  - ○ Is it possible that a physically attractive person might not be admired, accepted, and considered important?
  - ○ Are there attributes other than physical beauty (e.g. integrity, decency, or humor) that could be considered admirable, acceptable, and important?
- *Dr. Pepper is a product that makes people more attractive.*
  - ○ Does drinking Dr. Pepper contribute to the attractiveness of the main character?
  - ○ Would the main character be just as attractive even if he wasn't drinking Dr. Pepper?
  - ○ Would the main character be just as attractive if he was drinking another brand of soft drink or drinking nothing at all?
- *Drinking Dr. Pepper makes life more pleasurable.*
  - ○ Is it possible to experience pleasure without Dr. Pepper?
  - ○ Is Dr. Pepper the only brand of soft drink that can bring pleasure?
  - ○ Is it possible to be unhappy while drinking Dr. Pepper?
- *Drinking Dr. Pepper is key to a successful romance.*
  - ○ Would the romantic encounter have occurred if the character was drinking another brand of soft drink?
  - ○ Would the romantic encounter have occurred if the character was not drinking at all?
  - ○ Is it possible that the romantic encounter may not have occurred even though the young man was drinking a Dr. Pepper?
- *The characters need the product to be happy.*
  - ○ Can the characters be happy without the soft drink?
  - ○ Can the characters be unhappy even if they have purchased a Dr. Pepper?
  - ○ Is the product is "all they need" to be happy?
  - ○ Are other products found in the ad (e.g., the young man's jacket, hair gel, or shoes) also essential for happiness?

Thus, the Socratic method of inquiry discloses a number of illogical suppositions in the commercial that convey disconcerting messages. The worldview of this ad operates according to a hierarchy of appearance, in which physical attractiveness is the dominant criterion for attention, admiration, and romance. In this narcissistic world, the audience—as an extension of the main character—watches as others admire him.

Romance requires finding a partner who is equally attractive, so that they "look good together" walking down the street. Within this context, Dr. Pepper is a magic potion that "makes the world better" by transforming a person's appearance, therefore making romance possible.

However, under rational scrutiny, these product claims must be substantially reduced, as follows: *Dr. Pepper is a soft drink that some people may find pleasurable.*

Lines of Inquiry—Socratic Approach

In addition to the methodology described above, the Socratic approach to media literacy analysis offers several lines of inquiry for the analysis of media and media presentations.

The Contextual Line of Inquiry

The meaning of a narrative is often derived from understanding the context of the presentation. As an example, consider the following television ad for Tyson chicken:

The setting of the commercial is a junior high school dance. The tableau begins with a wide shot, showing young couples dancing. Although several white teenagers can be spotted, the crowd is predominantly African American.

The camera swoops in past the dancers to the far side of the gym, where several girls are standing, talking to each other. However, one tall, solitary figure stands out—a young African American girl in a yellow party dress. The girl looks shyly away from the camera, toward the floor. The camera moves closer to this "wall flower," drawing the attention of the audience and adding to the self-consciousness of this youngster. The narrator then proclaims that this young girl is a symbol of all of the daughters of the parents in the audience: "She's the apple of your eye . . . Your pride and joy." As the camera moves into a close-up of this fragile young lady, the narrator declares, "You'd make sure her heart was never broken . . . if you could."

The camera then fades, moving from her face to a shot of the Tyson Chicken Logo. The narrator smoothly affirms, "You'd give her Tyson— great tasting wholesome quality chicken . . . because you can." The voiceover is accompanied by shots of chicken on a grill, with the words "Quality" and "Wholesome" superimposed on the screen.

At this point, the camera returns to the dance, where we see a young African American boy finally approaching the girl, presumably to ask her to dance. The narrator explains, "It's what you expect from Tyson. And it's what your family deserves."

The Socratic approach calls for, first, identification of the implicit assumptions behind the ad, and then questioning the viability of these suppositions (that is, identifying situations in which the statement would not be true):

- Being a good parent is contingent on being able to protect one's child against all dangers.
  - Can you be a good parent and still be unable to protect your child against all threats?
  - If you are unable to protect your child against all dangers, are you a bad parent?
- It is possible to insulate children from all societal threats.
  - Is it possible that it is not possible to insulate children from all societal threats?
  - Is it possible that being a good parent does not require insulating their children?
  - Is it possible that being overprotective does not prepare children to face societal challenges?
- Good parents can shield their daughters from social disappointments by giving them Tyson's chicken.
  - Is it possible that one's daughter could eat Tyson's chicken and still be disappointed?
  - Is it possible that one's daughter could eat another brand of chicken and avoid social disappointments?
  - Will a person's daughter be able to avoid other disappointments by eating Tyson chicken?
  - Are other products in the commercial (e.g., the party dress or hair products) essential in protecting the young girl?
  - Can other products not seen in the ad (e.g., laundry detergent or toothpaste) help one's daughter avoid social disappointments?
  - Is it possible to be a good parent and not serve chicken for dinner?
  - Is it possible to be a good parent and give another brand of chicken?
  - Is it possible to be a good parent and serve another main course (e.g., a beef or vegetarian dish)?

Thus, the Socratic analysis of the ad exposes an illogical leap from parental love to purchasing Tyson chicken. A latent message in the ad is that even if parents cannot orchestrate the social life of their children to ensure that he or she will never be hurt, at least they can control what their children eat for dinner. Thus, serving Tyson chicken is presented as a symbolic gesture that offers reassurance for stressed-out parents.

But in addition, this ad makes another supposition:

Tyson Foods takes care of the African American community.

In the commercial, Tyson specifically answers the prayers of the African American parents in the audience who have been agonizing over the discomfiture of their "daughter" during the commercial.

In the absence of any context, the question then emerges: *Why* is it important that Tyson Foods convey the message that they take care of the African American community? Research reveals a 2005 news article that provides perspective into this commercial message:

> Black Workers Sue Tyson over "Whites Only" Sign
> *WASHINGTON—The way black workers tell it in the suit . . . , the "Whites Only" sign was posted on the door of the renovated bathroom at Tyson's poultry plant in Ashland, Ala. Only white employees had the keys . . .*
>
> *The regional office of the U.S. Equal Employment Opportunity Commission is also suing Tyson for violating Title VII of the Civil Rights Act of 1964, which prohibits workplace discrimination. The nonpartisan Lawyers' Committee for Civil Rights Under Law also stepped in on the workers' behalf.* (Berry, 2005)

Thus, beyond the commercial message uncovered by the Socratic analysis, the contextual line of inquiry serves as point of departure for research that can provide insight into the messages in a media presentation.

Media Stereotyping Line of Inquiry

The Socratic approach is a particularly useful way to examine media stereotypes, which are based on associations and suppositions applied to particular groups.

The first step involves identifying the initial assumptions behind a media stereotype. To illustrate, one of the initial suppositions of the stereotype of scientists is: "Scientists are dangerous."

Applying Socratic questions challenge the implicit suppositions underlying this supposition:

- Are all scientists necessarily dangerous?
- Is it possible that some scientists are not dangerous?
- Are all dangerous people scientists?

A third step, then, is to examine the appearance of this illogical supposition in the media:

- Where does it appear in media presentations?
- Why does it appear in media presentations?

Images: Socratic Analysis

Although images contain a good deal of information, they are ambiguous. Photos only capture an instant, which may not represent the reality occurring before and after the shot was taken. Who the subjects are, and why they appear in the photo frequently goes unexplained. Moreover, photographs are defined by the arbitrary boundary of the frame, which can either eliminate essential elements or distort their importance.

Within this context, the Socratic approach can help to identify the essential suppositions in the photograph. To illustrate, an ad for Sara Lee bread consists of a photograph of four people (a male and female adult, and two girls), who are smiling broadly at the camera. Superimposed over the faces of the group is a huge slice of white bread, with the center of the piece carved in the shape of a smile, revealing the smiling visages of the two adults. To the right of this photo is the logo, "Sara Lee," which is also shaped in a smile. Below the logo are the following graphics:

A Good Thing
YOU CAN EAT
With a Smile
ON YOUR FACE

Homestyle Goodness
Pure Ingredients
Great Sara Lee Taste

It's Just Better With
Sara Lee

Below these graphics are photos of two loaves of Sara Lee bread.

The ad conveys the message that Sara Lee bread is a wholesome family product that brings happiness to the entire family and, indeed, helps to keep the family together. However, applying Socratic questions helps to identify the implicit assumptions underlying this supposition and raises questions regarding these assumptions.

Supposition 1: This is a family photograph

The four actors strike a pose that fits the portrait of the target audience—a young family situated in a traditional family pose. Further, the "family members" form a human chain of touch, suggesting that the bread is partly responsible for the bonding of the family.

- Is it possible that the people in the photo are not members of the same family?
- Even if these people are members of the same family, is the bread responsible for bringing the family together?

Supposition 2: This is a "found" photograph

The photograph has a natural, "snapshot" feel. The actors are casually dressed, and their poses are informal. Furthermore, the "border" of the snapshot is worn a bit on the edges. However, the composition of the ad is far from casual, consisting of two photos and graphics.

Again, applying Socratic questions challenges the implicit assumptions underlying this supposition:

- Have the technical aspects of the photograph been manipulated to create messages?
  - What lies outside of the frame?
  - Not just a snapshot but a carefully produced studio shot
  - Posing of the actors
- Why has this photograph been taken?
  - Is the purpose of the photo commercial (to sell bread) rather than as a "found" moment of family memorabilia?
  - What is the connection between the major images (the family and the bread)?
  - Is it possible that other factors are responsible for the happiness of the group?

Supposition 3: These people are happy as a result of eating Sara Lee bread

- Is the "smiley bread" necessarily responsible for the happiness of the family?
  - Is the bread genuinely making these people happy, or is this part of the commercial script?
  - Is it possible that other factors might be responsible for the happiness of the "family"?
  - Could other products (e.g., their drinks) be responsible for bringing the family together?
  - Is it possible that another brand of bread could bring the family together?

See also: Iconographic Analysis, Ideological Analysis

References

Berry, D. B. (2005, August 21). "Black Workers Sue Tyson over 'Whites Only' Sign." *St. Louis Post-Dispatch.*

de Botton, A. (2000). *The Consolations of Philosophy.* New York: Pantheon Books, 2000.

Translation Studies

Translation studies offer some useful ways to think about and discuss media presentations. The translation studies strategy is not to be confused with foreign language instruction, such as learning Italian, but instead focuses on how the choices made in translation from one language to another affect meaning.

As international communications becomes more pervasive, this approach can provide considerable insight into the construction of media messages. Global media communicators must be particularly sensitive to the nuances of language when translating text. To illustrate, in 2001, an American reconnaissance plane collided with a Chinese fighter plane over Chinese airspace, causing an international incident. In the collision, the Chinese plane was destroyed, and its pilot was killed. The American fighter plane was forced to land, and its crew was captured. The Chinese government demanded a formal apology from the United States as a condition for returning the American servicemen. The United States refused to apologize, and tensions grew. Finally, after a period of intense negotiations, U.S. Secretary of State Colin Powell issued a formal statement expressing "regret" over the incident.

Fortunately, this translation enabled both sides to save face. For Americans, the connotation of "regret" is an expression of sorrow, without admitting guilt. For the Chinese, this translation of the term admits a degree of culpability on the part of the Americans. William Safire (2002) explained,

> Using the syllable "qian" in his translation of (Powell's) letter . . . allowed the Chinese to infer an admission of wrongdoing. It's the informal alternative to sorrowful, based on sorg, which first appeared in "Beowulf" around 725, meaning "grief, sorrow, care."
>
> Sorry, with its -y suffix—meaning "full of" but also used to form pet names—seems more colloquial than regret. It was seized upon by the Chinese as "a form of apology," enabling them to claim satisfaction.

The issue of *equivalence in translation* is at the core of Translation Studies: is an exact version of the original text possible in translation? Three schools of thought exist with regard to this question: *Yes*, *No*, and a *Middle Way*.

- *Yes*. A literal translation is indeed possible. Translation Studies scholar Susan Bassnett (1998) describes this notion as the *Invariant Core*: "That which exists in common between all existing translations of a single work" (p. 33). There are, indeed, equivalent words and concepts in different languages. For instance, the French word for horse is *cheval*.
- *No*. According to this school of thought, it is not possible to render a faithful translation. As Bassnett (1998) explains, "It is an established fact in Translation Studies that if a dozen translators tackle the same poem, they will produce a dozen different versions" (p. 33).

A number of factors mitigate against a faithful rendering from one language to another. In some cases, words have no counterpart in another language. To illustrate, there is no term for *impeachment* in Russia, because the concept is foreign to its past and present systems of government. At the same time, the lexicon of the United States has no equivalent word for *Propiska*, a Russian term that refers to a national identification card.

In addition, the *form* of a language may not have a counterpart elsewhere. As an example, in 1980, the Australian film *The Gods Must Be Crazy* appeared in Tokyo, Japan, at a theater that catered to an English-speaking audience. But for some reason, rather than simply using the original title on its theater marquis, the management took the Japanese translation of the title and retranslated it *back* into English. Consequently, according to an American film patron, what appeared on the marquis was *Nice to Meet You, Mr. Bushman* (Michael Sprout, pers. comm., April 3, 2012).

Moreover, the *style* of a text may not be translated "accurately" (or as intended) in another culture. Although the words may reflect the intended meaning, translations often lose the rhythm that reinforces the meaning of the text—or conveys another, independent message. Author Michael Cunningham (2010) comments,

> As the author of "Las Horas," "Die Stunden" and "De Uren"—ostensibly the Spanish, German and Dutch translations of my book "The Hours," but actually unique works in their own right—I've come to understand that all literature is a product of translation. They have music. Here's where the job of translation gets more difficult. Language in fiction is made up of equal parts meaning and music. The sentences should have rhythm and cadence, they should engage and delight the inner ear. Ideally, a sentence read aloud, in a foreign language, should still sound like something, even if the listener has no idea what it is he or she is being told.

Finally, symbolic language often has no literal counterpart in another language.

- *Idiomatic* expressions are often tied to the cultural life of a nation and, consequently, cannot be translated into another language. For example, the American term "It's not a picnic" (which means "it's not easy") is unknown in countries that do not engage in this type of social function. Furthermore, American idioms such as "can't get to first base" and "hit a home run" are based on its national pastime, baseball, and make little sense to people who are not familiar with the sport.
- *Slang* expressions are an informal form of a language, which operates outside of the formal syntax and vocabulary of a language. A person receiving formal education in a language would not be exposed to these terms. Consequently, international audiences can easily be confused by slang expressions. Marc Lacey (2003) provides the following example:

  > When a Kenyan asks for a little tea, he may or may not have a hot beverage in mind. Tea is a popular drink here, usually served with healthy helpings of milk and sugar. But "a little tea" is also the slang used by bureaucrats, police officers or anyone else with an

outstretched palm to ask for a bribe. In "Ncluya Kitu Kidogo," a new Kiswahili song that has taken Kenya by storm, Eric Wainaina tells those desiring a little tea to visit a popular tea-growing area in central Kenya. He recommends that those in need of a soda—another word for bribe—refresh themselves with a Fanta.

- The third school of thought maintains that the way to remain true to the *spirit* of the language of origin is by altering the *letter* of the text. For example, in the United States, people often greet one another by saying, "How are you?" This can be confusing to foreigners who might question why someone would inquire about their health and then hurry on without waiting for an answer. The issue, then, becomes one of *loss* and *gain*.
  - What is lost in the translation of a text?
  - What is gained in the translation of a text?

In today's mass-mediated world, translation has become more widespread. Three types of translation are conducted in this mass-mediated environment:

- General information: e-mails, blogs, Web sites, news
- Marketing/advertising
- Global arts: music, films, plays

Products have become more information intensive, requiring instant translation into many languages. For instance, rental cars are equipped with GPS navigation systems, which must be able to provide directions in English, German, French, Chinese, and numerous other languages. Michael Cronin (2003) explains:

A car with a navigation system will need large amounts of geographical data or a pocket scanner which provides elementary translation will contain a considerable amount of linguistic information. (p. 16)

When watching foreign movies, subtitles affect how the audience experiences the film. The attention of the audience is focused on the bottom of the screen to read the subtitle, as opposed to the image on screen. Consequently, audience members cannot focus their attention on the immediate responses of the characters. Furthermore, given the amount of dialogue in a typical script, the subtitles must be condensed. In addition, the subtitles must be coordinated with the images that appear on screen.

Media Literacy Strategies

According to scholars of translation studies, several factors can affect the translation process. These variables can also be applied to the analysis of media presentations.

Function

The function, or purpose behind the translation has an impact on the translation process. The Skapos Theory addresses the issue of function in translation. *Skapos* is a Greek term meaning "aim" or "purpose." It was introduced into translation theory in the 1970s by Hans J. Vermeer as "a technical term for the purpose of a translation and of the action of translating" (Munday, 2003: 78–79). It deals with "a translational action . . . which has to be negotiated and performed, and which has a purpose and a result" (Vermeer, 1989–2000: 221). Jeremy Munday (2003) states: "According to the Skapos theory, the same text may be translated in different ways as a result of the purpose . . . and the commission which is given to the translator." Understanding the purpose behind a translation enables the translator to prioritize what information to include in the translation" (pp. 82–83). Thus, knowing why a narrative is to be translated and its function can have an impact on the way in which text is interpreted. For example, Katharina Reiss feels that it is more important for a metaphor to be retained in the translation of an artistic work ("expressive text") than in an informational narrative (p. 75).

Munday (2003: 75) has identified the following functions of translation:

- Plain communication of facts: information, knowledge, opinions, etc. The language dimension used to transmit the information is logical or referential, the content or "topic" is the main focus of the communication, and the text type is **informative**.
- "Creative composition"; the author uses the aesthetic dimension of language . . . the text type is **expressive**.
- "Inducing behavioral responses": the aim of the appellative function is to appeal to or persuade the reader or "receiver" of the text to act in a certain way. The form of language is dialogic, the focus is appellative and Reiss calls this text type **operative**.
- Audiomedial texts, such as films and visual and spoken advertisements which supplement the other three functions with visual images, music, etc.

To add to the complexity of international translation, the function of a text may be different between two cultures. Reiss cites the example of

Jonathan Swift's classic allegory, *Gulliver's Travels.* Munday (2003) explains, "Originally written as a satirical novel to attack the government of the day, . . . it is nowadays normally read and translated as 'ordinary entertaining fiction'" (p. 75).

In some political communications, words operate as a code, which necessitates that the translation be precise. To illustrate, the 2007 trial of suspected terrorist Jose Padilla focused on the accuracy of translated phone conversations wiretapped by the FBI. Three men were accused of using code words to plan the support of terrorist organizations abroad:

> Defense lawyers at the terrorism trial of Jose Padilla challenged the accuracy of some translations and interpretations used by prosecutors.
>
> In the first day of defense testimony, lawyers argued that some expressions used by terror suspects in conversations wiretapped by the F.B.I. were not code words for waging jihad, or holy war, but rather were common Arabic euphemisms for activities like collecting donations for Muslim orphans overseas.
>
> A professional Arabic translator, Kamal Yunis, told a defense lawyer, Jeanne Baker, that the surreptitiously recorded remarks made by her client, Adham Hassoun, also a terror suspect, were not about buying arms or supporting jihad, as translators and F.B.I. agents had testified for the prosecution, but were references to fund-raising for children whose parents were killed in conflicts like those in Kosovo, Lebanon and Somalia.
>
> Mr. Yunis said that a phone call in 1997 with a Lebanese religious leader in which Mr. Hassoun expressed a desire 'to send you two eggplants' was an expression understood by both men to mean $2,000 in donations for Muslim children abroad. Translators had testified for the prosecution that the eggplants were rocket-propelled grenades bought with Muslims' donations.
>
> Mr. Hassoun's references to 'football' were another way to say someone was 'kicked around,' Mr. Yunis testified, contradicting translations by prosecution experts who said football referred to jihad.
>
> Mr. Hassoun and another defendant, Kifah Jayyousi, were heard using those and other unusual expressions in thousands of hours of calls collected by the Federal Bureau of Investigation over nearly 10 years. (Gentile, 2007)

Another determinant of function involves *who* is engaged in the translation process. According to Justa Holz-Manttari, the major "players" in a translation consist of the following:

- The initiator: the company or individual who needs the translation
- The producer: The individual who writes the translation
- The person who uses the translation; for example as teaching material or sales literature (Munday, 2003: 77)

These players each have their own specific primary and secondary goals. Munday (2003) explains,

> What is functionally suitable has to be determined by the translator, who is the expert in translational action and whose role is to make sure that the intercultural transfer takes place satisfactorily. . . . [The translation] is analyzed solely for its "construction and function profile". . . . The needs of the receiver are determining factors. . . . [For example], a technical term in [the original version] of a manual may require clarification for a non-technical user [of the translation]. (pp. 139–148)

Context

The choice of words in translation takes different forms for different situations. To illustrate, in 2003, French president Jacques Chirac was criticized for rebuking 13 Eastern European countries that had expressed support for the United States' actions in Iraq. Chirac said that these countries "ont manque une bonne occasion de se taire," which was translated in the American and British press as "missed a good opportunity to shut up." Authors Eleanor and Michel Levieux (2003) explain:

> Mr. Chirac's words were a significant notch above [a level of insult]. To be sure, he could have been quite formal and said "ont manque une bonne occasion de s'absentir de tout commentaire" ("refrain from making any comment"), or "garder le silence" or "se garder de s'exprimer" ("keep silent" or "say nothing"). And of course, he also could have taken a much lower road and said "ont manque une bonne occasion de fermer leur gueule" or "de la fermer," which would indeed mean "to shut up." The verb Mr. Chirac chose, "se taire," was neither elegant nor rude, simply neutral.

Computer programs currently are being designed to translate text. Google has adopted a statistical approach in which, by feeding millions of passages and their human-generated translations into the computer, it makes accurate guesses about how to translate new texts. However, the software continues to make errors when confronted with nuances in a language—particularly with business idioms and cultural references. However, computer scientist Rohini Srihari has developed software that recognizes emotions attached to concepts:

> When you are able to figure out what the topic of the conversation is, what kind of sentiment is being expressed around that, that's the goal of what we are trying to do . . . What I want is to determine who are the people, places and things being talked about. Is there an opinion being expressed? Is it a positive or negative opinion being expressed? (Joyce, 2011a)

Cultural Context

Cultural context can play an enormous role in the translation process. As an example, the native language of Finland includes a number of terms describing variations of snow. This would complicate translation efforts between Finland and a country whose language does not have a comparable set of words for "snow."

Conversely, considering the context of translations can provide considerable insight into the *cultural experience* of the country of origin. Thus, defining these terms can furnish perspective into contemporary U.S. culture. To illustrate, according to linguist Ben Zimmer, the word "occupy" has been invested with a new meaning as a powerful call to action, starting with "Occupy Wall Street" (Joyce, 2011b). Indeed, the following words have become so ingrained into the American experience that they were added to the 2011 *Merriam-Webster Collegiate Dictionary*:

- *Mashup*: a musical recording made by combining elements from two or more different songs
- *Fantastical*: extremely fantastic
- *E-mailable:* able to be sent and received through an e-mail system
- *Fast-rope*: to descend from a flying helicopter by sliding down a thick rope

In addition, the principles of translation studies can provide insight into Intercultural Communication; that is, communication *within* a country. Subcultures maintain their own communication systems, including distinctive words and syntax. Thus, translation studies can be of value in terms of understanding subcultures, as defined by ethnic and racial identification, gender, and generational divisions within a larger culture.

Translation studies can also be of value with regard to analysis of media presentations produced in different time periods. Although contemporary audiences can watch films produced during World War II, the films of that era were undoubtedly interpreted differently by the audience of that time. In the process of "translation," the modern audience will undoubtedly learn more about the values, context, and media messages that defined World War II culture.

Performance is another contextual element that influences how content is interpreted. General statements such as "that was a swell idea" derive their meaning largely within the context of the sentences surrounding this expression. In addition, voice inflexion can also play a role in how a performer "translates" a script.

Point of View. The choice of words in translations can furnish perspective into the point of view of the media communicator. To illustrate, as part of the ongoing Middle East conflict, a number of Palestinians have strapped explosives on their bodies, killing Israelis (and themselves in the process). While the Israeli and American press described these individuals as *suicide bombers*, the American press referred to them as *martyrs* and *self-sacrificers* who were carrying out acts of "resistance" against their Israeli oppressors.

The *Usborne Cookery School's Cooking for Beginners* (Wilkes, 2007), an illustrated book of recipes to help British children learn to cook, illustrates how various factors influence the translation process.

- Function has had an impact on the *form* of the translations to European audiences. For instance, the English language commonly employs the imperative form of verbs (e.g., "cut the tomatoes, add the onion") whereas other languages typically use the infinitive form ("to cut the onion").
- The *context* of the translation affects the content of the cookbook. For example, cooking utensils such as kettles, garlic presses, and potato mashers are not used in all cultures. In a recipe for creamy fish piece (p. 12), a drawing of a potato masher is followed by the caption: "Crush the potato by pressing a potato masher down, again and again, on the chunks. Do it until there are no lumps left." Thus, the translator has to find a translation for potato masher that matches the picture, the recipe instructions and the caption space (Wilkes, 2007: 86).

See also: Cultural Context; Production Analysis Approach; Values Clarification Approach

References

Bassnett, S. (1998). *Translation Studies*. London and New York: Routledge.

Cronin, M. (2003). *Translation and Globalization*. London and New York: Routledge.

Cunningham, M. (2010, October 2). "Found in Translation." *New York Times.* Retrieved from http://www.nytimes.com/2010/10/03/opinion/03cunningham. html?pagewanted=all

Gentile, C. (2007, July 24). "Defense at Padilla Trial Raises a Dispute Over Translations." *New York Times.* Retrieved from http://www.nytimes.com/2007/07/24/us/24padilla.html

Joyce, C. (2011a, December 16). "American Dialect Society to Choose Word of the Year." Morning Edition, National Public Radio. Retrieved from http://benzimmer.com/morning-edition-npr-american-dialect-society-to-choose-word-of-the-year/

Joyce, C. (2011b, April 5). "Computer Translator Reads between the Tweets." Morning Edition, National Public Radio. Retrieved from http://www.npr.org/2011/04/05/135049784/computer-translator-reads-between-the-tweets

Lacey, M. (2003, February 16). "To the Beat of a Hit Song, the New Kenya Sends Spirits Off the Charts." *New York Times.* Retrieved from http://www.nytimes.com/2003/02/16/world/to-the-beat-of-a-hit-song-the-new-kenya-sends-spirits-off-the-charts.html

Levieux, E., & Levieux, M. (2003, February 23). "No, Chirac Didn't Say "Shut Up." *New York Times.* Retrieved from http://www.nytimes.com/2003/02/23/weekinreview/the-world-no-chirac-didn-t-say-shut-up.html

Munday, J. (2003). *Introducing Translation Studies.* London and New York: Routledge.

Safire, W. (2002, April 29). "Walk Back the Cat." *New York Times.* Retrieved from http://www.nytimes.com/2002/04/29/opinion/walk-back-the-cat.html

Vermeer, H. (1989–2000). "Skopos and Commission in Translational Action." In L. Venuti (Ed.), *The Translation Studies Reader* (pp. 221–232). London: Routledge.

Wilkes, A. (2007). *Usborne Cookery School's Cooking for Beginners.* London: Usborne.

Values Clarification Approach

Values clarification is a qualitative approach to media literacy analysis that focuses on the identification and analysis of the values systems operating in a media presentation or genre. Values clarification analysis can serve as a useful way to approach the analysis of media content, in several respects:

- Identifying the value system operating in a media presentation or body of media presentations, so that individuals can understand the origin and influence of their personal values system

- Comparing/contrasting the value system of a media presentation with one's personal value system
- Recognizing the influence of the media on the development of an individual's personal values system
- Considering the *irreality* of media presentations with regard to the promotion of cultural values
- Deciding which prevailing values in a media presentation to adopt (if any); individuals can examine their own values system in response to choices made by characters in media presentations
- Serving as a springboard for personal values clarification, providing opportunities for reflection on a range of topics involving media and ethics, such as privacy versus right to know, conflicts of interest, and responsibilities to the public versus benefit to the media company
- To account for why people are attracted to certain kinds of media programming, such as violent programs
- Examining the media of a foreign culture can serve as a source of information about its value system

An essential aspect of an individual's psychological makeup is their personal values system. A values system consists of the relative importance that an individual attaches to the objects, events, thoughts, and feelings that he or she has encountered. In *The Audacity of Hope*, Barack Obama (2007) defines values as "the standards and principles that (individuals) deem important in their lives, and in the life of the country" (p. 52).

Individuals' behavior is often predicated on the value that they place on their environment. Consequently, the study of the formation and implementation of core values systems is a way to better understand individuals and their behaviors.

The process of forming a personal values system involves establishing a *hierarchy* of abstract principles, from positive values (i.e., that which is good, right, or correct), to negative standards (i.e., that which is bad, wrong, or incorrect). An individual's values come into conflict every day; the decision to assert or modify these values is always the result of the strength of these values and the conviction with which the individual holds them.

In some cases, defining a personal values system is made easier by clear choices between positive and negative values. In other cases, values formation is complicated by choices between two positives or two negative values. Kannenberg (n.d.) explains,

Most of us hold thousands of individual values in our value system. Some of these values are held with strong conviction, while others are held but questioned. Consider an individual who values honesty. In this person's everyday life, she attempts to tell the truth even in situations where it might be easier to tell a "little lie." However, consider a situation in which this person becomes involved in a workplace dispute in which telling the truth will mean dismissal from her job. If, on the other hand, if she were to say nothing or lie, her job will not only be secure but she would be likely to receive a promotion. For this individual, her position at work is of primary importance in her life, and she chooses to lie in this situation. In this example, we see a common dilemma for many of us. Do we adhere to a value that is important to us (i.e., telling the truth) or do we 'modify' that value in order to maintain another value (i.e., having a good job)? (p. 27)

Cultural Values

As is the case with individuals, cultures also develop their own distinctive value systems. The value system that characterizes a culture is the value system held (or at least, understood) by most individuals in the culture. These values serve as the basis of shared cultural attitudes, behaviors, roles, and norms. In *The Audacity of Hope*, Barak Obama (2007) refers to cultural values as "the glue upon which every healthy society depends," describing the American values system as follows:

> Our individualism has always been bound by a set of communal values. . . . We value the imperatives of family and the cross-generational obligations that family implies. We value community, the neighborliness that expresses itself through raising the barn or coaching on the soccer team. We value patriotism and the obligations of citizenship, a sense of duty and sacrifice on behalf of our nation. We value a faith in something bigger than ourselves, whether that something expresses itself in formal religion or ethical precepts. And we value the constellation of behaviors that express our mutual regard for one another: honesty, fairness, humility, kindness, courtesy, and compassion. (p. 55)

An individual's identity is strongly influenced by the culture's mainstream values system. But at the same time, *subcultures*, defined by social class, gender, and race, give rise to their own distinct values systems. Individuals may adhere to several different values systems simultaneously, based on their membership in more than one subculture. For instance, a 60-year-old working-class male from the northwestern United States is influenced by at least four distinct sets of values: age, social class, gender, and region. Furthermore, the interaction between these values systems can create or result in a distinctive way of experiencing the world. Changing one of these demographic categories alters the broad values system of the individual. To return to the example above, two individuals may share three of the four demographic categories. However, if one is male the other female, then their general values systems would be different.

Authority: Sources of Value Systems

The designation of an *authority* is integral to the development of both personal and cultural value systems. The authority is the embodiment of a particular value system. An authority can be human, spiritual, societal (e.g., the legal system), or institutional (e.g., school, the church). Individuals and groups look to authorities to justify their value systems.

An authority serves as a central concept in core value exploration. Identifying the authority is essential for both understanding and predicting an individual's values and behaviors. *Internal* authorities are found in primary relationships, such as family, longstanding beliefs (from childhood, second-generation, or spiritual models of ethical behavior). An *External* authority refers to a secondary or indirect source of values that influences our personal values. People are particularly susceptible to the influence of authorities during infancy, childhood, and early adulthood.

In Western culture, people look to the media as a major external source of values. The media legitimize people and events; values look more appropriate simply because they appear in the media. The authority figures in media presentations are decisive and attractive. In addition, most narratives are scripted (including "reality" programs), meaning that the decisions that are made by the protagonists result in a successful resolution. Furthermore, consequences are frequently ignored in narratives. Consequently, the values and values systems that appear in media presentations can mislead the audience into wanting to adopt these values.

Lines of Inquiry

The values clarification approach can follow several lines of inquiry.

Core Values Exploration

One of the concerns expressed by media critics is that programs impart "negative values" that corrupt our young people. But is this claim accurate?

Core Values Exploration (CVE) is an approach that can assess the values system operating in a particular media program or genre. CVE originally was devised by Dr. Gary Kannenberg as a research instrument that identifies an individual's personal values system. Applying this methodology to the study of media provides a way to identify the belief system(s) embedded in a media presentation or body of media presentations. Moreover, CVE can furnish insight into how a person's values system is influenced by the media.

Media presentations often involve conscious efforts to influence the value systems of the target audience. Kannenberg (n.d.) declares, "An example of intentional influence is seen in the media area of advertising."

The goals of CVE are (a) to enable individuals to see where their values system comes from and (b) to understand the implications and consequences of their values system. Individuals are then in a position to modify their existing value system and authority in line with their interests and concerns, thus making the adoption of a values system the result of active choice on the part of the individual (Kannenberg: 87).

CVE can furnish perspective into a range of media presentations, including the following:

- The values system that is operating in a particular media presentation
- The values system characteristic of the body of work of a particular media communicator
- The values system characteristic of a genre (e.g., Action-Adventure, Horror, News)
- Cumulative media messages: that is, characters and performances that are independent of individual media presentations (e.g., the films of John Wayne, Clint Eastwood, and the Rock share values that make up the Macho Male stereotype)
- Values attached to a particular issue or behavior (e.g., violence)
- International media presentations: the values systems characterizing a national media presentation

CVE provides a method for assessing media presentations, sections of media presentations, or individual characters within a performance using CVE. In addition, media text can be a springboard for personal values clarification, providing opportunities for reflection on a range of topics involving media and ethical dilemmas, such as privacy versus right to know, conflicts of interest, and responsibilities to the public versus benefit to the media company.

A CVE approach to media literacy analysis has the following goals:

- To identify the value system operating in a media presentation or media genre
- To compare and contrast the value system of a media presentation with one's personal value system

In this approach, media presentations are assessed on the basis of six variables:

1. The major authority
2. The individual's attitude toward the authority
3. The clarity of values presented
4. The consistency of the values presented
5. The type of values presented
6. The locus or control encouraged in the media presentation (Kannenberg, n.d.)

One of the major areas of focus in CVE involves identifying the authority in media presentations:

- Who is the authority in the media presentation?
- What values and value systems does the authority represent?

The authority figure in media presentations is not necessarily the hero. For example, mentors such as Professor Albus Dumbledore (Harry Potter series, 2001–2011), Mr. Miyagi (*The Karate Kid*, 1984), and Ben Obi-Wan Kenobi (*Star Wars*, 1977) are mythic figures who appear as secondary figures, providing support and direction for the hero.

A final important variable is the *relative power* that the Authority represents to the individual. Strong authorities represent powerful validation of the values expressed by that authority in the media presentation. On the other hand, authorities who do not exercise much influence offer little validation for the values expressed by that authority.

Values Hierarchy

A second line of inquiry examines the *values hierarchy* of a media presentation. In media presentations, heroes and heroines embody those qualities that society considers admirable. These protagonists are generally in media entertainment programming because they embody the values that are esteemed within the culture. In contrast, villains personify values that pose a threat to the worldview of the presentation. As the protagonists and villains engage in conflict, the values that they personify are also in opposition.

As the protagonists and villains engage in conflict, the values that they personify are also in opposition:

- Good vs. Evil
- Justice vs. Injustice
- Truth vs. Falsehood
- Love vs. Hate
- Internal Satisfaction vs. Material Acquisition

The resolution of a presentation establishes a hierarchy of values: the good guy wins, happiness is restored, and the values embodied in the protagonist are reaffirmed. As Chandler (n.d., p. 79) observes, "The structure of the text works to position the reader to 'privilege one set of values and meanings over the other'."

Embedded Values

A close examination of media programming can divulge the value system of the media communicator, as well as widely held cultural values. Values such as ethnocentrism, altruistic democracy, and the preservation of social order are seldom overt in news products but are often present. Media communicators convey meaning by manipulating production elements such as editing decisions, word choice, and connotative images. Thus, a consideration of these elements can reveal the values of the media communicators. To illustrate, consider the following headlines for two newspaper stories reporting on the a car bombing incident in Baghdad on October 28, 2003:

- "Five Consecutive Martyrdom Operations Rock Baghdad" (*Al Gumhuria*)
- "Bloodied Baghdad; Four Coordinated Suicide Car Bombings Kill 34, Wound 224" (*Newsday*)

In the first headline, which appeared in an Egyptian government–owned newspaper, the word *martyrdom* is an indication that the media communicator regarded this action as morally justifiable. In contrast, the term *suicide bombings* in *Newsday*, a mainstream American publication, reveals that, according to the reporter, this was a brutal and senseless attack.

Illogical Conclusion

The conclusion of a narrative can also furnish perspective into the values system of the media presentation. In the course of a narrative, characters are rewarded or punished for certain behaviors, which are predicated on particular values. However, the conclusions of many media presentations are often false, confused, or simply illogical when considered within the flow of the program. One explanation can be found in the audience's desire for a happy ending. Mindful of the demand for a satisfying resolution, media communicators feel compelled to insert an artificial ending that makes the audience leave the theater with smiles on their faces. Indeed, film studios compete to release the "feel good movie of the year." As a result, the artificial conclusion often undermines the manifest message of the media presentation.

Envisioning a conclusion consistent with the logical flow of the narrative can provide insight into the cultural values of the period about marriage and relationships: Given the initial premise, characters, and worldview, how *should* the presentation logically end?

A related line of inquiry is *preferred conclusion*: How do individuals *want* the story to end? Their responses to this question provide insight into their personal values systems.

See also: Autobiographical Analysis; Character Analysis; Dialectical Analysis; Mythic Analysis

References

Bazzi, M. (2003, October 23). "Bloodied Baghdad; Four Coordinated Suicide Car Bombings Kill 34, Wound 224." *Newsday*. Retrieved from www.newsday.com

Chandler, D. (n.d.). *Semiotics for Beginners*. Retrieved from http://aber.ac.uk/dgc/semioti.html

"Five Consecutive Martyrdom Operations Rock Baghdad." (2003, October 23). *Al Gumhuria*. Retrieved at www.Algomhuria.net

Kannenberg, G. D. (n.d.). "The Influence of Media Communications on Human Behavior." Unpublished manuscript. Webster University, St. Louis, Missouri.

Obama, B. (2007). *The Audacity of Hope*. New York: Random House.